VICTIMS' RIGHTS

Recent Titles in
Documentary and Reference Guides

Islamism: A Documentary and Reference Guide
John Calvert

The Patriot Act: A Documentary and Reference Guide
Herbert N. Foerstel

Abortion: A Documentary and Reference Guide
Melody Rose

Immigration: A Documentary and Reference Guide
Thomas Cieslik, David Felsen, Akis Kalaitzidis

Gun Control: A Documentary and Reference Guide
Robert J. Spitzer

Culture Wars in America: A Documentary and Reference Guide
Glenn H. Utter

Civil Liberties and the State: A Documentary and Reference Guide
Christopher Peter Latimer

The Politics of Sexuality: A Documentary and Reference Guide
Raymond A. Smith

U.S. Election Campaigns: A Documentary and Reference Guide
Thomas J. Baldino and Kyle L. Kreider

U.S. Foreign Policy: A Documentary and Reference Guide
Akis Kalaitzidis and Gregory W. Streich

White-Collar and Corporate Crime: A Documentary and Reference Guide
Gilbert Geis

Homelessness: A Documentary and Reference Guide
Neil Larry Shumsky

VICTIMS' RIGHTS

A Documentary and Reference Guide

Douglas E. Beloof

Documentary and Reference Guides

AN IMPRINT OF ABC-CLIO, LLC
Santa Barbara, California • Denver, Colorado • Oxford, England

Library of Congress Cataloging-in-Publication Data

Beloof, Douglas E., 1955–
    Victims' rights : a documentary and reference guide / Douglas E. Beloof.
      p. cm. — (Documentary and reference guides)
    Includes bibliographical references and index.
    ISBN 978-0-313-39345-7 (hard copy : alk. paper) — ISBN 978-0-313-39346-4 (ebook)
1. Victims of crimes—Legal status, laws, etc.—United States. I. Title.
KF9763.B454   2012
345.73'05046—dc23   2011043292

ISBN: 978-0-313-39345-7
EISBN: 978-0-313-39346-4

16 15 14 13 12   1 2 3 4 5

This book is also available on the World Wide Web as an eBook.
Visit www.abc-clio.com for details.

Greenwood
An Imprint of ABC-CLIO, LLC

ABC-CLIO, LLC
130 Cremona Drive, P.O. Box 1911
Santa Barbara, California 93116-1911

This book is printed on acid-free paper ∞
Manufactured in the United States of America

This book is dedicated to Rodney Knight Houser and Lois Shurts Houser.
And, to their steadfast relatives including Doug, Lucy, David, and Sue, with my greatest
respect and admiration.

CONTENTS

Preface   ix

Acknowledgments   xi

1. Background and History of Victims' Rights   1

2. To Include Victims in the Criminal Process?   39

3. The President's Task Force on Victims of Crime   63

4. The Federal Constitutional Context of Victims' Rights   83

5. The Oklahoma City Bombing and the Failure of Federal Victims' Rights   121

6. The Federal Constitutional Victims' Rights Effort   133

7. The Crime Victims' Rights Act   207

8. Present Status and the Future of Victims' Rights   261

Conclusion   303

Index   305

PREFACE

Crime victims have a long and venerable history of participation in the criminal process. At the time of the founding of America, victims prosecuted their own cases. For a variety of reasons explained in this book, victims were gradually excluded. Ultimately, by 1975, victims were significantly marginalized into the role of witness. Victims could not attend trials, could not speak at sentencing, and were not provided notice of proceedings unless they received a subpoena to testify. The exclusion of victims from the criminal process led to victims experiencing increasing resentment and dissatisfaction with the criminal justice system. Sometime during the 1970s, the Victims' Rights Movement was born.

On the one hand, the Victims' Rights Movement has led the greatest law reform in criminal procedure of the last 30 years—victims' rights. The Movement has successfully enacted victims' rights statutes and state constitutional amendments. On the other hand, victims' rights in many jurisdictions still suffer from significant dysfunction. That dysfunction is the inability to enforce victims' rights in many jurisdictions. Where rights cannot be enforced, they are illusory. Illusory rights may be ignored with impunity by police, prosecutors, and judges.

Recognizing this problem, in the 1990s, the Victims' Rights Movement began to seek passage of a federal constitutional amendment giving crime victims rights in the Bill of Rights. While this amendment effort came close to passing the United States Senate, it ultimately was clear it would not garner the two-thirds vote needed for passage. An experimental statute was passed instead, the Crime Victims' Rights Act (CVRA). Unlike a federal amendment, which would apply equally around the nation, the CVRA applies only to federal prosecutions, which comprise only 2 percent of all criminal prosecutions brought in the United States.

Today, federal courts are busy interpreting the CVRA. It remains a very open question whether the CVRA will provide meaningful remedy for violations of victims' rights. Ultimately, this issue will be decided by the United States Supreme Court. If the Court interprets the CVRA narrowly, the CVRA will be a failed experiment. In that event, the Victims' Rights Movement will go back to the drawing board, continuing the effort to pass a constitutional amendment.

The motivation to create this text comes from the realization that no similar text is in print today. The key documents concerning victims' rights have been difficult for the nonexpert to identify until now. These documents are quite varied in nature and include histories, a Presidential Task Force report, Supreme Court cases, Reports of the United States Senate, observations of legal scholars, and legislation, among other things. Having been identified, the text gathers the documents into one volume, thus saving the reader many hours of research time. Furthermore, the documents are analyzed and put in context so the reader does not need to struggle with understanding the context and central significance of the documents.

This text puts modern victims' rights in historical perspective. Chapter 1 of this text contains histories of victims from colonial times to the present. Additionally, a history of the movement itself, as provided by some of the movement's early pioneers, is set forth. From there, the text moves to providing conceptual context of victims' rights in Chapter 2 by examining a model of criminal justice that is inclusive of the victim and a thorough explanation of the reasons why victims should or should not be included in the criminal justice process. President Reagan's Task Force on Victims of Crime and the recommendations it made are the subject of Chapter 3. The task force report provided momentum to the nascent Crime Victims' Rights Movement. The constitutional context of victims' rights is discussed in Chapter 4 by setting forth and analyzing two Supreme Court cases and a federal circuit case. Chapter 5 reveals the dismal treatment of the Oklahoma City Bombing victims under then-existing federal victims' rights. These rights turned out to be unenforceable and inspired the third wave of victims' rights, a move to enforceable rights. The effort to enact a federal constitutional amendment is examined in Chapter 6, including the Senate Majority and Minority reports on the draft amendment. Chapter 7 sets forth and examines the Crime Victims' Rights Act and reveals that while the CVRA held out the hope of enforceable rights, it may be a failed experiment. Finally, Chapter 8 details the present status and future of victims' rights.

The text is arranged both chronologically and in an order easily accessible to the reader. There are two primary ways to utilize this book. Using the index, the text can be used to locate specific, commonly referenced documents. Alternatively, the reader may choose to read the entire book or, using the table of contents, view the sections that reflect specific topic areas. Using it the latter way, the reader can see larger trends that are only understandable with a comprehensive perspective.

There are several central issues discernable for the reader of the entire book. The American criminal justice system has had periods of significant victim inclusion and exclusion. Today, neither complete exclusion nor complete inclusion is desired. This raises several questions: How can we consciously integrate crime victims' interests into the criminal process through the creation of victims' rights? What should those rights be? Should the rights be illusory or real? And, if real, how should the rights be enforced so government actors will respect those rights?

This text will assist the reader in reaching his or her own answers to these questions.

ACKNOWLEDGMENTS

Thanks are given to my talented research assistant Jacqueline Swanson, whose excellent editorial skills greatly facilitated the creation of the book. Thanks also to my assistant Dianne Viales for collecting the copyright permissions and keeping me laughing. Finally, thanks for the support of Lewis and Clark Law School, without which this project would not have come about. I am also pleased to have been selected as an author by the editors of the Documentary and Reference Guides series.

1

BACKGROUND AND HISTORY OF VICTIMS' RIGHTS

HISTORY

Crime victims' rights represent the greatest revolution in criminal procedure of the last several decades. It is a populist revolution driven by the will of the people and their representatives. This revolution has dramatically changed a criminal system that, by 1975, had exiled the victim from the criminal process. In 1975, the system focused only on the defendant and the state. As a result, legislation and court opinions gave consideration almost exclusively to the two formal parties, prosecutor and defendant, with little thought given to the victim. Today, victims' rights in the criminal process are commonplace and expanding. Some victims' rights are even taken for granted today. However, these procedures are the result of the hard civil rights struggle of the Crime Victims' Rights Movement begun in the 1970s, which is very much alive today.

The Crime Victims' Rights Movement seeks to establish victims' rights of participation, protection, and privacy in American criminal procedure. As a result of these efforts, victims participate by speaking at sentencings, plea bargains, and parole board hearings. Victim protections include, for example, the ability to obtain restraining orders, notification of release or escape of the offender, notification of sex offenders residing nearby, and Amber Alerts. Privacy rights include rape shield laws that prohibit the use of irrelevant evidence of a victim's sexual history at trial.

Rights are held by an individual victim. Thus, it is only the victim of a particular crime who can exercise his victims' rights in the proceedings involving that crime. Moreover, only that victim can waive, or choose not to exercise, his rights. Of course, in cases involving homicide, surviving family members are given victim status, and in cases involving minor children, a responsible adult or agency is authorized to exercise the victims' rights.

There are multiple sources of victims' rights, laws, and accommodations. First, while modern victims' rights make up a substantial part of these laws, the history of victim involvement is important in identifying all rights. At the time of the founding of America, victims participated actively as private prosecutors, acting as public prosecutors do now. Today, public prosecution dominates and victims privately prosecute only misdemeanors and petty offenses in some states. However, there are victim accommodations that remain from the founding era. For example, in many jurisdictions, victims can directly report a crime to the grand jury, and victims' attorneys can assist a public prosecution by working under the authority of the public prosecutor. These are accommodations surviving as judge-made law, referred to as "common law," or as statutes that have codified common law.

A second type of victim participation comes in the form of third-party practice. Victims and other witnesses are not formal parties to the criminal process. Nevertheless, they are able to defend certain types of interests in court. For example, the law of evidence, which governs what information is allowed in trial, grants certain privileges, such as the psychiatrist-patient privilege. A privilege means no one can access the information protected by the privilege without the victim's or witness's permission. If the defense or prosecution in a criminal case subpoenas a victim's psychiatric records, the victim can seek to quash or invalidate the subpoena request. Similarly, if the same victim is asked about the psychiatric care on the witness stand, the victim can independently enforce her privilege against disclosure.

Third, the limits of courts' jurisdiction or authority over victims can also be an important source of privacy or protection for the victim. Because victims are not full parties to a criminal proceeding, there may be limits on what a court and the parties can make a victim do. For example, can a court order a sexual assault victim to submit to a physical examination? Whether the court has jurisdiction over the victim is the first, but not the only, legal inquiry made in finding the answer.

Fourth are the modern victims' rights, consisting of federal and state statutes and state constitutional rights. These are the laws enacted by the modern Victims' Rights Movement. These rights include, for example, the right to attend trial and speak at sentencing.

Finally, judges and prosecutors operate with a great deal of discretion in making many decisions. Even if a victim does not have any of the modern rights, historical accommodations, or third-party interests, prosecutors and judges often can use their discretion to grant or deny accommodation to crime victims. Discretion means that it is up to the official whether the victim is accommodated or not. There is no legal recourse for the victim if the authorities do not exercise discretion in the victim's favor.

Because victims' rights are not (yet) in the federal constitution, victims' rights are not universally the same throughout the nation. Instead, each state and the federal government has its own set of victims' rights. However, all of the victims' laws in these different jurisdictions fall into at least one of the source categories outlined above. Each state's and the federal supreme court has the independent authority to interpret the meaning, scope, and enforceability of the rights that exist in their respective jurisdictions. Among different jurisdictions, courts have been quite mixed in their interpretation of victims' rights. Some have been very restrictive, while others have been quite expansive. Thus, the scope and application of rights can vary greatly among jurisdictions.

Having just described the sources of victim laws, is it is also important to be aware of the difference between victims' *laws* and victims' *rights*. Rights are protections against government power. In the context of modern crime victims' rights, the government powers against which victims have rights are courts, prosecutors, prison and parole authorities, and the police.

For a victim law to be a victim right, the victim must be able to both *exercise* and *enforce* the right. Exercising a right means the victim takes advantage of the right. For example, if the victim has a right to speak at sentencing and the victim does speak at sentencing, the victim is exercising the right. When the victim exercises his right, he is acting as a *participant* in the criminal process. A victim acting as a participant is not a full party. The full *parties* in the criminal process are the public prosecution and the criminal defendant. For example, victims do not try the case; instead, the full parties try the case. Victims are participants exercising their rights intermittently at some but not all procedural stages in the criminal process. Thus, for example, a victim might object in court to a pretrial release of the defendant, object to or support a plea bargain in court, or speak at sentencing.

Enforcing the victim's right means something quite different than *exercising* the right. When the victim is denied the opportunity to exercise the right, enforcement means the victim can seek a ruling from a higher court authority to restore the victim's right to exercise the right. For example, if the victim was denied the ability to exercise her right by speaking at sentencing, she would enforce her right by asking an appellate court or higher court to overrule the trial court's decision. The appellate court would order the trial court to allow the victim to exercise her right and to conduct a resentencing with the opportunity for the victim to exercise the right to speak.

While the victim is a *participant* in exercising his right in front of the criminal trial court, the lowest-level court, when the right is denied by that court, the victim becomes a *party* to enforcement of the right in the appellate courts. That is to say, when going to a higher court to enforce a right that has been violated, the victim is a full party in the higher-court proceeding.

Furthermore, victims must have *standing* in court before they can enforce the right. Standing is the ability to present to the court and have the court rule on the issue of whether the right was violated. In order to have standing, there must be a remedy that is provided by statute or that the courts can craft. Standing and remedies can be provided for specifically in law or, in some circumstances, courts can determine that standing and remedy exist even without a specific remedy.

The term *victims' rights* is used in different places in the documents set forth in this book to mean different things. When lawyers and judges talk about rights, they mean the type of rights outlined above. That is, rights can be exercised and are enforceable in courts. However, in public discourse, the term *victims' rights* is also used to describe accommodations or laws that improve the status of crime victims but fall short of enforceable legal rights.

When you, the reader, are trying to tell the difference between real and unenforceable rights, look to see if the law in question gives victims participation, privacy, or protection in the criminal process. Then, look to see if it is enforceable. If so, it is a real right. If the law gives victims participation, privacy, or protection in the criminal process but there is no way to enforce the law, then the victim does not have real legal rights. Instead, these laws are only advisory and the government has discretion to ignore them. Also, if the victim law involves access to social services or to funds outside the criminal process, while important, these are not legal rights in the criminal process. Again, people often use the term *victims' rights* to describe all of these things. Nevertheless, the only real victims' rights are rights of participation, protection, and privacy that can be exercised and are enforceable in the courts.

The distinction between real victims' rights and other victim laws is very important. The states are divided between those that have enforceable victims' rights and states that have unenforceable rights. For example, in some states, the right to attend trial is enforceable, thus making it a legal right. In other states, similar laws permit attendance, but the law is unenforceable. When unenforceable, attendance is an accommodation the court may grant or deny at its discretion. Where the government can deny attendance at will, there is no real right to attend.

While many states have enforceable rights, there are active ongoing efforts by the Crime Victims' Rights Movement to turn victims' laws in states without enforceable rights into real victims' rights. For example, this has happened recently in California and Oregon. What were formerly unenforceable state constitutional laws for crime victims in those states have since become enforceable, real victims' rights. The effort to ensure that legislated rights are enforceable is but one area in which the struggle for civil liberties for victims in the criminal process is ongoing. Efforts such as those of the nonprofit National Crime Victim Law Institute (NCVLI.org) are ongoing to obtain favorable court opinions interpreting these rights. We will look at some of these efforts through the documents in this book.

While many fine prosecutors have the best interests of victims in mind, prosecutors do not represent victims. Instead, prosecutors represent the public interest. Although television conveys the opposite impression, crime victims are not the prosecutors' clients. Judges are also not obligated to victims. Judges are supposed to remain above the fray of the adversarial system, neutral and impartial. This raises at least two issues. First, who represents the victim? For the vast majority of victims, the answer is that no one formally represents them, although in most jurisdictions, prosecutors may, if they choose to and the victim consents, enforce a victim's rights. However, the lack of legal representation is an ongoing challenge. The second issue is, who opposes victims' rights? Because victims' rights are rights against government, and in particular against prosecutors and judges, most instances of formal opposition in the legal process come from prosecutors and courts, and, less frequently, from criminal defendants.

In History

The English concept that a crime harmed both the state and the victim crossed the ocean to the American colonies. In his influential *Commentaries on the Laws of*

England, Blackstone (1979) explained, "[i]n all cases the crime includes an injury: every public offense is also a private wrong, and somewhat more; it affects the individual, and it likewise affects the community." Proceeding on the basis that crime harms individuals, early American criminal prosecutions were (as in England) often brought by the victim—a private prosecutor—rather than by a government agency. Histories of eighteenth-century criminal justice in the United States, including the period before, during, and after the framing of the Constitution, reveal that victims directly prosecuted criminal cases.

THE VICTIM PARTICIPATION MODEL

Criminal procedure has been described with reference to two conceptual models: the crime control model and the due process model. These models were developed by law professor Herbert Packer to explain underlying fundamental tensions in the criminal process. His models are at the beginning of many criminal procedure casebooks. As victims' rights and interests continue to grow in significance, a third model is needed to explain the process more accurately and completely. This next document acknowledges and describes Professor Packer's models while adding a third model, the victim participation model, to explain the rise of victims' rights.

- **Document:** "The Third Model of Criminal Process: The Victim Participation Model" by Douglas Evan Beloof
- **Date:** 1999
- **Significance:** Professor Beloof's paper examines the need for an addition to Packer's two-value system: a third victim-participation model acknowledging the importance of victim participation in the criminal process.
- **Source:** Beloof, Douglas Evan. "The Third Model of Criminal Process: The Victim Participation Model." *Utah Law Review* (1999): 289.

* * *

Thirty-[three] of the states have chiseled victims' rights into their respective constitutions. The federal government and the rest of the states have statutory rights for victims. (Beloof 1999; National Victim Center 1996; Siegelman and Tarver 1988) [. . .] [Make no mistake about it,] [t]he inclusion of the victim as a participant has shaken conventional assumptions about the criminal process to their foundation. *Compare Booth v. Maryland*, 482 U.S. 496, 502-07 (1987) (holding that introduction of victim impact statement at sentencing phase of capital murder trial violated Eighth Amendment), *with Payne v. Tennessee*, 501 U.S. 808, 821-27 (1991) (holding that Eighth Amendment did not erect per se bar prohibiting capital sentencing jury from considering victim impact evidence). [In light of laws of victim participation,] [o]ne core assumption that has occupied the field for many years is no longer true. This core assumption is that only two value systems compete with each other in the criminal process. Professor Packer identified and then labeled these two value systems the "Crime Control Model" and the "Due Process Model" (Packer 1968). The crime control model has as its value the efficient suppression of crime. (See id. at 158.) The due process model has as its value the primacy of the defendant and the related concept of limiting governmental power. (See id. at 163, 165.) Thirty years ago, Professor Packer stated:

> The kind of model we need is one that permits us to recognize explicitly the value choices that underlie the details of the criminal process. In a word what we need is a normative model or models. It will take more than one model, but it will not take more than two. (Id. at 153.)

This last assertion is no longer true. Today, it takes more than two models to recognize explicitly the value choices that underlie the criminal process.

[Professor Packer attempted to illuminate the values underlying our criminal process, by articulating the crime control model and the due process model. These models have been modified by some and criticized by others.] (Arenella 1983; Mirjan 1973; Griffiths 1970). It is not the function of this Article to support or detract from these, or other, critiques. Nevertheless, the models remain useful constellations above the sea of the criminal process. Taken together, the crime control model and the due process model have comprised a dominant two-model universe of values. Aranella at 209. The models were created by Packer to serve [several] functions. . . . [T]he models explicitly recognize "the value choices that underlie the details of the criminal process." Packer at 153. This, in turn, provides a "convenient way to talk about the . . . process" that operates between the "competing demands" of the two value systems. (Id.) . . . [T]he models allow us to "detach ourselves from the . . . details" of the process so we can see how the entire system may be able to deal with the various tasks it is expected to accomplish. (Id.) at 152. . . . [T]he models assist in understanding the process as dynamic, rather than static. [And], the models may assist in revealing the relationship of criminal process to substantive criminal law. (Id.)

[Of course,] Professor Packer did not anticipate laws of formal victim participation. . . . Thus, it is hardly surprising that his two models do not include a conceptual framework in which victim participation in the criminal process can be understood (Hall 1975). . . . [B]ecause victim participation does not rest primarily on the values underlying the [two models], the two models [alone do not] and cannot facilitate an understanding of victim participation. [Thus, it is time for] a shift in a dominant paradigm of criminal procedure. . . . [The victim's formal participation does not harken the demise of either the crime control model or the due process model. To understand the operation of victim participation,] a third model—the Victim Participation Model—is needed as a complement to, but [not as a replacement for], Packer's two models.

* * *

How the Values of the Three Models Differ

The Values Underlying the Crime Control Model

The primary value underlying the crime control model is the efficient suppression of crime. Efficiency is the capacity to process criminal offenders rapidly. Professor Packer provides an image of the crime control model:

> The image that comes to mind is an assembly line conveyor belt which moves an endless stream of cases, never stopping, carrying the cases to workers who stand at fixed stations and who perform on each case . . . the same small but essential operation that brings it one step closer to being finished product, or, to exchange the metaphor for the reality, a closed file. The criminal process, in this model, is seen as a screening process in which each successive stage . . . involves a series of routinized operations whose success is gauged primarily by their tendency to pass the case along to a successful conclusion. (Packer 1968, 159–60.)

The Values Underlying the Due Process Model

Underlying the due process model is the value of the primary importance of the individual defendant and the related concept of limiting government power. Again, Professor Packer's image is helpful:

> If the crime control model resembles an assembly line, the due process model looks very much like an obstacle course. Each of its successive stages is designed to present formidable impediments to carrying the accused any further along in the process . . . the aim of the process is as much to protect the factually innocent as it is to convict the factually guilty. It is a little like quality control in industrial technology. . . . The due process model resembles a factory that has had to devote a substantial part of its input to quality control. This necessarily cuts down on quantitative output. (Id. at 163–65.)

[Unlike the crime control model in which the primary value is to effectively, swiftly and with finality suppress crime, the value of the primacy of the defendant seeks to assure reliability in determinations of guilt.]

The Values of the Victim Participation Model

[The mere existence of victim participation values which are external to the two-model concept is not sufficient justification for the creation of a new model. For a modern discussion to be worthwhile there needed to be a consensus in law that the values underlying the victim's role are genuine and significant. This consensus exists now. The consensus that victim participation values exist, are genuine and are significant, is revealed in the laws that have created rights for victims of crime in all fifty states and the federal government.]

The values underlying the Victim Participation Model [are expressly stated in the language of constitutional rights in many states and in federal and state statutes].

[These values include]: fairness to the victim, respect for the victim, and dignity of the victim. Two or more of these three concepts appear in the vast majority of state constitutional victims' rights provisions. [Twenty states expressly set forth two or more of these values in their respective constitutional amendments. Seven other states have created constitutional civil rights for victims. These amendments implicitly recognize the value of the dignity of the victim. We have then a majority of twenty-seven states recognizing the value of the dignity of a victim on a constitutional level. A separate group of eight states have expressly set forth one or more of these values in statutory victims' rights provisions. A federal statute expressly sets forth victim dignity as a value. Thus, we are presented with legitimization of the dignity of the victim which is further illuminated by the nature of particular rights granted.]

Generally, these rights are rights to notice and attendance, [and an opportunity to be heard]. (See Sourcebook, at §§2, 5, 10 [discussing three different rights of participation]). [These rights resemble due process rights.]

The fundamental justification for providing due process-like rights of participation . . . is to prevent the two kinds of harm to which the victim is exposed. The first is primary harm, which results from the crime itself. The other harm is secondary harm, which comes from governmental processes and governmental actors within those processes. (See *Calderon v. Thompson*, 523 U.S. 538, 1998). Together, primary and secondary harm provide the justification for victim participation in the criminal process. . . . The primary harm is a basis for victim participation in the same way that harm to an individual, coupled with a legitimate theory of the liability of another, is the basis for standing in other legal contexts. [Secondary harm provides justification most particularly for] victim civil rights against government authority. The primacy of the individual victim [—reflected in values of fairness, dignity and respect—] is the value underlying the victim participation model. [The value of primacy of the victim derives from primary harm that is causally linked to the alleged criminal liability of another], taken together with the concept of minimizing secondary harm (governmental harm) to the victim. [. . .]

[I will borrow from Packer's use of a factory image to dramatize the function of the victim participation model.] The image of the victim participation model is that of a victim following their own case down the assembly line. [In the investigatory stage the victim] consults with police and prosecutor. At formal proceedings the victim, when appropriate and in an appropriate manner, may speak and address the court. Victims are [consulted] by the prosecutor and the court before pretrial dispositions are finalized. Victims may speak at sentencing and at release hearings.

[The consultant function] of the victim is designed to ensure that the interest of the individual victim in the case is promoted. A core interest of the victim is that the truth be revealed and an appropriate disposition reached. However, there is a significant limit to the victim's [consultant] role. [The victim is a consultant about their case, but] cannot control the critical decisions made in the factory by grand and petit juries, prosecutors, or judges. (*See East v. Scott*, 55 F.3d 996, 1001 (5th Cir. 1995) (finding defendant made out prima facie case for additional discovery of whether private prosecutor hired by victim's family had controlled prosecution); *Person v. Miller*, 854 F.2d 656, 663–64 (4th Cir. 1988) (holding participation by private counsel appropriate so long as it consists of subordinate role to government counsel). At [every critical stage] in the factory [victims are consulted by government actors].... [This victim consultation] may indirectly result in greater or lesser efficiency and victim participation may or may not conflict with the value of the primacy of the individual defendant...

* * *

Analysis

Neither Packer's nor Beloof's models comprehensively explain all that is involved in the criminal process. But for the person seeking to understand the fundamental dynamics among prosecutors, defendants, and victims, the models are extremely useful. In a system with no victim participation model, the rights and interests of crime victims cannot be integrated into Professor Packer's influential models, which were created to explain the criminal process.

The victim participation model is reflective of the growing significance of victims' rights. Packer's former paradigm of two sets of interests, the state and defendant, respectively represented by the efficiency and due process models, has yielded to a new paradigm. The new paradigm contains the original set of state and defendant interests but also includes the interests of crime victims. It is this paradigm change in the criminal process, from two sets of interests to three, that explains why victims' rights are fundamentally revolutionary to the criminal process. What underlie the victim participation model are the values underlying victims' rights. These values and where they exist in each jurisdiction are set out in Table 1.1.

THE HISTORICAL BACKGROUND OF VICTIMS' RIGHTS

Victims of crime have a rich history in American criminal justice. At the time of the founding, crime victims investigated and prosecuted their own cases. Gradually, over a hundred years or so, as professional police, prosecutors, and defense attorneys took over criminal justice functions, the crime victim was removed from the criminal process. Around 1975, the exile of victims from the criminal process became complete. In 1975, the Federal Rules of Evidence (FRE) were enacted by Congress. FRE 615 prevented witnesses, including victims, from attending trial upon the motion of either the prosecution or the defense.

The increasing domination of the criminal process by professionals resulted in significant minimization of the interests of crime victims. Crime victims' only function was to appear as witnesses and, after testifying, to go home. For example, victims had no rights to attend trials, to speak at sentencing, or to be consulted about plea bargains. Typically, victims did not even receive notice of proceedings unless they were

Table 1.1 The Presence of Values of Fairness, Respect, Dignity, Privacy, Freedom from Abuse, and Due Process in State Constitutions and Federal and State Statutes

		Values in Constitution						Values in Statutes					
	C / S	F	R	D	P	FA	DP	F	R	D	P	FA	DP
United States	C												
	S							X	X	X	X		
Alabama	C												
	S												
Alaska	C	X	X	X									
	S												
Arizona	C	X	X	X		X	X						
	S												
Arkansas	C												
	S												
California	C	X	X										
	S								X	X			
Colorado	C												
	S							X	X	X		X	X
Connecticut	C	X	X										
	S												
Delaware	C												
	S												
Florida	C												
	S												
Georgia	C												
	S												
Hawaii	C												
	S								X	X			
Idaho	C	X	X	X	X								
	S							X	X	X	X		
Illinois	C	X	X	X	X								
	S							X					
Indiana	C	X	X	X									
	S								X	X			
Iowa	C												
	S												
Kansas	C												
	S							X	X	X	X		
Kentucky	C												
	S												
Louisiana	C	X	X	X									
	S												
Maine	C												
	S												
Maryland	C		X	X									
	S												
Massachusetts	C												
	S										X		
Michigan	C	X	X	X	X								
	S												
Minnesota	C												
	S												
Mississippi	C	X	X	X									
	S							X					
Missouri	C												
	S												
Montana	C												
	S								X				
Nebraska	C												
	S												
Nevada	C												
	S												

Table 1.1   (Continued)

			Values in Constitution						Values in Statutes					
	C	S	F	R	D	P	FA	DP	F	R	D	P	FA	DP
New Hampshire		S							X	X	X	X		
New Jersey	C	S	X	X							X			
New Mexico	C	S	X	X	X	X				X	X			
New York		S							X					
North Carolina	C	S												
North Dakota		S												
Ohio	C	S	X	X	X									
Oklahoma	C	S	X	X	X		X	X						
Oregon	C	S		X	X				X					
Pennsylvania		S								X	X			
Rhode Island	C	S		X	X					X	X			
South Carolina	C	S	X	X	X		X	X		X	X			
South Dakota		S												
Tennessee	C	S						X			X			
Texas	C	S	X	X	X	X						X		
Utah	C	S	X	X	X		X	X		X	X			
Vermont		S								X	X			
Virginia	C	S	X	X	X					X	X	X		
Washington	C	S		X	X					X	X			
West Virginia		S												
Wisconsin	C	S	X	X	X	X				X	X			
Wyoming		S								X				

C = Constitution; S = Statute; F = Fairness; R = Respect; D = Dignity; P = Privacy; FA = Freedom from Abuse; DP = Due Process called as witnesses. By our bicentennial in 1976, the pendulum had swung so far away from recognizing the crime victim's interest that concern about the dignity of and respect for crime victims began to crystallize into the Victims' Rights Movement. The following document reflects the state of affairs in 1976.

A HISTORICAL OVERVIEW OF VICTIMS IN THE CRIMINAL PROCESS

General History from the Founding to 1976

- **Document:** "Towards a Bicentennial Revolution in Criminal Justice: The Return of the Victim" by William F. McDonald
- **Date:** 1976
- **Significance:** McDonald's article illustrates the status quo of victims' rights in 1976.
- **Source:** McDonald, William F. "Towards a Bicentennial Revolution in Criminal Justice: The Return of the Victim." *American Criminal Law Review* 13 (1976): 649. Reprinted with permission.

* * *

The Role of the Victim in Colonial American Justice

The formal machinery of law enforcement in Colonial America was largely derived from the English, pre-urban past (Lane 1967). This system functioned without a public prosecutor or an effective police force but, rather, was conducted by the private individuals victimized by crime, with the aid of officials who charged fees for their services. (Id. at 7–8.)

Thus, during the 18th century, to obtain an arrest the victim of a crime called a watchman [footnote 15 omitted], if available, and afterwards applied to a justice of the peace for a warrant and a constable to help in making the arrest. Id at 7. The victim paid for the warrant and for the services of the constable. (Id. at 7–9.) The burden of investigation also rested on the victim. He either performed his own detective work, usually with the aid of paid informers, or posted a reward for the successful prosecution of the offender. (Id. at 7.) Except through the coroner's inquest, the state or town provided no help in identifying the unknown offender. Even after identification and arrest, the victim carried the burden of prosecution. He retained an attorney and paid to have the indictment written and the offender prosecuted. (Id.)

Although revenge on the part of the victim surely was a motivating force behind these private prosecutions, so too was a system of restitution by the offender to the victim which was an accepted goal of the system (Bridenbaugh 1955; Holdsworth 1936; Nelson 1974). For many criminal offenses, the victim was awarded multiple damages. (See Nelson.) Where the offender was indigent, the victim was usually authorized to sell the defendant into service for a period corresponding to the amount of multiple damages. If the victim could not sell the convict within a reasonably short period of time, the offender would be released unless the victim compensated the government for the costs of keeping the defendant in jail. (Id.)

Although this system of law enforcement was highly inadequate, it was preferred to the establishment of a professional prosecutor and police force for two important reasons. One was the fear of tyranny that colonists associated with a system of prosecutors and policemen paid by the government as was evidenced by the French experience. Second, the colonists followed the English approach of reducing costs by relying heavily on citizen initiative and funding the system only when necessary.

This system of private initiative underwent a radical change as the commercial revolution progressed throughout the colonies. In former times, law enforcement had relied greatly upon the ancient institution of the "hue and cry" whereby victims called upon their fellow townsmen to assist in pursuing criminals. However, this practice became unworkable as the growth of urban centers inhabited by increasingly mobile populations developed in response to commercial needs (Chambliss 1964; Hall 1952). As people lost communication and kinship with their neighbors, their sense of social responsibility diminished. In an effort to restore this lost sense of responsibility, laws were passed making communities responsible for the financial losses of victims caused by certain crimes (Hibbert 1963). However, these laws proved increasingly unpopular and unsuccessful and were later replaced by a system of rewards to those who brought criminals to justice. By the middle of the 18th century, this system was firmly established as governments, insurance companies, businesses, and private individuals each offered rewards for specified convictions. (Id. at 91–92.) This led eventually to a prosperous "information trade" in which common informers acting as free-lance policemen made handsome livings by convicting people of violations of numerous petty, usually regulatory, offenses. In addition, another species of private policeman known as "thief-takers" developed. These individuals made an occupation out of hunting and prosecuting the more dangerous law-violators, the professional criminals, who also brought the largest rewards.

Unfortunately, this system of law enforcement was unable to satisfy any of the affected interests in the community. Businessmen and property-owners were unable to prevent losses. Governments were frustrated in their desire to reduce crime and citizen complaints. Citizens were frequently unable to obtain redress for crimes committed against them. Finally, officers of the system were dissatisfied with their low status and pay. In this state, the colonial system that relied principally on private initiative was ready for reform.

The Decline of the Victim's Role in the Criminal Justice System

Beccaria and the Enlightenment

By the time of the American Revolution, the inadequacies and inequities of the existing criminal justice system had become apparent to many. Suggestions for reform were made and significant changes instituted during the 19th century. Gradually, reform of the police, prosecutorial and correctional systems occurred

Cesare Beccaria published his *Essay on Crimes and Punishments* in 1764, in which he argued that a crime is a state harm, and should not be cognizable as a harm to the individual. (Beccaria, Cesare. *Opere di Cesare Beccaria*, 1821)

both in the colonies and in England. These changes followed closely the lines suggested by Enlightenment writers, particularly Cesare Beccaria, whose work, *Essay on Crimes and Punishment*, was the most influential of the time (Beccaria 1983).

As a member of the Enlightenment, Beccaria sought to re-examine the proper role of the criminal justice system. He regarded society as being created by social contract and viewed the criminal justice system as a necessary expedient in obtaining protection against those members who sought to breach that contract. (Id. at 74.) Applying the standard of the maximization of social good, Beccaria analyzed the system and took issue with many of the existing principles of criminal justice. (Id.)

* * *

Further, Beccaria took issue with the proposition that the primary purpose of the criminal justice system was to serve as an aid to private action in obtaining redress from the criminal. (Id. at 74.) Since the system arose from a social contract, it should serve the interests of society, not the individual victim. Punishments inflicted by the system should primarily serve to deter the criminal, to repay his debt to society, or to deter others from committing similar acts. Punishments should not be imposed to redress private damages. (Id.)

In making this argument, Beccaria distinguished the criminal from the civil suit. The society is damaged by crime and the criminal justice system should serve to prevent this social damage. Thus, the victim should not be allowed to control the decisions concerning prosecution and punishment. (Id. at 58.) Take for example the case in which it would be beneficial to society to prosecute the criminal, but harmful to the victim, such as a sexual assault case where testimony by the victim might be psychologically damaging. To Beccaria, the only choice would be to prosecute because that course of action maximized social utility. (Id. at 87; McDonald 1976; Pincoffs 1966).

Overall, Beccaria's principles evidenced the start of the declining role of the victim in the criminal justice system. This new system required that the victim's roles as policeman, prosecutor, and punishment beneficiary be reduced to that of informant and witness only. These ideas strongly appealed to Americans who sought to emphasize the principles of rationality and utilitarianism, and had an enormous influence on the development of the American criminal justice system during the 19th century.

American Correctional Reform

* * *

This passing of the victim from his former place in corrections went unnoticed and uneventfully. It was not until the end of the 19th century that the victim's disappearance was noticed and some thought was given to restoring him to some role in the correctional process. One proposal was that instead of going to prison the defendant should work for the state, retaining for himself only enough to keep from starving. The balance would go into a fund for compensating the victim (Schafer 1976). If the offender were solvent, his property should be confiscated and restitution made therefrom by order of the court. (Id.) Another proposal suggested that the convict should perform services for compensation for the state while in prison, and that the convict should remain in prison until restitution to the victim was completed. (Id.)

These suggestions, however, met with little success. First, they were based on the assumption that prisoners would be able to earn a reasonable wage through prison labor. However, by the end of the 19th century, the emergence of the labor union movement in America and adverse publicity from a series of investigations into the prisons' abuses of prisoner labor helped foster strong opposition to these proposals (Allen and Simonsen 1975). Later, the economic crises of the Great Depression prompted 33 states to quickly pass laws which forbade the sale of prison products on the open market. These laws severely limited most prison industry. (Id.)

The second obstacle to the return of the victim through such compensation proposals was the fact that the honeymoon with the penitentiary was not over. While it had become clear by the 1850's that penitentiaries not only failed to reform inmates but had degenerated into places of corruption and cruelty, the solution advanced by the new generation of penologists was not to restore the victim's role in the system. Instead, they advocated modification of the great white elephants that had been erected. (Id. at 60–61, nn. 1 & 10.) They urged early release for well-behaved prisoners, and the use of parole and separate institutions for young first offenders. But few of these proposals were enacted. Incarceration had become a value in its own right, and even if it did not rehabilitate it served a useful custodial function (Rothman 1971). By the end of the 19th century, the victim ceased to be a concern for the correctional authorities and the criminal justice system.

The Public Prosecutor

Another important change that occurred shortly after the Revolution that further displaced the victim from his former role in criminal justice was the emergence of the office of public prosecutor. The history of the development of this office in America is a puzzle. English common law made no provision for a public prosecutor such as our district attorney. All prosecutions were private prosecutions brought in the name of the king (Stephen 1883). The right and power to accuse, collect evidence, and manage prosecutions for the state rested with the individual citizen. (Id.) The victim or whoever brought the prosecution retained his own counsel and had charge of the case as in a civil proceeding except that the Attorney General, as representative of the king, could refuse to allow it to go on. In addition to this system of private prosecutions there were prosecutions at the instance of the Crown brought by law officers of the Crown. (Id.) But the powers of these officers were regarded at law as no different from those of a private prosecutor.

In Colonial America where the English common law was the law of the land, the system of private prosecutions was widely used; and no doubt it shared many of the same weaknesses as the English system. But, in America there also existed an office of public prosecutor. [Footnote 61 omitted]. The office was first established by statute in Connecticut in 1704, whose example was soon followed by the other colonies. However, it was not until shortly after the Revolution that this office emerged as the predominant method of prosecution. [Note to reader: This point has been disputed by later historians who place the rise of the public prosecution at a later time.] During the 1780's the rebel government had brought numerous political prosecutions. These declined after 1790 but by then the government's interest in the outcome of many criminal cases continued for other reasons. With the imposition of hard labor instead of treble damages as the usual punishment for theft, the victim of theft no longer was the party of interest in theft prosecution. The government became the truly interested party. After 1805, when fines or imprisonment were the punishments in all cases, the government's interest was even greater.

The history of the role of the victim in the prosecution of criminal cases from 1810 to the present is difficult to trace. Unlike corrections and the police, the office of the public prosecutor has received only limited scholarly treatment. Thus, attention herein is focused upon the relationship between the victim and the public prosecutor during the 20th century.

Today [1976], in the opinion of many commentators, both victims and witnesses of crimes receive from public prosecutors what has been called the "administrative runaround" (Ash 1972). Both are required to make numerous trips to the courthouse to tell and retell their stories to a series of prosecutors responsible for different stages of the case, and often to sit for prolonged periods of time in dirty waiting rooms or corridors, frequently with the defendant nearby. (Id.) Witness fees are generally inadequate to cover actual expenses, much less to compensate for the emotional stress. In many jurisdictions they are not paid at all. (Id.)

Criticism has also been leveled at the legal profession for its pattern of neglect with regard to the interests of victims and witnesses. Victims and witnesses do not receive even a fraction of the protections and defenses that are accorded an accused. (Id. at 401.) Typically, the interests of the victim and witnesses are subordinated to what are regarded as more important interests. A good example is the character cross-examination of a victim in rape cases. While the defendant has an interest in the introduction of relevant evidence on his behalf, the victim has important interests as well, such as freedom from intimidation, harassment, and further degradation, and the preservation of privacy. Yet, the legal profession seems remarkably willing to sacrifice such interests of the victim to those of the defendant in every instance.

Another area in which the victim gets little satisfaction from the public prosecutor is the matter of criminal fraud. This crime was not unknown at the time of the Revolution, but since then with the development of the modern marketplace the opportunity for such fraud has vastly increased. When the victim of such a crime seeks the public prosecutor's assistance, he is usually treated to a lecture on the difference between civil and criminal law. Thus, while the victim was the subject of a criminal law violation, he is encouraged only to hire a private attorney and file a civil suit. Generally, the prosecutor's position is that he lacks the resources to conduct such prosecutions; but even if he had them, the criminal prosecution would be conducted in the interests of society and no attempt would be made to recover the victim's losses. For example, if the prosecution showed chances of success, the defendant would probably be offered the opportunity to plead nolo contendere. This would supposedly serve the interests of the community by making conviction certain and reducing the costs of prosecution, but does a disservice to the interests of the victim who then would be unable to use the criminal conviction as prima facie evidence of guilt in a subsequent civil suit. Of course, in legal theory, the public prosecutor is not supposed to serve the particular interests of private individuals; nor, for that matter, is he to serve the public interest. Instead, he has the much greater burden of seeing that justice is done (American Bar Association 1971).

It is usually in these terms, for instance, that the practice of plea bargaining is justified. Although plea bargaining is the means by which most criminal convictions are obtained, it does not occur in an open hearing at which the victim could, if he wished, be present (Alschuler 1968; Newman 1966). Instead, it is usually conducted informally in hallways, private offices, and sometimes even by telephone (see Alschuler). Not only is the victim seldom present but he is usually not consulted. Even worse, he is rarely informed of the outcome.

Therein lies the exquisite irony of modern law. The age-old struggle of civilization has been to persuade people not to take justice into their own hands but rather to let their vengeance and righteous indignation be wrought by the law. Western civilization had by the Middle Ages succeeded in substituting private prosecutions for blood feuds. The next step was to replace private prosecution with public prosecution, while asking the victim to forego whatever satisfaction he might derive from personally prosecuting his transgressor and settling for the more intangible satisfaction of knowing that justice would be done. Now, the modern criminal justice system operates in an age of computers and instant telecommunications, disposing of large numbers of cases without trial and without bothering to give the victim even the minimal satisfaction of knowing what happened to his case and why.

This ill-treatment afforded the victim of crime by the modern public prosecutor and the neglect to provide the victim with the information concerning the handling of his case reflects an historical and constricted understanding of his function. While the prosecutor is quick to state that his purpose is to maintain law and order in society, he sees his responsibility for doing this entirely in terms of punishing those who violate the law. However, while pursuing this ideal of impersonal justice, the system has neglected the continuing struggle of all societies to convince their members not to resort to personal vengeance to settle their grievances. Lawfulness in society is increased or diminished to the extent that this struggle is successful.

The Professional Police

The advent of professional police further diminished the victim's prominence in law enforcement. By the middle of the 18th century the inadequacies of a policing system composed of part-time, privately paid law enforcement officers and bounty-seeking private citizens led slowly to the development of government operated police forces (see Hibbet at 99–102).

Several factors combined to make the development of professional police inevitable. Traditional notions of community responsibility for mutual welfare had vanished in the impersonality of large urban concentrations (Rothman at 57).

Citizens rarely aided peace officers in making arrests (Lane at 12). Even monetary rewards had lost their power to motivate citizen cooperation, and toward the end of the 1820's payments of criminal fines to private informers had virtually ceased (Id. at 37). Moreover, the traditional system had been singularly ineffective in preventing crime. The reformers touted the advantages of professional police who could uncover potential crime on their own initiative without being barred from action until some public disturbance or private complaint came to their attention. (Id. at 35.)

Further, law enforcement financed by private fees had become not only inefficient but corrupt. Victims able to pay higher fees commanded disproportionate attention (Richardson 1970). The competitiveness of the fee system discouraged cooperation among lawmen in apprehending criminals. (Id.) As victims were primarily interested in the return of their property, officers had little incentive to bring offenders to justice. Illicit arrangements between police and criminals were being made even in advance of the crime. (Id.) Thus, a salaried police force responsible to the whole community became an increasingly attractive prospect.

A final development in the early 19th century enhanced the authority of the police to combat crime. Traditionally, both peace officers and private citizens could make arrests without warrants when a felony had been committed if there was reasonable suspicion that the arrestee was the guilty party (Hall 1936). However, police and citizens alike were liable in a civil action for false arrest if they were mistaken that a crime in fact occurred. (Id.) In 1827, a court decision (*Beckwith v. Philby*, 6 B&C 635 (K.B. 1827)) established the power of police to make warrantless arrests on reasonable suspicion that a felony had been committed, insulating the police from false arrest suits if their reasonable suspicion proved unfounded (Hall at 575). Police were thus able to pursue suspected criminal activity far more aggressively than before and private citizens were simultaneously encouraged to rely on the police to apprehend criminals (see Lane at 8).

Although the advent of the professional police curtailed the victim's direct role in law enforcement, he still retained a role in the detection and solution of crime. Successful police work depends greatly upon the victims' identification of their assailants (President's Commission 1967). Moreover, victims generally initiate police responses to crime (Reiss 1971).

However, it is also understood that as many as two-thirds or more of all crimes committed are never reported to the police (President's Commission 1967). This is attributed to victims' fears that the police would not want to be bothered with their cases, or would be unable to do anything about the crimes. Studies have found that victims are critical of the professional attitude of modern police and find them cold and impersonal (see MacDonald, *Introduction*). Further, victims are disturbed by the failure of police to offer advice on how to prevent the crime from reoccurring, or to inform them of the progress of their cases (Freemont, Calif. Police Dep't 1974). Police are also criticized for confiscating property without explaining that it is needed for evidence or explaining the procedure for regaining the property after trial. (Id.) Victims also resent repeating their stories to various officers. (Id.)

In part these criticisms reflect the intractable fact that the police do approach crime, and victims, professionally. For the police, a particular crime is simply one crime among many; for the victim, his crime is a personal calamity. Perhaps the burden should fall more heavily on the police to offer victims some solicitude. To a greater extent, however, the criticisms reflect misunderstanding and misinformation among the public about police and legal procedures, and this is being addressed by a variety of new efforts to ease the victim's involuntary confrontation with the criminal law.

* * *

In the contemporary American criminal justice system, the victim no longer controls the investigation and prosecution of crime. In many respects this evolution in law enforcement has benefitted the victim, who is no longer required to bear the risk of apprehending criminals, nor to expend his own funds and energy to bring offenders to justice. These responsibilities are entrusted to the particular expertise of police, prosecutors, and correctional officials, and society as a whole now bears the costs of enforcing the criminal law.

While the victim has been relieved of his responsibilities as law enforcer, the criminal justice system itself has become an institution designed to serve the entire society, and not the individual victim. It has been too easy to forget that the victim suffers peculiarly personal emotional and economic damage as a direct result of the crime, and that he is often bewildered by a complex prosecutorial system which he is powerless to control. The recent efforts to provide victims with personal support, and to clarify and expand their role in the prosecutorial process, reflects a growing awareness that a just and humane society cannot ignore the toll which crime exacts upon individual victims. The third century of American development will be enriched if these first tentative steps lead to a new accommodation for the victim within the criminal justice process.

* * *

Analysis

Professor McDonald's historical survey provides description and analysis of the state of affairs for victims culminating in 1976, the year of the nation's bicentennial. At the time of the article, the Victims' Rights Movement had barely begun. Thus, McDonald looks backward, describing and analyzing the reasons and rationales for the decline of the role of the victim. Necessarily an ambitious undertaking, the article grasps the big-picture developments leading to victim exclusion. In doing so, the article is important as a 1976 baseline from which the subsequent evolution of victims' rights may be measured. That baseline is that the victim's only role was to enter the courtroom at the time he or she was called to testify. When the testimony was finished, he or she would leave.

The exclusion of the victim from the trial addressing his or her victimization was of particular concern to the modern Victims' Rights Movement. This exclusion came about gradually and was fully achieved in 1975 through the adoption of Federal Rule of Evidence 615, which permitted either party as a matter of right to exclude from the trial any witnesses, including victims.

The History of the Modern Victims' Rights Movement

The following document is a summary of the history of the Victims' Rights Movement as told by some important pioneers in the Movement. The document describes the origins of the Victims' Rights Movement as a collection of unlikely allies and examines the special interests that oppose the Movement.

- **Document:** "History of the Crime Victims' Rights Movement in the United States" by Steven Derene, Steve Walker, and John Stein
- **Date:** 2007
- **Significance:** This document reviews the influence of significant legal and social codes on today's Victims' Movement and provides an overview of movements that were precursors of the Crime Victims' Movement.
- **Source:** Derene, Steven, Steve Walker, and John Stein. "History of the Crime Victims' Rights Movement in the United States." *Participant's Text*. Washington D.C.: Office of Justice Programs, National Victim Assistance Academy, 2007.

---

* * *

Today's view of violent crime and victimization is quite different than in the 1970s. The nation's emotional and legal reaction to criminals has changed dramatically. Why have personal and political responses changed during this period? This chapter . . . will focus on the historical development of the crime victims' movement and the reasons for the public's more recently altered perceptions of crime and the treatment of crime victims.

In the last three decades, the crime victims' movement has emerged as a powerful source of social, legal, and political change. Many early pioneers of the crime victims' movement were influenced by the cultural environment created by the civil rights and antiwar movements. Meanwhile, the women's movement, as well as the law and order movement, led more directly to the emergence of a clearly defined crime victims' movement. The history of the movement can be divided into six stages, each denoting new developments in victim involvement and services, changes in service providers' attitudes, new theoretical concepts, and ongoing legal changes. This description is, by necessity, not inclusive of all historical facts; rather, its purpose is to acquaint the reader with the *zeitgeist*, or spirit, of each stage of the crime victims' movement.

* * *

Starting in the 1970s, the societal view of criminals' and victims' rights began changing dramatically and not always on parallel tracks, given the differing kinds of reforms that advocates sought for victims. In 1972, an assistant district attorney in Milwaukee County, Wisconsin, published an article in the *Notre Dame Law Review* that described the "pattern of blindness and neglect" with which witnesses were treated (Ash 1972). The article drew attention to the critical role of crime victims in the criminal justice system and encouraged the development of what was then referred to as "witness appearance-control projects" (Ash, at 411–12).

Victim issues gradually moved back into the mainstream of the criminal justice system and led to the creation of entirely new kinds of social services. The following sections delineate the reasons for these changes and describe the movements that helped precipitate this return to the victims' rights of the late 1700s and early 1800s.

Emerging Social Movements

It was not until the 1800s that women like Susan B. Anthony began to rebel against male domination and abuse. Most known for her zeal in promoting the right for women to vote, Anthony was also creating the first women's movement in this country by addressing domestic violence, the victimization of prostitutes, and the battle for equal pay for women. She published a newspaper edited by and for women, cautioning workers about sexual harassment while railing against substance abuse and pointing out that women beaten by their intoxicated husbands were its most common victims (Sherr 1995).

> Friends, when we come before you to advocate the Cause popularly termed "Women's Rights," we simply ask that woman not be wronged. We ask for her justice and equality—not favor and superiority—the rights and privileges her humanity charters to her equally with man, not arbitrary power and selfish domination. (Id. at 50.)

In 1866, the American Society for the Prevention of Cruelty to Animals was formed, followed by the Society for the Prevention of Cruelty to Children in 1975, both predating any formal organization to prevent cruelty to women in the United States. In spite of the noble efforts of Susan B. Anthony and Elizabeth Cady Stanton, and, one generation later, Jane Addams, who founded Hull House in Chicago, not much changed for women in the United States until the first protective shelters for battered women were established 100 years later.

Beginning in the early 1960s and preceding renewed focus on crime victims, four social/political movements set the stage for the crime victims' movement as it exists today. The first two—the civil rights movement and the antiwar movement—created a cultural environment that, along with the inspiration of President John F. Kennedy's "New Frontier" idealism, greatly influenced the philosophical, legal, and tactical background of many pioneers of the crime victims' movement. Two other movements—the women's movement and the law and order movement—had more direct bearing on the evolution of the crime victims' movement.

The Civil Rights Movement

Dr. Martin Luther King, Jr., and other leaders of the civil rights movement changed this country's view of civil disobedience, clarifying that all Americans have rights under the U.S. Constitution, and focusing on nonviolent change. Even though this country has had a long history of civil disobedience dating back to the Boston Tea Party and 19th century literary figures like Thoreau and Whitman, this approach diminished as a result of 20th century patriotism engendered by two world wars. Civil disobedience was, therefore, not new in 1963 but reemerged and was applied to a new group: American minorities. The civil rights movement enabled society's disenfranchised minorities to exert power over American governmental and private institutions and demand equal rights and equal access to society's opportunities and institutions. This movement helped establish the principles that constitutional rights should apply to all citizens, and that nonviolent methods of advocacy can be productive in changing American society (Karmen 2004).

The Antiwar Movement

This movement organized to oppose American participation in the war in Vietnam. It pointed to America's propensity for violence and the influence of the military-industrial complex, as President Dwight D. Eisenhower called it. A key component of this movement was distrust of authority, which continues today. Through its well orchestrated marches in cities across America, the antiwar movement showed that grassroots politics could influence and even overpower conventional politics. More importantly, the movement raised questions not only about governmental decisionmaking but also about the moral implications of these decisions.

Even more than proponents of the civil rights movement, antiwar proponents used the media, especially television, to publicize their issues and concerns. The women's movement later used this tool efficiently in publicizing the plight of rape and domestic violence victims. Both of these populist political movements empowered citizens, especially young people, to speak out publicly for what they believed was right. Both served as incubators of grassroots organizations that would awaken groups and organizations concerned with sexual assault, domestic violence, and homicide.

The Women's Movement

A focus on child abuse and neglect led to attention to women as well. This child protection concern initially focused on physicians, social workers, and public-sector personnel. The attention of child advocates and Congress to the work of Dr. C. Henry Kempe, who made his first presentation about the "battered child syndrome" in 1961, led to the creation of the National Center on Child Abuse and Neglect in the Department of Health, Education, and Welfare in 1974.

Attention to women as a group had diminished after they were given the right to vote by the 19th Amendment to the U.S. Constitution. Not until the early 1970s did the women's movement reexamine American family values and traditional male/female roles by spotlighting sexism in bureaucracy (including, very importantly, the criminal justice system) and economic discrepancies between men and women. This perspective and insight have been considered the most significant precursor ("the mother") of the crime victims' movement. "The idea that women should organize to combat rape (and domestic violence) was an invention of the women's movement" (Burgess 2004). The victimization of women and the bureaucratic facilitation of this violence in all areas of society were clarified and politicized. The long overdue recognition that women were entitled to equal social, political, and economic opportunity and power became a national focus.

Susan Brownmiller's book *Against Our Will: Men, Women and Rape* gave credence to the sexual assault movement. It broadened the understanding of "rape" from a crime against "sexual morality" to one of "physical assault" and called attention to society's and, in particular, the criminal justice system's maltreatment of sexual assault victims (Brownmiller 1975).

A direct result of this increase in women's power and attention to women's issues was the formation of rape crisis centers and domestic violence shelters in the early 1970s (Burgess 2004). These community-based grass-roots programs were started by rape and domestic violence victims in their own living rooms and basements. The common agenda was to right the wrongs for other victims, but the programs met strong resistance. In one community after another, rape crisis counselors faced countless negative encounters with the criminal justice system and other bureaucracies. Meanwhile, they developed descriptions of "crisis counselors," as they called themselves. "They began with no role models and became role models for themselves and for other

Susan Brownmiller poses with her book *Against Our Will–Men, Women and Rape*, in New York, October 18, 1975. This book was the most influential work against sexual assault. (AP Photo/Suzanne Vlami)

crime victims" (Burgess 2004). This important manifestation of the women's movement led to some of its earliest, most publicized political events, such as Take Back the Night and numerous candlelight vigils for women's rights to facilitate consciousness-raising.

The Law and Order Movement

The law and order movement in 1968 slightly predated the beginning of the crime victims' movement (often marked at 1972, when the first three official crime victim service agencies were formed), and its alliance with the women's movement did not develop until 1974. The law and order movement focused on increasing the rights of the common citizen to achieve parity with the rights of the criminal. However, many supporters felt that common citizens could manage their own protection and believed that justice should be accomplished without expanding governmental assistance and monetary support (Karmen 2004). Law and order supporters believed that criminals should be punished more rigorously; potential victims should be more careful; and victims, once victimized, should be self-sufficient and not dependent on the government for assistance.

The mid-1970s brought the development of victim/witness assistance programs located in prosecutors' offices. The earliest programs were designed to help victims who were witnesses in criminal cases navigate the criminal court system and to encourage them to cooperate and thereby improve conviction rates. The emotional distress of many victims led some members of the victim/witness staff to offer counseling as part of their job. As they tried to make the road through the justice system smoother, some of them began to see themselves as advocating on behalf of victims as well.

By the early 1980s, a shift developed placing more emphasis on victims' needs. Programs emerged to respond to the crises of all victims of violence—some in grassroots settings and some in law enforcement agencies. The support for increased offender accountability and a back-to-the-basics constitutional approach produced a new emphasis on restitution and individual rights. The law and order movement has been particularly influential in the later stages of the crime victims' movement. Its call for participation by victims as a way to protect their own interests was hastened along by new victim activists—including some within the system who were allied to this cause, as were an increasing number of veterans of the law and order movement who broadened their focus from the offender to the victim.

Sometimes in unison, more often in parallel ways, the women's movement and the law and order movement greatly accelerated the pace and success of the victims' movement in the 1980s.

The following section outlines and describes six stages of the crime victims' movement, detailing critical events in its history. This description denotes changes concerning victim involvement and services, service providers' attitudes, new theoretical concepts, and ongoing legal changes. The changes associated with these stages did not always occur in neat, discrete epochs but evolved out of earlier developments and continued through subsequent stages.

The identification and role of broad movements should not overlook or diminish the contributions of individuals, not necessarily acting in concert with others, to the development of the crime victims' movement. For example, Margery Fry originated the concept of government-run crime victim compensation programs and invented domestic violence shelters. Also important, was the power of personal stories, such as those of Candy Lightner, John Walsh, and Roberta Roper, in fostering a broader appreciation and support for crime victims' rights and services.

Historical Stages of the Crime Victims' Movement

Stage 1: Response to Crime

In the early 1960s, crime rose steadily in the United States, reaching its highest point in 1981 (FBI 1981). Its effect on American life was evident. In response, the crime victims' movement mobilized on multiple fronts (Young 1988).

In 1965, the first crime victims' compensation program was established by the California legislature. However, the major strides of this period were accomplished not by legislatures but by the energy of volunteers, many of whom were crime victims themselves. In many cases, they had been victimized again due to less-than-adequate assistance and services within the criminal justice system.

In 1972, volunteers founded the first three official victim assistance programs that still exist today:

- Aid for Victims of Crime, St. Louis, Missouri (now the Crime Victim Advocacy Center of St. Louis).
- Bay Area Women Against Rape, San Francisco, California.
- Rape Crisis Center, Washington, DC.

Throughout the 1960s and early 1970s, many state and federal commissions were established to study crime and urban riots and their consequences. Following these efforts, the federal government took two significant steps to address the problem: the creation of the first national victimization survey, *National Crime Survey*, in 1972 (renamed the *National Crime Victimization Survey* in 1990) and the formation of the Law Enforcement Assistance Administration (LEAA; Young 1988).

The *National Crime Survey* gathered crime data from randomly selected individuals and households all across America, an approach that was very different from the FBI's *Uniform Crime Report* (UCR), which compiles only crime statistics reported to law enforcement agencies. The new information made it devastatingly clear that the rates of rape and other violent crimes were much higher than those reported to law enforcement. The *National Crime Survey* showed that actual crime rates were three or four times higher than the UCR's published official rates (Bureau of Justice Statistics 1998).

LEAA monies were intended to combat victimization by increasing law enforcement funding and establishing the first victim/witness programs across the United States in 1974. Funds were also used to help educate and increase the sensitivity of police officers in dealing with victims.

In 1974, the first battered women's shelter was established in Denver, Colorado. It was operated by volunteers who used their own funds and a few donations. Their major focus, as in the women's movement, was to provide victim support using the approach of self-help groups. Their goals quickly expanded to target insensitive and unfair treatment of victims by the criminal justice system, an evolution from helping to advocacy and activism that was occurring in other sectors of the movement (Young 1998).

- LEAA called together leading victim activists to discuss methods of increasing victim assistance and created some pilot victim/witness programs in 1974.
- James Rowland, chief probation officer in Fresno, California, developed the first victim impact statement used by the criminal justice system to clearly ascertain and specify a victim's losses.
- In Fort Lauderdale, Florida, and Indianapolis, Indiana, the first law enforcement-based victim assistance programs were established.

In 1975, Frank Carrington's book *The Victims* promoted "the proposition that the victim's current sorry status in the criminal justice system *need not be so* [italics added] and that something can and must be done to enhance the rights of the victim" (Carrington 1975). The National Organization for Victim Assistance (NOVA) was founded in 1975. In 1976, about 100 leaders met at the Second National Victim Assistance Conference in Fresno, California.

During this first stage, mental health providers had limited involvement at the grassroots level. However, practitioners working with victims of sexual assault recognized characteristics common to many victims. In 1974, Ann Burgess coined the term *rape trauma syndrome* (Burgess and Holstrom 1974). Although not universally accepted until years later, its initial use during this time would later facilitate better services for victims in both the mental health and criminal justice systems.

By the late 1970s, mental health providers became more aware of victim trauma. Research began to show the efficacy of peer support groups; some research indicated that these groups were often much more helpful than mental health professionals, partly because the professionals had little training in the grieving process and crisis therapy. *The Crime Victim's Book*, written by Morton Bard and Dawn Sangrey and first published in 1979, was an early, influential primer on understanding and recognizing victims' emotional responses to crime victimization.

As specialized service providers gained new insights into victimization, mental health practitioners began to acknowledge their lack of expertise and began to listen to advocates and victims. For example, the description of the "battered woman syndrome," formulated by Lenore Walker in 1979, provided a theoretical framework for working with victims of domestic violence.

During this period, a number of the pioneers in understanding and treating the mental health problems of crime victims began comparing notes with colleagues treating Vietnam veterans suffering from what seemed to be related aftereffects of trauma.

By the end of this stage, the groundwork was laid from two sources for the development of a full-fledged movement. The women's movement created grassroots rape counseling and domestic violence programs, and within the criminal justice system through LEAA funding, victim assistance programs were emerging.

Stage 2: Conflict and Unstable Funding

At the outset of this second stage, it appeared that many of the gains of the fledgling victims' movement might be lost. In 1979, LEAA was defunded by Congress, and thus the first stream of federal support abruptly ended. As is often the case when limited funding is paired with too many needs, community-based and government-based programs began to compete for limited resources (Young 1988).

Professionalism and training emerged as competing themes, partly to define differing approaches to victim services and partly to propose that their own perspective was most worthy of the dwindling dollars. Despite their common purpose of assisting victims, the contrasting perspectives, purposes, structure, and operation of grassroots victim programs versus criminal justice-based programs increasingly became issues. This was exacerbated by the frequent complaint of grassroots victim advocates that the criminal justice system did not adequately support victims of rape and domestic violence. Even today, some of the residual tension from this grassroots-versus-system perspective remains, as do critiques of both perspectives from those without ties to either camp.

In 1978, sexual assault programs and domestic violence programs created their own national organizations to pursue their specific agendas (Young 1988). These organizations include the following:

- National Coalition Against Sexual Assault (NCASA).
- National Coalition Against Domestic Violence (NCADV).

Believing that change in rape and domestic violence law was not happening quickly enough, these organizations decided not to work within the criminal justice system, which, they felt, was not listening. At the same time, however, they fought successfully for the first round of victims' rights reforms, namely rape shield laws and a ban on the exemption for marital rape.

During this period, program leaders and administrators debated the strengths and weaknesses of the various programs.

Many movements fail (including some of the precursors of the victims' movement) because no "second generation" is trained to continue with the original fervor and energy. Fortunately, this was not true for the victims' movement. In spite of the dissension among the established programs, the system-based programs were proving their worth, and important new grassroots organizations arose. Often led by victims, these new groups directly challenged the indifference of the criminal justice system and the stigmatizing approaches of the mental health system.

Two new grassroots programs grew in response to a void in services to family members of those killed. The cumulative effect was a new infusion of energy into the movement. These two programs were:

- Parents of Murdered Children (POMC), founded by Robert and Charlotte Hullinger in 1978.
- Mothers Against Drunk Driving (MADD), founded by Candy Lightner and Cindy Lamb in 1980.

In 1979, Frank Carrington founded the Crime Victims' Legal Advocacy Institute, which was renamed the Victims' Assistance Legal Organization (VALOR) in 1981, to advocate for the legal rights of crime victims. While his main contribution was getting the civil courts to make it easier for victims to get monetary redress, Carrington was also among those seeking reform in the criminal justice system.

On the legislative front, crime victim advocates pressed for reforms, and state legislators enacted laws that increasingly supported victims, such as the following:

- In 1977, Oregon passed the first law mandating arrest in domestic violence cases.
- In 1978, Minnesota enacted legislation to allow warrantless arrest in domestic violence cases, regardless of whether there was a prior protection order.
- In 1980, Wisconsin enacted the first statutory bill of rights for victims and witnesses of crime, including state funding for county victim/witness assistance programs (National Center for Victims of Crime 1994a).

In 1981, Ronald Reagan became the first president to proclaim National Victims' Rights Week. Later that year, the Attorney General's Task Force on Violent Crime issued its report. The task force, which included Frank Carrington, recommended that a separate task force be created to consider victims' issues.

Stage 3: Public Awareness:

As the revitalized crime victims' movement learned better ways to access the news media, public awareness of victims' issues increased. The 1981 Uniform Crime

Reports had clearly shown the increase in victimization, and the movement actively used these new statistics for its cause (FBI 1981).

In response to the Attorney General's Task Force recommendation, President Reagan appointed a Task Force on Victims of Crime in 1982. Chaired by Lois Haight Herrington, this task force made 68 recommendations to improve the treatment of crime victims. The recommendations were directed at all segments of the public and private sectors, including the criminal justice system. The report included, for the first time, a recommendation for a constitutional amendment for crime victims' rights and federal funding for state crime victim compensation and victim/witness assistance programs.

Later that year, Congress passed the Victim and Witness Protection Act. Borrowing from new victims' rights precepts in state laws, this act provided for witness protection, restitution, and fair treatment for federal victims and witnesses of violent crimes (NCVC 1994a).

Likewise, changes at the federal level encouraged legislative changes at state levels, including victims' bills of rights, proposals for training and education, and expansion of existing victim/witness programs. The single greatest legislative event in the victims' movement to date was the 1984 Victims of Crime Act (VOCA). This act established the Crime Victims Fund to provide funds for local victim assistance programs and state victim compensation as well as services for victims of federal crimes. The fund was made up of money from federal criminal fines, penalties, and bond forfeitures.

The Office for Victims of Crime (OVC), created in the Department of Justice in 1983 to implement the 68 recommendations of the President's Task Force, was designated to administer VOCA, including the distribution of VOCA funds to states for existing victim programs (NCVC 1994a).

With increased public awareness and high-level political support for victims' issues, numerous programs were started and laws passed during the 1980s. The greatest increase in victim/witness programs occurred in this third stage. Some highlights of this stage were:

- National Conference of the Judiciary on Victims of Crime (1983).
- Missing Children's Assistance Act, which included the establishment of the National Center for Missing and Exploited Children by Congress (1984).
- Attorney General's Task Force on Family Violence (1984).
- Family Violence Prevention and Services Act (1984).
- National Institute of Mental Health (NIMH) and NOVA national colloquium, "Aftermath of Crime: A Mental Health Crisis" (1985).
- National Center for Victims of Crime (formerly Sunny von Bulow National Victim Center) (1985).
- NOVA Constitutional Amendment Meeting (1986).
- President's Child Safety Partnership (1987).

Changes in rape and domestic violence laws during this period helped to influence attitudes in the criminal justice system and local communities. However, grassroots rape counseling and domestic violence advocates felt that citizens were still inclined to view these crimes in morality terms rather than criminal terms (Burgess 2004).

As the movement spread to bring services to other victims as well as victims of domestic and sexual violence, second-generation grassroots organizations—including the newer ones—feared that increased governmental involvement and new competition for funding of victim programs would lead to dissension as in previous years. These fears were not realized, however. A floor amendment to VOCA in 1984 had mandated that priority be given to victims of child abuse, but this led to complaints from groups representing victims of spousal abuse, sexual assault, and other crimes. And so a fourth priority, for "previously underserved victims of violent crimes," was later added. In 1988, VOCA was reauthorized, and the OVC was established permanently. Crime victim compensation was expanded to include victims of both domestic violence and drunk driving.

In addition, during this stage, theoretical concepts were put to more practical use in both the criminal justice and mental health systems. The concept of *second victimization* as originally enunciated by psychiatrist and former New York City police officer Martin Symonds—that victims were often harmed as much by the system's response as by the crime itself—became generally recognized and accepted. Even dealings with friendly justice professionals could generate acute stress in victims, leading many in prosecutors' offices to learn the same crisis intervention techniques as were used by colleagues who saw victims much closer to the original trauma.

The various syndromes identified earlier were being discussed within the context of a new diagnosis—posttraumatic stress disorder (PTSD). With the identification of PTSD, a general diagnosis was now developed that did not stigmatize the victim but, rather, clarified and legitimized the victim's normal response to an abnormal situation. In 1980, this diagnosis was recognized when the description of PTSD was placed in the *Diagnostic and Statistical Manual* (third edition) of the American Psychiatric Association (APA), the authoritative diagnostic tool of mental health professionals.

In addition, better training in trauma and crisis intervention enabled mental health professionals to learn about victims' issues. Mental health professionals also began to provide better supportive services. Peer support groups began to be seen as a useful adjunct to successful individual therapy.

A major development occurred in 1986 when NOVA was asked to send a team of experienced crisis counselors to help the community of Edmond, Oklahoma, immediately after a mass murder. Tens of thousands of caregivers have been trained in the NOVA model that emerged under the rubric of Community Crisis Response Teams. A similar set of short-term services, called Critical Incident Stress Debriefings, emerged at about the same time, which focused principally on the stresses of first responders in cases of mass violence. Volunteers from both disciplines became the victims' movement's special contribution to disaster services.

During this period, the crime victims' movement came of age, becoming more focused and sophisticated (Andrews 1992). The first 10 years had been initiated and perpetuated by strong leaders with forthright personalities; however, in this period, an important paradigm shift was taking place. The movement expanded beyond the dynamics of individual-level politics to group-level national politics, resulting in the change into a more formalized profession.

Stage 4: Expanding Legislative Agenda

In the 1900s, three major legislative issues emerged:

- Victim service funding.
- Victims' rights.
- Law and order concerns.

The growing sophistication of the victims' movement enabled advocates to exert power and influence on several fronts. Thanks to state networks and coalitions, political efforts during this time became much more organized and presented clearer and more cohesive agendas, such as:

- Removing the limit on deposits into the Crime Victims Fund for VOCA to provide expanded and more stable funding for state crime victim compensation and victim assistance programs.
- Expanding victims' rights through more extensive and effective state legislation.
- Adopting crime victims' rights amendments in state constitutions.
- Successful results of this agenda at the federal level included the following:
- As of 1995, all 50 states, the District of Columbia, and three territories had enacted crime victim compensation programs.
- As of 1998, 33 states had passed constitutional amendments.
- The U.S. Congress passed major legislation that addressed hate crimes, campus security, child protection, violence against women, sexual assault, kidnapping, and gun control.
- The U.S. Supreme Court upheld the use of victim impact statements in capital cases.
- Currently, all states have passed victims' rights legislation in the form of a victims' bill of rights or a series of statutory protections.

This legislative agenda has continued to grow and expand. The recent serious congressional consideration to a federal constitutional victims' rights amendment exemplifies this. The women's movement's rape and domestic law reform agenda has been embraced by both women and men in the lawmaking professions (Burgess 2004). Activities and issues in this stage continue into the sixth stage.

Stage 5: Emerging Professionalism

One of the most salient issues in recent years has been the emerging professionalism in the field of victim services. As with other grassroots movements, there is some apprehension about professionalizing a community-based service system that originated and developed its strength through the dedication of volunteers who extended themselves personally to victims in need. Most victim service programs, however, have not diluted their passion and are led by dedicated professionals who have years of experience working with victims in specialized settings while still relying heavily on trained, committed volunteers.

The historical distrust of other professionals who have no specialized training or experience in victim treatment issues has persisted in many areas. Experience has made some of these concerns both legitimate and urgent. However, salary issues, increased availability of training, and a growing interest in program evaluation and quality services have led to significant professionalism in the field.

Victim service providers work in very diverse settings. Advocates typically perform a variety of tasks that require an understanding of social, psychological, and legal principles. In addition:

- The areas of expertise and the training needed are multidisciplinary in nature.
- There is a growing recognition that to be accepted by other professionals, certification or some other form of credentialing is necessary.
- Increased professionalization of this field will potentially create professional-level salaries for experienced victim advocates and administrative staff.
- Credentialing by victim groups, with help from allied government agencies to support training called for in the credentialing program, is seen by many as a way to overcome the fear of traditional degree-centered credentials that might be imposed on the field by one of the licensed professions. The trend toward credentialing by advocates' groups and their allies in government has been hastened by (unsuccessful) proposals in a few states that only members of a licensed mental health profession should be allowed to perform certain counseling services.

The changes in this area have often been small but significant and growing. By the early 21st century, a dozen or more states have established their own credentialing systems, with the required educational units designed and taught mostly by peers. (States with such systems include Ohio, Florida, California, Connecticut, Kansas, and South Carolina.)

In 1987, the NOVA Board of Directors adopted a *Code of Professional Ethics for Victim Service Providers*, which covers practitioners' relationship with clients, colleagues, other professionals, and the public. Using NOVA's Code as a template, MADD developed a Code of Ethics for its victim advocates in 1988.

Academic programs were offered in increasing numbers during the 1990s. California State University (CSU), Fresno developed the first academic program in victim services/victimology in the United States. By the summer of 1989, CSU, Fresno had started the first Victim Services Summer Institute to make its certificate program available to professionals in other states. By 1990, the number of graduates from this program had more than tripled. Finally, by 1991, CSU, Fresno developed the first victimology major in the nation and then began developing the first doctorate in 1996 (NCVC 1994a).

Eight states have established clinics to offer free legal services for victims seeking to enforce their rights. Nurturing this development is the National Crime Victims Law Institute (NCVLI.org), founded in 2000 at Lewis and Clark Law School in Oregon, which also fosters teaching courses on victims' rights in law schools around the country.

Academic credit and the development of more degree programs will continue to be important for the next phases of the crime victims' movement. Some victimology programs have developed legal advocacy components in addition to their training, technical assistance, and educational activities, such as the Center for the Study of Crime Victims' Rights, Remedies, and Resources of the University of New Haven in Connecticut. This program, part of the School of Public Safety and Professional Studies, provides amicus briefs in selected appellate cases dealing with victims' rights issues.

Based on the template for performance ethics and standards developed by the National Victim Assistance Standards Consortium, the next potential step could be the development of curriculum standards for education at the national and state levels. The National Victim Assistance Academy (NVAA) curriculum was created to offer this opportunity. The original NVAA began in 1995 by offering a 45-hour core course of work in victim services that could be taken for academic credit. It formed the basis for the first state-level academy in Michigan in 1998. Then, OVC initiated a multiyear funding strategy for the development of state victim assistance academies in 1999. As of 2006, state victim assistance academies have been offered or are in the process of development in 30 states, most which have received OVC financial support and technical assistance.

A sign of the growing recognition of the need to enhance the professional status of victim service providers was the creation in 2003 of the National Advocate Credentialing Program (NACP) by a consortium of national victim organizations. By 2006, more than 500 victim service providers have received NACP credentials based on their experience and training.

In 1996, the National Domestic Violence Hotline (1-800-799-SAFE) was established to provide crisis intervention information and assistance to victims of domestic violence. OVC launched a number of international crime victim initiatives in 1996, including working to foster worldwide implementation of a United Nations declaration on victims' rights and initiatives to better assist Americans victimized abroad.

In 1997, OVC representatives joined the U.S. Delegation to the United Nations Commission on Criminal Justice and Crime Prevention. OVC played a leadership role in the development of an International Victim Assistance Training Manual to implement the United Nation's *Declaration of Basic Principles of Justice for Victims of Crime and Abuse of Power*.

In 1997, the National Center for Victims of Crime (formerly National Victim Center) used its extensive legislative database to create the *Legislative Sourcebook*, a comprehensive compendium of victims' rights laws in all 50 states and the District of Columbia.

In 1998, *New Directions from the Field: Victims' Rights and Services for the 21st Century* was released to the field by OVC. The report was developed with support from OVC and input from more than 1,000 individuals across the nation. It assessed the nation's progress in meeting the recommendations set forth in the *Final Report* of the 1982 President's Task Force on Victims of Crime and issued more than 250 new recommendations from the field for the next millennium. OVC disseminated the 1998 report widely to many programs across the nation.

Stage 6: Advancing Advocacy

During this stage, additional significant developments have occurred on the national and state levels with respect to victims' rights constitutional amendments, legislation, expanded VOCA funding, and creation of national programs affecting crime victims.

U.S. Victims' Rights Constitutional Amendments

In the spring of 1996, bipartisan federal victims' rights constitutional amendments were introduced in both the U.S. House of Representatives and the Senate. The amendment was reintroduced in the Senate in January 1997, but no formal action was taken. Hearings on the amendment were then held in Congress in 1996, 1997, and 1998. In 2004, after being unable to break a potential filibuster on their proposal, Senators Jon Kyl and Dianne Feinstein crafted—and Congress passed—a federal statute modeled on their proposed amendment that allowed the general rights of restitution, notification, allocution, and protection with specific measures to enforce its provisions. Additionally, by 1998, a total of 33 states had adopted crime victims' rights constitutional amendments.

* * *

Analysis

The rise of the Victims' Movement was due centrally to several factors. First was the colossal failure of governments to invest enough resources to provide an acceptable level of public safety. Second was the exile of victims from the criminal process. The document reveals that a tremendous need existed for crime victim services and rights.

In History

The need for criminal justice reforms was deeply felt by the public, who overwhelmingly approved state constitutional victims' rights. Table 1.2 reveals the passage rates of state constitutional amendments.

Table 1.2 States' Passage of Victims' Rights Constitutional Amendments (Popular Vote Passage Percentage of State Constitutional Victims' Rights)

Alabama	1994	80%
Alaska	1994	87%
Arizona	1990	58%
California	1982 (2008)	56% (54%)
Colorado	1992	86%
Connecticut	1996	78%
Florida	1988	90%
Idaho	1994	79%
Illinois	1992	77%
Indiana	1996	89%

(continued)

Table 1.2   (Continued)

Kansas	1992	84%
Louisiana	1998	69%
Maryland	1994	92%
Michigan	1988	84%
Mississippi	1998	93%
Missouri	1992	84%
Montana	1998	71%
Nebraska	1996	78%
New Jersey	1991	85%
New Mexico	1992	68%
Nevada	1996	74%
North Carolina	1996	78%
Ohio	1994	77%
Oklahoma	1996	91%
Oregon	1999 (2008)	58% (75%)
Rhode Island	1986	passed by Const. Convention
South Carolina	1996	89%
Tennessee	1998	89%
Texas	1989	73%
Utah	1994	68%
Virginia	1996	84%
Washington	1989	78%
Wisconsin	1993	84%
33 States	Average	79%

REFERENCES

Allen, H. E. and C. E. Simonsen. *Corrections in America: An Introduction.* Beverly Hills, CA: Glencoe, 1975, 55–56.

Alschuler, A. *The Prosecutor's Role in Plea Bargaining,* 36 U. Chi. L. Rev. 50 (1968).

American Bar Association Project on Standards for Criminal Justice. *Stands Relating to the Prosecution Function and the Defense Function* § 1.1(c) (Approved Draft 1971).

Andrews, A. *Victimization and Survivor Services: A Guide to Victim Assistance.* New York: Springer Publishing Co., 1992.

Arenella, Peter. *Rethinking the Functions of Criminal Procedure: The Warren and Burger Courts' Competing Ideologies,* 72 Geo L.J. 185 (1983).

Ash, Michael. "On Witnesses: A Radical Critique of Criminal Court Procedures." In No. 48 *Notre Dame Lawyer,* 386–425, 1972.

Bard, Morton, and Dawn Sangrey. *The Crime Victim's Book.* 2nd ed. New Jersey: Citadel Press, 1986.

Beccaria, Cesare. *Essay on Crimes and Punishments.* 4th ed. Translated from Italian. London: Printed for E. Newberry, 1775. Reprinted New Jersey: The Lawbook Exchange, Ltd., 2006.

Beckwith v. Philby, 6 B&C 635 (K.B. 1827).

Bellamack v. State, 294 P. 622 (Ariz. 1930).

Beloof, Douglas E. *The Third Model of Criminal Process: The Victim Participation Model.* 1999 Utah L. Rev. 289 (1999).

Beloof, Douglas E. *The Third Wave of Crime Victims' Rights: Standing, Remedy and Review.* 2005 B.Y.U. L. Rev. 255 (2005).

Beloof, Douglas E. *Victims in Criminal Procedure.* NC: North Carolina Press, 1999.

Beloof, Douglass E. and Paul Cassell. *The Crime Victim's Right to Attend the Trial: The Reascendant National Consensus.* 9 Lewis & Clark L. Rev. 481 (2005).

Bishop's New Criminal Procedure. Vol. 1, 1188.1 4th Edition. Chicago: TH Flood and Co., 1895.

Blackstone, William. *Commentaries on the Laws of England.* Facsimile edition with introductions by Stanley N. Katz. Vol. 4. Chicago: University of Chicago Press, 1979.

Booth v. Maryland, 482 U.S. 496 (1987).

Bridenbaugh, C. *Cities in the Wilderness.* New York: Capricorn, 1955.

Brownmiller, S. *Against Our Will: Men, Women and Rape.* New York: Simon and Schuster, 1975.

Bureau of Justice Statistics. *National Crime Victimization Survey.* Washington, DC: U.S. Department of Justice, 1998.

Bureau of Justice Statistics. *Sourcebook of Criminal Justice Statistics.* Washington, DC: U.S. Department of Justice, 1998.

Burford v. Commonwealth, 20 S.E.2d 509 (Va. 1942).

Burgess, A. and L. Holstrom. 1974. *Rape Trauma Syndrome.* 131 American Journal of Nursing. 981 (1974).

Burgess, A. "Research and Practice in Victim Services: Perspective from Education and Research." In *American Society of Victimology Symposium Proceedings,* A. Burgess and T. Underwood. Topeka, Kansas: Washburn University, 2004.

Butler v. State, 97 N.E.2d 492 (Ind. 1951).

Cal. P.C. Code 868.

Calderon v. Thompson, 523 U.S. 538 (1998).

Carrington, F. G. *The Victims.* New Rochelle, NY: Arlington House Pub., 1975.

Chambliss, W. *A Sociological Analysis of the Law of Vagrancy,* 12 Soc. Prob. 67–77 (1964).

Clary v. State, 150 S.W. 919 (Tex. Crim 1912).

Commonwealth v. Harris, 171 A.2d 850 (Pa. Super. Ct. 1961).

Coolman v. State, 72 N.E. 568 (Ind. 1904).

Cornett v. Williams, 87 U.S. 226 (1873).

Cronan ex rel. State v. Cronan, 774 A.2d 866 (R.I. 2001).

Dale v. State, 15 S.E. 287, 289 (Ga. 1892).

Damaska, Mirjan. *Evidentiary Barriers to Conviction and Two Models of Criminal Procedure: A Comparative Study,* 121 U. PA. L. Rev. 506 (1973).

Dangel, Stephanie. *Is Prosecution a Core Executive Function? Morrison v. Olsen and the Framer's Intent.* 99 Yale L.J. 1069 (1990).

Derene, Steven, Steve Walker, and John Stein. "History of the Crime Victims' Rights Movement in the United States." In *Participant's Text.* Office of Justice Programs: National Victim Assistance Academy, 2007.

Dickens v. State, 398 P.2d 1008 (Alaska 1965).

Driscoll v. State, 232 S.W.2d 28 (Tenn. 1950).

Dye v. State, 137 S.E.2d 465 (Ga. 1964).

East v. Scott, 55 F.3d 996 (5 h Cir. 1995).

Federal Bureau of Investigation. *Crime in the United States Uniform Crime Reports, 1981.* Washington, DC: U.S. Department of Justice, 1981.

Fed. R. Evid. 615

Freddy v. State, 229 S.W. 533 (Tex. Crim. App. 1921).

Gaskins, Richard. *Changes in the Criminal Law in Eighteenth Century Connecticut.* 25 Am. J. Legal Hist. 309 (1981).

Greenleaf, Simon. *A Treatise on the Law of Evidence*. 1st Edition. Boston: Boston Daily Atlas, 1842.

Greenleaf, Simon. *A Treatise on the Law of Evidence*, 12th Edition. New York: Little, Brown and Co., 1866.

Griffiths, John. *Ideology in Criminal Procedure or a Third Model of the Criminal Process*. 79 Yale L.J. 359, 367–91 (1970).

Gunn v. State, 243 A.2d 15 (Md. 1968).

Hall, Donald J. *The Role of the Victim in the Prosecution and Disposition of a Criminal Case*. 28 Vand. L. Rev. 931 (1975).

Hall, Jerome. *Legal and Social Aspects of Arrest Without a Warrant*, 49 Harv. L. Rev. 566, 567 (1936).

Hall, J. *Theft, Law and Society*. 2nd ed. Indianapolis, IN: Bobbs-Merrill, 1952.

Hibbert, C. *The Roots of Evil: A Social History of Crime and Punishment*. Boston: Little, Brown, 1963.

Hindus, Michael. *The Contours of Crime and Justice in Massachusetts and South Carolina*. 1767–1878, 21 Am. J. Legal Hist. 212 (1977).

Holder v. State, 187 So. 781 (Fla. 1939).

Holdsworth, W. *A History of English Law*. Vol. 2, 4th ed. London: Methuen, 1936.

Ireland, Robert M. *Privately Funded Prosecution of Crime in the Nineteenth-Century United States*. 39 Am. J. Legal Hist. 43 (1995).

Jackson v. State, 115 S.W. 262 (Tex. Crim. App. 1908).

Joseph, Gregory P. & Stephen A. Saltzburg, *Evidence in America: The Federal Rules in the States*. Washington, DC: American Bar Association, 1987 & 1994 supp.

Karmen, A. *Crime Victims: An Introduction to Victimology*. Belmont, CA: Wadsworth/ Thomson, 2004.

Keller v. State, 31 S.E. 92 (Ga. 1898).

Kemper, Kurtis. *Exemption of Witnesses Under Rule 615 of Federal Rules of Evidence*. 181 A.L.R. Fed. 484 (2005).

Krent, Harold J. *Executive Control Over Criminal Law Enforcement: Some Lessons From History*. 38 Am. U. L. Rev. 275 (1989).

Lane, R. *Policing the City—Boston 1822–1885*. Cambridge, MA: Harvard University Press, 1967.

Leache v. State, 3 S.W. 539 (Tex. Crim. App. 1886).

LeBlanc v. Gauthier, 174 So. 2d 353 (Fla. Dist. Ct. 1965).

Lee v. State, 488 P.2d 365 (Okla. Crim. App. 1971).

Leigh, and J. E. Hall Williams. *International Encyclopaedia of Laws*, vol. 3, Criminal Law. United Kingdom, 1993.

Loyd, William. *The Courts of Pennsylvania in the Eighteenth Century Prior to the Revolution*. 56 U. Pa. L. Rev. 28 (1908).

Malek v. Fed. Ins. Co., 944 F.2d 49 (2d Cir. 1993).

Marcum v. Commonwealth, 1 S.W. 727 (Ky. 1886).

Massy v. State, 142 S.E.2d 832 (Ga. 1965).

McDonald, William F. "Criminal Justice and the Victim: An Introduction," in *Criminal Justice and the Victim*. Thousand Oaks, CA: Sage, 1976: 43.

McDonald, William F. *Towards a Bicentennial Revolution in Criminal Justice: The Return of the Victim*. 13 Amer. Crim. L. Rev. 649 (1976).

McDonald, William F. "The Victim and Correctional Theory: Integrating Victim Reparation with Offender Rehabilitation," in Stephen Shafer (Ed.), *Criminal Justice and the Victim*. Thousand Oaks, CA: Sage, 1976: 47.

McGuff v. State, 7 So. 35 (Ala. 1889).

McKinnon v. State, 299 P.2d 535 (Okla. 1956).

McManus, Edgar. *Law and History in Early New England: Criminal Justice and Due Process*. Massachusetts: University of Massachusetts Press, 1993.

Milo v. State, 214 S.W.2d 618 (Tex. Crim. App. 1948).

Mitchell v. United States, 126 F.2d 550 (10th Cir. 1942).

Mueller, Christopher & Laird Kirkpatrick. *Evidence*. 3rd Edition. New York: Aspen Publishers, 2003.

National Center for Victims of Crime. *Crime Victims' Rights in America: An Historical Overview*. Arlington, VA: Author, 1994a.

National Victim Center. *The 1996 Victim's Rights Sourcebook: A Compilation and Comparison of Victim Rights*. Washington, DC: Laws National Victim Center, 1996.

Nelson, William E. *Emerging Notions of Modern Criminal Law in the Revolutionary Era: An Historical Perspective*. 42 N.Y.U. L. Rev. 450 (1967).

Newman, D. *Conviction: The Determination of Guilt or Innocence Without Trial*. Boston, Mass: Little Brown Pub, 1966.

Norman v. State, 175 S.E. 2d 199 (Ga. Ct. App. 1970).

Office for Victims of Crime. *President's Task Force on Victims of Crime: Final Report*. Washington DC: U.S. Government Printing Press, 1982.

Oliver B. Cannon and Son, Inc. v. Fid & Cas. Co. of New York, 519 F. Supp. 668 (Del. 1981).

Opus 3 Ltd. v. Heritage Park, Inc., 91 F.3d 625 (4th Cir. 1996).

Packer, Herbert L. *The Limits of the Criminal Sanction*. Palo Alto, CA: Stanford University Press, 1968.

Packer, Herbert. *Two Models of Criminal Process*. 113 U. PA. L. Rev. 1 (1964).

Payne v. Tennessee, 501 U.S. 808 (1991).

People v. Cooke, 54 N.E.2d 357 (N.Y. 1944).

People v. Tanner, 44 P.2d 324 (Cal. 1935).

People v. Tidwell, 12 P. 61 (Utah Terr. 1886).

People v. Winchester, 185 N.E. 590 (Il. 1933).

Person v. Miller, 854 F.2d 656 (4th Cir. 1988).

Pincoffs, E. *The Rationale of Legal Punishment*. New York: Humanities Press, 1966.

Polythane Sys., Inc v. Marina Ventures Int'l Ltd., 993 F.2d 1201 (5th Cir. 1993).

Powell v. United States, 208 F.2d 618 (6th Cir. 1953).

President's Commission on Law Enforcement and Administration of Justice. *Task Force Report: The Police*. Washington, DC: U.S. Government Printing Office, 1967.

Ramsey, Carolyn. *The Discretionary Power of "Public" Prosecutors in Historical Perspective*. 39 Am. Crim. L. Rev. 1309 (2002).

Reiss, A. *The Police and the Public*. New Haven and London: Yale University Press, 1971.

Richardson, J. F. *The New York Police: Colonial Times to 1901*. New York: Oxford University Press, 1970.

Roach v. State, 221 Ga. 783 (1966).

Rothman, D. J. *The Discovery of the Asylum*. Chicago and London: University of Chicago Press, 1971, 65.

Ryan v. Couch, 66 Ala. 244 (1880).

Salisbury v. Commonwealth, 79 Ky. 425 (1881).

Schoppel v. United States, 270 F.2d 413 (4th Cir. 1959).

Sherr, L. *Failure Is Impossible: Susan B. Anthony in Her Own Words*. New York: Times Books, 1995.

Siegelman, Don and Courtney W. Tarver, *Victims' Rights in State Constitutions*, 1 Emerg. Issues St. Const. L. 163, 167 (1988).

S.J. Res. 35, 107th Cong. 143 (2002).

Smartt v. State, 80 S.W. 586 (Tenn. 1904).

State v. Bishop, 492 P.2d 509 (Or. Ct. App. 1971).

State v. Brevelle, 270 So. 2d 852 (La. 1972).

State. Bonza, 269 P. 480 (Utah 1928).

State v. Ede, 117 P.2d 235 (Or. 1941).

State v. Hughes, 71 Mo. 633 (1880).

State v. Lewis, 199 So. 2d 907 (La. 1967).

State v. Paolella, 561 A.2d 111 (Conn. 1989).

State v. Pell, 119 N.W. 154, 158 (Iowa 1909).

State v. Ray, 143 N.E.2d 484 (Ohio Ct. App. 1956).

State v. Sampson, 261 N.W. 769, 770 (Iowa 1935).

State v. Smith, 180 0N.W. 4 (Iowa 1920).

State v. Whitworth, 29 S.W. 595 (Mo. 1895).

State v. Williams, 346 So. 2d 181 (La. 1977).

Steinberg, Allen. *From Private Prosecution to Plea Bargaining: Criminal Prosecution, The District Attorney, and American Legal History*. 30 Crim. & Delinq. 568 (1984).

Steinberg, Allen. *The Transformation of Criminal Justice: Philadelphia 1800–1890*. North Carolina: University of North Carolina Press, 1989.

Stephen, J. A *History of the Criminal Law of England*, Originally published 1883. Lenox Hill Pub., 1973.

Stith, Kate. *The risk of Legal Error in Criminal Cases: Some Consequences of Asymmetry in the Right to Appeal*. 57 U. Chi. L. Rev. 1 (1990)

Swartz v. State, 238 N.W. 312 (Neb. 1931).

Trammell v. State, 97 S.W. 2d 902 (Ark. 1936).

Transworld Metals v. Southwire Co., 769 F.2d 902 (2d Cir. 1985).

United States v. Escobedo, 430 F.2d 603 (7th Cir. 1970).

United States v. Machor, 879 F.2d 945 (1st Cir. 1989).

United States v. Frazier, 417 F.2d 1138 (4th Cir. 1969).

United States v. Pellegrino, 470 F.2d 1205 (2nd Cir. 1972).

United States v. Wells, 437 F.2d 1144 (6th Cir. 1971).

Victims' Assistance Legal Organization (VALOR). 1995–1999. *National Crime Victims' Rights Week Resource Guide*. Washington, DC: U.S. Department of Justice, Office for Victims of Crime.

Warren, Charles. *New Light on the History of the Federal Judiciary Act of 1789*. 37 Harv. L. Rev. 49 (1924).

Wigmore, J. *Evidence in Trials at Common Law* 1841, vol. 6., at 475 (Chadbourn rev. 1976).

Wigmore, J. *Sequestration of Witnesses*, 14 Harv. L. Rev. 475, 491 (1901).

William, Richard. *A National Strategy Against Crime*. 20 Harv. J.L. & Pub. Pol'y 543 (1997).

Young, M. "The Crime Victims' Movement," in F. Ochberg (Ed.), *Post-Traumatic Therapy and Victims of Violence*, New York: Brunner/Mazel, 1988: 319–329.

2

TO INCLUDE VICTIMS IN THE CRIMINAL PROCESS?

WHY VICTIMS WERE EXCLUDED FROM THE CRIMINAL PROCESS

As Professor McDonald explained in Chapter 1, our criminal justice process has evolved from one in which crime victims were central players to one in which, until quite recently, victims were essentially excluded. In addition to such historical reasons, why did the process evolve to exclude victims? Various explanations from different authorities examining the question all seem plausible.

Victim Exclusion as an Historical Misunderstanding

- **Document:** "Defining the Role of the Victim in Criminal Prosecution" by Abraham Goldstein
- **Date:** 1982
- **Significance:** In this article, Goldstein elaborates on the expanding role of victims in criminal prosecution as it was at the beginning of the 1980s.
- **Source:** Goldstein, Abraham. "Defining the Role of the Victim in Criminal Prosecution." *Mississippi Law Journal* 52 (1982): 515. Reprinted with permission.

* * *

The victim currently [1982] is denied a formal role—party status—at each of these [restitution] hearings. He has no right to present his views—the right of "allocution"—and he has no right to present evidence, to argue the issues, or to appeal. The victim's complaint may give rise to the prosecution and his testimony may be essential to sustain it, but he has no formal relation to the criminal case. The prosecutor alone is said to represent the public interest in criminal law. He has been endowed by the courts with a broad and virtually unreviewable discretion in these matters of charging and dismissal and restitution (Goldstein 1981; McDonald 1975).

This "monopoly" of criminal prosecution by the district attorney is more the result of a misunderstanding of history than of explicit legislative direction. It traces to a time when the procedure for invoking criminal law was largely in private hands, as it is in England even today. When our system of public prosecution evolved, most statutes merely authorized the district attorney to prosecute all criminal cases in his county; they were silent as to whether the victim or anyone else could prosecute on his own. In a series of early opinions, however, the courts described the district attorney as exercising on the county level the powers of prosecution of the Attorney General of England whose actions could not be reviewed by the courts. From that historical analogy, the courts inferred that the district attorney's actions—particularly in deciding whether or not to initiate a prosecution—were also not reviewable (see generally McDonald 659–61).

These opinions overlooked the fact that the English Attorney General was not a public prosecutor in our sense at all. Except for a limited class of cases, he did not initiate prosecutions. That was (and is) generally left to the victim and to the police as members of the public. He did have an unreviewable power in criminal cases—but only to enter a writ of *nolle prosequi*. That is, he could terminate prosecutions brought by private parties and the courts could not review his actions in doing so, and he could take over a private prosecution if he regarded it as in the public interest to do so. In short, the Attorney General of England exercised a reviewing authority over private prosecution, to ensure that criminal processes and criminal sanctions were not used for harassment or in a manner inconsistent with the public interest (see Goldstein at 12–24).

The American historical error confused the power to intervene and dismiss cases already initiated by private parties with the exclusive power to decide whether they should be initiated at all. It transformed the assertion of the public interest at a secondary review stage into a rationale for total control of the initial stage, the charge itself. In the United States, victims trying to prosecute or participate in criminal cases came to be regarded as pursuing private interests; only district attorneys, therefore, could be entrusted with the conduct of criminal prosecutions.

* * *

Victim Exclusion as a Practicality

The exclusion of the victim might also be explained as the practical result of a criminal system whose purpose is to punish wrongdoers.

- **Document:** "An Essay on the Civil Criminal Distinction with Special Reference to Punitive Damages" by Gail Heriot
- **Date:** 1996
- **Significance:** Heriot explores the evolution and significance of the criminal justice system in precluding victims from participation.
- **Source:** Heriot, Gail. "An Essay on the Civil Criminal Distinction with Special Reference to Punitive Damages." *Journal of Contemporary Legal Issues* 7 (1996): 43, 47–51. Copyright © 1996 *The Journal of Contemporary Legal Issues.* Reprinted with the permission of *The Journal of Contemporary Legal Issues.*

* * *

If one were to ask a person on the street about the basic structure of a criminal proceeding, the explanation given might go something like this: A criminal proceeding is a legal proceeding brought by the state against a defendant who is alleged to be a wrongdoer. If the allegation is proven, the defendant is punished for his wrongdoing.

If the same question were asked with regard to a civil proceeding, the reply might be that it is a legal proceeding brought by an injured person, called plaintiff, against a defendant who plaintiff alleges to have wrongfully caused his injury. [Footnote 19 omitted]. If the allegation is proven, the defendant is ordered to compensate the plaintiff. [Footnote 20 omitted].

Let us accept this view of what is basic in the structure of criminal and civil cases. (We do have to start somewhere, and common understandings tend to be a more propitious starting point than most legal academics are willing to admit.) What is at the root of the distinction between civil and criminal proceedings? What accounts for their separate basic structure?

Fundamental Purposes and Extent to Which They Compel Basic Structure

Perhaps the most frequently identified single distinction is that the "purpose" of the civil law is compensation and the "purpose" of the criminal law is punishment. The civil law confronts a situation in which a loss has occurred and determines who shall bear it. It does not seek to punish—or at least so the argument runs. The criminal law, on the other hand, inflicts a loss that did not exist before, and it does so in order to effect a punishment (see *Kennedy v. Mednoza-Martinez*, 372 U.S. 144 (1963)). [Footnote 21 omitted].

Let us suppose for the moment that these are indeed in some sense the respective "purposes" [Footnote 22 omitted] of civil and of criminal law, rather than simply the tools used by them to achieve some deeper purpose or purposes. Surprisingly little concerning the basic structure of those great bodies of law follows as a matter of necessity from these purposes. Indeed, perhaps only two things result:

First, with regard to the civil law, the compensation purpose requires that there always be on hand an identifiable person who claims injury and is thus the potential recipient of compensation. No such person is necessary in order to carry out the criminal law's punishment purpose. Indeed, modern American criminal cases frequently involve activities that are considered essentially victimless (e.g., gambling [*see, e.g.*, Ill. Rev. Stat. ch. 720, para 5/28-1 (1993)] and prostitution [*see, e.g.*, Ill. Rev. Stat. ch. 720, para. 5/11-15 (1993)]), or that are considered victimless on the facts of the particular case (e.g., reckless endangerment [see, e.g., Model Penal Code § 211.2 (Official Draft 1962)] and attempt [see, e.g., Model Penal Code § 5.01]). In either case, the absence of a victim is no obstacle to punishment.

Second, with regard to the criminal law, the punishment goal requires that there must always be an identifiable person who allegedly should be punished. Such a person is not necessary to the goal of compensation in civil law. It is easy to imagine an institution that fulfills the purpose of compensation without obtaining that compensation from the person who caused the injury. Social insurance agencies and private insurers do it all the time.

That may be all: civil law needs an alleged victim; criminal law needs an alleged wrongdoer. The simple compensation/punishment distinction cannot account for the rest of the differences in the basic structure of the two bodies of law. These must be explained some other way.

Practicality and How It Compels Basic Structure

If conceptual necessity does not explain the whole of the basic structure of civil and criminal law, maybe practicalities can. For example, in the criminal law, it is not conceptually necessary to vest sole authority to initiate and direct the proceedings in the state. The purpose of punishment could be carried out without the state. Indeed, we know from the appeal of felony that there have been times in which the authority to bring proceedings to inflict punishment has been primarily vested in victims rather than in state. [Footnote 27 omitted].

Why victims? Relying upon victims to initiate and direct criminal proceedings may simply have been a practicality; it was probably less costly than establishing a prosecuting bureaucracy. Practicalities have a lot to do with the adoption of legal procedures.

Why did it change over time? Why did the state become the primary initiator of criminal prosecutions? For one thing, victims can be relied upon to initiate criminal actions only when they exist. For wrongdoing without specific identifiable victims, someone other than the victim must initiate the proceeding if that wrongdoing is going to be punished by the criminal law. [Footnote 28 omitted]. The state is the only obvious party. Thus, once the decision is made to punish conspiracies, attempts and other conduct that does not necessarily lead to an identifiable victim, the state must be ready to step in.

That, of course, does not explain why the state would become the exclusive initiator of criminal proceedings as it has in American law or the near-exclusive initiator of criminal proceedings as it has in Great Britain. [Footnote 29 omitted] One explanation that is consistent with the punishment purpose is again a practical one rooted in social changes. The costs of initiating a prosecution have changed significantly as a consequence of urbanization. When private prosecutions were common, a higher proportion of crimes occurred in small towns and rural areas, simply because an overwhelmingly higher proportion of the population lived in such places. In such cases, victim, wrongdoer and witnesses were often personally acquainted. Little detective work was necessary or even possible. When the victim saw her husband's cousin setting her house afire, there was no need for police sketches, lineups, or other elaborate means to identify the perpetrator. A victim with even a weak taste for vengeance might be willing to undertake the costs necessary to initiate the prosecution.

As society became more urbanized, however, the likelihood that victim, wrongdoer and witnesses would be strangers increased significantly. Hence the need for serious detective work increased. [Footnote 30 omitted]. Victims would thus be much more inclined to "chalk it up to experience" and refrain from prosecution. This is simply human nature. Why undertake the cost of prosecuting a criminal when the benefits of so doing will accrue to the community at large rather than the private prosecutor? It seems far more sensible for the victim to let these costs be borne by all who benefit.

After a while this was bound to increase the need for the state to act as prosecutor. At some point, these practical pressures created the basis for the development of the criminal legal proceeding that we are all familiar with: The state brings an action against a defendant-wrongdoer whose alleged wrongdoing may or may not have caused an actual harm to someone. If the state proves that the defendant wrongdoer should be punished, he is executed, imprisoned, fined or otherwise made to feel unpleasant. The victim, if any, is relegated to a supporting role. He may bring a civil action if he pleases, but he may not control the criminal proceeding. Indeed, the victim who is insistent upon a central role is viewed with suspicion. There is something vaguely distasteful about a victim who is too interested in punishing a wrongdoer.

Practical pressures probably also explain some of the basic structure of the civil law. For example, the civil law's putative compensatory purpose does not mandate that the victim be a "plaintiff" in the sense that he must be the person who initiates and in part directs the action. One could just as well imagine a legal proceeding concerned with compensation in which the state is the initiating party and the victim, although a necessary player, is simply a bystander. [Footnote 31 omitted].

Yet, the plaintiff is no bystander in the civil law and for good reason: Hundreds of years ago, it was probably less costly to rely upon victims to pursue their own remedy than it was to hire government officials and vest them with that authority. Indeed, this probably remains so today for most cases we would label "civil." [Footnote 32 omitted]. Under such circumstances, one would expect the plaintiff-victim concept to evolve. Moreover, one would expect it to be stable. Unlike the prosecutor-victim in the criminal law, the plaintiff-victim in a civil case reaps the benefits of a successful case. She thus has no incentive to shirk.

* * *

Victim Exclusion as Fairness to the Defendant

Victims may have become excluded from the criminal justice system by virtue of a focus on defendants' interests. An argument for excluding victims from the process, other than as witnesses, rests on the understanding that the purpose of criminal trials is to determine the guilt or innocence of the criminal defendant. To reach a fair determination of guilt, public institutions detached from the crime should present the evidence. A criminal process constructed of public institutions (prosecutors, judges, and parole boards) and representatives of the community (jurors) is removed from the direct trauma of victimization. This distance arguably results in more neutral procedures and punishments and promotes a public perception of a fair procedure. Allowing a victim's participation could introduce the risk of vindictiveness and emotion and, thus, potential unfairness into the process.

To some extent, some actors in the criminal justice system may have reached a conclusion that fairness to defendants requires exclusion of victims. But even if the system has not consciously decided to exclude victims, exclusion may be a byproduct of increasing focus on defendants' rights. In the 1960s, defendants' rights developed considerably as the Warren Court expansively interpreted federal constitutional protections for criminal defendants. Even when the Supreme Court slowed this expansion, some state courts picked up the slack and interpreted state constitutions generously to protect defendants' interests. No comparable development has taken place for victims because victims' rights are not protected in the federal constitution and are absent (at least until recently) from state constitutions. This expansion and constitutionalization of defendants' rights left little room for victims and may have eliminated some of the informal accommodations to victims that were possible in earlier years.

Victim Exclusion as Truth Seeking

- **Document:** "The Trouble with Trials, the Trouble with Us" by Stephen J. Schulhofer
- **Date:** 1995
- **Significance:** This excerpt seeks to illustrate the potential costs of reshaping the criminal justice system to accommodate the victim.
- **Source:** Schulhofer, Stephen J. "The Trouble with Trials, the Trouble with Us." *Yale Law Journal* 105 (1995): 825. Reprinted with permission.

---

* * *

... The purpose of the trial is to determine whether the defendant is factually and legally responsible for an offense (see, e.g., *Wainwright v. Sykes*, 433 U.S. 72, 90 (1977; "The trial of a criminal case [is] a decisive and portentious event ... Society's resources have been concentrated at that time and place in order to decide, within the limits of human fallibility, the question of guilt or innocence of one of its citizens."). Indeed, the Supreme Court has sometimes implied that this truth-determining function should be virtually the sole task of the criminal trial. [Footnote 75 omitted]. Presently, our society remains committed to a small number of devices that can sometimes interfere (mostly in modest ways) with the primary truth-seeking function of the trial (see Arenella 1983; noting that no American court could adopt a pure guilt-or-innocence model and that functions other than guilt determination are intrinsic to criminal procedure).But we remain acutely aware of the costs of procedural rules that serve goals other than determining the truth, and we are rightly suspicious of efforts to burden our trial process by adding more rules of that sort. [Footnote 77 omitted].

Any thoroughgoing effort to reshape the criminal trial to serve the victim, at the expense of truth seeking, would have dramatic and totally unacceptable costs. [Footnote 78 omitted].

* * *

Victim Exclusion as a Cultural and Institutional Dynamic

Victim exclusion may also be the result of cultural and institutional dynamics. Crime victims tend to be disproportionately drawn from the ranks of the disempowered and disfavored. Moreover, actors at all of levels of the criminal justice system may tend to blame victims for the misfortune of being victimized. The facts can produce cultural and institutional dynamics that, at the very least, tend to lead the system to ignore the interests of victims.

The first problem is that crime victims tend to be people who are least able to cope with the victimization and assert their rights in the process. Victims are disproportionately the poor, the young, and people of color. The most recent victimizations surveys show that racial minorities—particularly African-Americans—are far more likely to be the victims of violent crime than are whites (Bureau of Justice Statistics 2003–2004). For example, the national crime survey has repeatedly shown that blacks are victims of completed robbery at over four times the rate than whites. Given that victims frequently come from racial and socioeconomic groups that tend to lack access to government machinery generally, it should come as no surprise that they are excluded in the criminal process.

A second barrier to appreciation of the "victim problem" is that people tend to believe that good is rewarded and evil punished (Lerner 1970). Furthermore, vestiges of Puritanism (the strong survive and the wicked do not) and of social Darwinism (people who suffer misfortune are naturally inferior) continue to this day (Bard and Sangrey 1979). This may produce a subconscious tendency to blame the victim and to focus primarily on other interests besides those of the victim.

Third, the instinctive human reaction to the crime victim is one of avoidance: "It is not hard to turn away from victims, their pain is discomforting, their anger is sometimes embarrassing, their mutilations are upsetting" (President's Task Force on Victims of Crime 1982).

Fourth, people have been conditioned to think about and react to crime by focusing on the criminal's actions and how he will be treated in the justice system (see *The Crime Victims Book*). For example, most media treatment of crime is devoted to the exploits of criminals and consequent effort of police officers to catch them. (Id.)

Finally, bureaucratic pressures may also play a role: "From the perspective of a system that must handle a large number of cases with limited resources, victims are a nuisance" (McCabe 1982).

Analysis

These documents, taken together with the histories in Chapter 1, provide the reader with broad perspective on how and why victims came to be excluded from the criminal process. The histories describe increasing professionalization: Lawyers started running the show and victim significance was substantially diminished. Industrialization and personal mobility meant such professionalization was key to ensuring the process was basically functional. As Professor Heriot observes, victims may have been excluded to preserve a practical process, although other practical processes might work as well.

As the process gradually became a two-party process, attention shifted to the only individual left in it: the criminal defendant. Fairness to the defendant became the exclusive individual interest. Moreover, history is subject to interpretation, and as Professor Goldstein observes, it was misinterpreted to reinforce the rising two-party procedure.

The principle of treating similarly situated defendants equally raises questions about whether individual victims, with their individual harms and views, should be allowed to participate in the process. As Professor Schulhofer points out, the principle of truth seeking—that is, determining the truth about whether the defendant is guilty—should provide some check on victim involvement. Finally, cultural forces such as social Darwinism and the Puritan legacy provide ready excuses for minimizing the role of the victim.

JUSTIFICATIONS FOR INCLUDING VICTIMS IN CRIMINAL PROCEDURES

Whatever the historical, cultural, or educational explanations for leaving victims outside of the criminal process, recent assessments have found several compelling justifications for bringing victims back inside the process.

Fairness to the Victim

The overarching justification for victim participation in the process is that fundamental fairness demands it. Modern criminal procedure tends to view the party injured by crime as merely the State. Increasingly, however, both the public and the participants in the criminal justice process have recognized that this paradigm inadequately captures the full range of interests in the criminal process. Victimization frequently involves psychological and physical trauma. Sometimes the trauma is obvious, as in cases involving violent crime. In other cases, the trauma may be psychological yet pervasive, involving disruption of personal relationships or the loss of economic security. In short, whatever the legal understanding of the parties to a criminal action is, in the realm of common sense, victims are harmed by crimes—sometimes grievously so.

Because victims are the persons harmed by the crime, a number of commentators have argued that their exclusion from the criminal justice process is unfair.

- **Document:** *With Justice For Some: Protecting Victims' Rights in Criminal Trials* by George P. Fletcher
- **Date:** 1995
- **Significance:** Fletcher argues that standing by the victim should be a central tenant of the criminal justice system.
- **Source:** Fletcher, George P. *With Justice For Some: Protecting Victims' Rights in Criminal Trials*. Boston, Mass: Addison Wesley, 1995.

---

* * *

The theme that runs through all [my] proposals is that we develop a new conception of why we prosecute and punish criminals. The standard debate on this subject fluctuates between grandiose ambitions of social engineering and abstract propositions about punishing simply for the sake of justice and, as the philosopher Hegel put it, vindicating right over wrong. I have urged . . . a more realistic purpose of punishment. The primary task of the criminal trial is neither to change society nor to rectify a metaphysical imbalance in the moral order. The purpose of the trial is to stand by the victim. . . .

A just legal system must stand by its victims. We may neither deter future offenders, nor rehabilitate present inmates, nor achieve justice in the eyes of God. But by seeking to punish the guilty, we do not abandon the innocent who suffer. We do not become complicitous in the crimes against them. We seek justice not only for offenders but for all of us.

* * *

Protecting the Interests of Society

In some areas, protecting victims' interests might more effectively protect society's interests. In the modern era, the public prosecutor has been the sole representative of society. For example, in the context of plea-bargaining, the prosecutor has traditionally decided what plea offer is in the best interests of society. Yet some debatable plea bargains have lead to questions about whether a single representative of the government—the prosecutor—always act in society's best interests and whether giving victims an oversight role in the plea process might lead to results more representative of the interests of society. As a result, in areas such as plea-bargaining, victim participation can be justified as protecting society.

Avoiding Secondary Victimization

In addition to the death itself, victims cope with the violence of death, loss of intimacy, financial stresses and the destruction of the family structure, among other things (Lord 1987). For example, Professor Bard writes: "The violation . . . can hardly be called a positive experience, but it does represent an opportunity for change. One of two things will happen, either victims will become reordered or their experiences will promote further disorder with long term consequences" (Bard and Sangrey 1979).

The victim may experience further disorder by the criminal justice system through *secondary victimization*: "Victims' accounts of their encounters with the criminal justice system range from positive experiences resulting in feelings of satisfaction to tales of horror best described as a further victimization by the criminal justice system" (McCabe 1982)

Dean Kilpatrick, Ph.D. in Psychology and Director of the Crime Victim's Research and Treatment Center at the Medical University of South Carolina, states that failure to give victims an opportunity for meaningful input at sentencing can increase secondary victimization (Kilpatrick 1986). These secondary victimizations continue to occur despite the fact that "crime related trauma is a major contributing factor to the victim's failure to cooperate with the criminal justice system?" (Id. at 5.)

Facilitating Truth Seeking

- **Document:** "The Crime Victim's Right to Attend the Trial: The Reascendant National Consensus" by Douglas E. Beloof and Paul G. Cassell
- **Date:** 2005
- **Significance:** Professors Beloof and Cassell contend that crime victims should have an unequivocal right to attend a criminal trial, as it furthers the truth-seeking process.
- **Source:** Beloof, Douglas E. and Paul G. Cassell. "The Crime Victim's Right to Attend the Trial: The Reascendant National Consensus." 9 *Lewis & Clark Law Review* 9 (2005): 481, 544.

* * *

In considering victim sequestration and the truth-seeking process, it is important to understand that claims can be made in both directions. On balance, it appears that allowing victims to attend trials can actually facilitate the truth-seeking process more than harm it.

It is worth remembering that even in states without a victim's right to attend trial, victims still may be admitted where their presence is essential to the prosecution. Courts have long recognized that victims can be useful to prosecutors. Victims can assist the prosecution in many ways. In busy urban courtrooms, prosecutors often have to juggle dozens of cases at any one time, and likely will not have complete mastery of the facts at issue, even with the assistance of a case agent. A victim, on the other hand, has only one case to remember. Indeed, the events of that case may be seared into the mind of the victim. Apart from the defendant, no one knows more about the crime than the victim herself. The victim, therefore, may be useful—if not indispensable—in crafting appropriate direct and cross-examination questions. As the Justice Department has concluded: "the presence of victims in the courtroom can be a positive force in furthering the truth-finding process by alerting prosecutors to misrepresentations of the testimony of other witnesses" (U.S. Dept. of Justice 1988). State prosecutors report similar experiences (see, e.g.,Telephone interview with Carolyn Hanson, Deputy State's Attorney in Chittenden County, Vt. (June 1, 2005; victims in the courtroom are helpful to organizing the government's rebuttal case and spotting inaccuracies in a defendant's testimony).

* * *

Preventing Victim Alienation

- **Document:** "Victims' Perceptions of Criminal Justice" by Deborah P. Kelly, Ph.D.
- **Date:** 1984
- **Significance:** This brief excerpt illustrates the victim's harsh reality— that he or she has no standing in court or power over his or her case.
- **Source:** Kelly, Deborah P., Ph.D. "Victims' Perceptions of Criminal Justice." *Pepperdine Law Review* 11 (1984): 15, 16.

* * *

. . . Consider the judicial process from the victim's perspective: Victims are introduced to a system grounded on the legal fiction that victims are not the injured party. Victims soon learn they have no standing in court, no right to counsel, no control over the prosecution of their case and no voice in its disposition.

* * *

- **Document:** "The Alienation of the Victim" from "Defining the Role of the Victim in Criminal Prosecution" by Abraham Goldstein
- **Date:** 1982
- **Significance:** Goldstein traces the theme of alienation in contemporary criminal procedure, which relegates the victim to a secondary role.
- **Source:** Goldstein, Abraham. "Defining the Role of the Victim in Criminal Prosecution." *Mississippi Law Journal* 52 (1982): 515, 518-19. Reprinted with permission.

* * *

The Alienation of the Victim

A key assumption underlying the victims' movement is that the failure of victims to cooperate with the criminal justice system has reached epidemic proportions. Recent statistical studies of victimization confirm what we have known for some time. Victims often do not report to the police the crimes that have been committed against them. And the more crime we have, the larger this "dark figure" of unreported crime becomes. Even when they report crimes, a remarkably large proportion of victims later refuse to testify, which leads prosecutors to dismiss or reduce charges. Conversely, victims often find police unwilling to investigate and prosecutors unwilling to charge. In short, each—authorities and victims—finds the other uncooperative, resulting in a reciprocal cycle of decline. Confidence in justice is eroded, enforcement efforts are impeded, and conviction rates, when measured against crimes actually committed, tumble downward.

This theme of alienation, which runs through the victims' movement, traces to a deeply held feeling that the victim has been so much separated from the crime against him that the crime is no longer "his." The sense of alienation probably began when the civil action for damages was split off from the criminal prosecution. A fine paid to the King became a substitute, at least in the criminal process, for compensation previously paid by the offender to the victim and his family. Alienation was accentuated when private prosecution—by victims or by any member of the public—was abandoned in the United States and the public prosecutor was given a monopoly of the criminal charge (see generally Goldstein 1983; Hall 1943).

The victim has been left to play a distinctly secondary role. He reports crimes to public officials and leaves it to them to decide whether offenders should be prosecuted and punished. His injury becomes the occasion for a public cause of action, but he has no "standing" to compel prosecution of the crime against him or to contest decisions to dismiss or reduce the charges or to accept plea bargains, or to challenge the sentence imposed on the offender who injured him, or to participate in hearings on restitution. He is, in a sense, represented by the district attorney, but if his interest in pressing the charge comes into conflict with the prosecutor's conception of the public interest, the latter will prevail. And what is seen to be in the public interest may consist of elements that have little or nothing to do with the victim's case—its strength or weakness—or the nature of the victim's injuries or his outrage against the defendant or even his fear that the crime may be repeated. It may turn on the utility of the defendant as a state witness in another case, or on correctional factors that make it seem preferable to abandon the victim's case rather than prosecute the offender on a serious charge or on any at all. It may turn on whether the particular offense has a high priority at the moment. Thefts and burglaries and consumer frauds may be low on the priority list, crimes of violence high. Spouse abuse may be a disfavored charge, assaults by the ghetto resident against another not worth bothering with. The decision may not be made on qualitative grounds at all. The victim's interest may be subordinated to the more amorphous administrative objective of making the most of the prosecutor's limited resources, or keeping the court's dockets from being clogged, or keeping the prisons from overflowing (see generally Goldstein 1981; Hal 1975; Miller 1969).

It is easy to understand both the prosecutor's difficulties and the victim's frustrations. To the prosecutor, the victim is one among many competing interests. To the victim, the prosecutor is a bureaucrat who holds decisive power over his use of the criminal law—whether to give him emotional satisfaction or to deter the offender or to obtain financial reparation for his injuries. And the bureaucrat is often busy with things other than the victim's case—much more so today when the number of crimes and criminals is much greater than when public prosecution first supplanted the victim's right to prosecute on his own.

In any event, a collective memory has developed by now that makes the victim feel uninvolved in the crime against him and that makes him regard the criminal law as unresponsive to his concerns. He is told that he is not a "party" but a "mere witness": His complaints are often not investigated. The prosecutor need not tell him whether a charge has been filed or why it has been reduced from the offense complained of to a lesser one. Neither prosecutor nor judge need advise him of the terms of plea arrangements or sentences. And little or nothing need be done in the criminal case to facilitate his obtaining financial compensation for his injuries.

Though the victim may begin with the assumption that it is the wrong against him that is to be requited by the criminal law—that the prosecutor is his surrogate, proceeding in his place and on his behalf—he is too often persuaded by the "system" that the criminal prosecution is not really "his" business at all. It is little wonder that so many victims do not bring their complaints to the police or, if they do, that they become unwilling witnesses who are responsible for the high rate of dismissals of prosecution.

* * *

Analysis

In this section, the justifications for including victims in the process are laid out. Professor Fletcher, in saying that the purpose of the criminal trial is to stand by the victim, challenges the view that the only individual the process should concern itself with is the defendant. This view goes against recent conventional wisdom and provides room for the victim to be an individual considered by the process. Indeed, the problems of victim alienation and secondary victimization, described by Professor Goldstein and others, originate from a process that has not seen the victim as a significant individual. Viewed in this light, not standing by the victim is a fundamental failing of the criminal process.

The interests of society are, in theory, protected by the prosecution. But do prosecutors, who have to expediently process many cases, always have the interests of society in mind? The overwhelming passage of state constitutional rights (documented at the end of Chapter 1), which include the victim's right to speak at sentencing, indicate that the public may not believe that public prosecutors are always adequately protecting the society's interest. Finally, truth seeking is not necessarily served by victim exclusion. For example, truth seeking can be facilitated by victim inclusion in the form of victims' attendance at trial.

The effort to enact victims' rights has not been easy. Many interests oppose rights for crime victims. The following document identifies and discusses the opposition to victims' rights.

- **Document:** "Who's Against Victims' Rights—The Nature of the Opposition to Pro-Victim Initiatives in Criminal Justice" by Andrew A. Karmen
- **Date:** 1992
- **Significance:** In the document below, Karmen explores the myriad opposition to victims' rights and the driving forces behind such opposition.
- **Source:** Karmen, Andrew A. "Who's Against Victims' Rights—The Nature of the Opposition to Pro-Victim Initiatives in Criminal Justice." *St. John's Journal of Legal Commentary* 8 (1992): 157. Reprinted with permission.

---

* * *

. . . [I]n their quest to secure rights they believe they are entitled to, [victim] activists and advocacy organizations have encountered considerable opposition, and continue to meet resistance from many quarters. Not much opposition comes from criminals, who are their natural enemies in this conflict, chiefly because offenders are not organized into interest groups. But the victims' movement's pursuit of its goals has been thwarted, slowed down, coopted, and derailed by its ostensible partners and allies in government, and also by ideologically-oriented groups concerned with the larger issues of criminal justice policy.

A Capsule History of the Problem and the Movement to Solve It

For most of [recent] American history, the legal system did not grant crime victims any rights whatsoever. A victim was simply a complainant who activated the machinery of the criminal justice system by bringing evidence and information about illegal acts to the attention of the authorities. If the police solved the case and made an arrest, the victim then played an additional role as a witness for the prosecution—helping the government to secure a conviction. Since crime was conceptualized as an event that threatened and offended the entire community, and was prosecuted by the state on behalf of an abstraction (i.e., "the People"), the real flesh-and-blood victim was treated like just another piece of evidence, a mere exhibit to be discarded after the trial (see President's Task Force on Victims of Crime 1982).

To address these injustices and imbalances, crime victims began to seek each other out. Individuals joined together to form "consciousness-raising" groups, self-help support groups, and organizations to engage in public education, outreach, research and lobbying. Working together in coalitions and meeting periodically in conferences, the activists and advocacy groups emerged as a loosely constituted, highly de-centralized social movement in the early 1970s (McNamara 1992). Ideologically, socially, and politically, it was unusually diverse. The movement's leading activists and core groups did not have a clear philosophy. They were not bound together by any unifying set of principles, or a shared vision of a better world. Rank and file supporters were attracted to the cause from all walks of life—from all ages, racial and ethnic groups, and political persuasions. They acknowledged that all they had in common, really, besides being former victims recovering from a criminal incident, was a burning desire to turn their misfortunes into something positive, so that others who found themselves in the same predicament would not have to suffer as much as they had (Friedman 1985; Smith 1985).

. . . [I]t appears that most participants [in the victims' rights movement] would agree upon this basic critique:

1) That criminal justice personnel—the police, prosecutors, defense attorneys, judges, probation officers, parole boards, corrections administrators—were systematically overlooking or neglecting the legitimate needs of crime victims until they began their campaign; 2) that there was a prevailing tendency on the part of the public as well as agency officials to unfairly blame victims for facilitating or even provoking crimes; 3) that explicit standards of fair treatment were required to protect the interests of complainants and prosecution witnesses, as well as injured parties whose cases were not solved; 4) that people who suffered injuries and losses inflicted by criminals ought to receive reimbursement from one source or another; and 5) that the best way to make sure that victims could pursue their personal goals and protect their own best interests was by granting them formal rights within the criminal justice system. . . .

Three contemporaneous social movements—two from the political Left and one from the Right—influenced the initial directions and thinking of the fledgling victims' movement. The women's liberation movement challenged the way the male-dominated criminal justice system handled violence against girls and women. They responded by setting up rape crisis centers and then by establishing shelters for battered women. The civil rights movement questioned the way that white authorities treated minority victims of Klan terrorism, segregationist mobs, and brutal police officers. And the conservative law and order movement attacked the landmark decisions of the Warren Court that extended new rights to criminal suspects, defendants, and prisoners—which put victims at an even greater disadvantage in the adversarial process (Carrington 1975). These three distinct political movements have been competing, over the past few decades, for support within the ranks of the victims' movement.

The Crux of the Problem: The Victim's Contradictory Role

The drive for victims' rights has encountered opposition from two distinct sources. Resistance to progress in the field of victims' rights arises out of the inherently contradictory role of victims within the criminal justice system. The contradiction is as follows:

1) On the one hand, victims are allies of the government in the state's effort to suppress lawbreaking through punishment or compulsory treatment.

To the degree that victims are junior partners "on the same side" as the police and the prosecution, reforms intended to empower victims might end up facilitating the government's ability to convict and punish those persons that officials choose to pursue selectively. If it turns out that changes designed to strengthen the position of victims in the criminal justice process actually strengthen the position of law enforcement agencies and the prosecution in the adversarial system, then these proposals will be resisted by civil libertarians. Such enhancements of potentially repressive state power provoke distrust, alarm, and opposition from individuals and groups concerned with constitutional rights, procedural safeguards, and due process guarantees.

2) On the other hand, victims are independent actors in the criminal justice process. In defense of their own best interests, they may advocate courses of action that are rejected by a police officer, the assistant district attorney, the judge, the warden, or the parole board. What victims define as their own best interests in "their cases" often diverges from or directly clashes with the goals of the state. . . .

Granting new rights to crime victims necessitates a shake-up in the balance of power within the adversarial system (but see Pliskin 1992). Since all the political territory has already been staked out, the situation becomes a zero-sum game. A gain by the victims' movement can only be at another's expense. Some demands for a greater role in the criminal justice process pit victims against their natural adversaries, namely the suspects accused of harming them or criminals already convicted. Other demands for input into the process, however, are secured at the expense of those agencies, officials, and professionals who are responsible for law enforcement, prosecution, adjudication, and corrections (Karmen 1990; full discussion of how victims are treated within criminal justice system and movement for victims' rights).

Power to Do What?—What Victims Might Want from the System

What do victims want from the criminal justice system—retribution, rehabilitation of the offender, or restitution? Some victims certainly want the system to help them "get even" with those offenders who made them suffer. But retaliation or revenge is only one possible goal.

Some victims have come to the realization that they do not get much satisfaction—and certainly no material benefits—from the knowledge that a convict has been punished on their behalf. The deprivations endured by an inmate behind bars in no way eliminates the emotional, physical, or financial harm endured by the victim. Victims who reach this conclusion seek to be restored to the condition they were in before the crime occurred. Restitution by the offender becomes essential for their recovery. In this view, only through hard work and sacrifice, perhaps as a condition of probation or parole, can the offender make amends.

In addition, aside from retribution and/or restitution, some victims may press for rehabilitation of the offender. This course of action is especially likely if the victim and the offender had a positive *prior* relationship—as lovers, friends, neighbors, co-workers, or classmates. If the victim and the offender are going to continue to be in contact with each other in the future, it is in the best interest of the victim that the offender be rehabilitated. Victims who are of a less vindictive mind may believe that an offender with a psychological problem, violent temper, drug habit, or a lack of marketable skills, needs help, treatment, and support, rather than punishment.

Opposition When Victims Challenge the Prerogatives of the Crime Control Establishment

There are a number of scenarios where victims can have a falling-out with their "allies" in the criminal justice system. One frequent problem arises when the victim wants his case to be pursued but the police or prosecutors seek to drop the charges. Conversely, some victims may want charges to be dropped but the authorities want to press on. In some cases, the victim seeks restitution while the government is more concerned with incarceration. Occasionally the victim seeks the rehabilitation of the offender while the state seeks punishment, but more often the converse is sought (Holten and Lamar 1991).

These potentially divergent goals sow the seeds of conflict between victims and officials. As victims are granted influence within the criminal justice process they will begin to behave as independent actors. The result is that victim advocacy organizations may find themselves at odds with important figures within the criminal justice establishment when they insist that such "insiders" relinquish control over the outcome of each stage in the proceedings (Elias 1986, full discussion of conflicting goals and politics of victimology; Elias 1990, full evaluation of victim policy, involvement in criminal process and politics of movement; Hillenbrand, 1997, full discussion of victim restitution; Kelly, 1997, describing victims' goals at different levels in justice system).

Area of Conflict: The Victim's Right to Be Informed

Carved in stone over the entrance to many college libraries is the inspiring message "Knowledge Is Power." The slogan overstates the relationship between information and influence. "In order to wield power, a person must be well informed" is a less catchy but more accurate message. Knowledge is a prerequisite for effective action. If victims are going to be meaningfully empowered within the criminal justice process, officials must undertake the additional effort to tell them all that they need to know.

Until recently, officials never perceived an obligation to inform victims about important developments in "their" cases. Now this is supposed to change, as more and more states and localities enact statutes designed to keep victims informed of the progress of "their" cases as they wind their way through the criminal justice process (Colo. Rev. Stat. § 24-4. 1-303 (1992, guidelines for informing victims and witnesses of crimes of their rights); N.J. Stat § 52:4B-44 (1992, services available to victims on request); N.D. Cent. Code § 12/1-34-02 (1991), (details information that state *must* provide victims and witnesses); Wyo. Stat. § 1-40-203 (1992) (provides notification and information regarding status of case).

Police departments have been pressured to "read victims their rights," perhaps not in the immediate aftermath of the crime, when they are dazed and bleeding, but shortly thereafter, when they have regained their composure. Victims need to know what they are getting into when they ask that the machinery of criminal justice be set in motion. Victims need to be advised about their potential responsibilities and duties, for example, to attend a line-up . . .

* * *

. . . When victims call for improvements in the way in which they are treated, they question the existing way of doing business—which might be more accurately described as "disposing of cases" rather than as "genuinely dispensing justice." Enacting reforms means directly confronting the practices of police officers and law enforcement agencies; assistant district attorneys and prosecutor's offices; probation officers and departments; judges; corrections officials; and members of parole boards. What victims are really asking for when they demand pledges of fair treatment and explicit guarantees of participatory input are intrusions upon the latitude and discretion (i.e., "the turf") of these criminal justice decisionmakers. It is therefore not surprising that these authorities would resist demands to share power when it comes to agency priorities, budgetary allotments, standards of evaluation for departmental and individual performance, and sheer personal inconvenience. The contested terrain includes such decisions as whether or not to investigate a complaint, to press or drop charges, and to grant or deny bail. Victims want the right to play an active role in negotiating the terms of a guilty plea, in deciding upon an appropriate sentence after a successful trial, and in determining the conditions of release for a prisoner on parole (*see* Austern 1987, outlining and discussing full range of victim problems and limited solutions available; Stark and Goldstein 1985, reviewing rights gained by victims within criminal justice system).

Area of Conflict: The Victims' Movement v. the Police

Various constituencies in the victims' movement have demanded better treatment from the first representatives of the criminal justice system they encounter, namely the police.

Parents of missing children, for example, have challenged the professional judgment of department policymakers over the issue of how much time must elapse before an investigation and a full-scale search is begun. Policy generally allows for hours or even days to pass before action is taken, while distraught parents want immediate action. Advocates for battered women have demanded that the police immediately arrest wife-beaters rather than tell the offender to "take a walk and cool off," or to attend marriage counseling. Battered women have requested the police to diligently enforce orders of protection issued on their behalf by judges. Supporters of

victims of racial, religious, or homophobic bigotry have requested local policy departments to set up special anti-bias squads to more effectively investigate hate-motivated
crimes of vandalism and violence. Advocates for rape victims have demanded that
departments establish sex crime investigation units staffed by specially-trained detec-
tives and policewomen. This is demanded to assure victims that they will be questioned with sensitivity and that their complaints will be taken seriously.

By demanding improved service, victimized members of the general public are
pressuring police administrators to reorder institutional priorities, reallocate resources, and redeploy officers. Law enforcement decisionmakers find it difficult to
openly oppose these calls for greater responsiveness by the people they are sworn
to protect and serve. When these decisionmakers resist pro-victim initiatives, they
argue that their department doesn't have the manpower or money; or that not
enough cases arise to justify such redeployments; or that the demands are impractical or unreasonable in terms of additional workloads.

* * *

. . . [P]rosecutors have balked at real power-sharing by denying victims the right to
be present at the negotiations or to play a direct and active part in the bargaining
process.

The reasons for prosecutorial reluctance are obvious. Victims (like offenders) are
outsiders, and the courtroom work-group, composed of the prosecutor, defense attorney, and judge, are insiders, who have arrived at certain understandings about what
the "going rate" should be in their jurisdiction for a particular type of charge. If the
victim insisted on harsher terms or mandatory restitution—or compulsory treatment
for the offender—these options would be considered disruptive since they would
undermine the work-group's standardization of the disposal of cases. The root of
the problem is that the victims' movement takes at face value the description of
adjudication as an "adversarial process," whereas in reality, out-of-court settlements
are meant to be an administrative routine carried out with assembly-line precision
(see Dow 1981, court may pressure prosecution or defense to accept plea offer judge
deems reasonable; Walker 1989).

Area of Conflict: The Victims v. Other Criminal Justice Professionals

Although judges are supposed to be impartial, they are not immune from the
demands of victims. When it comes to setting bail, victims want judges to keep their
safety in mind. Victims would like judges to warn defendants on pre-trial release to
have no contact with complainants, and that acts of intimidation or threats of
retaliation will be grounds for revoking bail.

On the rare occasion where plea negotiations break down and a formal trial
before a jury must be staged, victims want a chance to shape the sentence should a
conviction result. They do not want to have to rely on the prosecutor to represent
their views when the prosecution makes its sentence recommendation. In many
states, victims of serious felonies now have a right to allocution, that is, to appear
before the judge and recommend an appropriate sentence. If they are not allowed
to address the court in person, they are sometimes granted the opportunity to put
their opinions in writing, as part of a victim impact statement in the probation

Eleven-year-old twins sit at the prosecution table as their aunt reads their victim impact statement during the sentencing of Robert and Brenda Matthey, May 10, 2007, in Flemington, New Jersey. Seated is Rich Pompelio, attorney and victim advocate. Robert and Brenda Matthey were each sentenced to four years in prison for causing the death of their adopted son, Viktor, the twins' brother, more than six years before. Attorney Richard Pompelio is one of the original victims' rights attorneys. He is the father of a murdered son. (AP Photo/Matt Rainey)

department's pre-sentence investigation report (MADD 1988; NOVA 1987). Hard feelings towards unresponsive judges can result if victims perceive, rightly or wrongly, that they are exercising an empty right "to let off steam" that has no discernible impact on the sentence that is handed down (see Lewis and Peoples 1978, "The sentence imposed usually reflects the judge's own commitment to a particular sentencing philosophy; retribution, isolation, or deterrence"). Of course, many other sources of input, besides the victim's notion of justice coupled with the judge's own predilections may influence the sentencing process. . . .

Similarly, when parole boards meet to decide whether to release a convict ahead of schedule, victims want the right to attend the hearing and address members of the board (see e.g., 1992 Conn. Pub. Acts 92-153(4) (Reg. Sess., qualified right to appear before parole board and make statement regarding parole and conditions attached thereto). A victim might argue that parole should not be granted because the inmate has not suffered sufficiently; or that the terms of conditional liberty should include mandatory participation in a treatment program; or that there be some form of restitution. But again, the board may decide on the basis of other priorities rather than what is best for the victim.

The demands of the victims' movement for input—into the way the police investigate, district attorneys prosecute, probation officers make sentence recommendations, judges hand down sentences, and parole boards set conditions for release—are intended to transform the privileges that are sometimes extended to a select group of "first class" victims (see Dow at 97) into formal rights that can be routinely exercised by all victims. But these demands for institutionalized participation meet resistance for another reason, less often acknowledged but statistically unavoidable. In "street crime" cases like aggravated assault, robbery, and burglary, many of the victims are drawn from the ranks of the underprivileged—the poor, the young, and oppressed racial minorities. Some victims might even be from *marginalized* groups, such as homeless persons, drug abusers, street gang members, or prostitutes. It seems unlikely that criminal justice personnel will honor commitments to victims' rights and willingly share decisionmaking with members of these groups. It is even more likely that officials will resist attempts by these "street crime" victims to exercise any rights, and they will receive instead second class treatment (see Karmen at 208-10, noting problems encountered by underprivileged segments of society).

In summary, the demand for empowerment—the ability to influence the course of events within the criminal justice process—inevitably brings the victims' movement into confrontation with existing power bases, hegemonic ideologies, key decisionmakers, and privileged professionals. . . .

The Victims' Movement v. Civil Libertarians

Civil libertarians believe that the criminal justice system in every society contains within it dangerous authoritarian tendencies. They fear that . . . a police state could emerge in the United States as it has in so many other societies. These civil libertarians seek to ensure that the laws of criminal procedure, embodying the separation of powers, checks and balances, and due process guarantees, are scrupulously followed. The struggle to contain the repressive tendencies of government often takes the form of safeguarding the rights of suspects, defendants, and even prisoners. Thus civil libertarians find themselves on the opposite side of the "zero sum" fence whenever victims try to secure additional rights for themselves by whittling down the rights of criminals (see Henderson 1985, discussing efforts to redress imbalance between crime victims and criminal defendants); (Viano 1987, stating that conservative approaches to victims' rights balance rights of accused with safety of community).

* * *

Analysis

Professor Karmen's article describes the groups that founded the Victims' Rights Movement as well as the groups opposing victims' rights. Since the publication of this article, victims' rights efforts have become increasingly less about law and order interests and more about granting victims' intermittent enforceable rights of participation, privacy, and protection in the criminal process. There was a significant difference in the approaches of the Victims' Rights Movement and the criminal justice reforms of the Feminist Movement. Historically, the Women's Movement has not sought participation rights for female victims of sexual assault and domestic violence. Instead, feminist law reform was content to leave the exclusive role of enforcing these reforms to the public prosecutor. So, for example, in most jurisdictions, rape victims typically cannot directly defend their privacy by enforcing rape shield laws. The purpose of rape shield laws is to prevent irrelevant sexual history from being introduced in the present rape trial. In all but three jurisdictions, only the public prosecutor can enforce these laws. However, sexual assault victims frequently take advantage of the modern victims' rights of participation, privacy, and protection developed by the Victims' Rights Movement.

Two of Professor Karmen's observations are open to criticism. First, his article pits civil libertarians against victims' rights. Such categorization is an outmoded view. This is because victims' rights, like defendant's rights, are increasingly viewed as civil liberties. For example, 33 states provide constitutional rights to victims in their respective Bills of Rights. Thus, the civil libertarians Karmen describes are those who highly value the civil liberties in existence before victims' rights, mainly the civil liberties of defendants. Second, his assumption that victims' rights exist in the context of a zero-sum game has been contradicted by others. A *zero-sum game* is a descriptive term that means if anyone is added to the game, someone else loses out. An apt analogy is a pizza: There are only so many slices, and the more who sit down to eat, the fewer slices each person gets. Applying the analogy, if a victim eats a slice, there is less for the prosecution and defense. This argument has been contradicted, most notably by the Human Rights Watch Report set out in the final chapter of this book.

REFERENCES

1992 Conn. Pub. Acts 92-153(4) (Reg. Sess.).

Arenella, Peter. *Rethinking the Functions of Criminal Procedure: The Warren and Burger Courts' Competing Ideologies.* 72 Geo. L.J. 185, 196–205 (1983).

Austern, David. *The Crime Victim's Handbook.* Maryland: Wonderbook, 1987.

Bard, M. & D. Sangrey, *The Crime Victims Book.* New York: Bruner/Mazel Publishers, 1979.

Beloof, Douglas E. & Paul G. Cassell, *The Crime Victim's Right to Attend the Trial: The Reascendant National Consensus.* 9 Lewis & Clark L. Rev. 481 (2005).

Bureau Of Justice Statistics, National Crime Victimization Survey, Criminal Victimization. Washington, DC: Bureau of Justice, 2003–2004.

Carrington, Frank. *The Victims.* New York: Arlington House, 1975.

Colo. Rev. Stat. § 24-4. 1–303 (1992).

Dow, Paul. *Discretionary Justice.* Cambridge, Ma: Ballinger, 1981.

Elias, Robert. *The Politics of Victimization: Victims, Victimology, and Human Rights.* USA: Oxford University Press, 1986.

Elias, Robert. *Which Victim Movement? The Politics of Victim Policy,* in *Victims of Crime: Problems, Policies and Programs,* edited by Arthur Lurigio et al. Thousand Oaks, CA: Sage Publications, Inc., 1990.

Fletcher, George P. *With Justice for Some: Protecting Victims' Rights in Criminal Trials.* Mass: Addison Wesley, 1995.

Friedman, Lucy. *The Crime Victim Movement at Its First Decade*. Pub. Admin. Rev., Nov. 1985.

Goldstein, Abraham. *Defining the Role of the Victim in Criminal Prosecution*. 52 Miss. L. J. 515 (1982).

Goldstein, A. *The Passive Judiciary: Prosecutorial Discretion and the Guilty Plea*. Baton Rouge and London: Louisiana State University Press, 1981.

Goldstein, A. *Prosecution: History of the Public Prosecutor*, in Encyclopedia of Crime and Justice, edited by S. Kadish. New York: The Free Press, 1983.

Hall. *Interrelations of Criminal Law and Torts: I*, 43 Colum. L. Rev. 753, 753 (1943).

Hall. *Interrelations of Criminal Law and Torts: II*, 43 Colum. L. Rev. 967, 967–1001 (1943).

Hall. *The Role of the Victim in the Prosecution and Disposition of a Criminal Case*. 28 Vand. L. Rev. 931 (1975).

Hanson, Carolyn. Telephone interview with. Deputy State's Attorney in Chittenden County, Vt. (June 1, 2005).

Henderson, Lynne. *The Wrongs of Victims' Rights*. 37 Stan. L. Rev. 937, 937–1021 (1985).

Heriot, Gail. *An Essay on the Civil Criminal Distinction with Special Reference to Punitive Damages*. 1 J. Contemporary Legal Issues 43 (1996).

Hillenbrand, Susan. "Restitution and Victim Rights in the 1980s." In *Victims of Crime*, edited by W. Skogan, A. Lurgio, & R. Davis. Thousand Oaks, CA: Sage, 1990.

Holten, Gary N. & Lawson L. Lamar, *The Criminal Courts: Structures, Personnel, and Processes*. New York: McGraw-Hill, 1991.

Ill. Rev. Stat. ch. 720, para. 5/11–15 (1993).

Ill. Rev. Stat. ch. 720, para 5/28–1 (1993).

Karmen, Andrew. *Who's Against Victims' Rights—The Nature of the Opposition to Pro-Victim Initiatives in Criminal Justice*. 8 St. John's J. L. Comm.157 (1992).

Karmen, Andrew. *Crime Victims: An Introduction to Victimology* 2nd edition. Belmont, CA: Wadsworth, 1990.

Kelly, Deborah. "Victim Participation in the Criminal Justice System." In *Victims of Crime*, edited by W. Skogan, A. Lurgio, & R. Davis. Thousand Oaks, CA: Sage, 1990.

Kelly, Deborah. *Victims' Perceptions of Criminal Justice*. 11 Pepperdine L. Rev. 15 (1984).

Kennedy v. Mendoza-Martinez, 372 U.S. 144 (1963).

Kilpatrick, D. "Addressing the Needs of Traumatized Victims." In *The Practical Prosecutor*. 1986. Houston: National College of District Attorneys, University of Houston Law Center, 1986.

Lerner, M. "The Desire for Justice and Reactions to Victims." In *Altruism And Helping Behavior*, Edited by J. Macaulay & L. Berkowitz. New York: Academic Press, Inc., 1970.

Lewis, Peter & Kenneth D. Peoples. *The Supreme Court and the Criminal Process*. Philadelphia, PA: Saunders, 1978.

Lord, J. *No Time for Goodbyes: Coping with Sorrow, Anger and Injustice after a Tragic Death*. Oxnard: Pathfinder Publishing of California, 1987.

McCabe, E. "The Quality of Justice: Victims in the Criminal Justice System." In *Victimization of the Weak*, Edited by J. Scherer & G. Shepherd. Springfield: Charles Thomas, 1982.

McDonald, William. *Towards a Bicentennial Revolution in Criminal Justice: The Return of the Victim*. 13 Am. Crim. L. Rev. 649 (1975).

McNamara, Eileen. "Revenging Angels." In *Boston Globe Magazine*, Feb. 23 1992.

Miller, F. *Prosecution: The Decision to Charge a Suspect with a Crime*. Boston: Little Brown & Co., 1969.

Model Penal Code (Official Draft 1962).

Mothers Against Drunk Driving (MADD). *Victims' Rights: How Far Have We Come?*, in Maddvocate, Irving, TX: MADD, Spring 1998.

National Organization for Victim Assistance (NOVA). *Victims' Rights and Services: A Legislative Directory*. Washington, DC: NOVA, 1987.

N.D. Cent. Code § 12/1-34-02 (1991).

N.J. Stat § 52:4B-44 (1992).

Office for Victims of Crime, President's Task Force on Victims of Crime. *Final Report.* Washington, DC: U.S. Government Printing Press, 1982.

Pliskin, Richard. *Where Are All the Victims?* 132 N.J.L.J., 781 (1992).

Schulhofer, Stephen J. *The Trouble with Trials, the Trouble with Us.* 105 Yale L.J. 825 (1995).

Smith, Brent. *Trends in the Victims' Rights Movement and Implications for Future Research.* 10 Victimology 34 (1985).

Stark, James & Howard Goldstein, *The Rights of Crime Victims.* New York: Bantam Books, 1985.

Statement of the Chairman, President's Task Force on Victims of Crime. *Final Report.* Washington DC: U.S. Government Printing Press, 1982.

U.S. Dept. Of Justice, Office for Victims of Crime. *New Directions from the Field: Victims' Rights and Services for the 21st Century.* Washington, DC: U.S. Government Printing Press, 1998.

Viano, Emilio. *Victim's Rights and the Constitution: Reflections on a Bicentennial.* 33 Crime & Delinq. 438, 443 (1987).

Wainwright v. Sykes, 433 U.S. 72, 90 (1977).

Walker, Samuel. *Sense and Nonsense About Crime*, 2d Edition. California: Brooks/Cole, 1989.

Wyo. Stat. § 1-40-203 (1992).

Additional Reading

Carrington, Frank, and George Nicholson. *The Victims' Movement: An Idea Whose Time Has Come.* 11 Pepp. L. Rev. 1 (1984).

Erez, Edna, and Julian Roberts. "Victim Participation in the Criminal Justice System." In *Victims of Crime*, edited by Robert Davis, Arthur J. Lurigio, Susan Herman. 3rd ed. California: Sage Publications, Inc., 2007.

Roland, David L. *Progress in the Victim Reform Movement: No Longer the Forgotten Victim.* 17 Pepp. L. Rev. 35 (1989).

3

THE PRESIDENT'S TASK FORCE ON VICTIMS OF CRIME

THE TASK FORCE

Ronald Reagan's *Presidential Task Force Report on Victims of Crime* is perhaps the most significant document in the history of modern victims' rights. First and foremost, the mere fact that President Ronald Reagan felt that victims' interests were important enough to warrant presidential attention is significant. His attention was so focused on the issue that he appointed a task force to investigate crime victim issues. The importance of the president's focus on a domestic issue like crime victims' rights cannot be overstated.

The legitimacy given to the Victims' Rights Movement provided by President Reagan's attention to crime victims' interests, his creation of the Task Force to investigate victim issues, and the *Task Force Report* itself were tremendous. The national level of attention given to the issue gave a profound boost of momentum to the nascent Crime Victims' Rights Movement. For example, beginning in 1982—the year of the report—the first states enacted state constitutional rights for crime victims. This was possible in no small measure because of the legitimacy and momentum provided by the president and the task force. The first document presented is an excerpted portion of the *Task Force Report* that focuses on recommendations for victims' rights in the criminal process.

- **Document:** *President's Task Force on Victims of Crime, Final Report*, Office for Victims of Crime
- **Date:** 1982
- **Significance:** This task force report granted a tremendous amount of legitimacy to the Crime Victims' Rights Movement and spurred awareness of victims' rights issues nationally.

Ronald Reagan, U.S. politician and president of the United States (1981–1989). President Reagan was a strong proponent of victims' rights. (U.S. Department of Defense)

- **Source:** Office for Victims of Crime. *President's Task Force on Victims of Crime, Final Report.* Washington, DC: Government Printing Office, 1982.

* * *

Victims of Crime in America

I.

Before you, the reader, can appreciate the necessity of changing the way victims are treated, you must confront the essential reality that almost all Americans, at some time in their lives, will be touched by crime. Among the most difficult obstacles are the myths that if people are wise, virtuous, and cautious, they will escape, and that those who are victimization somehow responsible for their fate. These are pernicious falsehoods. First, for every person mugged on a dark street at 3 a.m., many more are terrorized in their homes, schools, offices, or on main thoroughfares in the light of day. Second, to adopt the attitude of victim culpability is to accept that citizens have lost the right to walk their streets safely regardless of the hour or locale; it is to abandon these times and places to be claimed as the hunting preserves of the lawless.

Violent crime honors no sanctuary. It strikes when least expected, often when the victim is doing the most commonplace things. Victims testified at hearings of the President's Task Force on Victims of Crime about these occurrences:

- As she walks across campus on her first afternoon at college, a young woman is murdered.
- A pharmacist turns to wait on a customer and is confronted by a robber wearing a ski mask.
- A child is molested by the driver of his school bus.
- A man answers the front door and is shot in the chest.
- As a mother shops in a department store, her child, looking at books an aisle away, is kidnapped.
- Walking down the street at lunchtime, an elderly man is assaulted from behind and left permanently blind.
- While a woman is leaving a shopping center someone jumps into her car; 5 hours of rape and torture follow.
- An elderly woman's purse is snatched and she is thrown to the ground, suffering injuries that prevent her from walking again.

- In the restroom of a hotel, a woman is raped by an attacker who is hiding in an adjoining cell.
- A couple returning home from work opens the door to discover that the house has been ransacked.
- A cabdriver, working in the afternoon, turns to collect a fare and is shot.

Based on the testimony of these and other victims, we have drawn a composite of a victim of crime in American today. This victim is every victim; she could be you or related to you.

II.

You are a 50-year-old woman living alone. You are asleep one night when suddenly you awaken to find a man standing over you with a knife at your throat. As you start to scream, he beats and cuts you. He then rapes you. While you watch helplessly, he searches the house, taking your jewelry, other valuables, and money. He smashes furniture and windows in a display of senseless violence. His rampage ended, he rips out the telephone line, threatens you again, and disappears into the night.

At least, you have survived. Terrified, you rush to the first lighted house on the block. While you wait for the police, you pray that your attacker was bluffing when he said he'd return if you called them. Finally, what you expect to be help arrives. The police ask questions, take notes, dust for fingerprints, make photographs. When you tell them you were raped, they take you to the hospital. Bleeding from your cuts, your front teeth knocked out, bruised and in pain, you are told that your wounds are superficial, that rape itself is not considered an injury. Awaiting treatment, you sit alone for hours, suffering the stares of curious passersby. You feel dirty, bruised, disheveled, and abandoned. When your turn comes for examination, the intern seems irritated because he has been called out to treat you. While he treats you, he says that he hates to get involved in rape cases because he doesn't like going to court. He asks you if you "knew the man you had sex with."

The nurse says she wouldn't be out alone at this time of night. It seems pointless to explain that the attacker broke into your house and had a knife. An officer says you must go through this process, then the hospital sends you a bill for the examination that the investigators insisted upon. They give you a box filled with test tubes and swabs and envelopes and tell you to hold onto it. They'll run some tests if they ever catch your rapist.

Finally, you get home somehow, in a cab you paid for and wearing a hospital gown because they took your clothes as evidence. Everything that the attacker touched seems soiled. You're afraid to be in your house alone. The one place where you were always safe, at home, is sanctuary no longer. You are afraid to remain, yet terrified to leave your home unprotected.

You didn't realize when you gave the police your name and address that it would be given to the press and to the defendant through the police reports. Your friends call to say they saw this information in the paper, your picture on television. You haven't yet absorbed what's happened to you when you get calls from insurance companies and firms that sell security devices. But these calls pale in comparison to the threats that come from the defendant and his friends.

You're astonished to discover that your attacker has been arrested, yet while in custody he has free and unmonitored access to a phone. He can threaten you from jail. The judge orders him not to annoy you, but when the phone calls are brought to his attention, the judge does nothing.

At least you can be assured that the man who attacked you is in custody, or so you think. No one tells you when he is released on his promise to come to court. No one ever asks you if you've been threatened. The judge is never told that the defendant said he'd kill you if you told or that he'd get even if he went to jail. Horrified, you ask how he got out after what he did. You're told the judge can't consider whether he'll be dangerous, only whether he'll come back to court. He's been accused and convicted before, but he always comes to court; so he must be released.

You learn only by accident that he's at large; this discovery comes when you turn a corner and confront him. He knows where you live. He's been there. Besides, your name and address were in the paper and in the reports he's seen. Now nowhere is safe. He watches you from across the street; he follows you on the bus. Will he come back in the night? What do you do? Give up your home? Lose your job? Assume a different name? Get your mail at the post office? Carry a weapon? Even if you wanted to, could you afford to do these things?

You try to return to normal. You don't want to talk about what happened, so you decide not to tell your co-workers about the attack. A few days go by and the police unexpectedly come to your place of work. They show their badges to the receptionist and ask to see you. They want you to look at some photographs, but they don't explain that to your co-workers. You try to explain later that you're the victim, not the accused.

The phone rings and the police want you to come to a line-up. It may be 1:00 a.m. or in the middle of your workday, but you have to go; the suspect and his lawyer are waiting. It will not be the last time you are forced to conform your life to their convenience. You appear at the police station and the line-up begins. The suspect's lawyer sits next to you, but he does not watch the stage; he stares at you. It will not be the last time you must endure his scrutiny.

III.

You have lived through the crime and made it through the initial investigation. They've caught the man who harmed you, and he's been charged with armed burglary, robbery, and rape. Now he'll be tried. Now you expect justice.

You receive a subpoena for a preliminary hearing. No one tells you what it will involve, how long it will take, or how you should prepare. You assume that this is the only time you will have to appear. But you are only beginning your initiation in a system that will grind away at you for months, disrupt your life, affect your emotional stability, and certainly cost you money; it may cost you your job, and, for the duration, will prevent you from putting the crime behind you and reconstructing your life.

Before the hearing, a defense investigator comes to talk to you. When he contacts you, he says he's "investigating your case," and that he "works for the county." You assume, as he intends you to, that he's from the police or the prosecutor's office. Only after you give him a statement do you discover that he works for the man who attacked you.

This same investigator may visit your neighbors and co-workers, asking questions about you. He discusses the case with them, always giving the defendant's side. Suddenly, some of the people who know you seem to be taking a different view of what happened to you and why.

It's the day of the hearing. You've never been to court before, never spoken in public. You're very nervous. You rush to arrive at 8 a.m. to talk to a prosecutor you've never met. You wait in a hallway with a number of witnesses. It's now 8:45. Court starts at 9:00. No one has spoken to you. Finally, a man sticks his head out a door, calls out your name and asks, "Are you the one who was raped?" You're aware of the stares as you stand and suddenly realize that this is the prosecutor, the person you expect will represent your interests.

You only speak to the prosecutor for a few minutes. You ask to read the statement you gave to the police but he says there isn't time. He asks you some questions that make you wonder if he's read it himself. He asks you other questions that make you wonder if he believes it.

The prosecutor tells you to sit on the bench outside the courtroom. Suddenly you see the man who raped you coming down the hall. No one has told you he would be here. He's with three friends. He points you out. They all laugh and jostle you a little as they pass. The defendant and two friends enter the courtroom; one friend sits on the bench across from you and stares. Suddenly, you feel abandoned, alone, afraid. Is this what it's like to come to court and seek justice?

You sit on that bench for an hour, then two. You don't see the prosecutor, he has disappeared into the courtroom. Finally, at noon he comes out and says, "Oh, you're still here? We continued that case to next month."

You repeat this process many times before you actually testify at the preliminary hearing. Each time you go to court, you hire a babysitter or take a leave from work, pay for parking, wait for hours, and finally are told to go home. No one ever asks you if the new dates are convenient to you. You miss vacations and medical appointments. You use up sick leave and vacation days to make your court appearances. Your employer is losing his patience. Every time you are gone is business is disrupted. But you are fortunate. If you were new at your job, or worked part-time, or didn't have an understanding boss, you could lose your job. Many victims do.

The preliminary hearing was an event for which you were completely unprepared. You learn later that the defense is often harder on a victim at the preliminary hearing than during the trial. In trial, the defense attorney cannot risk alienating the jury. At this hearing, there is only the judge—and he certainly doesn't seem concerned about you. One of the first questions you are asked is where you live. You finally moved after your attack; you've seen the defendant and his friends, and you're terrified of having them know where you now live. When you explain that you'd be happy to give your old address, the judge says he'll dismiss the case or hold you in contempt of court if you don't answer the question. The prosecutor says nothing. During your testimony, you are also compelled to say where you work, how you get there, and what your schedule is.

Hours later you are released from the stand after reliving your attack in public, in intimate detail. You have been made to feel completely powerless. As you sat facing a smirking defendant and as you described his threats, you were accused of lying and inviting the "encounter." You have cried in front of these uncaring strangers. As you leave no one thanks you. When you get back to work they ask what took you so long.

You are stunned when you later learn the defendant also raped five others; one victim was an 8-year-old girl. During her testimony she was asked to describe her attacker's anatomy. Spectators laughed when she said she didn't understand the words being used. When she was asked to draw a picture of her attacker's genitalia the girl fled from the courtroom and ran sobbing to her mother, who had been subpoenaed by the defense and had to wait outside. The youngster was forced to sit alone and recount, as you did, each minute of the attack. You know how difficult it was for you to speak of these things; you cannot imagine how it was for a child.

Now the case is scheduled for trial. Again there are delays. When you call and ask to speak with the prosecutor, you are told the case has been reassigned. You tell your story in detail to five different prosecutors before the case is tried. Months go by and no one tells you what's happening. Periodically you are subpoenaed to appear. You leave your work, wait, and are finally told to go home.

Continuances are granted because the courts are filled, one of the lawyers is on another case, the judge has a meeting to attend or an early tennis match. You can't understand why they couldn't have discovered these problems before you came to court. When you ask if the next date could be set a week later so you can attend a family gathering out of state, you are told that the defendant has a right to a speedy trial. You stay home from the reunion and the case is continued.

The defense attorney continues to call. Will you change your story? Don't you want to drop the charges?

Time passes and you hear nothing. Your property is not returned. You learn that there are dozens of defense motions that can be filed before the trial. If denied, many of them can be appealed. Each motion, each court date means a new possibility for delay. If the defendant is out of custody and fails to come to court, nothing can happen until he is re-apprehended. If he is successful in avoiding recapture, the case may be so compromised by months or years of delay that successful prosecution is impossible. For as long as the case drags on, your life is on hold. You don't want to start a new assignment at work or move to a new city because you know that at any time the round of court appearances may begin again. The wounds of your attack will never heal as long as you know that you will be asked to relive those horrible moments.

No one tells you anything about the progress of the case. You want to be involved, consulted, and informed, but prosecutors often plea bargain without consulting victims. You're afraid someone will let the defendant plead guilty to a lesser charge and be sentenced to probation. You meet another victim at court who tells you that she and her family were kidnapped and her children molested. Even though the prosecutor assured her that he would not accept a plea bargain, after talking with the attorneys in his chambers, the judge allowed the defendant to plead as charged with the promise of a much reduced sentence. You hope that this won't happen in your case.

IV.

Finally the day of trial arrives. It is 18 months since you were attacked. You've been trying for a week to prepare yourself. It is painful to dredge up the terror again, but you know that the outcome depends on you; the prosecutor has told you that the way you behave will make or break the case. You can't get too angry on the stand because then the jury might not like you. You can't break down and sob because then you will appear too emotional, possibly unstable. In addition to the tremendous pressure of having to relive the horrible details of the crime, you're expected to be an actress as well.

You go to court. The continuances are over; the jury has been selected. You sit in a waiting room with the defendant's family and friends. Again you feel threatened, vulnerable, and alone.

You expect the trial to be a search for the truth; you find that it is a performance orchestrated by lawyers and the judge, with the jury hearing only half the facts. The defendant was found with your watch in his pocket. The judge has suppressed this evidence because the officer who arrested him didn't have a warrant.

Your character is an open subject of discussion and innuendo. The defense is allowed to question you on incidents going back to your childhood. The jury is never told that the defendant has two prior convictions for the same offense and has been to prison three times for other crimes. You sought help from a counselor to deal with the shattering effect of this crime on your life. You told him about your intimate fears and feelings. Now he has been called by the defense and his notes and records have been subpoenaed.

You are on the stand for hours. The defense does its best to make you appear a liar, a seductress, or both. You know you cannot relax for a moment. Don't answer unless you understand the question. Don't be embarrassed when everyone seems angry because you do not understand. Think ahead. Be responsive. Don't volunteer. Don't get tired.

Finally you are finished with this part of the nightmare. You would like to sit and listen to the rest of the trial but you cannot. You're a witness and must wait outside. The jury will decide the outcome of one of the major events of your lie. You cannot hear the testimony that will guide their judgment.

The verdict is guilty. You now look to the judge to impose a just sentence.

V.

You expect the sentence to reflect how terrible the crime was. You ask the prosecutor how this decision is reached, and are told that once a defendant is convicted he is interviewed at length by a probation officer. He gives his side of the story, which may be blatantly false in light of the proven facts. A report that delves into his upbringing, family relationships, education, physical and mental health, and employment and conviction history is prepared. The officer will often speak to the defendant's relatives and friends. Some judges will send the defendant to a facility where a complete psychiatric and sociological work-up is prepared. You're amazed that no one will ever ask you about the crime, or the effect it has had on you and your family. You took the defendant's blows, heard his threats, listened to him brag that he's "beat the rap" or "con the judge." No one ever hears of these things. They never give you the chance to tell them.

At sentencing, the judge hears from the defendant, his lawyer, his mother, his minister, his friends. You learn by chance the day the hearing was. When you do attend, the defense attorney says you're vengeful and it's apparent that you over-reacted to being raped and robbed because you chose to come and see the sentencing. You ask permission to address the judge and are told that you are not allowed to do so.

The judge sentences your attacker to three years in prison, less than one year for every hour he kept you in pain and terror. That seems very lenient to you. Only later do you discover that he'll probably serve less than half of his actual sentence in prison because of good-time and work-time credits that are given to him immediately. The man who broke into your home, threatened to slit your throat with a knife, and raped, beat, and robbed you will be out of custody in less than 18 months. You are not told when he will actually be released, and you are not allowed to attend the parole release hearing anyway.

VI.

For this victim the ordeal of the trial is over, but the ordeal of being a victim is far from over; it continues with unrelenting pressure. The consequences for the victim described in this essay were found by the Task Force to be very real and very commonplace. Even at the point of conviction of the defendant, the system can now place new burdens on the victim; if the defendant wins an appeal, the victim may have to go through the trial process all over again. There might have been more than one defendant, or one might have been a juvenile. This would have meant two or three trials, two or three times as many court appearances and hours of cross-examination, double or triple the harassment. There might have been two or three law enforcement agencies involved in the case who did not cooperate with each other. The defendant's every right has been protected, and now he serves his time in a public facility, receiving education at public expense. In a few months his sentence will have run. Victims receive sentences too; their sentences may be life long.

If you were the victim, you may now be crippled or blind as a result of brutality. You may have lost a limb and may have to undergo surgery repeatedly to repair the body your attacker nearly destroyed. You were active, healthy, full of life; now you may be dependent and destitute.

The economic impact on you can be devastating. You may have been hospitalized and unable to return to work for months, if ever. You may have used all your sick leave and vacation. You may need braces, a wheelchair, a ramp to get into your home, a hearing aid, or a special bed. You may not be able to afford them, because you may well be in debt. You may have lost what took you years to build. You may have lost what you treasured most—the locket with your mother's picture that can never be replaced. Your business may be bankrupt, or you may have run through your savings. Your once excellent credit rating may now be gone.

You may have to leave your home. If you cannot leave, you may no longer feel safe there; you may no longer be able to sleep in the room where you were raped. Every time you open your door you may feel anew the sense of invasion.

The psychological scars are perhaps the hardest to bear. These are the hardships that those untouched by crime find the most difficult to understand. Before the crime you felt reasonably safe and secure; the world is now a violent and deadly place to you. It seems you must either accept guilt for what happened to you or condemn yourself to the realization that you have no control. Everything seems to reinforce these feelings of inadequacy. Doctors dictate part of your days; lawyers and creditors dominate the rest. You may sleep badly, eat poorly, be continually afraid, depressed, ill. The most mundane occurrences make you flash back to the crime. Before the crime you were bright, attractive, talented, competent; now you may feel as though you are none of these. The criminal has taken from you your sense of security, your sense of humor, your sense of self. You are fearful and you are angry.

You may well be isolated in your anguish. You can't believe that this could happen to you. Others want to believe that the aftermath is not as bad as you claim. If it should happen to them, they could handle it better, be stronger, recover sooner. You have become a shadow of their own vulnerability. They must deny you. So they tell you that your anger, your desire for justice, your suspicion and fear are unreasonable. But when you are beaten and robbed, your home destroyed, or your husband or child murdered, who has standing to label your anger irrational?

Many people can accept tragedy that comes through natural disaster or accident, but you know that your victimization was intentional. They say that by now you should be back to normal. But they don't have to see your scars in the mirror every morning. The court system doesn't call them once a month for years to dredge it all up again.

Having survived all this, you reflect on how you and your victimizer are treated by the system that is called justice. You are aware of inequities that are more than merely procedural. During trial and after sentencing the defendant had a free lawyer; he was fed and housed; given physical and psychiatric treatment, job training, education, support for his family, counsel on appeal. Although you do not oppose any of these safeguards, you realize that you helped to pay for all these benefits for the criminal. Now, in addition and by yourself, you must try to repair all that his crime has destroyed; and what you cannot repair, you must endure.

Recommendations for State and Federal Action

* * *

1. Legislation should be proposed and enacted to ensure that addresses of victims and witnesses are not made public or available to the defense, absent a clear need as determined by the court.
2. Legislation should be proposed and enacted to ensure that designated victim counseling is legally privileged and not subject to defense discovery or subpoena.
3. Legislation should be proposed and enacted to ensure that hearsay is admissible and sufficient in preliminary hearings, so that victims need not testify in person.

4. Legislation should be proposed and enacted to amend the bail laws to accomplish the following:

   a. Allow courts to deny bail to persons found by clear and convincing evidence to present a danger to the community;

   b. Give the prosecution the right to expedited, and appeal of adverse, bail determinations, analogous to the right presently held by the defendant;

   c. Codify existing case law defining the authority of the court to detain defendants as to whom no conditions of release are adequate to ensure appearance at trial;

   d. Reverse, in the case of serious crimes, any standard that presumptively favors release of convicted persons awaiting sentence of appealing their convictions;

   e. Require defendants to refrain from criminal activity as a mandatory condition of release; and

   f. Provide penalties for failing to appear while released on bond or personal recognizance that are more closely proportionate to the penalties for the offense with which the defendant was originally charged.

5. Legislation should be proposed and enacted to abolish the exclusionary rule as it applies to Fourth Amendment issues.

6. Legislation should be proposed and enacted to open parole release hearings to the public.

7. Legislation should be proposed and enacted to abolish parole and limit judicial discretion in sentencing.

8. Legislation should be proposed and enacted to require that school officials report violent offenses against students or teachers, or the possession of weapons or narcotics on school grounds. The knowing failure to make such a report to the police, or deterring others from doing so, should be designated a misdemeanor.

9. Legislation should be proposed and enacted to make available to businesses and organizations the sexual assault, child molestation, and pornography arrest records of prospective and present employees whose work will bring them in regular contact with children.

10. Legislation should be proposed and enacted to accomplish the following:

    a. Require victim impact statements at sentencing;

    b. Provide for the protection of victims and witnesses from intimidation;

    c. Require restitution in all cases, unless the court provides specific reasons for failing to require it;

    d. Develop and implement guidelines for the fair treatment of crime victims and witnesses; and

    e. Prohibit a criminal from making any profit from the sale of the story of his crime. Any proceeds should be used to provide full restitution to his victims, pay the expenses of his prosecution, and finally, assist the crime victim compensation fund.

11. Legislation should be proposed and enacted to establish or expand employee assistance programs for victims of crime employed by government.

12. Legislation should be proposed and enacted to ensure that sexual assault victims are not required to assume the cost of physical examinations and materials used to obtain evidence.

* * *

A Proposed Constitutional Amendment

* * *

[The President's Task Force on Victims of Crime also recommended an Amendment to the United States Constitution. It consisted of one sentence added to a preexisting amendment for criminal defendants (the Sixth Amendment).]

In all criminal prosecutions the accused shall enjoy the right to a speedy and public trial, by an impartial jury of the State and district wherein the crime shall have been committed, which district shall have been previously ascertained by law, and to be informed of the nature and cause of the accusation; to be confronted with the witnesses against him; to have compulsory process for obtaining witnesses in his favor and to have the Assistance of Counsel for his defense. *Likewise, the victim in every criminal prosecution, shall have the right to be present and to be heard at all critical stages of judicial proceedings.*

* * *

Analysis

The importance of Ronald Reagan's creation of a task force on victims of crime cannot be overstated. The mere act of creating the Task Force elevated crime victims' rights, interests, and credibility to the highest level of American government. Moreover, the Task Force recommendations for federal and state action created legitimacy and gave momentum to the Victim's Rights Movement. Many of the recommendations have since been enacted in law in federal and state jurisdictions. The recommendation for an amendment to the United States Constitution providing crime victims' rights was a shot in the arm for victim activists. Beginning in 1982, two-thirds of the states would adopt state constitutional rights for crime victims. Federal and state statutory law includes many victims' rights.

The scenarios and stories set out in the *Task Force Report* are important in a number of respects. First, the use of true stories to describe outrageous treatment of victims by government officials and a process largely indifferent to victim interests and dignity was an effective method of awareness raising that would be repeatedly utilized by victims' rights activists throughout the United States. These stories, and many more like them, told in state legislatures and to the Congress have facilitated the development of crime victims' civil liberties.

The momentum created by the Task Force recommendations and the enactment of state constitutional rights went to the effort to create federal constitutional rights for crime victims. While such federal constitutional rights have not yet been enacted, the effort resulted in the Crime Victims' Rights Act of 2004 (CVRA). The CVRA provides victims' rights in federal criminal procedures. The CVRA serves as model legislation for states' crime victims' rights. Since its enactment, California has amended its constitutional victims' rights provision to provide victims with enumerated and enforceable rights. Oregon has amended its victim constitutional rights to make the rights enforceable.

As interesting as the Task Force recommendations are, there are a variety of victims' rights commonly available today that were not included in the *Task Force Report* recommendations. The *Task Force Report* was a strong beginning, but, ultimately, did not serve to define the scope or limit of victims' rights.

The recommendations of the *Task Force Report* represented a substantial call for change. What follows is the present status of each recommendation.

Present Status on Task Force Recommendations

1. Legislation should be proposed and enacted to ensure that addresses of victims and witnesses are not made public or available to the defense, absent a clear need as determined by the court.
   Present status: This recommendation has been followed and made the subject of statutes in many jurisdictions.

2. Legislation should be proposed and enacted to ensure that designated victim counseling is legally privileged and not subject to defense discovery or subpoena.
   Present status: This recommendation has been followed in some but not all jurisdictions. Moreover, where enacted, such laws have been rigorously enforced by courts in some states and undermined by courts in other states.

3. Legislation should be proposed and enacted to ensure that hearsay is admissible and sufficient in preliminary hearings, so that victims need not testify in person.
   Present status: Some states have enacted this recommendation.

4. Legislation should be proposed and enacted to amend the bail laws to accomplish the following:
   a. Allow courts to deny bail to persons found by clear and convincing evidence to present a danger to the community;
   b. Give the prosecution the right to expedited appeal of adverse bail determinations, analogous to the right presently held by the defendant;
   c. Codify existing case law defining the authority of the court to detain defendants as to whom no conditions of release are adequate to ensure appearance at trial;
   d. Reverse, in the case of serious crimes, any standard that presumptively favors release of convicted persons awaiting sentence or appealing their convictions;
   e. Require defendants to refrain from criminal activity as a mandatory condition of release; and

f. Provide penalties for failing to appear while released on bond or personal recognizance that are more closely proportionate to the penalties for the offense with which the defendant was originally charged.

Present status: Congress passed and the president has signed the Bail Reform Act of 1984. About half the states have since enacted their own versions of bail reform. Many of these acts implement reforms suggested by the Task Force.

5. Legislation should be proposed and enacted to abolish the exclusionary rule as it applies to Fourth Amendment issues.
   Present status: The exclusionary rule is a very controversial rule that calls for the suppression of reliable evidence found or seized as a result of a Fourth Amendment search or seizure violation. The rule was created by the Supreme Court to deter unlawful police conduct. It is questionable whether any legislation could trump the Supreme Court's use of the exclusionary rule. In any event, court opinions have weakened both the application and scope of the use of the exclusionary rule. It is unlikely the *Task Force Report* had any major influence over these developments.

6. Legislation should be proposed and enacted to open parole release hearings to the public.
   Present status: In an increasing number of states, parole hearings are open to the press and victims may address the parole board either through written or oral testimony or both.

7. Legislation should be proposed and enacted to abolish parole and limit judicial discretion in sentencing.
   Present status: This recommendation is in response to the victim's interest in truth in sentencing. When convicts are sentenced in a parole system, they typically do much less time than they are sentenced to. Many jurisdictions have abandoned parole systems in favor of both the sentencing guidelines and mandatory minimum sentences.

8. Legislation should be proposed and enacted to require that school officials report violent offenses against students or teachers, or the possession of weapons or narcotics on school grounds. The knowing failure to make such a report to the police, or deterring others from doing so, should be designated a misdemeanor.
   Present status: While not necessarily criminalized, requirements for such reporting are now commonplace.

9. Legislation should be proposed and enacted to make available to businesses and organizations the sexual assault, child molestation, and pornography arrest records of prospective and present employees whose work will bring them in regular contact with children.
   Present status: Generally, an employer can require an applicant to sign a release granting access to criminal records.

10. Legislation should be proposed and enacted to accomplish the following:
    a. Require victim impact statements at sentencing;
    b. Provide for the protection of victims and witnesses from intimidation;
    c. Require restitution in all cases, unless the court provides specific reasons for failing to require it;
    d. Develop and implement guidelines for the fair treatment of crime victims and witnesses; and
    e. Prohibit a criminal from making any profit from the sale of the story of his crime. Any proceeds should be used to provide full restitution to his victims, pay the expenses of his prosecution, and finally, assist the crime victim compensation fund.

    Present status:

    a. Victim impact statements in written or oral testimony or in presentence reports are authorized in every state and federal jurisdictions;
    b. Many state constitutional and federal and state statutory victims' rights schemes provide this right;
    c. Restitution is now mandatory in many jurisdictions, and the number is increasing;
    d. Generally, many agencies have established policies and procedures concerning fair treatment of victims. These vary greatly in efficacy and enforceability.
    e. The problem of criminal profit is an ongoing problem. Early efforts to limit profiting were deemed in violation of First Amendment freedoms by the United States Supreme Court. States have been slow to rewrite these laws to conform to the constitution.

11. Legislation should be proposed and enacted to establish or expand employee assistance programs for victims of crime employed by government.
    Present status: This exists in various forms in some jurisdictions.

12. Legislation should be proposed and enacted to ensure that sexual assault victims are not required to assume the cost of physical examinations and materials used to obtain evidence.
    Present status: Most jurisdictions have shifted the cost of sexual assault physical exams to the government.

13. The Constitutional Amendment: *"Likewise, the victim, in every criminal prosecution shall have the right to be present and to be heard at all critical stages of judicial proceedings."*
    Present status: There is no federal constitutional amendment, although efforts are likely to resurface. Two-thirds of the states have created constitutional rights for crime victims. All jurisdictions allow the victim to be heard at sentencing. This right likely extends to plea hearings. In many states, victims can be heard at release hearings, at parole hearings, and in other contexts as well. Victims are allowed to attend trial in most jurisdictions but do not have an active role at trial other than as a witness. The amendment effort is responsible for the passage of the Crime Victim's Rights Act, the subject of Chapter 7 of this book.

In History

The crime victims' rights movement frequently makes reference to a famous historical quote of the United States Supreme Court: "The law, as we have seen, is sedulous in maintaining for a defendant charged with crime whatever forms of procedure are of the essence of an opportunity to defend. Privileges so fundamental as to be inherent in every concept of a fair trial that could be acceptable to the thought of reasonable men will be kept inviolate and inviolable, however crushing may be the pressure of incriminating proof. But justice, though due to the accused, is due to the accuser also. The concept of fairness must not be strained till it is narrowed to a filament. We are to keep the balance true" Justice Cardozo, writing for the majority, in *Snyder v. Commonwealth of Massachusetts*, 291 U.S. 97 (1934). It is this balance that the movement is trying to achieve.

Proposed Model Legislation

The *Task Force Report* inspired other significant documents. Among the most important were the Justice Department, Office of Justice Programs, Office for Victims of Crime, Proposed Model Legislation. The chair of the President's Task Force on Victims of Crime was Lois Haight-Herrington. After serving in that capacity, she became an assistant attorney general. She wrote the following letter, preceding the introduction to the model legislation.

- **Document:** *Proposed Model Legislation* by Lois Haight-Harrington
- **Date:** May 1986
- **Significance:** The following letter, penned by Lois Haight-Herrington, precedes the proposed model legislation for crime victim rights offered by the Office of Justice Programs and the Office for Victims of Crime.
- **Source:** Haight-Harrington, Lois. *Proposed Model Legislation*. Washington, DC: Office of Justice Programs, Office for Victims of Crime, 1986.

* * *

Office for Justice Programs
Office for Victims of Crime
Victims of Crime
Proposed Model Legislation
In Cooperation with
The National Association of Attorneys General,
Crime Victims Project
and
The American Bar Association,

Criminal Justice Section,
Victim Witness Project

* * *

U.S. Department of Justice
Office of Justice Programs
Office of the Assistant Attorney General, Washington, D.C. 20531

"That night I changed from a law-abiding citizen, with a child-like belief in the justice system, to someone awakened to the reality of crime, criminal rights and injustice for the victim."

These words of an innocent victim of crime manifest a serious crisis in the American criminal justice system. The United States is a nation of laws. If laws are to be obeyed, they must be respected; to be respected, they must be just. A system that fails to be equitable cannot survive. Our system was designed to be the fairest in history but in recent years, it has lost the balance that has been the cornerstone of its wisdom.

In the wake of a violent crime, a person naturally turns to the justice system for help. Too often he has instead been met by further harm. Frightened by the potential for future attacks, many victims have not felt adequately protected. Confused by a complex system, often they have neither been informed nor consulted about their case. Anxious to put their lives back to some semblance of what they were before the crime occurred, victims frequently have been made to endure endless questioning, intimidation, and harassment. If they have survived the ordeal to see the offender convicted and sentenced, victims have often been shocked to learn by accident that the criminal has been released without having served his full sentence.

By the end of this process, the victims have felt more despair than justice. Many vow never to cooperate again, and they tell their friends and families to stay away from the courts. More than half of all violent crime victims never report the offense to law enforcement. The system is absolutely dependent upon the victims' cooperation to hold criminals accountable, thereby preventing future crimes as well. In return for their great sacrifice, the victims of crime deserve to be treated with dignity and compassion.

With this understanding, the President's Task Force on Victims of Crime made 68 recommendations to improve the treatment of the victims. Some proposals require only common sense and courtesy. Others require changes of law. The desire to enact these changes is growing in the states, and the need for careful analyses of the related legal and public policy issues is needed. The model statutes which follow were written to provide that assistance. In general they meet three basic needs of innocent citizens stricken by crime: to be consulted, to be respected, and to be protected. If enacted, these laws specifically would:

- maintain the confidentiality of a victim's discussions in counseling
- require that the effect of the crime on the victim be considered at the defendant's sentencing
- open parole hearings
- permit hearsay at preliminary hearings
- limit the disclosure of victim addresses and phone numbers
- extend the statute of limitations for offenses against children

- declare children to be competent witnesses regardless of their age
- reform procedures for defendant's pre-trial release
- establish guidelines for determinate sentencing
- disclose any sex offense history of those employed in child-related positions.

These dramatic reforms have been carefully proposed and researched. They are among the recommendations of two national studies, by the President's Task Force on Victims of Crime and the Attorney General's Task Force on Family Violence. They were prepared by the Victim Witness Project of the Criminal Justice Section of the American Bar Association and the Crime Victims Project of the National Association of Attorneys General, with support from the Office for Victims of Crime in the U.S. Justice Department. Although these statutes are comprehensive, they are intended to encourage rather than dictate reforms on behalf of victims. Legislators, victim advocates and criminal justice professionals may use all or part of these measures according to their needs. Many states have already taken action to ensure fair treatment of victims, but they could do more.

They must. Justice Oliver Wendell Holmes once said, "The law is the witness and the external deposit of our moral life. Its history is the history of the moral development of the race." Judging from the response of innocent victims who experience the application of criminal law, our moral deposit has decayed. Our criminal laws have often been applied not according to right and wrong, but according to "rights," of which the victim had few. These model statutes do not intend to diminish the sacred constitutional safeguards for defendants. They merely provide equal protection for victims and balance to our system of justice. If we value human dignity and condemn its violation, then we must act to cast these values into laws on behalf of the innocent victims of crime.

Lois Haight-Herrington, Chair of the President's Task Force on Victims of Crime (1981–1982) and Assistant Attorney General of the United States (1983–1986). She was a powerful advocate for victims' rights. (Courtesy Ronald Reagan Library)

Lois Haight-Herrington
Assistant Attorney General
May 1986

* * *

Analysis

The proposed model legislation is important because it reflects efforts to take the recommendations of the President's Task Force and turn them into model legislation. Model legislation provides a template that the federal and state jurisdictions can look at without having to reinvent the wheel. Typically, the template will be somewhat modified in each jurisdiction.

Moreover, the document is the product of a significant partnership. The Victim Witness Project of the Criminal Justice Section of the American Bar Association and the Crime Victims Project of the National Association of Attorneys General, with support from the Office for Victims of Crime in the U.S. Justice Department, engaged in a collective effort to draft the model legislation.

The model legislation is a foundation for enacting victims' rights. Like the President's *Task Force Report*, it represents efforts in the early 1980s to accommodate and recognize crime victims' rights. The scope of victims' rights has not been limited to this model legislation—on the contrary, it has expanded beyond it.

The American Bar Association created a project called the Victim Witness Project. This project was one of the groups working on the model legislation previously reviewed. In addition to contributing to that document, the ABA project generated the following policy recommendations for victims of crime. Presented below is solely the language of the guidelines, without the accompanying commentary.

- **Document:** *Guidelines for Fair Treatment of Victims and Witnesses in the Criminal Justice System*, American Bar Association
- **Date:** 1983
- **Significance:** This document represents the recognition of victims' rights and accommodations by the American Bar Association.
- **Source:** American Bar Association (ABA). *Guidelines for Fair Treatment of Victims and Witnesses in the Criminal Justice System*. Washington, DC: Author, 1983.

---

* * *

1. Victims or their representatives should be provided appropriate information about:

   (a) availability of social and medical services, especially emergency services; and
   (b) availability of crime victim compensation and restitution.

2. Victims and witnesses should be provided information about their role in the criminal justice process, including what they can reasonably expect from the system and what the system expects from them.

3. Victims and witnesses should be advised of available protections against unlawful intimidation.

4. Victims and witnesses should be notified as soon as practicable of scheduling changes which will affect their required attendance at criminal justice proceedings, or be given access to a system providing up-to-date scheduling information.

5. Victims and witnesses who request it should be provided with employer and creditor intercession to seek employer cooperation in minimizing employees' loss of pay and other benefits resulting from their participation in the criminal justice process, and to seek consideration from creditors if the victim is unable, temporarily, to continue payments.

6. Victims of serious crimes should be given the opportunity to enter a standing request for and receive timely notice of the date, time and place of the defendant's initial appearance before a judicial officer, submission to the court of plea agreements, the trial, and sentencing. It is, however, the responsibility of the victim to provide a current address and telephone number to the appropriate official.

7. As soon after an arrest as possible, victims or their representatives in serious cases should be given the opportunity to enter a standing request and subsequently receive timely notification of the case disposition, including the trial and sentencing. It is, however, the responsibility of the victim to provide a current address and telephone number to the appropriate official.

8. As soon after an arrest as possible, victims or their representatives should be given the opportunity to enter a standing request for and subsequently receive prompt notification of any decision or action in the case which results in the defendant's provisional or final release from state custody. It is, however, the responsibility of the victim to provide a current address and telephone number to the appropriate official.

9. At any time from the commission of the crime to final disposition or release of the defendant or offender, victims and witnesses who request it should be provided with information about the status of their case.

10. Victims or their representatives in serious cases should have the opportunity to consult with the prosecutor prior to dismissal of the case or filing of a proposed plea negotiation with the court, and should be advised of this opportunity as soon as feasible.

11. Prior to the sentencing of an offender in a serious case, victims or their representatives should have the opportunity to inform the sentencing body of the crime's physical, psychological, and financial repercussions on the victim or the victim's family. Jurisdictions may do this in one of several ways, including:

    a. written statement prepared by the victim to be included in the probation department's presentence report on the offender;

    b. written statement prepared by the probation department after consultation with the victim or the victim's representative; and/or

    c. oral statement by the victim or the victim's representative before the sentencing body. In utilizing this alternative, courts or jurisdictions shall fully

evaluate the conflicting considerations, on the one hand, of citizen participation, public confidence in law enforcement, and the victim's understandable interest; and, on the other, the potentially inflammatory impact in
some matters of the victim's courtroom statement and appearance.

12. Victims of a crime involving economic loss, loss of earnings, or earning
capacity should be able to expect the sentencing body to give priority consideration to restitution as a condition of probation.

13. Victims of property crimes should have their property returned as expedi-
tiously as possible, e.g., through photographing such property for use in
evidence.

* * *

Analysis

Written at roughly the same time as the Presidential Task Force Report on
Victims of Crime, the American Bar Association Guidelines for Treatment of Victims and Witnesses are now quite dated. Nevertheless, the Guidelines are important
in several respects. First, it is significant that such a project was undertaken by the
ABA during a time when victims had not previously been considered by that organization. The ABA's undertaking was groundbreaking, because it meant that lawyers
in the country were becoming concerned with the status of victims.

Since then, the ABA has had a permanent victims' subcommittee within the
Criminal Justice Committee. However, its influence is limited because the ABA
remains very defense and prosecution centered. One reason for prosecution and
defense centrality is the small number of lawyers who represent victims in criminal
cases. Victims' lawyers are numerically overwhelmed by prosecution and defense
interests. The topic of lawyers for victims is taken up in Chapter 8 of this book.

REFERENCES

American Bar Association (ABA). *Guidelines for Fair Treatment of Victims and Witnesses in the Criminal Justice System*. Author, 1983.
Bibas, Stephanos. *Assembly-Line Criminal Justice*. Under contract withOxford University Press, forthcoming 2011.
Dubber, Marcus D. *Victims in the War on Crime: The Use and Abuse of Victims' Rights*. New York: New York University Press, 2002.
Haight-Harrington, Lois. *Proposed Model Legislation*. Washington, DC: Office of Justice Programs, Office for Victims of Crime, 1986.
Office for Victims of Crime. *President's Task Force on Victims of Crime, Final Report*. Washington, DC: U.S. Government Printing Press, 1982.
Synder v. Commonwealth of Massachusetts, 291 U.S. 97 (1934).
Young, Marlene. "The Crime Victims' Movement." In *Post-Traumatic Therapy and Victims of Violence*, edited by Frank Ochberg, 319–29. New York: Brunner/Mazel, 1988.

4

THE FEDERAL CONSTITUTIONAL CONTEXT OF VICTIMS' RIGHTS

THE CONSTITUTIONAL CONTEXT OF VICTIMS' RIGHTS

The United States Constitution is the highest law of the land. It is the role of the Supreme Court to interpret the Constitution. The Constitution is important to victims' rights in several different ways. First, can the existing Constitution be interpreted to provide for some role for the victim in the criminal process? Second, how must victims' rights be created in light of the constraints imposed by the Constitution?

The answers to these questions is explored in the three documents that make up this chapter. These three documents are court cases, two from the Supreme Court of the United States and one from a federal circuit court. The first case is *Payne v. Tennessee*, 501 U.S. 808 (1991), which reversed the Court's own holding in *Booth v. Maryland* case just four years earlier. *Booth* had held that victim impact statements in capital cases were unconstitutional, and *Payne* effectively reversed that limitation.

Modern victims' rights were in the early stages of development when a United States Supreme Court opinion, *Booth v. Maryland*, 482 U.S. 496 (1987), cast doubt over the constitutionality of victim impact statements. *Booth* was a death penalty case in which the Court concluded that victims could not give impact statements because they were composed of constitutionally irrelevant information. In essence, the *Booth* case held that the only relevant harm was the harm defined in the criminal charge. Because the charge was murder, the death of another human being was the only harm that could be considered. The Court was "troubled by the implication that defendants whose victims were assets to the community are more deserving of punishment that those whose victims are perceived to be less worthy."

The Court decided that the impact on the surviving relatives, the characteristics of the victim, and the victim's opinion were all constitutionally irrelevant. The *Booth* court opinion controlled only death penalty cases, but there was reason for concern in the Crime Victims' Rights Movement. They worried that the unlawful-ness of victim impact in death penalty cases would expand to other crimes, or that the state jurisdictions would use the *Booth* opinion as a foundation to declare victim impact statements unconstitutional under their respective state constitutions. The *Booth* court had been a 5-to-4 split opinion. Over the next four years, two justices were replaced. This shift in the makeup of the court set the stage for *Payne v. Tennessee*, the 1991 case that overruled *Booth*.

- **Document:** *Payne v. Tennessee*
- **Date:** June 27, 1991
- **Significance:** *Payne v. Tennessee* overruled *Booth v. Maryland*, holding that the Eighth Amendment did not erect a per se bar prohibiting a capital sentencing jury from hearing victim impact evidence.
- **Source:** *Payne v. Tennessee*, 501 U.S. 808 (1991).

---

* * *

Chief Justice Rehnquist delivered the opinion of the Court.

In this case we reconsider our holdings in *Booth v. Maryland*, 482 U.S. 496 (1987) and *South Carolina v. Gathers*, 490 U.S. 805 (1989), that the Eighth Amendment bars the admission of victim impact evidence during the penalty phase of a capital trial.

Petitioner, Pervis Tyrone Payne, was convicted by a jury on two counts of first-degree murder and one count of assault with intent to commit murder in the first degree. He was sentenced to death for each of the murders and to 30 years in prison for the assault.

The victims of Payne's offenses were 28-year-old Charisse Christopher, her 2-year-old daughter Lacie, and her 3-year-old son Nicholas. The three lived together in an apartment in Millington, Tennessee, across the hall from Payne's girlfriend, Bobbie Thomas. On Saturday, June 27, 1987, Payne visited Thomas' apartment several times in expectation of her return from her mother's house in Arkansas, but found no one at home. On one visit, he left his overnight bag, containing clothes and other items for his weekend stay, in the hallway outside Thomas' apartment. With the bag were three cans of malt liquor.

Payne passed the morning and early afternoon injecting cocaine and drinking beer. Later, he drove around the town with a friend in the friend's car, each of them taking turns reading a pornographic magazine. Sometime around 3 p.m., Payne returned to the apartment complex, entered the Christophers' apartment, and began making sexual advances towards Charisse. Charisse resisted and Payne became violent. A neighbor who resided in the apartment directly beneath the Christophers heard Charisse screaming, " 'Get out, get out,' as if she were telling the children to leave" Brief for Respondent 3. The noise briefly subsided and then began, " 'horribly loud' " (Id). The neighbor called the police after she heard a "blood curdling scream" from the Christopher's apartment (Id).

When the first police officer arrived at the scene, he immediately encountered Payne, who was leaving the apartment building, so covered with blood that he appeared to be " 'sweating blood.' " The officer confronted Payne, who responded, " 'I'm the complainant.' " When the officer asked, " 'What's going on up there?' " Payne struck the officer with the overnight bag, dropped his tennis shoes, and fled (*State v. Payne*, 791 S.W.2d 10, 12 (Tenn. 1990)).

Inside the apartment, the police encountered a horrifying scene. Blood covered the walls and floor throughout the unit. Charisse and her children were lying on the floor in the kitchen. Nicholas, despite several wounds inflicted by a butcher knife that completely penetrated through his body from front to back, was still breathing. Miraculously, he survived, but not until after undergoing seven hours of surgery and a transfusion of 1,700 cc's of blood—400 to 500 cc's more than his estimated normal blood volume. Charisse and Lacie were dead.

Charisse's body was found on the kitchen floor on her back, her legs fully extended. She had sustained 42 direct knife wounds and 42 defensive wounds on her arms and hands. The wounds were caused by 41 separate thrusts of a butcher knife. None of the 84 wounds inflicted by Payne were individually fatal; rather, the cause of death was most likely bleeding from all of the wounds.

Lacie's body was on the kitchen floor near her mother. She had suffered stab wounds to the chest, abdomen, back, and head. The murder weapon, a butcher knife, was found at her feet. Payne's baseball cap was snapped on her arm near her elbow. Three cans of malt liquor bearing Payne's fingerprints were found on a table near her body, and a fourth empty one was on the landing outside the apartment door.

Payne was apprehended later that day hiding in the attic of the home of a former girlfriend. As he descended the stairs of the attic, he stated to the arresting officers, " 'Man, I ain't killed no woman.' " According to one of the officers, Payne had " 'a wild look about him. His pupils were contracted. He was foaming at the mouth, saliva. He appeared to be very nervous. He was breathing real rapid.' " He had blood on his body and clothes and several scratches across his chest. It was later determined that the blood stains matched the victims' blood types. A search of his pockets revealed a packet containing cocaine residue, a hypodermic syringe wrapper, and a cap from a hypodermic syringe. His overnight bag, containing a bloody white shirt, was found in a nearby dumpster.

At trial, Payne took the stand and, despite the overwhelming and relatively uncontroverted evidence against him, testified that he had not harmed any of the Christophers. Rather, he asserted that another man had raced by him as he was walking up the stairs to the floor where the Christophers lived. He stated that he had gotten blood on himself when, after hearing moans from the Christophers' apartment, he had tried to help the victims. According to his testimony, he panicked and fled when he heard police sirens and noticed the blood on his clothes. The jury returned guilty verdicts against Payne on all counts.

During the sentencing phase of the trial, Payne presented the testimony of four witnesses: his mother and father, Bobbie Thomas, and Dr. John T. Hutson, a clinical psychologist specializing in criminal court evaluation work. Bobbie Thomas testified that she met Payne at church, during a time when she was being abused by her husband. She stated that Payne was a very caring person, and that he devoted much time and attention to her three children, who were being affected by her marital difficulties. She said that the children had come to love him very much and would miss him, and that he "behaved just like a father that loved his kids." She asserted that he did not drink, nor did he use drugs, and that it was generally inconsistent with Payne's character to have committed these crimes.

Dr. Hutson testified that based on Payne's low score on an IQ test, Payne was "mentally handicapped." Hutson also said that Payne was neither psychotic nor schizophrenic, and that Payne was the most polite prisoner he had ever met. Payne's parents testified that their son had no prior criminal record and had never been arrested. They also stated that Payne had no history of alcohol or drug abuse, he worked with his father as a painter, he was good with children, and he was a good son.

The State presented the testimony of Charisse's mother, Mary Zvolanek. When asked how Nicholas had been affected by the murders of his mother and sister, she responded:

> "He cries for his mom. He doesn't seem to understand why she doesn't come home. And he cries for his sister Lacie. He comes to me many times during the week and asks me, Grandmama, do you miss my Lacie. And I tell him yes. He says, I'm worried about my Lacie."

In arguing for the death penalty during closing argument, the prosecutor commented on the continuing effects of Nicholas' experience, stating:

> But we do know that Nicholas was alive. And Nicholas was in the same room. Nicholas was still conscious. His eyes were open. He responded to the paramedics. He was able to follow their directions. He was able to hold his intestines in as he was carried to the ambulance. So he knew what happened to his mother and baby sister.
>
> There is nothing you can do to ease the pain of any of the families involved in this case. There is nothing you can do to ease the pain of Bernice or Carl Payne, and that's a tragedy. There is nothing you can do basically to ease the pain of Mr. and Mrs. Zvolanek, and that's a tragedy. They will have to live with it the rest of their lives. There is obviously nothing you can do for Charisse and Lacie Jo. But there is something that you can do for Nicholas.
>
> Somewhere down the road Nicholas is going to grow up, hopefully. He's going to want to know what happened. And he is going to know what happened to his baby sister and his mother. He is going to want to know what type

of justice was done. He is going to want to know what happened. With your verdict, you will provide the answer."

In the rebuttal to Payne's closing argument, the prosecutor stated:

You saw the videotape this morning. You saw what Nicholas Christopher will carry in his mind forever. When you talk about cruel, when you talk about atrocious, and when you talk about heinous, that picture will always come into your mind, probably throughout the rest of your lives. . . .

. . .

. . . No one will ever know about Lacie Jo because she never had the chance to grow up. Her life was taken from her at the age of two years old. So, no there won't be a high school principal to talk about Lacie Jo Christopher, and there won't be anybody to take her to her high school prom. And there won't be any-body there—there won't be her mother there or Nicholas' mother there to kiss him at night. His mother will never kiss him good night or pat him as he goes off to bed, or hold him and sing him a lullaby.

. . .

[Petitioner's attorney] wants you to think about a good reputation, people who love the defendant and things about him. He doesn't want you to think about the people who love Charisse Christopher, her mother and daddy who loved her. The people who loved little Lacie Jo, the grandparents who are still here. The brother who mourns for her every single day and wants to know where his best little playmate is. He doesn't have anybody to watch cartoons with him, a little one. These are the things that go into why it is especially cruel, heinous, and atrocious, the burden that that child will carry forever.

The jury sentenced Payne to death on each of the murder counts.

The Supreme Court of Tennessee affirmed the conviction and sentence (791 S.W.2d 10 (Tenn. 1990)). The court rejected Payne's contention that the admission of the grandmother's testimony and the State's closing argument constituted preju-dicial violations of his rights under the Eighth Amendment as applied in *Booth v. Maryland* and *South Carolina v. Gathers*. The court characterized the grandmother's testimony as "technically irrelevant," but concluded that it "did not create a consti-tutionally unacceptable risk of an arbitrary imposition of the death penalty and was harmless beyond a reasonable doubt" (791 S.W.2d, at 18).

The court determined that the prosecutor's comments during closing argument were "relevant to [Payne's] personal responsibility and moral guilt" (Id., at 19). The court explained that "[w]hen a person deliberately picks a butcher knife out of a kitchen drawer and proceeds to stab to death a twenty-eight-year-old mother, her two and one-half year old daughter and her three and one-half year old son, in the same room, the physical and mental condition of the boy he left for dead is surely relevant in determining his 'blameworthiness.' " The court concluded that any violation of Payne's rights under *Booth* and *Gathers* "was harmless beyond a rea-sonable doubt" (Ibid.).

We granted certiorari, 498 U.S. 1080, 111 S.Ct. 1031, 112 L.Ed.2d 1032 (1991), to reconsider our holdings in *Booth* and *Gathers* that the Eighth Amendment prohibits a capital sentencing jury from considering "victim impact" evidence relating to the personal characteristics of the victim and the emotional impact of the crimes on the victim's family.

In *Booth*, the defendant robbed and murdered an elderly couple. As required by a state statute, a victim impact statement was prepared based on interviews with the victims' son, daughter, son-in-law, and granddaughter. The statement, which described the personal characteristics of the victims, the emotional impact of the crimes on the family, and set forth the family members' opinions and characterizations of the crimes and the defendant, was submitted to the jury at sentencing. The jury imposed the death penalty. The conviction and sentence were affirmed on appeal by the State's highest court.

This Court held by a 5-to-4 vote that the Eighth Amendment prohibits a jury from considering a victim impact statement at the sentencing phase of a capital trial. The Court made clear that the admissibility of victim impact evidence was not to be determined on a case-by-case basis, but that such evidence was per se inadmissible in the sentencing phase of a capital case except to the extent that it "relate[d] directly to the circumstances of the crime" (482 U.S., at 507, n.10). In *Gathers*, decided two years later, the Court extended the rule announced in *Booth* to statements made by a prosecutor to the sentencing jury regarding the personal qualities of the victim.

The *Booth* Court began its analysis with the observation that the capital defendant must be treated as a " 'uniquely individual human bein[g]' " (482 U.S., at 504 (quoting *Woodson v. North Carolina*, 428 U.S. 280, 304 (1976)), and therefore the Constitution requires the jury to make an individualized determination as to whether the defendant should be executed based on the " 'character of the individual and the circumstances of the crime' " (482 U.S., at 502 (quoting *Zant v. Stephens*, 462 U.S. 862, 879 (1983)). The Court concluded that while no prior decision of this Court had mandated that only the defendant's character and immediate characteristics of the crime may constitutionally be considered, other factors are irrelevant to the capital sentencing decision unless they have "some bearing on the defendant's 'personal responsibility and moral guilt' " (482 U.S., at 502 (quoting *Edmund v. Florida*, 458 U.S. 782, 801 (1982)). To the extent that victim impact evidence presents "factors about which the defendant was unaware, and that were irrelevant to the decision to kill," the Court concluded, it has nothing to do with the "blameworthiness of a particular defendant" (482 U.S., at 504, 505). Evidence of the victim's character, the Court observed, "could well distract the sentencing jury from its constitutionally required task [of] determining whether the death penalty is appropriate in light of the background and record of the accused and the particular circumstances of the crime" (Id., at 507, and n.10). The Court concluded that, except to the extent that victim impact evidence relates "directly to the circumstances of the crime," the prosecution may not introduce such evidence at a capital sentencing hearing because "it creates an impermissible risk that the capital sentencing decision will be made in an arbitrary manner" (Id., at 505).

Booth and *Gathers* were based on two premises: that evidence relating to a particular victim or to the harm that a capital defendant causes a victim's family do not in general reflect on the defendant's "blameworthiness," and that only evidence relating to "blameworthiness" is relevant to the capital sentencing decision. However, the assessment of harm caused by the defendant as a result of the crime charged has understandably been an important concern of the criminal law, both in determining the elements of the offense and in determining the appropriate punishment. Thus, two equally blameworthy criminal defendants may be guilty of different offenses solely because their acts cause differing amounts of harm. "If a bank robber aims his gun at a guard, pulls the trigger, and kills his target, he may be put to death. If the gun unexpectedly misfires, he may not. His moral guilt in both cases is identical, but his responsibility in the former is greater" (*Booth*, 482 U.S., at 519, 107 S.Ct., at 2541 (Scalia, J., dissenting)). The same is true with respect to two defendants, each of whom participates in a robbery, and each of whom acts with reckless disregard for human life; if the robbery in which the first defendant participated results in the death of a victim, he may be subjected to the death penalty, but if the robbery in which the second defendant participates does not result in the death of a victim, the death penalty may not be imposed (*Tison v. Arizona*, 481 U.S. 137, 148 (1987)).

The principles which have guided criminal sentencing—as opposed to criminal liability—have varied with the times. The book of Exodus prescribes the Lex talionis, "An eye for an eye, a tooth for a tooth" (Exodus 21:22–23). In England and on the continent of Europe, as recently as the 18th century, crimes which would be regarded as quite minor today were capital offenses. Writing in the 18th century, the Italian criminologist Cesare Beccaria advocated the idea that "the punishment should fit the crime." He said that "[w]e have seen that the true measure of crimes is the injury done to society" (Farrer 1880, 199).

Gradually the list of crimes punishable by death diminished, and legislatures began grading the severity of crimes in accordance with the harm done by the criminal. The sentence for a given offense, rather than being precisely fixed by the legislature, was prescribed in terms of a minimum and a maximum, with the actual sentence to be decided by the judge. With the increasing importance of probation, as opposed to imprisonment, as a part of the penological process, some States such as California developed the "indeterminate sentence," where the time of incarceration was left almost entirely to the penological authorities rather than to the courts. But more recently the pendulum has swung back. The Federal Sentencing Guidelines, which went into effect in 1987, provided for very precise calibration of sentences, depending upon a number of factors. These factors relate both to the subjective guilt of the defendant and to the harm caused by his acts.

Wherever judges in recent years have had discretion to impose sentence, the consideration of the harm caused by the crime has been an important factor in the exercise of that discretion:

"The first significance of harm in Anglo-American jurisprudence is, then, as a prerequisite to the criminal sanction. The second significance of harm—one no less important to judges—is as a measure of the seriousness of the offense and therefore as a standard for determining the severity of the sentence that will be meted out" (Wheeler, Mann, and Sarat 1988, 56).

Whatever the prevailing sentencing philosophy, the sentencing authority has always been free to consider a wide range of relevant material (*Williams v. New York*,

337 U.S. 241 (1949)). In the federal system, we observed that "a judge may appropriately conduct an inquiry broad in scope, largely unlimited either as to the kind of information he may consider, or the source from which it may come" (*United States v. Tucker*, 404 U.S. 443, 446 (1972)). Even in the context of capital sentencing, prior to Booth the joint opinion of Justices Stewart, Powell, and Stevens in *Gregg v. Georgia*, 428 U.S. 153, 203–204 (1976), had rejected petitioner's attack on the Georgia statute because of the "wide scope of evidence and argument allowed at presentence hearings." The joint opinion stated:

"We think that the Georgia court wisely has chosen not to impose unnecessary restrictions on the evidence that can be offered at such a hearing and to approve open and far-ranging argument. . . . So long as the evidence introduced and the arguments made at the presentence hearing do not prejudice a defendant, it is preferable not to impose restrictions. We think it desirable for the jury to have as much information before it as possible when it makes the sentencing decision."

The Maryland statute involved in *Booth* required that the presentence report in all felony cases include a "victim impact statement" which would describe the effect of the crime on the victim and his family (*Booth*, 482 U.S., at 498). Congress and most of the States have, in recent years, enacted similar legislation to enable the sentencing authority to consider information about the harm caused by the crime committed by the defendant. The evidence involved in the present case was not admitted pursuant to any such enactment, but its purpose and effect were much the same as if it had been. While the admission of this particular kind of evidence, designed to portray for the sentencing authority the actual harm caused by a particular crime, is of recent origin, this fact hardly renders it unconstitutional (*Williams v. Florida*, 399 U.S. 78 (1970, upholding the constitutionality of a notice-of-alibi statute, of a kind enacted by at least 15 States dating from 1927; *United States v. DiFrancesco*, 449 U.S. 117, 142 (1980; upholding against a double jeopardy challenge an Act of Congress representing "a considered legislative attempt to attack a specific problem in our justice system, that is, the tendency on the part of some trial judges 'to mete out light sentences in cases involving organized crime management personnel' ").

We have held that a State cannot preclude the sentencer from considering "any relevant mitigating evidence" that the defendant proffers in support of a sentence less than death (*Eddings v. Oklahoma*, 455 U.S. 104, 114 (1982); see also *Skipper v. South Carolina*, 476 U.S. 1 (1986)). Thus we have, as the Court observed in *Booth*, required that the capital defendant be treated as a "uniquely individual human bein[g]." But it was never held or even suggested in any of our cases preceding *Booth* that the defendant, entitled as he was to individualized consideration, was to receive that consideration wholly apart from the crime which he had committed. The language quoted from *Woodson* in the *Booth* opinion was not intended to describe a class of evidence that could not be received, but a class of evidence which must be received. Any doubt on the matter is dispelled by comparing the language in *Woodson* with the language from *Gregg v. Georgia*, quoted above, which was handed down the same day as Woodson. This misreading of precedent in *Booth* has, we think, unfairly weighted the scales in a capital trial; while virtually no limits are placed on the relevant mitigating evidence a capital defendant may introduce concerning his own circumstances, the State is barred from either offering "a quick glimpse of the life" which a defendant "chose to extinguish" (*Mills v. Maryland*, 486 U.S. 367, 397 (1988)) or demonstrating the loss to the victim's family and to society which has resulted from the defendant's homicide.

The *Booth* Court reasoned that victim impact evidence must be excluded because it would be difficult, if not impossible, for the defendant to rebut such evidence without shifting the focus of the sentencing hearing away from the defendant, thus creating a "'mini-trial' on the victim's character" (*Booth*, 482 U.S., 506–507). In many cases the evidence relating to the victim is already before the jury at least in part because of its relevance at the guilt phase of the trial. But even as to additional evidence admitted at the sentencing phase, the mere fact that for tactical reasons it might not be prudent for the defense to rebut victim impact evidence makes the case no different than others in which a party is faced with this sort of a dilemma. As we explained in rejecting the contention that expert testimony on future dangerousness should be excluded from capital trials, "the rules of evidence generally extant at the federal and state levels anticipate that relevant, unprivileged evidence should be admitted and its weight left to the factfinder, who would have the benefit of cross-examination and contrary evidence by the opposing party" (*Barefoot v. Estelle*, 463 U.S. 880, 893 (1983)).

Payne echoes the concern voiced in *Booth*'s case that the admission of victim impact evidence permits a jury to find that defendants whose victims were assets to their community are more deserving of punishment than those whose victims are perceived to be less worthy (*Booth*, 482 U.S. at 506, n.8). As a general matter, however, victim impact evidence is not offered to encourage comparative judgments of this kind—for instance, that the killer of a hardworking, devoted parent deserves the death penalty, but that the murderer of a reprobate does not. It is designed to show instead each victim's "uniqueness as an individual human being," whatever the jury might think the loss to the community resulting from his death might be. The facts of *Gathers* are an excellent illustration of this: The evidence showed that the victim was an out of work, mentally handicapped individual, perhaps not, in the eyes of most, a significant contributor to society, but nonetheless a murdered human being.

Under our constitutional system, the primary responsibility for defining crimes against state law, fixing punishments for the commission of these crimes, and establishing procedures for criminal trials rests with the States. The state laws respecting crimes, punishments, and criminal procedure are, of course, subject to the overriding provisions of the United States Constitution. Where the State imposes the death penalty for a particular crime, we have held that the Eighth Amendment imposes special limitations upon that process.

First, there is a required threshold below which the death penalty cannot be imposed. In this context, the State must establish rational criteria that narrow the decisionmaker's judgment as to whether the circumstances of a particular defendant's case meet the threshold. Moreover, a societal consensus that the death penalty is disproportionate to a particular offense prevents a State from imposing the death penalty for that offense. Second, States cannot limit the sentencer's consideration of any relevant circumstance that could cause it to decline to impose the penalty. In this respect, the State cannot challenge the sentencer's discretion, but must allow it to consider any relevant information offered by the defendant." (*McCleskey v. Kemp*, 481 U.S. 279, 305–306 (1987)).

But, as we noted in *California v. Ramos*, 463 U.S. 992, 1001 (1983), "[b]eyond these limitations . . . the Court has deferred to the State's choice of substantive factors relevant to the penalty determination."

"Within the constitutional limitations defined by our cases, the States enjoy their traditional latitude to prescribe the method by which those who commit murder shall be punished" (*Blystone v. Pennsylvania*, 494 U.S. 299, 309 (1990)). The States remain free, in capital cases, as well as others, to devise new procedures and new remedies to meet felt needs. Victim impact evidence is simply another form or method of informing the sentencing authority about the specific harm caused by the crime in question, evidence of a general type long considered by sentencing authorities. We think the *Booth* Court was wrong in stating that this kind of evidence leads to the arbitrary imposition of the death penalty. In the majority of cases, and in this case, victim impact evidence serves entirely legitimate purposes. In the event that evidence is introduced that is so unduly prejudicial that it renders the trial fundamentally unfair, the Due Process Clause of the Fourteenth Amendment provides a mechanism for relief. (See *Darden v. Wainwright*, 447 U.S. 168, 179-183 (1986).) Courts have always taken into consideration the harm done by the defendant in imposing sentence, and the evidence adduced in this case was illustrative of the harm caused by Payne's double murder.

We are now of the view that a State may properly conclude that for the jury to assess meaningfully the defendant's moral culpability and blameworthiness, it should have before it at the sentencing phase evidence of the specific harm caused by the defendant. "[T]he State has a legitimate interest in counteracting the mitigating evidence which the defendant is entitled to put in, by reminding the sentencer that just as the murderer should be considered as an individual, so too the victim is an individual whose death represents a unique loss to society and in particular to his family" (*Booth*, 482 U.S., at 517 (White, J., dissenting; citation omitted)). By turning the victim into a "faceless stranger at the penalty phase of a capital trial" (*Gathers*, 490 U.S., at 821 (O'Connor, J., dissenting)), *Booth* deprives the State of the full moral force of its evidence and may prevent the jury from having before it all the information necessary to determine the proper punishment for a first-degree murder.

The present case is an example of the potential for such unfairness. The capital sentencing jury heard testimony from Payne's girlfriend that they met at church; that he was affectionate, caring, and kind to her children; that he was not an abuser of drugs or alcohol; and that it was inconsistent with his character to have committed the murders. Payne's parents testified that he was a good son, and a clinical psychologist testified that Payne was an extremely polite prisoner and suffered from a low IQ. None of this testimony was related to the circumstances of Payne's brutal crimes. In contrast, the only evidence of the impact of Payne's offenses during the sentencing phase was Nicholas' grandmother's description—in response to a single question—that the child misses his mother and baby sister. Payne argues that the Eighth Amendment commands that the jury's death sentence must be set aside because the jury heard this testimony. But the testimony illustrated quite poignantly some of the harm that Payne's killing had caused; there is nothing unfair about allowing the jury to bear in mind that harm at the same time as it considers the mitigating evidence introduced by the defendant. The Supreme Court of Tennessee in this case obviously felt the unfairness of the rule pronounced by *Booth* when it said: "It is an affront to the civilized members of the human race to say that at sentencing in a capital case, a parade of witnesses may praise the background, character and good deeds of Defendant (as was done in this case), without limitation as to relevancy, but nothing may be said that bears upon the character of, or the harm imposed, upon the victims" (791 S.W.2d, at 19).

In *Gathers*, as indicated above, we extended the holding of *Booth* barring victim impact evidence to the prosecutor's argument to the jury. Human nature being what it is, capable lawyers trying cases to juries try to convey to the jurors that the people involved in the underlying events are, or were, living human beings, with something to be gained or lost from the jury's verdict. Under the aegis of the Eighth Amendment, we have given the broadest latitude to the defendant to introduce relevant mitigating evidence reflecting on his individual personality, and the defendant's attorney may argue that evidence to the jury. Petitioner's attorney in this case did just that. For the reasons discussed above, we now reject the view—expressed in *Gathers*—that a State may not permit the prosecutor to similarly argue to the jury the human cost of the crime of which the defendant stands convicted. We reaffirm the view expressed by Justice Cardozo in *Snyder v. Massachusetts*, 291 U.S. 97, 122 (1934): "[J]ustice, though due to the accused, is due to the accuser also. The concept of fairness must not be strained till it is narrowed to a filament. We are to keep the balance true."

We thus hold that if the State chooses to permit the admission of victim impact evidence and prosecutorial argument on that subject, the Eighth Amendment erects no per se bar. A State may legitimately conclude that evidence about the victim and about the impact of the murder on the victim's family is relevant to the jury's decision as to whether or not the death penalty should be imposed. There is no reason to treat such evidence differently than other relevant evidence is treated.

* * *

Justice O'Connor, with whom Justice White and Justice Kennedy join, concurring

In my view, a State may legitimately determine that victim impact evidence is relevant to a capital sentencing proceeding. A State may decide that the jury, before determining whether a convicted murderer should receive the death penalty, should know the full extent of the harm caused by the crime, including its impact on the victim's family and community. A State may decide also that the jury should see "a quick glimpse of the life petitioner chose to extinguish" (*Mills v. Maryland*, 486 U.S., at 397), to remind the jury that the person whose life was taken was a unique human being.

Given that victim impact evidence is potentially relevant, nothing in the Eighth Amendment commands that States treat it differently than other kinds of relevant evidence. "The Eighth Amendment stands as a shield against those practices and punishments which are either inherently cruel or which so offend the moral consensus of this society as to be deemed 'cruel and unusual'" (*South Carolina v. Gathers*, 490 U.S., at 821). Certainly there is no strong societal consensus that a jury may not take into account the loss suffered by a victim's family or that a murder victim must remain a faceless stranger at the penalty phase of a capital trial. Just the opposite is true. Most States have enacted legislation enabling judges and juries to consider victim impact evidence. The possibility that this evidence may in some cases be unduly inflammatory does not justify a prophylactic, constitutionally based rule that this evidence may never be admitted. Trial courts routinely exclude evidence that is unduly inflammatory; where inflammatory evidence is improperly admitted, appellate courts carefully review the record to determine whether the error was prejudicial.

We do not hold today that victim impact evidence must be admitted, or even that it should be admitted. We hold merely that if a State decides to permit consideration of this evidence, "the Eighth Amendment erects no per se bar." If, in a particular case, a witness' testimony or a prosecutor's remark so infects the sentencing proceeding as to render it fundamentally unfair, the defendant may seek appropriate relief under the Due Process Clause of the Fourteenth Amendment.

That line was not crossed in this case. The State called as a witness Mary Zvolanek, Nicholas' grandmother. Her testimony was brief. She explained that Nicholas cried for his mother and baby sister and could not understand why they did not come home. I do not doubt that the jurors were moved by this testimony—who would not have been? But surely this brief statement did not inflame their passions more than did the facts of the crime: Charisse Christopher was stabbed 41 times with a butcher knife and bled to death; her 2-year-old daughter Lacie was killed by repeated thrusts of that same knife; and 3-year-old Nicholas, despite stab wounds that penetrated completely through his body from front to back, survived—only to witness the brutal murders of his mother and baby sister. In light of the jury's unavoidable familiarity with the facts of Payne's vicious attack, I cannot conclude that the additional information provided by Mary Zvolanek's testimony deprived petitioner of due process.

Nor did the prosecutor's comments about Charisse and Lacie in the closing argument violate the Constitution. The jury had earlier seen a videotape of the murder scene that included the slashed and bloody corpses of Charisse and Lacie. In arguing that Payne deserved the death penalty, the prosecutor sought to remind the jury that Charisse and Lacie were more than just lifeless bodies on a videotape, that they were unique human beings. The prosecutor remarked that Charisse would never again sing a lullaby to her son and that Lacie would never attend a high school prom. In my view, these statements were permissible. "Murder is the ultimate act of depersonalization" (Brief for Justice For All Political Committee et al. as *Amici Curiae* 3). It transforms a living person with hopes, dreams, and fears into a corpse, thereby taking away all that is special and unique about the person. The Constitution does not preclude a State from deciding to give some of that back.

I agree with the Court that *Booth v. Maryland* and *South Carolina v. Gathers* were wrongly decided. The Eighth Amendment does not prohibit a State from choosing to admit evidence concerning a murder victim's personal characteristics or the impact of the crime on the victim's family and community. *Booth* also addressed another kind of victim impact evidence—opinions of the victim's family about the crime, the defendant, and the appropriate sentence. As the Court notes in today's decision, we do not reach this issue as no evidence of this kind was introduced at petitioner's trial. Nor do we express an opinion as to other aspects of the prosecutor's conduct. As to the victim impact evidence that was introduced, its admission did not violate the Constitution. Accordingly, I join the Court's opinion.

Justice Scalia, with whom Justice O'Connor and Justice Kennedy join as to Part II, concurring.

I.

The Court correctly observes the injustice of requiring the exclusion of relevant aggravating evidence during capital sentencing, while requiring the admission of all relevant mitigating evidence (see, e.g., *Eddings v. Oklahoma*, 455 U.S. 104 (1982); *Lockett v. Ohio*, 438 U.S. 586 (1978; plurality opinion)). I have previously expressed my belief that the latter requirement is both wrong and, when combined with the remainder of our capital sentencing jurisprudence, unworkable (see *Walton v. Arizona*, 497 U.S. 639, 671–673 (1990)). Even if it were abandoned, however, I would still affirm the judgment here. True enough, the Eighth Amendment permits parity between mitigating and aggravating factors. But more broadly and fundamentally still, it permits the People to decide (within the limits of other constitutional guarantees) what is a crime and what constitutes aggravation and mitigation of a crime.

II.

. . . If there was ever a case that defied reason, it was *Booth v. Maryland*, imposing a constitutional rule that had absolutely no basis in constitutional text, in historical practice, or in logic. Justice Marshall has also explained that "[t]he jurist concerned with public confidence in, and acceptance of the judicial system might well consider that, however admirable its resolute adherence to the law as it was, a decision contrary to the public sense of justice as it is, operates, so far as it is known, to diminish respect for the courts and for law itself" (*Flood v. Kuhn*, 407 U.S. 258, 293 n.4 (1972; dissenting opinion; citation omitted)). *Booth*'s stunning ipse dixit, that a crime's unanticipated consequences must be deemed "irrelevant" to the sentence (482 U.S., at 503), conflicts with a public sense of justice keen enough that it has found voice in a nationwide "victims' rights" movement.

Today, however, Justice Marshall demands of us some "special justification"—beyond the mere conviction that the rule of *Booth* significantly harms our criminal justice system and is egregiously wrong—before we can be absolved of exercising "[p]ower, not reason." I do not think that is fair. In fact, quite to the contrary, what would enshrine power as the governing principle of this Court is the notion that an important constitutional decision with plainly inadequate rational support must be left in place for the sole reason that it once attracted five votes.

It seems to me difficult for those who were in the majority in *Booth* to hold themselves forth as ardent apostles of stare decisis. That doctrine, to the extent it rests upon anything more than administrative convenience, is merely the application to judicial precedents of a more general principle that the settled practices and expectations of a democratic society should generally not be disturbed by the courts. It is hard to have a genuine regard for stare decisis without honoring that more general principle as well. A decision of this Court which, while not overruling a prior holding, nonetheless announces a novel rule, contrary to long and unchallenged practice, and pronounces it to be the Law of the Land—such a decision, no less than an explicit overruling, should be approached with great caution. It was, I suggest, *Booth*, and not today's decision, that compromised the fundamental values underlying the doctrine of stare decisis.

* * *

Justice Stevens, with whom Justice Blackmun joins, dissenting.

The novel rule that the Court announces today represents a dramatic departure from the principles that have governed our capital sentencing jurisprudence for decades. Justice Marshall is properly concerned about the majority's trivialization of the doctrine of stare decisis. But even if *Booth v. Maryland* and *South Carolina v. Gathers* had not been decided, today's decision would represent a sharp break with past decisions. Our cases provide no support whatsoever for the majority's conclusion that the prosecutor may introduce evidence that sheds no light on the defendant's guilt or moral culpability, and thus serves no purpose other than to encourage jurors to decide in favor of death rather than life on the basis of their emotions rather than their reason.

Until today our capital punishment jurisprudence has required that any decision to impose the death penalty be based solely on evidence that tends to inform the jury about the character of the offense and the character of the defendant. Evidence that serves no purpose other than to appeal to the sympathies or emotions of the jurors has never been considered admissible. Thus, if a defendant, who had murdered a convenience store clerk in cold blood in the course of an armed robbery, offered evidence unknown to him at the time of the crime about the immoral character of his victim, all would recognize immediately that the evidence was irrelevant and inadmissible. Evenhanded justice requires that the same constraint be imposed on the advocate of the death penalty.

I.

In *Williams v. New York*, 337 U.S. 241 (1949), this Court considered the scope of the inquiry that should precede the imposition of a death sentence. Relying on practices that had developed "both before and since the American colonies became a nation" (Id., at 246), Justice Black described the wide latitude that had been accorded judges in considering the source and type of evidence that is relevant to the sentencing determination. Notably, that opinion refers not only to the relevance of evidence establishing the defendant's guilt, but also to the relevance of "the fullest information possible concerning the defendant's life and characteristics" (Id., at 247). "Victim impact" evidence, however, was unheard of when *Williams* was decided. The relevant evidence of harm to society consisted of proof that the defendant was guilty of the offense charged in the indictment.

Almost 30 years after our decision in *Williams*, the Court reviewed the scope of evidence relevant in capital sentencing. See *Lockett v. Ohio*, 438 U.S. 586 (1978). In his plurality opinion, Chief Justice Burger concluded that in a capital case, the sentencer must not be prevented "from considering, as a mitigating factor, any aspect of a defendant's character or record and any of the circumstances of the offense that the defendant proffers as a basis for a sentence less than death" (Id. at 604; emphasis deleted). As in *Williams*, the character of the offense and the character of the offender constituted the entire category of relevant evidence. "Victim impact" evidence was still unheard of when *Lockett* was decided.

As the Court acknowledges today, the use of victim impact evidence "is of recent origin." Insofar as the Court's jurisprudence is concerned, this type of evidence made its first appearance in 1987 in *Booth v. Maryland*. In his opinion for the Court, Justice Powell noted that our prior cases had stated that the question whether an individual defendant should be executed is to be determined on the basis of " 'the character of the individual and the circumstances of the crime' " (Id., at 502; internal quotations omitted). Relying on those cases and on *Enmund v. Florida*, 458 U.S. 782, 801 (1982), the Court concluded that unless evidence has some bearing on the defendant's personal responsibility and moral guilt, its admission would create a risk that a death sentence might be based on considerations that are constitutionally impermissible or totally irrelevant to the sentencing process (482 U.S., at 502). Evidence that served no purpose except to describe the personal characteristics of the victim and the emotional impact of the crime on the victim's family was therefore constitutionally irrelevant.

Our decision in *Booth* was entirely consistent with the practices that had been followed "both before and since the American colonies became a nation" (*Williams*, 337 U.S., at 246). Our holding was mandated by our capital punishment jurisprudence, which requires any decision to impose the death penalty to be based on reason rather than caprice or emotion (see *Gardener v. Florida*, 430 U.S. 349, 362 (1977; opinion of Stevens, J.)). The dissenting opinions in *Booth* and in *Gathers* can be searched in vain for any judicial precedent sanctioning the use of evidence unrelated to the character of the offense or the character of the offender in the sentencing process. Today, however, relying on nothing more than those dissenting opinions, the Court abandons rules of relevance that are older than the Nation itself and ventures into uncharted seas of irrelevance.

II.

Today's majority has obviously been moved by an argument that has strong political appeal but no proper place in a reasoned judicial opinion. Because our decision in *Lockett*, 438 U.S., at 604, recognizes the defendant's right to introduce all mitigating evidence that may inform the jury about his character, the Court suggests that fairness requires that the State be allowed to respond with similar evidence about the victim. [Footnote 1 omitted]. This argument is a classic non sequitur: The victim is not on trial; her character, whether good or bad, cannot therefore constitute either an aggravating or a mitigating circumstance.

Even if introduction of evidence about the victim could be equated with introduction of evidence about the defendant, the argument would remain flawed in both its premise and its conclusion. The conclusion that exclusion of victim impact evidence results in a significantly imbalanced sentencing procedure is simply inaccurate. Just as the defendant is entitled to introduce any relevant mitigating evidence, so the State may rebut that evidence and may designate any relevant conduct to be an aggravating factor provided that the factor is sufficiently well defined and consistently applied to cabin the sentencer's discretion.

The premise that a criminal prosecution requires an even-handed balance between the State and the defendant is also incorrect. The Constitution grants certain rights to the criminal defendant and imposes special limitations on the State designed to protect the individual from overreaching by the disproportionately powerful State. Thus, the State must prove a defendant's guilt beyond a reasonable doubt (see *In Re Winship*, 397 U.S. 358 (1970)). Rules of evidence are also weighted in the defendant's favor. For example, the prosecution generally cannot introduce evidence of the defendant's character to prove his propensity to commit a crime, but the defendant can introduce such reputation evidence to show his law-abiding nature (see, e.g., Fed. Rule Evid. 404(a)). Even if balance were required or desirable, today's decision, by permitting both the defendant and the State to introduce irrelevant evidence for the sentencer's consideration without any guidance, surely does nothing to enhance parity in the sentencing process.

III.

Victim impact evidence, as used in this case, has two flaws, both related to the Eighth Amendment's command that the punishment of death may not be meted out arbitrarily or capriciously. First, aspects of the character of the victim unforeseeable to the defendant at the time of his crime are irrelevant to the defendant's "personal responsibility and moral guilt" and therefore cannot justify a death sentence (see *Enmund v. Florida*, 458 U.S., at 801; see also id., at 825 (O'Connor, J., dissenting; "[P]roportionality requires a nexus between the punishment imposed and the defendant's blameworthiness"); *Tison v. Arizona*, 481 U.S. 137, 149 (1987; "The heart of the retribution rationale is that a criminal sentence must be directly related to the personal culpability of the criminal offender); *California v. Brown*, 479 U.S. 538 (1987; O'Conner, J., concurring)).

Second, the quantity and quality of victim impact evidence sufficient to turn a verdict of life in prison into a verdict of death is not defined until after the crime has been committed and therefore cannot possibly be applied consistently in different cases. The sentencer's unguided consideration of victim impact evidence thus conflicts with the principle central to our capital punishment jurisprudence that, "where discretion is afforded a sentencing body on a matter so grave as the determination of whether a human life should be taken or spared, that discretion must be suitably directed and limited so as to minimize the risk of wholly arbitrary and capricious action" (*Gregg v. Georgia*, 428 U.S. 153, 189 (1976; joint opinion of Stewart, Powell, and Stevens, JJ.)). Open-ended reliance by a capital sentencer on victim impact evidence simply does not provide a "principled way to distinguish [cases], in which the death penalty [i]s imposed, from the many cases in which it [i]s not" (*Godfrey v. Georgia*, 446 U.S. 420, 433 (1980; opinion of Stewart, J.)).

The majority attempts to justify the admission of victim impact evidence by arguing that "consideration of the harm caused by the crime has been an important factor in the exercise of [sentencing] discretion." This statement is misleading and inaccurate. It is misleading because it is not limited to harm that is foreseeable. It is inaccurate because it fails to differentiate between legislative determinations and judicial sentencing. It is true that an evaluation of the harm caused by different kinds of wrongful conduct is a critical aspect in legislative definitions of offenses and determinations concerning sentencing guidelines. There is a rational correlation between moral culpability and the foreseeable harm caused by criminal conduct. Moreover, in the capital sentencing area, legislative identification of the special aggravating factors that may justify the imposition of the death penalty is entirely appropriate. [Footnote 2 omitted]. But the majority cites no authority for the suggestion that unforeseeable and indirect harms to a victim's family are properly considered as aggravating evidence on a case-by-case basis.

The dissents in *Booth* and *Gathers* and the majority today offer only the recent decision in *Tison v. Arizona*, and two legislative examples to support their contention that harm to the victim has traditionally influenced sentencing discretion. *Tison* held that the death penalty may be imposed on a felon who acts with reckless disregard for human life if a death occurs in the course of the felony, even though capital punishment cannot be imposed if no one dies as a result of the crime. The first legislative example is that attempted murder and murder are classified as two different offenses subject to different punishments. The second legislative example is that a person who drives while intoxicated is guilty of vehicular homicide if his actions result in a death but is not guilty of this offense if he has the good fortune to make it home without killing anyone (see *Booth*, 482 U.S., at 516 (White, J., dissenting)).

These three scenarios, however, are fully consistent with the Eighth Amendment jurisprudence reflected in *Booth* and *Gathers* and do not demonstrate that harm to the victim may be considered by a capital sentencer in the ad hoc and post hoc manner authorized by today's majority. The majority's examples demonstrate only that harm to the victim may justify enhanced punishment if the harm is both foreseeable to the defendant and clearly identified in advance of the crime by the legislature as a class of harm that should in every case result in more severe punishment.

In each scenario, the defendants could reasonably foresee that their acts might result in loss of human life. In addition, in each, the decision that the defendants should be treated differently was made prior to the crime by the legislature, the decision of which is subject to scrutiny for basic rationality. Finally, in each scenario, every defendant who causes the well-defined harm of destroying a human life will be subject to the determination that his conduct should be punished more severely. The majority's scenarios therefore provide no support for its holding, which permits a jury to sentence a defendant to death because of harm to the victim and his family that the defendant could not foresee, which was not even identified until after the crime had been committed, and which may be deemed by the jury, without any rational explanation, to justify a death sentence in one case but not in another. Unlike the rule elucidated by the scenarios on which the majority relies, the majority's holding offends the Eighth Amendment because it permits the sentencer to rely on irrelevant evidence in an arbitrary and capricious manner.

The majority's argument that "the sentencing authority has always been free to consider a wide range of relevant material," thus cannot justify consideration of victim impact evidence that is irrelevant because it details harms that the defendant could not have foreseen. Nor does the majority's citation of *Gregg v. Georgia* concerning the "wide scope of evidence and argument allowed at presentence hearings," 428 U.S., at 203, support today's holding. The *Gregg* joint opinion endorsed the sentencer's consideration of a wide range of evidence "[s]o long as the evidence introduced and the arguments made at the presentence hearing do not prejudice a defendant" (428 U.S., at 203–204). Irrelevant victim impact evidence that distracts the sentencer from the proper focus of sentencing and encourages reliance on emotion and other arbitrary factors necessarily prejudices the defendant.

The majority's apparent inability to understand this fact is highlighted by its misunderstanding of Justice Powell's argument in *Booth* that admission of victim impact evidence is undesirable because it risks shifting the focus of the sentencing hearing away from the defendant and the circumstances of the crime and creating a " 'mini-trial' on the victim's character" (482 U.S., at 507). *Booth* found this risk insupportable not, as today's majority suggests, because it creates a "tactical" "dilemma" for the defendant, but because it allows the possibility that the jury will be so distracted by prejudicial and irrelevant considerations that it will base its life-or-death decision on whim or caprice (see 482 U.S., at 506–507).

IV.

* * *

V.

The notion that the inability to produce an ideal system of justice in which every punishment is precisely married to the defendant's blameworthiness somehow justifies a rule that completely divorces some capital sentencing determinations from moral culpability is incomprehensible to me. Also incomprehensible is the argument that such a rule is required for the jury to take into account that each murder victim is a "unique" human being. The fact that each of us is unique is a proposition so obvious that it surely requires no evidentiary support. What is not obvious, however, is the way in which the character or reputation in one case may differ from that of other possible victims. Evidence offered to prove such differences can only be intended to identify some victims as more worthy of protection than others. Such proof risks decisions based on the same invidious motives as a prosecutor's decision to seek the death penalty if a victim is white but to accept a plea bargain if the victim is black (see *McCleskey v. Kemp*, 481 U.S., at 366).

Given the current popularity of capital punishment in a crime-ridden society, the political appeal of arguments that assume that increasing the severity of sentences is the best cure for the cancer of crime, and the political strength of the "victims' rights" movement, I recognize that today's decision will be greeted with enthusiasm by a large number of concerned and thoughtful citizens. The great tragedy of the decision, however, is the danger that the "hydraulic pressure" of public opinion that Justice Holmes once described [Footnote 3 omitted]—and that properly influences the deliberations of democratic legislatures—has played a role not only in the

Court's decision to hear this case, [Footnote 4 omitted] and in its decision to reach the constitutional question without pausing to consider affirming on the basis of the Tennessee Supreme Court's rationale, [Footnote 5 omitted] but even in its resolution of the constitutional issue involved. Today is a sad day for a great institution.

* * *

Analysis

The *Payne* decision cleared the way for victim impact statements. Now the law permitted victim impact statements in capital cases, with the exception, as interpreted by most courts, that the victim cannot give his or her opinion on whether the death sentence is appropriate. In other, noncapital cases, victims may also give their opinions on the proper sentence without running afoul of the Constitution.

The *Payne* case may well be the most important case for victims' rights. By allowing victim impact statements at sentencing, the *Payne* decision conferred constitutional clarity of other victims' rights. More specifically, because *Payne* did not allow the value of equal treatment of similarly situated defendants to constitutionally prohibit victim statements' impact at sentencing, the "equal treatment" argument is unlikely to succeed in defeating other victims' rights.

In *Payne*, the Court ruled 6–3 that certain victim impact statements were permissible, even in death penalty cases. The Court identified three types of victim impact information: characteristics of the victim, the resulting harm to the survivors and community, and the victim's opinion about the sentence. After *Payne*, the first two types of victim impact—the resulting harm to the victim and characteristics of the victim—are permissible, but lower courts have interpreted *Payne* as prohibiting victim opinion on the propriety of the death sentence. However, in non–death penalty cases, all three types of impact are constitutional. Thus, in non–death penalty cases, the States are free to permit victim opinion about the sentence.

The *Payne* opinion is also important because it equates defendants and victims as "unique individual human beings." This phrase had previously been used only to describe the defendant's interest in sentencing as an interest grounded in the prospect of punishment. Victims' interests in sentencing are now recognized by the court as grounded in the harm that results from the criminal act.

The *Payne* decision was as encouraging to the Victims' Rights Movement as the *Booth* opinion had been discouraging.

The next document is an example of a victim impact statement. Michael Luttig is the son of a murder victim and author of the impact statement.

- **Document:** Statement to the State Court of Texas by Michael Luttig
- **Date:** March 20, 1995
- **Significance:** This document serves as an example of a powerful victim impact statement that might be given or submitted during the sentencing stage of a criminal trial.

Michael Luttig, then a judge on the 4th U.S. Circuit Court of Appeals. He is author of a moving victim impact statement concerning the murder of his father and assault of his mother. (AP Photo/4th U.S. Circuit Court of Appeals)

- **Source:** Luttig, Michael. Statement to the Court. *State of Texas v. Napoleon Beazley* 144d. 4-94-22 (Texas 1997). Reprinted in *Texas Lawyer* (Mar. 20, 1995): 4.

* * *

May it please the Court. It is one of life's ironies that I appear before the court for the reason that I do. But I do so to represent my dad—who is not here—and his wife, and daughters. His family, my family.

More than anything else, I do this to honor him, because if the roles were reversed, he would be standing here today, of this I am certain.

I also owe this to the other victims of violent crime who either stand silently by, or who speak and are not heard.

I owe it to the public.

I owe it, as well, to Donald and Cedric Coleman, who may not yet understand the magnitude of the losses they inflicted on the night of April 19.

Words seem trite in describing what follows when your husband is murdered in your presence, when your father is stripped from your life, the horror, the agony, the emptiness, the despair, the chaos, the confusion, the sense—perhaps temporary, but perhaps not—that one's life no longer has any purpose, the doubt, the hopelessness. There are no words that can possibly describe it, and all it entails.

But being the victim of a violent crime such as this is the least of these things. Exactly these things in my family's case; the equivalent of these things in the countless other cases.

While it is happening and in the seconds and the minutes thereafter . . .

. . . it's the sheer horror of half-clothed people with guns storming up your driveway toward you in the dark of night, when you are totally defenseless.

. . . it's what must be the terrifying realization that you are first about to be, and then actually being, murdered.

. . . it's crawling on the floor of your own garage in the grease and filth, pretending you're dead, so that you won't be shot through the head by the person who just murdered your husband.

. . . it's realizing your husband has been gunned down in your driveway on your return from the final class you needed to complete your education—an education that had been the goal of both of you since the day you were married.

. . . it's knowing that the reason that your husband was with you—indeed, the reason that you were in the car that night at all—is that his Christmas gift to you the previous year was the promise you could take the class and that he would take you to and from, so that nothing would happen to you.

... it's mercilessly punishing yourself over whether you could have done something, anything at all, to have stopped the killing.

Moments later, across a continent . . .

... it's being frightened out of your mind in the middle of the night by a frantic banging on your door—calling the police, then canceling the call—and then answering the door. Your body goes limp as you see one of your best friends standing in the doorway. No words need even be spoken. For you know that the worst in life has happened. Then he tells you: "Your Mom just called. Father was just murdered in the driveway of your home."

... it's realizing that, at that very moment, the man who you have worshiped all your life is lying on his back in your driveway with two bullets through his head.

Across the globe . . .

... it's your husband taking the emergency international call, putting down the receiver, fumbling for the words, as he starts to deliver the news. "This is the hardest thing I will ever have to tell you," he begins.

Then, it is the calls home, or at least to what used to be home, first one, then the other. In eerie stunned calmness, you hear your mother utter the feared confirmation: "Yes, your dad was just murdered. You better come home." Now you believe.

Within hours . . .

... it's arriving home to television cameras in your front yard, to see your house cordoned off by police lines; police conducting ballistics and forensics tests, and studying the place in the driveway where your father had finally fallen dead—all as if it were a set from a television production.

... it's going down to the store where your dad had always shopped for clothes, to buy a shirt, a tie that will match his suit, and a package of three sets of underwear (you can only buy them in sets of three) so your dad will look nice when he is buried.

... it's being called by the funeral home and told that it recommends that the casket be closed and that perhaps your mom, sister, and wife should not see the body—and you know why, without even asking.

In the days that follow . . .

... it's living in a hotel in your own hometown, blocks away from where you have lived your whole life, because you just can't bear to go back.

... it's packing up the family home, item by item, memory by memory, as if all of the lives that were there only hours before are no more.

... it's reading the letters from you, your sister, and your wife, that your dad secreted away in his most private places, unbeknownst to you. Realizing that the ones he invariably saved were the ones that just said "thanks" or "I love you." And really understanding for the first time that that truly was all that he ever needed to hear or to receive in return, just as he always told you.

In the weeks thereafter . . .

. . . it's living in absolute terror, not knowing who had murdered your husband and tried to murder you, but realizing that often such people come back to complete the deed, and wondering if they would return this time.

. . . it's never spending another night in your own home because the pain is too great and the memories too fresh.

. . . it's all day every day, and all night, racking your brain to the point of literal exhaustion over who possibly could have done this. It's questioningly looking in the corners of every relationship, to the point that, at times, you are almost ashamed of yourself. Yet you have no choice but to continue, because, as they say, it could be anyone.

Then, they are finally found, and . . .

. . . it's collapsing on the kitchen floor when you are told—not from relief, but from the ultimate despair in learning that your husband was indeed killed for nothing but a car, and in an act so random as to defy comprehension.

. . . it's watching your mother collapse on the floor when she hears this news and knowing that she will not just have to relive the fateful night in her own mind, now she will have to relive it in public courtrooms, over and over again, for months on end.

In the months that follow . . .

. . . it's putting the family home up for sale and being told that everyone thinks it is beautiful, but they just don't think they could live there, because a murder took place in the driveway.

. . . it's the humiliation of being told by the credit card companies, after they closed your husband's accounts because of his death, that they are unable to extend your credit because you are not currently employed.

. . . it's receiving an anonymous letter that begins, "I just learned of the brutal carjacking and murder of your father," and that ends by saying, "I only wish your mother had been raped and murdered too."

. . . it's the crushing anxiety of awaiting the trauma and uncertainties of public trials.

The day arrives, and . . .

. . . it's listening, for the first time, to the tape of your mother's 9-1-1 call to report that her husband, your father, had been murdered. Hearing the terror in her voice, catching yourself before you pass out from the shock of knowing that, through the tape, you are present at the very moment it all happened.

. . . it's hearing the autopsy report on how the bullets entered your father's skull, penetrated and exited his brain, and went through his shoulder and arm.

. . . it's looking at the photographs of your dad lying in the driveway in a pool of blood, as they are projected on a large screen before your friends and family, and before what might as well be the whole world.

As the trauma of the trial subsides,

. . . it's getting down on your hands and knees and straightening your dad's new grave marker and packing the fresh dirt around it, so that it will be perfect, as he always insisted that things be for you.

. . . it's sitting across from each other at Thanksgiving dinner, each knowing that there is but one thing on the other's mind, yet pretending otherwise for their sake.

. . . it's wishing for the first time in your life that Christmas would never arrive.

. . . it's sitting beside your father's grave into the night in 30-degree weather, so that he won't be alone on the first Christmas.

. . . it's hearing your two-year-old daughter ask for "Pawpaw" and seeing your wife choke back the tears and tell her, "He's gone now, he's in heaven."

In the larger sense . . .

. . . it's feeling your body get rigid every time that you drive into a garage.

. . . it's being nervous every time you walk to your car, even in the open daylight.

. . . it's being scared to answer any phone call or any knock at the door at night (or for that matter during the day) because another messenger may be calling.

Finally, it's the long term effects . . .

. . . it's the inexplicable sense of embarrassment when you tell someone that your husband or your father was murdered—almost a sense of guilt over injecting ugliness into their lives.

. . . it's going out to dinner alone, knowing that you will be going out alone the rest of your life.

. . . it's that feeling—wrong, but inevitable—that you will always be the fifth wheel.

Of course, for my mother, my sister, my wife and I, the sun will come up again. But it will never come up again for the real victim of this crime. Not only will he never see what he worked a lifetime for, and was finally within reach of obtaining that would be tragedy enough. But, even worse, he died knowing that the only thing that ever could have ruined his life had come to pass—that his wife and his family might have to suffer the kind of pain that is now ours—and he was helpless to prevent it even as he saw its inevitability.

We live by law in this country so that, ideally, no one will ever have to know what it is like to be a victim of such violent crime. If I had any wish, any wish in the world, it would be that no one ever again would have to go through what my mother and father experienced on the night of April 19, what my family has endured since and must carry with us the rest of our lives.

Crimes such as that committed against my family are intolerable in any society that calls itself not only free, but civilized. The law recognizes as much, and it provides for punishment that will ensure at least that others will not suffer again at the same hands, even if it does not prevent recurrence at the hands of others.

On behalf of my dad, and on behalf of my mother and family, I respectfully request that these who committed this brutal crime receive the full punishment the law provides. There were no passive bystanders among the gang that executed my dad.

Thank you, Your Honor.

* * *

Analysis

Michael Luttig delivered an impact statement about the murder of his father, who was killed during a carjacking. At the time Luttig gave his victim impact statement, he was a federal judge for the Fourth Circuit Court of Appeals. Judge Luttig was able to give this impact statement due to the efforts of the Victims' Rights Movement, which worked hard to enact federal legislation permitting admission of impact statements.

Victim impact statements were controversial in the Supreme Court because they can have an emotional impact at sentencing. However, studies have revealed that juries in capital cases are not so swayed by emotion that the victim impact statement controls their decision.

The next document concerns the limits of victim participation in the criminal process. Historically, victims had been private prosecutors. Because this was commonplace at the time of the nation's founding, it is clear that the framers of the Constitution did not intend the Constitution to exclude such private prosecutions. However, history is only one basis upon which the federal courts interpret the Constitution. There is another method of interpretation called "evolving due process." The reasoning behind this approach is, as civilization evolves, more civilized standards of due process evolve along with it. Thus, a procedure acceptable one hundred years ago can be scrutinized as unconstitutional now, even though the actual words of the Constitution have not changed at all.

Because victims had been private prosecutors, a reasonable historically based assumption is that modern victims' rights could reintroduce private prosecution in felony cases. There has been no effort by the Victims' Rights Movement to reinstate private prosecution, and there is unlikely to be any such effort in the future. Nevertheless, it is important to develop a sense of what is and is not constitutionally possible in order to understand the scope of victims' rights.

The next document is a federal court of appeals case, one level below the authority of the Supreme Court. The Supreme Court has not yet ruled on whether a historical or evolvingdue process constitutional interpretation will be used to determine the potential constitutional scope of victim's rights. The case that follows, *East v. Scott*, utilizes an evolving due process standard.

- **Document:** *East v. Scott*
- **Date:** June 9, 1995
- **Significance:** *East v. Scott* is a significant case in that it uses an "evolving due process" interpretation to determine whether a defendant's due process rights were violated when a private prosecutor, hired by the victim's family, controlled the case.
- **Source:** *East v. Scott*, 55 F.3d 996 (5th Cir. 1995).

---

* * *

W. Eugene Davis, Circuit Judge

Wayne East, a Texas Death Row inmate, appeals the district court's dismissal of his §2254 habeas corpus petition. . . .

I.

In August 1982, a Taylor County, Texas jury convicted Wayne East of capital murder and sentenced him to die for the murder of Mary Eula Sears. Sears was killed during a burglary of her home. The linchpin of the state's evidence against East was the testimony of his accomplice, Dee Dee Martin. Martin testified that after she and East broke into Sears' house, East bound Sears and repeatedly stabbed her when she refused to remain quiet. The Texas Court of Criminal Appeals subsequently affirmed East's conviction and sentence on direct appeal and the U.S. Supreme Court denied certiorari (*East v. State*, 702 S.W.2d 606 (Tex.Crim.App 1985)).

East filed his first state habeas petition in May 1986 and the state trial court stayed East's June 1986 execution date. The trial court granted East's request for an evidentiary hearing, but denied his request for discovery. After the evidentiary hearing, the trial court entered findings of fact and recommended that East's application be denied. The Texas Court of Criminal Appeals subsequently denied East's habeas application without a written order. . . .

* * *

II.

East argues that the district court erred in denying his habeas petition in the following respects: (1) in dismissing his petition without allowing him the opportunity for discovery or an evidentiary hearing to resolve his claim that the participation of a private attorney in his prosecution violated the Due Process Clause. . . .

A.

The Private Prosecutor

East first contends that the district court should have permitted discovery and held an evidentiary hearing to resolve his claim that the involvement of a private prosecutor in his prosecution denied him due process. Prior to East's trial, the victim's family retained Russell Ormesher, a former Dallas County prosecutor, to assist the Taylor County district attorney in East's capital murder prosecution. East maintains that Mr. Ormesher essentially controlled all the critical trial strategy and prosecutorial decisions, and that Ormesher's role in the prosecution thus violated the Due Process Clause.

The opportunity for an evidentiary hearing in a federal habeas corpus proceeding is mandatory only where there is a factual dispute which, if resolved in the petitioner's favor, would entitle the petitioner to relief and the petitioner has not received a full and fair evidentiary hearing in state court (*Townsend v. Sain*, 372 U.S. 293 (1963)). . . . East's entitlement to an evidentiary hearing on this claim thus turns on whether his claim raises a question of fact which, if decided in his favor, would entitle him to relief. To resolve this issue, we must first examine the case law governing the participation of privately-retained attorneys in criminal prosecutions.

Powers v. Hauck, 399 F.2d 322, 325 (5th Cir. 1968), was the first decision by this court to expressly address whether the participation of a private prosecutor in a criminal prosecution violates the Due Process Clause. In *Powers*, a habeas petitioner convicted of capital murder alleged that the victim's family hired a private attorney to assist in his prosecution. The court adopted the district court's holding that "the mere participation of a special prosecutor alone is not sufficient grounds to show denial of due process, without some additional showing of a violation of the rules relating to prosecuting attorneys" (Id.). The court concluded that the private prosecutor's involvement did not violate due process because the elected district attorney retained control and management of the prosecution and the private prosecutor never acted without the district attorney's consent or supervision (Id.).

In *Woods v. Linahan*, 648 F.2d 973, 976 (5th Cir. 1981), the court similarly held that the participation of a privately-retained attorney in a murder prosecution did not offend due process even though the attorney exercised independent control over the prosecution during its pre-trial stages. The private prosecutor in *Woods* conducted the pre-trial investigation, interviewed witnesses, filed and argued pre-trial motions, and made pre-trial strategy decisions without the supervision or control of the district attorney. According to the court, the private prosecutor's pretrial activity "border[ed] on a constitutional violation" because "these activities were not carried out under the direction, control, or knowledge of the district attorney" (Id. at 976–977).

However, the court concluded that there was no due process violation in *Woods* because the district attorney assumed control of the prosecution once the trial started. After the trial started, the district attorney assumed control over trial strategy decisions, gave the state's opening and closing arguments, and examined all the witnesses. While the private prosecutor assisted the district attorney during the trial, he never acted without the district attorney's consent or supervision. Thus, as in *Powers*, the *Woods* court held that the private prosecutor's actions did not offend due process because he did not control important phases of the prosecution. [Footnote 2 omitted].

In *Person v. Miller*, 854 F.2d 656, 664 (4th Cir. 1988), the Fourth Circuit followed similar reasoning in concluding that a private prosecutor must effectively control a prosecution to violate the accused's due process rights. The court reasoned that, for purposes of due process, it is important to determine whether a private prosecutor controlled crucial prosecutorial decisions, such as "whether to prosecute, what targets of prosecution to select, what investigative powers to utilize, what sanctions to seek, plea bargains to strike, or immunities to grant" (Id.). According to the court,

> It is control over these critical prosecutorial decisions which determine the fairness of particular prosecutions that is the important consideration; operational conduct of the trial is actually of subordinate concern, except as it may actually impact upon the more fundamental prosecutorial decisions. The court reasoned that, while the quantitative division of trial work has some relevance to determining control, the ultimate question must be whether the private prosecutor controlled these crucial prosecutorial decisions. (Id.)

We agree with the Fourth Circuit's characterization of the proper framework for resolving East's claim. We therefore turn to East's pleadings to determine whether he alleges specific facts suggesting that Mr. Ormesher effectively controlled critical prosecutorial decisions throughout East's prosecution. East makes the following factual allegations regarding Mr. Ormesher's role:

- Ormesher controlled all the significant trial strategy decisions for the prosecution, including the decision to offer a plea bargain to Dee Dee Martin, the prosecution's key witness linking East to Sear's murder,
- Ormesher conducted an independent pre-trial investigation and maintained a separate case file,
- Ormesher interviewed all the state's key witnesses independent of the supervision or control of the Taylor County district attorney,
- Ormesher played a key role during the trial. According to East, Ormesher made the prosecution's opening and closing arguments and participated in the direct examination of the prosecution's most important witnesses,
- Ormesher was a "seasoned" veteran of capital murder prosecutions, while the district attorney prosecuting the case had little experience.

Applying the framework developed in *Powers*, *Woods*, and *Person*, we conclude that these factual allegations raise the inference that Ormesher effectively controlled East's prosecution and, consequently, are facially sufficient to establish a prima facie due process claim.

We now turn to East's contention that the district court erred in denying his discovery motion and in failing to hold an evidentiary hearing. Cases expressly provide for discovery in habeas proceedings if the petitioner shows "good cause" for discovery. According to the commentary to Rule 6,

[W]here specific allegations before the court show reason to believe that the petitioner may, if the facts are fully developed, be able to demonstrate that he is confined illegally and is therefore entitled to relief, it is the duty of the court to provide the necessary facilities and procedures for an adequate inquiry. While the district court generally has discretion to grant or deny discovery requests under Rule 6, a court's blanket denial of discovery is an abuse of discretion if discovery is "indispensable to a fair, rounded, development of the material facts." *Coleman v. Zant*, 708 F.2d 541, 547 (11th Cir. 1983; quoting *Townsend*, 372 U.S., at 322).

Given the nature of East's allegations, we agree that East has shown good cause for discovery under Rule 6. While the state court record reveals the extent to which Ormesher questioned witnesses and participated in the trial, the record is silent as to whether Ormesher effectively controlled critical prosecutorial decisions. Indeed, the Taylor County district attorney, the district attorney's staff, and Mr. Ormesher are likely the only witnesses who can shed any light on this issue. The record indicates that East has not, however, been able to obtain access to these witnesses or their files. The district court denied East's request to depose these witnesses and examine their files. Because access to these witnesses and their files is necessary to fully develop the facts needed to consider East's claim, we conclude that the district court abused its discretion in denying East's discovery requests.

* * *

Analysis

The *East* decision used an evolving due process standard to determine that a victim could not privately prosecute a felony case (victims still do privately prosecute petty offenses in many state jurisdictions). However, the *East* court reaffirmed the constitutionality of victims' attorneys assisting a public prosecutor. The assistance is limited by the fact that the public prosecutor must be in charge of all critical stage decisions. On remand, the trial court concluded that there was no evidence to indicate that the private prosecutor was in charge of the prosecution.

It remains to be seen whether the United States Supreme Court will use an historical or evolving due process analysis. If the court chooses an historical analysis, felony private prosecution would likely be constitutional. However, state and federal statutes may restrict such a practice.

In History

In 1986, under the supervision of the United States Attorney, the prominent civil rights attorney Morris Dees of the Southern Poverty Law Center prosecuted a case for criminal contempt against a white supremacist leader. The contempt complaint alleged that the defendant, Miller, and the White Patriot Party (WPP) had violated the court's order by operating a paramilitary organization and engaging in (unlawful) conduct. The district court ordered Miller and the WPP to show cause as to why they should not be found in contempt and set a hearing for July 1986. Dees was initially authorized by the court to prosecute the contempt action. From the time that the original complaint was filed until June 1986, Dees was actively engaged in preparing the case. He filed several amendments to the original complaint, moved the court to add various parties as defendants, one of whom was Stephen Miller, and conducted discovery. In June 1986, counsel for Miller moved to have Dees disqualified on the grounds that Dees would be a material witness at trial and that Dees's appointment as prosecutor violated the North Carolina Rules of Professional Conduct and Miller's right to be prosecuted by an impartial prosecutor as guaranteed by the Due Process Clause of the 14th Amendment. Noting a conflict in recent Circuit Court decisions on whether counsel for an interested party could prosecute a related criminal contempt action, the court ordered that the prosecution would be under the "direct supervision and control" of the United States Attorney's Office for the Eastern District of North Carolina. The court further ordered that Dees could "assist the United States Attorney prior to and during the course of the trial." Shortly after the entry of the court's order, the prosecution filed a composite complaint against Glen Miller and the WPP, which was signed by the United States Attorney for the Eastern District of North Carolina and Dees. The case came to trial in late July 1986. Miller was found guilty. In *Person v. Miller*, 854 F.2d 656 (4th Cir. 1988), the appellate court approved of Morris Dees's active participation in the case under the control of the U.S. Attorney.

Generally, the laws governing the conduct of the privately funded prosecutor are the same as the laws governing the public prosecutor. The role of the privately funded prosecutor is not limited to the examination of witnesses, as they may also address the jury in opening statements or closing arguments.

Not surprisingly, the beginning of the Victims' Rights Movement coincided with the exile of the victim from the criminal process, which is identified as occurring with the sequestration of witnesses as a right of either party provided in the 1975 enactment of Federal Rules of Evidence. This meant a victim, now merely a witness, could readily be excluded from observing the very trial concerning his or herown victimization. The next document is the case of *Linda R.S. v. Richard D.*, which implicitly framed the structure within which modern victims' rights emerged. Although victims had extensive roles in the criminal process before, during, and after the nation's founding, by 1975, the role of the victim had been diminished to the point where a victim was no different than a mere witness.

Linda R.S. is a case decided in the legal context of the 1970s, when the victim's role was at rock bottom.

- **Document:** *Linda R.S. v. Richard D.*
- **Date:** March 5, 1973
- **Significance:** This case helped frame the structure within which modern victim's rights emerged. The case implies that that it is necessary to legislate victims' rights via statutes and state constitutional amendments. As a result, modern victims' rights are legislated rights.
- **Source:** *Linda R.S. v. Richard D.*, 410 U.S. 614 (1973).

---

* * *

Mr. Justice Marshall delivered the opinion of the Court

Appellant, the mother of an illegitimate child, brought this action in United States District Court on behalf of herself, her child, and others similarly situated to enjoin the 'discriminatory application' of Art. 602 of the Vernon's Ann. Texas Penal Code. A three-judge court was convened pursuant to 28 U.S.C. s 2281, but that court dismissed the action for want of standing. [Footnote 1 omitted](335 F.Supp. 804 (N.D.Tex.1971)). We postponed consideration of jurisdiction until argument on the merits, and now affirm the judgment below.

Article 602, in relevant part, provides: "any parent who shall wilfully desert, neglect or refuse to provide for the support and maintenance of his or her child or children under eighteen years of age, shall be guilty of a misdemeanor, and upon conviction, shall be punished by confinement in the County Jail for not more than two years." The Texas courts have consistently construed this statute to apply solely to the parents of legitimate children and to impose no duty of support on the parents of illegitimate children (see *Home of Holy Infancy v. Kaska*, 397 S.W.2d 208, 210 (Tex. 1966); *Beaver v. State*, 96 Tex.Cr.R 179 (1923)). In her complaint, appellant alleges that one Richard D. is the father of her child, that Richard D. has refused to provide support for the child, and that although appellant made application to the local district attorney for enforcement of Art. 602 against Richard D., the district attorney refused to take action for the express reason that, in his view, the fathers of illegitimate children were not within the scope of Art. 602. [Footnote 2 omitted].

Appellant argues that this interpretation of Art. 602 discriminates between legitimate and illegitimate children without rational foundation and therefore violates the Equal Protection Clause of the Fourteenth Amendment (Cf. *Gomez v. Perez*, 409 U.S. 535 (1973); *Weber v. Aetna Casualty & Surety Co.*, 406 U.S. 164 (1972); *Glona v. American Guarantee & Liability Ins. Co.*, 391 U.S. 73 (1968); *Levy v. Louisiana*, 391 U.S. 68 (1968);but cf. *Labine v. Vincent*, 401 U.S. 532 (1971)). Although her complaint is not entirely clear on this point, she apparently seeks an injunction running against the district attorney forbidding him from declining prosecution on the ground that the unsupported child is illegitimate.

Before we can consider the merits of appellant's claim or the propriety of the relief requested, however, appellant must first demonstrate that she is entitled to invoke the judicial process. She must, in other words, show that the facts alleged present the court with a "case or controversy" in the constitutional sense and that she is a proper plaintiff to raise the issues sought to be litigated. The threshold question which must be answered is whether the appellant has "alleged such a personal stake in the outcome of the controversy as to assure that concrete adverseness which sharpens the presentation of issues upon which the court so largely depends for illumination of difficult constitutional questions" (*Baker v. Carr*, 369 U.S. 186, 204 (1962)).

Recent decisions by this Court have greatly expanded the types of "personal stake(s)" which are capable of conferring standing on a potential plaintiff (compare *Tennessee Electric Power Co. v. TVA*, 306 U.S. 118 (1939), and *Alabama Power Co. v. Ickes*, 302 U.S. 464 (1938), with *Barlow v. Collins*, 397 U.S. 159 (1970), and *Association of Data Processing Service Organizations, Inc. v. Camp*, 397 U.S. 150 (1970)). But as we pointed out only last Term, "broadening the categories of injury that may be alleged in support of standing is a different matter from abandoning the requirement that the party seeking review must himself have suffered an injury" (*Sierra Club v. Morton*, 405 U.S. 727, 738 (1972)). Although the law of standing has been greatly changed in the last 10 years, we have steadfastly adhered to the requirement that, at least in the absence of a statute expressly conferring standing [Footnote 3 reads: "It is, of course, true that 'Congress may not confer jurisdiction on Art. III federal courts to render advisory opinions,' *Sierra Club v. Morton*, 405 U.S. 727, 732 n.3 (1972). But Congress may enact statutes creating legal rights, the invasion of which creates standing, even though no injury would exist without the statute. *See, e.g., Trafficante v. Metropolitan Life Ins. Co.*, 409 U.S. 205, 212 (1972) (White, J., concurring); *Hardin v. Kentucky Utilities Co.*, 390 U.S. 1, 6 (1968)."], federal plaintiffs must allege some threatened or actual injury resulting from the putatively illegal action before a federal court may assume jurisdiction. [Footnote 4 omitted] (see, e.g., *Moose Lodge No. 107 v. Irvis*, 407 U.S. 163, 166-167 (1972); *Flast v. Cohen*, 392 U.S. 83, 101 (1968); *Baker v. Carr*, 369 U.S. 186, 204 (1962). Cf. *Laird v. Tatum*, 408 U.S. 1, 12 (1972)).

Applying this test to the facts of this case, we hold that, in the unique context of a challenge to a criminal statute, appellant has failed to allege a sufficient nexus between her injury and the government action which she attacks to justify judicial intervention. To be sure, appellant no doubt suffered an injury stemming from the failure of her child's father to contribute support payments. But the bare existence of an abstract injury meets only the first half of the standing requirement. "The party who invokes (judicial) power must be able to show ... that he has sustained or is immediately in danger of sustaining some direct injury as the result of (a statute's) enforcement" (*Massachusetts v. Mellon*, 262 U.S. 447, 488 (1923; emphasis added); see also *Ex Parte Levitt*, 302 U.S. 633, 634 (1937)). As this Court made plain in *Flast v. Cohen*, a plaintiff must show "a logical nexus between the status asserted and the claim sought to be adjudicated. ... Such inquiries into the nexus between the status asserted by the litigant and the claim he presents are essential to assure that he is a proper and appropriate party to invoke federal judicial power" (392 U.S., at 102).

Here, appellant has made no showing that her failure to secure support payments results from the non-enforcement, as to her child's father, of Art. 602. Although the Texas statute appears to create a continuing duty, it does not follow the civil contempt model whereby the defendant "keeps the keys to the jail in his own pocket" and may be released whenever he complies with his legal obligations. On the contrary, the statute creates a completed offense with a fixed penalty as soon as a parent fails to support his child. Thus, if appellant were granted the requested relief, it would result only in the jailing of the child's father. The prospect that prosecution will, at least in the future, result in payment of support can, at best, be termed only speculative. Certainly the "direct" relationship between the alleged injury and the claim sought to be adjudicated, which previous decisions of this Court suggest is a prerequisite of standing, is absent in this case.

The Court's prior decisions consistently hold that a citizen lacks standing to contest the policies of the prosecuting authority when he himself is neither prosecuted nor threatened with prosecution (see *Younger v. Harris*, 401 U.S. 37, 42 (1971); *Bailey v. Patterson*, 369 U.S. 31, 33 (1962); *Poe v. Ullman*, 367 U.S. 497, 501 (1961)). Although these cases arose in a somewhat different context, they demonstrate that, in American jurisprudence at least, a private citizen lacks a judicially cognizable interest in the prosecution or nonprosecution of another. Appellant does have an interest in the support of her child. But given the special status of criminal prosecutions in our system, we hold that appellant has made an insufficient showing of a direct nexus between the vindication of her interest and the enforcement of the State's criminal laws. The District Court was therefore correct in dismissing the action for want of standing [Footnote 5 omitted], and its judgment must be affirmed. [Footnote 6 omitted].

Judgment affirmed.

Mr. Justice White, with whom Mr. Justice Douglas joins, dissenting

Appellant Linda R.S. alleged that she is the mother of an illegitimate child and that she is suing "on behalf of herself, her minor daughter, and on behalf of all other women and minor children who have sought, are seeking, or in the future will seek to obtain support for so-called illegitimate children from said child's father."

Appellant sought a declaratory judgment that Art. 602 is unconstitutional and an injunction against its continued enforcement against fathers of legitimate children only. Appellant further sought an order requiring Richard D., the putative father, "to pay a reasonable amount of money for the support of his child."

Obviously, there are serious difficulties with appellant's complaint insofar as it may be construed as seeking to require the official appellees to prosecute Richard D. or others, or to obtain what amounts to a federal child-support order. But those difficulties go to the question of what relief the court may ultimately grant appellant. They do not affect her right to bring this class action. The Court notes, as it must, that the father of a legitimate child, if prosecuted under Art. 602, could properly raise the statute's underinclusiveness as an affirmative defense (see *McLaughlin v. Florida*, 379 U.S. 184 (1964); *Railway Express Agency v. New York*, 336 U.S. 106 (1949)). Presumably, that same father would have standing to affirmatively seek to enjoin enforcement of the statute against him (Cf. *Rinaldi v. Yeager*, 384 U.S. 305 (1966); see also *Epperson v. Arkansas*, 393 U.S. 97 (1968)). The question then becomes simply: why should only an actual or potential criminal defendant have a recognizable interest in attacking this allegedly discriminatory statute and not appellant and her class? They are not, after all, in the position of members of the public at large who wish merely to force an enlargement of state criminal laws (Cf. *Sierra Club v. Morton*, 405 U.S. 727 (1972)). Appellant, her daughter, and the children born out of wedlock whom she is attempting to represent have all allegedly been excluded intentionally from the class of persons protected by a particular criminal law. They do not get the protection of the laws that other women and children get. Under Art. 602, they are rendered nonpersons; a father may ignore them with full knowledge that he will be subjected to no penal sanctions. The Court states that the actual coercive effect of those sanctions on Richard D. or others "can, at best, be termed only speculative." This is a very odd statement. I had always thought our civilization has assumed that the threat of penal sanctions had something more than a "speculative" effect on a person's conduct. This Court has long acted on that assumption in demanding that criminal laws be plainly and explicitly worded so that people will know what they mean and be in a position to conform their conduct to the mandates of law. Certainly Texas does not share the Court's surprisingly novel view. It assumes that criminal sanctions are useful in coercing fathers to fulfill their support obligations to their legitimate children.

Unquestionably, Texas prosecutes fathers of legitimate children on the complaint of the mother asserting nonsupport and refuses to entertain like complaints from a mother of an illegitimate child. I see no basis for saying that the latter mother has no standing to demand that the discrimination be ended, one way or the other.

If a State were to pass a law that made only the murder of a white person a crime, I would think that Negroes as a class would have sufficient interest to seek a declaration that that law invidiously discriminated against them. Appellant and her class have no less interest in challenging their exclusion from what their own State perceives as being the beneficial protections that flow from the existence and enforcement of a criminal child-support law.

I would hold that appellant has standing to maintain this suit and would, accordingly, reverse the judgment and remand the case for further proceedings.

Mr. Justice Blackmun, with whom Mr. Justice Brennan joins, dissenting.

* * *

The standing issue now decided by the Court is, in my opinion, a difficult one with constitutional overtones. I see no reason to decide that question in the absence of a live, ongoing controversy (see *Rice v. Sioux City Memorial Park Cemetery*, 349 U.S. 70, 75 (1955)). . . . Under these circumstances, I would remand the case to the District Court for clarification of the status of the litigation.

* * *

Analysis

The case of *Linda R.S.* is important because it sets the stage for how victims would develop modern rights. Because the Court states that victims have "no interest in the prosecution or non-prosecution of another," victims have no standing to enforce their constitutional rights in the criminal process. Additionally, *Linda R.S.* implies that it is necessary to legislate victims' rights by statutes and state constitutional amendments. As a result, modern victims' rights are all legislated rights, although victims do have rights and accommodations predating modern victims' rights from several sources, such as common law and third-party practice.

The common law accommodation that remained available to Linda R.S., the plaintiff, was to pursue a prosecution by approaching a grand jury, rather than compelling the prosecutor to charge. The ability to approach a grand jury exists in most jurisdictions and is a common law accommodation that has been codified in some states. In Texas, this alternative was available to Linda R.S. by legislation that had codified the common law procedure.

Linda R.S. v. Richard D. provides an example of public prosecutorial discretion historically never ceded to citizens. In *Linda R.S.*, the mother of an illegitimate child alleged an equal protection violation and sought to compel a Texas county prosecutor to bring charges of criminal nonsupport after the prosecutor declined to do so because "in his view," the statute did not extend to children born out of wedlock. Holding that Linda R.S. had no standing to use a mandamus action to compel a prosecutor to charge, the Court stated that, "in American jurisprudence at least, a private citizen lacks a judicially cognizable interest in the prosecution or nonprosecution of another" (*Linda R.S.*, 410 U.S. at 619).

Although the *Linda R.S.* opinion is silent on the procedural point, its holding is consistent with traditional state mandamus limitations—that mandamus could not be used to compel a discretionary act of the public prosecutor. Even in the era of private prosecution, public prosecutors had discretion to direct, or not direct, state resources to prosecution. Citizens' common law private prosecution rights did not allow citizens to seek a writ of mandamus requiring a public prosecutor to exercise prosecutorial charging discretion.

Instead of compelling the public prosecutor to charge, citizens brought charges independently of the public prosecutor. For example, in the Maryland case of *Brack v. Wells*, 40 A.2d 319 (MD.App.1944), decided three decades before *Linda R.S.*, the state's high court ruled that mandamus could not be used to compel a public prosecutor to charge.

As a general rule, whether the State's Attorney does or does not institute a particular prosecution is a matter that rests in his discretion. Unless that discretion is grossly abused, or such duty is compelled by statute, or there is a clear showing that such a duty exists, mandamus will not lie.

Further, the *Brack* court stated that mandamus would not lie when there was another remedy available. That other remedy was for the complainant to independently approach the grand jury.

Unquestionably, Linda R.S., as a Texan, could have directly approached a Texas grand jury in an attempt to secure a charge. Written before *Linda R.S.*, the seminal Texas case of *Hott v. Yarbrough* opined: "Equally clear is the right of any one who may consider himself aggrieved by the actual or supposed commission of a crime to call the matter to the attention of the grand jury for investigation and action" *112 Tex. 179, 186 (Tex. Comm'n App. 1922)). The Fifth Circuit Court of Appeals, interpreting Texas case law after *Linda R.S.*, confirmed that Texas citizens had a common law right of direct access to the grand jury: "Under Texas law, the grand jury has the authority to conduct their own investigations, to subpoena evidence and witnesses, and to indict on matters as to which the district attorney has presented no evidence and sought no indictment" (*Smith v. Hightower*, 693 F.2d 359, 368 n.21 (5th Cir. 1982)). The Linda R.S. case did not alter Linda R.S.'s personal right to independently approach the Texas grand jury. Nor did it alter the fact that her right to seek grand jury charging was judicially cognizable. Instead, Linda R.S. involved a procedurally inappropriate challenge to public prosecutorial discretion because she sought to compel the public prosecutor to bring charges. This approach failed her as it had failed the Maryland victim in *Brack* and victims in other jurisdictions. It failed her because citizen actions to compel public prosecutors to charge invaded the unceded discretion of the government not to initiate charging procedures.

The *Linda R.S.* case is limited to procedural contexts where state public prosecutors already exercise lawful discretion. Put another way, *Linda R.S.* means "that, in American jurisprudence at least, a private citizen lacks a judicially cognizable interest in the prosecution or nonprosecution of another" in procedures where public prosecutorial discretion already exists (*Linda R.S.*, 410 U.S., at 619).

The cases cited in *Linda R.S.* also support the idea that government discretion must already exist before citizens can be said to have "no judicially cognizable interest in the prosecution or non-prosecution of another" (Id.). The *Younger v. Harris* court held that no standing existed for persons to join with the criminal defendant as interveners in a civil injunction to halt prosecution when those persons were neither prosecuted nor threatened with prosecution (*Younger v. Harris*, 401 U.S. 37, 39, 42 (1971)). In *Bailey v. Patterson*, the court held that plaintiffs had no standing to enjoin prosecution where there was no allegation that plaintiffs were being prosecuted or threatened with prosecution (*Bailey v. Patterson*, 364 U.S. 31, 32–33 (1962; per curiam)). In both *Younger* and *Bailey*, the uncharged citizen had no standing to challenge the public prosecutor's exercise of already existing lawful discretion to bring charges. Finally, in *Poe v. Ullman*, 367 U.S. 497, 501, 507–09 (1961), plaintiffs were denied standing to bring a civil declaratory judgment action to invalidate state criminal statutes because plaintiffs were neither prosecuted nor threatened with prosecution. While *Poe* involved a civil challenge to a criminal statute, rather than a challenge to a prosecution, prosecutorial discretion remains centrally relevant to the decision. In *Poe*, where the prosecution exercised its already existing discretion not to seek a charge, plaintiff had no standing to challenge the criminal statute.

The procedural context, the internal citations, and the reality of citizens' judicially cognizable interests in grand jury charging in Texas all support the interpretation that the *Linda R.S.* case indicates that where prosecutors already exercise lawful discretion, citizens lack an interest in prosecution or nonprosecution of another that is sufficient to trump that discretion. Thus, *Linda R.S.* did not establish any new area of public prosecutorial discretion; rather, it preserved preexisting discretion.

Although *Linda R.S.* limited victims' constitutional standing, the case also implies that any victim right can be legislated as long as it does not conflict with the federal and state constitution. This would become the approach of the Victims' Rights Movement—to legislate modern victims' rights. Such legislation is presently in the form of state constitutional rights and state and federal statutes.

In sum, the cases in this chapter provide that victims may give victim impact statements at sentencing. The probable exception is that, in capital cases, victims may not give their opinion on the death sentence. Victims may not force the prosecutor to charge, but they may pursue other avenues to charging, such as the grand jury. Finally, victims may not directly try felony cases but may assist the public prosecutor, as long as the public prosecutor controls critical decisions.

REFERENCES

Alabama Power Co. v. Ickes, 302 U.S. 464 (1938).
Association of Data Processing Service Organizations, Inc. v. Camp, 397 U.S. 150 (1970).
Bailey v. Patterson, 369 U.S. 31 (1962).
Baker v. Carr, 369 U.S. 186 (1962).
Barefoot v. Estelle, 463 U.S. 880 (1983).
Barlow v. Collins, 397 U.S. 159 (1970).
Beaver v. State, 96 Tex.Cr.R 179 (1923).
Blystone v. Pennsylvania, 494 U.S. 299 (1990).
Booth v. Maryland, 482 U.S. 496 (1987).
Brack v. Wells, 40 A.2d 319 (MD. App. 1944).
Brief for Justice For All Political Committee et al. as *Amici Curiae* to *Payne v. Tenn.*
California v. Brown, 479 U.S. 538 (1987).
California v. Ramos, 463 U.S. 992 (1983).
Coleman v. Zant, 708 F.2d 541 (11th Cir. 1983).
Darden v. Wainwright, 447 U.S. 168 (1986).
East v. Scott, 55 F.3d 996 (5th Cir. 1995).
East v. State, 702 S.W.2d 606 (Tex.Crim.App. 1985).
Eddings v. Oklahoma, 455 U.S. 104 (1982).
Enmund v. Florida, 458 U.S. 782 (1982).

Epperson v. Arkansas, 393 U.S. 97 (1968).
Ex Parte Levitt, 302 U.S. 633 (1937).
Farrer, J. *Crimes and Punishments*. London: Chatto & Windus, 1880.
Fed. Rule Evid. 404(a).
Flast v. Cohen, 392 U.S. 83 (1968).
Flood v. Kuhn, 407 U.S. 258 (1972).
Gardener v. Florida, 430 U.S. 349 (1977).
Glona v. American Guarantee & Liability Ins. Co., 391 U.S. 73 (1968).
Godfrey v. Georgia, 446 U.S. 420 (1980).
Gomez v. Perez, 409 U.S. 535 (1973).
Gregg v. Georgia, 428 U.S. 153 (1976).
Hardin v. Kentucky Utilities Co., 390 U.S. 1 (1968).
Home of Holy Infancy v. Kaska, 397 S.W.2d 208 (Tex. 1966).
Hott v. Yarbrough, 112 Tex. 179 (Tex. Comm'n App. 1922).
In Re Winship, 397 U.S. 358 (1970).
Labine v. Vincent, 401 U.S. 532 (1971).
Laird v. Tatum, 408 U.S. 1 (1972).
Levy v. Louisiana, 391 U.S. 68 (1968);
Linda R.S. v. Richard D, 410 U.S. 614 (1973).
Lockett v. Ohio, 438 U.S. 586 (1978) (plurality opinion).
Luttig, Michael, Statement of, Reprinted in *Texas Lawyer*, Mar. 20, 1995.
Massachusetts v. Mellon, 262 U.S. 447 (1923).
McCleskey v. Kemp, 481 U.S. 279 (1987).
McLaughlin v. Florida, 379 U.S. 184 (1964).
Mills v. Maryland, 486 U.S. 367 (1988).
Moose Lodge No. 107 v. Irvis, 407 U.S. 163 (1972).
Payne v. Tennessee, 501 U.S. 808 (1991).
Person v. Miller, 854 F.2d 656 (4th Cir. 1988).
Poe v. Ullman, 367 U.S. 497 (1961).
Powers v. Hauck, 399 F.2d 322 (5th Cir. 1968).
Railway Express Agency v. New York, 336 U.S. 106 (1949).
Rice v. Sioux City Memorial Park Cemetery, 349 U.S. 70 (1955).
Rinaldi v. Yeager, 384 U.S. 305 (1966).
Sierra Club v. Morton, 405 U.S. 727 (1972).
Skipper v. South Carolina, 476 U.S. 1 (1986).
Smith v. Hightower, 693 F.2d 359, 368 n.21 (5th Cir. 1982)
Snyder v. Massachusetts, 291 U.S. 97 (1934).
South Carolina v. Gathers, 490 U.S. 805 (1989).
State v. Payne, 791 S.W.2d 10 (Tenn. 1990).
Tennessee Electric Power Co. v. TVA, 306 U.S. 118 (1939).
Tison v. Arizona, 481 U.S. 137, 148 (1987).
Townsend v. Sain, 372 U.S. 293 (1963).
Trafficante v. Metropolitan Life Ins. Co., 409 U.S. 205 (1972).
United States v. DiFrancesco, 449 U.S. 117 (1980).
United States v. Tucker, 404 U.S. 443 (1972).
Walton v. Arizona, 497 U.S. 639 (1990).
Weber v. Aetna Casualty & Surety Co., 406 U.S. 164 (1972).
Wheeler, S, K. Mann, & A. Sarat. *Sitting in Judgment: The Sentencing of White-Collar Criminals*. London: Yale University Press, 1988.
Williams v. Florida, 399 U.S. 78 (1970).
Williams v. New York, 337 U.S. 241 (1949).
Woods v. Linahan, 648 F.2d 973 (5th Cir. 1981).
Younger v. Harris, 401 U.S. 37 (1971).

Additional Reading

Beloof, Douglas E., Paul Cassell, and Steve Twist. *Victims in Criminal Procedure*. 3rd ed. Durham, NC: Carolina Academic Press, 2010.

Cronan ex rel State v. Cronan, 774 A.2d 866 (R.I. 2001).

Ireland, Robert M. *Privately Funded Prosecution of Crime in the Nineteenth Century United States*. 39 Am. J. Legal Hist. 43 (1995).

5

THE OKLAHOMA CITY BOMBING AND THE FAILURE OF FEDERAL VICTIMS' RIGHTS

THE OKLAHOMA CITY BOMBING

In History

At 9:02 AM on April 19, 1995, 5,000 pounds of ammonium nitrate were detonated outside the Alfred P. Murrah Federal Building in downtown Oklahoma City. The building housed many federal agency offices and contained a child-care center.

The explosion ripped through the building, reducing the entire north side to pieces. It took weeks to clear the rubble and discover all the victims. It was, before 9/11, by far the largest domestic terrorist attack in the United States. The bombers of Oklahoma City were United States citizens, born in the United States.

The human carnage of the Oklahoma City Bombing was staggering. The Oklahoma Governor's Office reported that 168 people were killed, of which 19 were children. Thirty children were orphaned; 219 children lost at least one parent; 850 people were injured; 462 were left homeless; 7,000 were left without a workplace; and 12,384 volunteers and rescue workers participated in rescue recovery and support.

One of the tragic consequences of the Oklahoma City Bombing was that the surviving family members of the victims would learn that they had no enforceable victims' rights in federal law. Timothy McVeigh was ultimately captured, put on trial, and executed. However, the criminal process was not kind to the crime victims. The trial judge ruled that, under existing federal victims' "rights," the victims of the Oklahoma City Bombing could not attend McVeigh's trial. When the United States appealed this ruling to the federal circuit court, the following opinion resulted.

Emergency workers search through the debris after an explosion at the Alfred Murrah Federal Building in Oklahoma City on April 19, 1995. (AP Photo/David J. Phillip)

- **Document:** *United States v. McVeigh*
- **Date:** February 4, 1997
- **Significance:** *US v. McVeigh* held that the Crime Victims' Rights Act did not give victim-impact witnesses standing to contest a sequestration order and that a sequestration order did not violate any constitutional right on the part of witnesses to be present at trial.
- **Source:** *United States v. McVeigh*, 106 F.3d 325 (10th Cir. 1997).

* * *

[Oklahoma City Bombing Victims] v. Honorable Richard P. Matsch, District Judge, Respondent. United States of America; Timothy James McVeigh; Terry Lynn Nichols; Real Parties In Interest,

Before Porfilio, Kelly, and Briscoe, Circuit Judges.

Per Curiam.

In these consolidated proceedings, we address an important question of criminal procedure involving significant interests of the defendants, prosecution, crime victims, and public, which has thus far received virtually no judicial attention: whether a pretrial order prohibiting victim-impact witnesses from attending the criminal prosecution in which they are slated to testify is subject to review at the urging of either the government or the nonparty witnesses themselves. Upon careful consideration of the various constitutional and statutory ramifications, we conclude as a general matter, and hold in this particular case, that it is not, though we do not categorically rule out the possibility of mandamus relief for the government in the event of a patently unauthorized and pernicious use of the sequestration power.

In early pretrial hearings, the district court invoked, originally on its own initiative and, thereafter, at the insistence of defense counsel, the traditional rule authorizing the sequestration of witnesses.*seeFed.R.Evid. 615 ("At the request of a party the court shall order witnesses excluded so that they cannot hear the testimony of other witnesses, and it may make the order of its own motion"). Later, in response to an extensively briefed and formally argued request for reconsideration, the district court reaffirmed its adherence to Rule 615, prompting the current proceedings for review.

The government and the excluded witnesses filed separate appeals, . . . which defendants moved to dismiss on procedural grounds. The excluded witnesses then filed a petition for a writ of mandamus, and the government added an informal request for mandamus consideration, both seeking to secure an alternative avenue of review in the event their appeals were deemed defective. This court consolidated all of the proceedings and granted expedited review. The briefs of the parties and amici [Footnote 1 omitted] have now been filed, putting the case at issue [Footnote 2 omitted]. On de novo consideration of the fundamental threshold questions raised by defendants' motions, *see Wilson v. Glenwood Intermountain Properties, Inc.*, 98 F.3d 590, 593 (10th Cir. 1996); *Comanche Indian Tribe v. Hovis*, 53 F.3d 298, 302 (10th Cir.1995) . . . we dismiss the government's appeal on jurisdictional grounds, deny as inappropriate its request for mandamus review, and dismiss the excluded witnesses' appeal and mandamus petition for lack of standing.

I.

The government's right to appeal in criminal cases is subject to unique limitations.

Recently, in *United States v. Carrillo-Bernal*, 58 F. 3d 1490 (10th Cir. 1995), we surveyed in detail the historical evolution of the government's right to appeal in criminal cases(Id. at 1494–97) . . . Before the turn of this century, government appeals in criminal cases were considered verboten. Since then, Congress has progressively loosened the government's ability to receive appellate review of unfavorable district court decisions in criminal matters (Id. at 1494–95). However, two general rules have survived this historical evolution: the government may only initiate criminal appeals based on specific statutory authority; and there is a presumption against government criminal appeals (Id.). *United States v. Roberts*, 88 F.3d 872, 883 (10th Cir. 1996).

Because the general jurisdictional statute governing the federal appellate courts, 28 U.S.C. § 1291, does not supply the requisite authorization for the government's appeal, we look to the Criminal Appeals Act, 18 U.S.C. § 3731, to resolve the jurisdictional question raised here. . . . We approach this inquiry mindful of the Supreme Court's "insist[ence] that Congress speak with a clear voice when extending to the Executive a right to expand criminal proceedings [by appeal]" *Arizona v. Manypenny,* 451 U.S. 232, 247 (1981)).

Since its last substantive amendment in 1984, § 3731 has expressly authorized government appeals:

> [1] from a decision, judgment, or order . . . dismissing an indictment or information or granting a new trial after a verdict or judgment, as to any one or more counts, except . . . where the double jeopardy clause . . . prohibits further prosecution[;]
>
> [2] from a decision or order . . . suppressing or excluding evidence or requiring the return of seized property in a criminal proceeding, not made after the defendant has been put in jeopardy and before the verdict or finding on an indictment or information, if the United States attorney certifies to the district court that the appeal is not taken for purposes of delay and that the evidence is a substantial proof of a fact material in the proceeding[; and]
>
> [3] from a decision or order . . . granting the release of a person charged with or convicted of an offense, or denying a motion for revocation of, or modification of the conditions of, a decision or order granting release.

These conditions permitting appeal have been "carefully circumscribed by Congress out of a desire (among other reasons) to safeguard individuals from the special hazards inherent in prolonged litigation with the sovereign" (*Carrillo-Bernal,* 58 F.3d at 1497; see also *United States v. Martinez,* 681 F.2d 1248, 1251 (10th Cir. 1982; "The right to appeal is strictly circumscribed by [§ 3731]"). Accordingly, "[t]he statute plainly limits appeals by the United States to [the three] specified categories of district court orders" (*United States v. Patterson,* 882 F.2d 595, 598 (1st Cir.1989; quotation omitted); see *Di Bella,* 369 U.S. at 130, 82 S.Ct. at 659–60 (right of appeal under § 3731 "is confined to narrowly defined situations"); *United States v. Mavrokordatos,* 933 F.2d 843, 846 (10th Cir.1991; "The statute was intended to make appeals possible under the stated circumstances").

Nothing in § 3731 remotely suggests that the government may appeal a witness sequestration order. The circuit courts have repeatedly dismissed government appeals taken from similar preliminary rulings which, neither ordering nor practically effecting the dismissal of charges, exclusion of evidence, or release of the defendant, fell outside the categories specified in § 3731. [Footnote 3 omitted] . . . We likewise hold that § 3731 does not provide the necessary authorization for the government's appeal in this case.

B.

Perhaps anticipating this conclusion, the government has essentially ignored § 3731 and, instead, relied exclusively on a judicially recognized exception to the foregoing limitations on government appeals. In *Carroll v. United States*, 354 U.S. 394, 403 (1957), the Supreme Court acknowledged in the criminal context an interlocutory-appeal rule analogous to the *Cohen* collateral-order doctrine [footnote 4 omitted] familiar in civil cases: "[C]ertain orders relating to a criminal case may be found to possess sufficient independence from the main course of the prosecution to warrant treatment as plenary orders, and thus be appealable on the authority of 28 U.S.C. § 1291 without regard to the limitations of 18 U.S.C. § 3731." The Court cautioned, however, that "[t]he instances in criminal cases are very few" (Id.; see *United States v. Denson*, 588 F.2d 1112, 1126–27 (5th Cir. 1979; *Carroll* "emphasized the rareness of such orders"). Notwithstanding that admonition, and despite the absence of any authority applying *Carroll* to a witness-sequestration order, the government maintains the independent-proceeding exception supports its appeal here.

The government contends the sequestration order (1) "conclusively [determined] that victim-witnesses are not entitled to attend court proceedings," (2) impacts an "important right" that "is 'completely separate from the merits' of whether defendants are guilty and how they should be punished," and (3) "would be 'effectively unreviewable' after [trial]," and, therefore, that the "*Cohen* inquiry is easily satisfied here" (Brief of Plaintiff-Appellant, at 9-11; Reply Brief of Plaintiff-Appellant, at 3). The conclusion of this argument bespeaks its flaw. Given the severe limitations on the government's right of appeal from final criminal judgments—including the complete prohibition thereon following a jury acquittal—pretrial criminal rulings would as a routine matter arguably, if not "easily," satisfy the *Cohen* criteria. However, the pertinent case law does not countenance the evisceration of § 3731 by any such wholesale departure from the traditional presumption against government interlocutory appeals in criminal cases. Indeed, the Supreme Court has specifically noted that the considerations disfavoring such appeals are "made no less compelling . . . by the fact that the Government has no later right to appeal" (*Di Bella*, 369 U.S. at 130).

The basic problem with the government's *Cohen* argument arises from the government's consistent failure throughout this appeal to come to grips with the fundamental principle that for it to appeal in the criminal context, authorization under § 3731 is an independent requirement in addition to the finality demanded by § 1291. Obviously, it is only the latter condition that traditionally has been excused by the civil *Cohen* collateral-order doctrine. Thus, when the government seeks review in a criminal case, concerns unaddressed by *Cohen* come into play. The Second Circuit has acknowledged this same crucial point in rejecting the government's invocation of *Carroll* and *Cohen* in support of an appeal unauthorized by § 3731:

"The same considerations that have led the courts to avoid construing § 3731 broadly as authorizing appeals from new-trial orders [footnote 5 omitted] lead us to eschew expansion of the traditional scope of § 1291 to allow the present appeal [under *Carroll* and *Cohen*]. . . . This historic policy disfavoring government appeals in criminal cases, which has repeatedly been reaffirmed by the Court concurrently with its recognition of Congress's increasing allowance of interlocutory appeals, has a prudential basis, 'over and above the constitutional protection against double jeopardy,' *Di Bella*, 369 U.S. at 130. The principal prudential bases are the avoidance of undue delay, see *Carroll* . . . and the avoidance of harassment, see *Arizona v.*

Manypenny . . . Finding no express authority in § 1291 authorizing government appeals in criminal cases, and viewing the new trial order as a nondispositive part of the main stream of the prosecution, we decline to construe § 1291, or the *Cohen-Carroll* exception, so broadly as to give us jurisdiction in the present case." (*United States v. Sam Goody, Inc.*, 675 F.2d 17, 23-24 (2nd Cir. 1982)).

Similarly, when the First Circuit recently relied on *Carroll* and *Cohen* to hear a government appeal from a post-judgment order imposing monetary sanctions for prosecutorial misconduct, the court emphasized that its holding had to be "a narrow one" because of precisely the same point:

> Rather than importing the collateral order doctrine lock, stock, and barrel into our criminal jurisprudence, we hold only that when, as now, the conditions of the collateral order doctrine are satisfied, and the prudential concerns that traditionally militate against allowing the government to appeal in a criminal case favor, or are at least neutral in respect to, the availability of a government appeal, then section [§] 1291 affords a vehicle through which the government may seek appellate review in a criminal case. (*United States v. Horn*, 29 F.3d 754, 769 (1st Cir.1994)).

. . . Significantly, the *Horn* court found the additional "prudential concerns" regarding government criminal appeals satisfied for unique reasons completely inapposite here: "the determination of the defendants' guilt has been made, sentence has been imposed, the attempted appeal is not interlocutory in any sense, and no prospect of piecemeal litigation endures" (Id. at 768–69).

We need not now decide upon any comprehensive, sagacious formulation for resolving the validity of all attempts by the government to appeal from interlocutory orders falling outside the compass of § 3731. The Supreme Court's initial heuristic prescription, specifying "orders . . . found to possess sufficient independence from the main course of the prosecution to warrant treatment as plenary orders" (*Carroll*, 354 U.S. at 403), fully suffices for present purposes. While legislative expansion of § 3731 has superseded the particular holdings of the seminal Supreme Court decisions establishing and implementing this prescription (see Id. at 403–04 . . . dismissing appeal of suppression order and discussing limited circumstances when order returning seized property might be appealable; *Di Bella*, 369 U.S. at 130–32 (same)), the analysis informing those decisions still holds counsel for us today. Thus, we draw a keen sense of the strict "independence" required for application of the independent-proceeding rule from *Di Bella*'s pronouncement that even such a collateral criminal matter as a proceeding "solely for return of property" can be regarded as independent only if it "is in no way tied to a criminal prosecution *in esse*" (Id. at 131–32; see also *Hines*, 419 F.2d at 175, noting "narrow ground" for appeal carved out by *Carroll* and *Di Bella*, and paraphrasing Supreme Court's "unequivocal language" therein as requiring a matter "totally segregated from" and "[not] even remotely connected [to]" a "pending criminal prosecution").

The district court's sequestration order clearly is not independent from the ongoing criminal prosecution out of which the government's appeal arises. Indeed, the stated purpose of the order, consistent with the recognized policy underlying

Rule 615 generally [footnote 6 omitted], is to preserve the integrity of that very proceeding by eliminating a potential source of impermissible influence on proposed testimonial evidence. The fact that the victim-impact evidence involved here would relate only to sentencing matters does not alter our analysis. Far from being collateral to the main course of the prosecution, "[t]he sentencing process is the inevitable culmination of a successful prosecution; it is an integral aspect of a conviction" (*Denson* at 1126; see *United States v. Patterson*, 882 F.2d 595, 599 (1st Cir. 1989); *United States v. Hundley*, 858 F.2d 58, 65 (2d Cir. 1988)).

Accordingly, we hold that neither § 3731 nor the independent-proceeding exception thereto apply to the government's appeal. We therefore dismiss the appeal for lack of the requisite jurisdictional authorization, and turn to the government's alternative request for a writ of mandamus.

Ordinarily, the unavailability of appeal favors mandamus consideration. But the lack of appellate jurisdiction here is not a mere procedural contingency fortuitously precluding review; on the contrary, the government's right of appeal in this context has been "carefully circumscribed by Congress" to safeguard important interests (*Carrillo-Bernal* at 1497). The federal courts of appeal "are courts of limited jurisdiction . . . empowered to hear only those cases . . . entrusted to them . . . by Congress [,] . . . [which] possesses plenary power to confer or withhold appellate jurisdiction" (*Henry v. Office of Thrift Supervision*, 43 F.3d 507, 511 (10th Cir. 1994)). "Were we to accede to the government's request [for mandamus relief], we would be expanding the government's right to bring interlocutory criminal appeals beyond the terms of [§ 3731]. We do not believe mandamus provides the appropriate avenue for such expansion" (*Roberts* at 884; see *Will v. United States*, 389 U.S. 90, 97 (1967; "Mandamus . . . may never be employed as a substitute for appeal in derogation of the[ ] clear policies [embodied by the limitations in § 3731]"); *Margiotta*, 662 F.2d at 134 n. 8, "Mandamus is not to be employed to circumvent the limitations of the Criminal Appeals Act").

While mandamus may not be used to circumvent the policies effectuated by the restrictive provisions of § 3731, "[t]his is not to say that mandamus may never be used to review procedural orders in criminal cases" (*Will* at 97). Thus, as indicated at the outset of this opinion, we do not categorically preclude the use of mandamus to review any and all criminal rulings, however egregious, unauthorized, and prejudicial, which might fall outside the scope of § 3731(*Cf.* 389 U.S. at 97–98, 88 S.Ct. at 275, citing as proper use of mandamus instance in which district court had "overreached its judicial power" in denying government "rightful fruits of a valid conviction"; *United States v. Dooling*, 406 F.2d 192, 198–99 (2d Cir.1969, finding "compelling need for the issuance of mandamus" in order to prevent "gross disruption in the administration of criminal justice" caused by "highly improper and undesirable" action by district court)). However, "[w]e are unpersuaded this case presents the appropriate vehicle to [permit such review]" (*Roberts* at 883; *cf. Margiotta* at 134 n.8).

We acknowledge that our analysis has resulted in completely foreclosing review of the government's challenge to the sequestration order. Though it may perhaps be seen as overly technical and unduly severe by those focused only on this particular controversy, our judicial restraint is ultimately guided and informed by a very broad principle—the constitutional distribution of power between the legislative and judicial branches of our government. As the Supreme Court took pains to explain in *Carroll*:

> Many interlocutory decisions of a trial court may be of grave importance to a litigant, yet are not amenable to appeal at the time entered, and some are never satisfactorily reviewable. In particular is this true of the Government in a criminal case. . . .
>
> If there is serious need for appeals by the Government from [sequestration] orders, or unfairness to the interests of effective criminal law enforcement in the distinctions we have referred to, it is the function of the Congress to decide whether to initiate a departure from the historical pattern of restricted appellate jurisdiction in criminal cases. We must decide the case on the statutes that exist today, in the light of what has been the development of the jurisdiction. It is only through legislative resolution, furthermore, that peripheral questions regarding the conduct of government appeals in this situation can be regulated. (354 U.S. at 406-08, 77 S.Ct. at 1339-40 (footnotes omitted)).

II.

Defendants have raised numerous challenges to the proceedings for review brought by the sequestered victim-impact witnesses themselves. However, we find it necessary to address only the issue of standing. As "an essential and unchanging part of the case-or-controversy requirement of Article III" (*Lujan v. Defenders of Wildlife*, 504 U.S. 555, 560 (1992)), constitutional standing "is a threshold issue in every case before a federal court, determining the power of the court to entertain the suit" (*Boyle v. Anderson*, 68 F.3d 1093 1100 (8th Cir. 1995)). . . . Accordingly, the excluded witnesses' failure to satisfy constitutional standing requirements would preclude our consideration of both their appeal and their petition for mandamus relief [footnote 7 omitted].

Article III imposes three fundamental requirements for standing in federal court:

> First, the [complainant] must have suffered an injury in fact—an invasion of a legally protected interest which is concrete and particularized and actual or imminent. Second, a causal connection must exist between the injury and the conduct complained of; the injury must be fairly traceable to the challenged action. Third, it must be likely that the injury will be redressed by a favorable decision. (*Committee to Save the Rio Hondo v. Lucero*, 102 F.3d 445, 447 (10th Cir. 1996, quotations and citations omitted)).

Our disposition turns on the first.

Legally protected interests derive from various sources, including constitutional guarantees. . . . The victim-impact witnesses rely on two of these sources for their asserted interest in attending the criminal trial from which they have been excluded by the sequestration order. First, they cite the Victims' Rights and Restitution Act (Victims' Rights Act) for the particularized right of crime victims "to be present at all public court proceedings related to the offense" (42 U.S.C. § 10606(b)(4)). Second, they argue more generally that the right of public access to criminal proceedings, recognized in *Richmond Newspapers, Inc. v. Virginia*, 448 U.S. 555 (1980; plurality) and *Globe Newspaper Co. v. Superior Court*, 457 U.S. 596 (1982), provides a constitutional basis for their claim of injury.

A.

There are a number of problems with the excluded witnesses' reliance on the Victims' Rights Act [footnote 8 omitted]. The statute charily pledges only the "best efforts" of certain executive branch personnel to secure the rights listed (see § 10606 (a), "Officers and employees of . . . departments and agencies of the United States engaged in the detection, investigation, or prosecution of crime shall make their best efforts to see that victims of crime are accorded the rights described in subsection (b) of this section"). The district court judge, a judicial officer not bound in any way by this pledge, could not violate the Act. Indeed, the Act's prescriptions were satisfied once the government made its arguments against sequestration—before the district court even ruled.

Further, the specific right to attend criminal proceedings is expressly subject to the following qualification: "unless the court determines that testimony by the victim would be materially affected if the victim heard other testimony at trial" (§ 10606(b)(4)). In essence, the statute acknowledges that the policies behind Rule 615 inherently limit the victim's right to attend criminal proceedings.

Finally, and in any event, Congress explicitly instructed that the Act "does not create a cause of action or defense in favor of any person arising out of the failure to accord to a victim the rights enumerated in subsection (b)" (§ 10606(c)). The excluded witnesses argue this provision relates only to independent enforcement actions and does not bar appeal or mandamus challenges within the criminal proceeding itself, but this facially uncompelling contention is undercut further by a decision of this court in an analogous standing context. In *United States v. Kelley*, 997 F.2d 806, 807–08 (10th Cir. 1993) we joined a line of authority holding that crime victims do not have standing under the Victim and Witness Protection Act (VWPA), 18 U.S.C. § 3663, to appeal unfavorable restitution orders. Significantly, this case law rejects victims' arguments for standing under the VWPA because the history and plain language of the VWPA "do not indicate that Congress, either explicitly or implicitly, intended to provide a private cause of action to victims" (*Kelley* at 808, quoting *United States v. Johnson*, 983 F.2d 216, 221 (11th Cir. 1993)). A fortiori, the Victims' Rights Act, which explicitly denies any private cause of action, does not grant standing to seek review of orders relating to matters covered by the Act. . . .

* * *

Accordingly, we hold that the excluded witnesses lack Article III standing to seek review of the sequestration order entered by the district court. We therefore do not have jurisdiction to reach the merits of either their appeal or their mandamus petition.

The government's appeal . . . is dismissed, and its request for alternative mandamus consideration is denied. The victims' appeal . . . and their mandamus petition
. . . are dismissed.

* * *

Analysis

The *McVeigh* court's denial of standing to victims meant they could not assert
their rights in court. In essence, they did not have real rights at all but instead had
only advisory rights. As a result, a court could disregard any advisory rights that
the victim had. In other words, the trial court was acting within its discretion to
bar the victims from the courtroom.

The denial of rights provided motivation to seek enactment of a constitutional
amendment granting victims' rights. More immediately, the trial court and appellate
court rulings caused the Oklahoma congressional delegation to pursue the Victims'
Rights Clarification Act of 1997 (VCRA), which quickly became law.

- **Document:** *The Victim's Rights Clarification Act (VCRA)*
- **Date:** March 19, 1997
- **Significance:** This statute became law after the decision in the landmark case *United States v. McVeigh*, in an attempt to ensure that victims
  of crime will not be prevented from attending a criminal trial in federal
  court because of their intent to give a statement at sentencing.
- **Source:** *The Victim's Rights Clarification Act (VCRA)* 18 U.S.C.
  § 3510 (1997).

---

* * *

(a) Noncapital cases.—Notwithstanding any statute, rule, or other provision of
law, a United States district court shall not order any victim of an offense
excluded from the trial of a defendant accused of that offense because such victim
may, during the sentencing hearing, make a statement or present any information
in relation to the sentence.

(b) Capital cases.—Notwithstanding any statute, rule, or other provision of law, a
United States district court shall not order any victim of an offense excluded from
the trial of a defendant accused of that offense because such victim may, during
the sentencing hearing, testify as to the effect of the offense on the victim
and the victim's family or as to any other factor for which notice is required under
section 3593(a).

* * *

Analysis

On its face, the VRCA allowed the Oklahoma City bombing victims who were to testify at sentencing to attend the trial. It seemed as if the victims had a green light to attend the proceedings. In fact, it was only a yellow light. The trial court judge elected not to rule on the constitutionality of the VRCA until after the trial phase (*United States v. McVeigh*, 958 F.Supp. 512 (D. Colo. 1997)). According to Professor Paul Cassell, who represented some of these victims throughout their effort to attend the trial, the delay on the ruling of constitutionality left the victims in a quandary. If they attended the trial, they risked being excluded from testifying at sentencing. If they didn't attend the trial, they would be unable to observe one of the most important events of their lives.

As a result of the ruling, some victims stayed away from the trial. After the trial phase, the judge ruled that the VRCA was constitutional. Nevertheless, those victims who observed the trial were examined by the court in order to determine whether the testimony they were to offer at sentencing had become tainted by what they heard at the trial. Clearly, despite the new law, the trial judge had determined that he still had authority to prohibit the testimony of these victims if their testimony was tainted.

Paul Cassell, law professor and lawyer for many of the victims in the Oklahoma City bombing case. (Courtesy University of Utah College of Law)

The VRCA was limited in scope to a narrow class of crime victims. These are victims who are to testify at sentencing as "impact" witnesses but who have no testimony to offer during the trial as witnesses to the crime. This narrow class mostly covers surviving family members of people who are victims of homicide, terrorism, or both who are not witnesses to the crime. Most victims of violent crime witness the crime and live to tell about it. These victims could still be excluded from the trial by either the United States Justice Department or the defendant as a matter of right pursuant to Federal Rule of Evidence (FRE) 615.

The lack of victim "standing" identified by the Tenth Circuit in the *McVeigh* decision can be remedied by a statute specifically conferring standing. With the passage of the Victims' Rights Act in 2004, Congress sought to remedy this problem by giving crime victims standing in the federal system. The CVRA replaced the rights in the VRCA and specifically provides that "[t]he crime victim or law representative . . . may assert the rights described [under the Act]" (18 U.S.C. §3771(d)(1)). In discussing the importance of this provision, the sponsors of the CVRA stated that "[t]his legislation is meant to correct, not continue, the legacy of the poor treatment of crime victims in the criminal process. This legislation is meant to ensure that cases like the McVeigh case, where victims of the Oklahoma

City Bombing were effectively denied the right to attend the trial, [never occur again] and to avoid federal appeals courts from determining, as the Tenth Circuit Court of Appeals did, that victims had no standing to seek review of their right to attend the trial under the former victims' law that this bill replaces" (150 Conf. Rec. S4260, S4269 (Apr. 22, 2004, statement of Sen. Feinstein)).

REFERENCES

Arizona v. Manypenny, 451 U.S. 232 (1981).
Boyle v. Anderson, 68 F.3d 1093 (8th Cir. 1995).
Carroll v. United States, 354 U.S. 394 (1957).
Comanche Indian Tribe v. Hovis, 53 F.3d 298 (10th Cir. 1995).
Committee to Save the Rio Hondo v. Lucero, 102 F.3d 445 (10th Cir. 1996).
Crime Victim Rights Act. 18 U.S.C. §3771.
Criminal Appeals Act. 18 U.S.C. § 3731.
DiBella v. United States, 369 U.S. 121 (1962).
Fed.R.Evid. 615.
Final Decisions of District Courts. 28 U.S.C. § 1291.
Globe Newspaper Co. v. Superior Court, 457 U.S. 596 (1982).
Henry v. Office of Thrift Supervision, 43 F.3d 507 (10th Cir. 1994).
Lujan v. Defenders of Wildlife, 504 U.S. 555 (1992).
Public Health and Welfare. 42 U.S.C. § 10606.
Richmond Newspapers, Inc. v. Virginia, 448 U.S. 555 (1980) (plurality).
United States v. Carrillo-Bernal, 58 F. 3d 1490 (10th Cir. 1995).
United States v. Denson, 588 F.2d 1112 (5th Cir. 1979).
United States v. Dooling, 406 F.2d 192 (2d Cir. 1969).
United States v. Hines, 419 F.2d 173 (10th Cir. 1969).
United States v. Horn, 29 F.3d 754 (1st Cir. 1994).
United States v. Hundley, 858 F.2d 58 (2d Cir. 1988).
United States v. Kelley, 997 F.2d 806 (10th Cir. 1993).
United States v. Margiotta, 662 F.2d 131 (1981).
United States v. Martinez, 681 F.2d 1248 (10th Cir. 1982).
United States v. Mavrokordatos, 933 F.2d 843 (10th Cir. 1991).
United States v. McVeigh, 106 F.3d 325 (10th Cir. 1997).
United States v. Patterson, 882 F.2d 595 (1st Cir. 1989).
United States v. Roberts, 88 F.3d 872 (10th Cir. 1996).
United States v. Sam Goody, Inc., 675 F.2d 17 (2nd Cir. 1982).
Victim and Witness Protection Act (VWPA). 18 U.S.C. § 3663.
The Victim's Rights Clarification Act (VCRA). 18 U.S.C. § 3510 (1997).
Will v. United States, 389 U.S. 90 (1967).
Wilson v. Glenwood Intermountain Properties, Inc., 98 F.3d 590 (10th Cir. 1996).

Additional Reading

Brandeis, Louis. *Other People's Money*. Washington, DC: National Home Library Foundation, 1933, 62.
Kight, Marsha, ed. *Forever Changed: Remembering Oklahoma City, April 19, 1995*. New York: Prometheus Books, 1998.
"The Official Record of the Oklahoma City Bombing." *Oklahoma Today*. January 31, 2005.

6

THE FEDERAL CONSTITUTIONAL VICTIMS' RIGHTS EFFORT

THE EFFORT TO ENACT A FEDERAL CONSTITUTIONAL VICTIMS' RIGHTS AMENDMENT

Between 1994 and 2004, the Victims' Rights Movement labored in Congress to enact an amendment to the United States Constitution. The effort was coordinated through the National Victim Constitutional Amendment Network (NVCAN) and was led by attorney and victims' rights proponent Steven J. Twist. Over a decade of deliberations, the Amendment went through many versions. In the 1998 Senate, the Judiciary Committee issued a majority and minority report on Senate Joint Resolution 44. The report provides great insight into the motivations of the proponents and opponents of federal constitutional rights for crime victims.

The Text of S.J. Res. 44

- **Document:** Senate Joint Resolution 44
- **Date:** April 1, 1998
- **Significance:** Proposal of an amendment to the U.S. Constitution to protect the rights of crime victims.
- **Source:** Senate Joint Resolution 44, *Congressional Record* 105th Cong., 2d Sess., 1998, 105–409.

* * *

Resolved by the Senate and the House of Representatives of the United States of America in Congress assembled (two-thirds of each House concurring therein), That the following article is proposed as an amendment to the Constitution of the United States, which shall be valid for all intents and purposes as part of the Constitution when ratified by the legislatures of three-fourths of the several States within seven years from the date of its submission by the Congress:

Section 1. A victim of a crime of violence, as these terms may be defined by law, shall have the rights:

to reasonable notice of, and not to be excluded from, any public proceedings relating to the crime;

to be heard, if present, and to submit a statement at all such proceedings to determine a conditional release from custody, an acceptance of a negotiated plea, or a sentence;

to the foregoing rights at a parole proceeding that is not public, to the extent those rights are afforded to the convicted offender;

to reasonable notice of a release or escape from custody relating to the crime;

to consideration of the interest of the victim that any trial be free from unreasonable delay;

to an order of restitution from the convicted offender;

to consideration for the safety of the victim in determining any conditional release from custody relating to the crime; and

to reasonable notice of the rights established by this article.

Section 2. Only the victim or the victim's lawful representative shall have standing to assert the rights established by this article. Nothing in this article shall provide grounds to stay or continue any trial, reopen any proceeding or invalidate any ruling, except with respect to conditional release or restitution or to provide rights guaranteed by this article in future proceedings, without staying or continuing a trial. Nothing in this article shall give rise to or authorize the creation of a claim for damages against the United States, a State, a political subdivision, or a public officer or employee.

Section 3. The Congress shall have the power to enforce this article by appropriate legislation. Exceptions to the rights established by this article may be created only when necessary to achieve a compelling interest.

Section 4. This article shall take effect on the 180th day after the ratification of this article. The right to an order of restitution established by this article shall not apply to crimes committed before the effective date of this article.

Section 5. The rights and immunities established by this article shall apply in Federal and State proceedings, including military proceedings to the extent that the Congress may provide by law, juvenile justice proceedings, and proceedings in the District of Columbia and any commonwealth, territory, or possession of the United States.

* * *

Senate Majority Report on Victims' Rights Constitutional Amendment

- **Document:** *United States Senate Report on Senate Joint Resolution 44*
- **Date:** October 12, 1998
- **Significance:** This document carefully lays out the reasoning behind both the proponents' and opponents' views of a victims' rights amendment to the United States Constitution.
- **Source:** Senate Report. *United States Senate Report on Senate Joint Resolution 44.* S.J. Res. 44, 69-010, Calendar No. 455, 105th Congress, Report, Senate, 2d Session, 105–409. Washington, DC: United States Senate, 1998.

* * *

S.J. Res. 44—Proposing An Amendment To The Constitution Of The United States To Protect The Rights Of Crime Victims, October 12 (Legislative Day, October 2), 1998—ordered to be printed.

Mr. Hatch, from the Committee on the Judiciary, submitted the following Report together with additional and minority views [To accompany S.J. Res. 44].

The Committee on the Judiciary, to which was referred the joint resolution (S.J. Res. 44) to propose an amendment to the Constitution of the United States to protect the rights of crime victims, having considered the same, reports favorably thereon, with an amendment, and recommends that the joint resolution, as amended, do pass.

Purpose

The Crime Victims' Rights Constitutional Amendment is intended to establish and preserve, as a matter of right for the victims of violent crimes, the practice of victim participation in the administration of criminal justice that was the birthright of every American at the founding of our Nation.

It was decades after the ratification of the Constitution and the Bill of Rights that the offices of the public police and the public prosecutor would be instituted, and decades beyond that before the victim's role was fully reduced from that of the moving party in every criminal prosecution, to that of a party of interest in the proceedings, to that of mere witness, stripped even of membership in "the public" under the Constitutional meaning of "a public trial."

Much, of course, was gained in the transformation of criminal justice from one of private investigation and prosecution to an enterprise of government. The overall community's stake in how the System operated was recognized; the policies governing the System, the public servants hired by the System, and the resources needed by the System all became accountable to the democratic institutions of government. In many ways, crime victims themselves benefited from the change. They had the aid of public law enforcement, which was more skilled than the average victim in investigating the crime, and the aid of public prosecutors, who were more skilled than the average victim in pleading their case in court. No longer would the wealth of the violated party be a significant determinant as to whether justice was done.

However, in the evolution of the Nation's Justice System, something ineffable has been lost, evidenced in this plea of a witness speaking to the 1982 President's Task Force on Victims of Crime: "Why didn't anyone consult me? I was the one who was kidnapped—not the state of Virginia."

One of the most extraordinary aspects of the several hearings the Committee has held on this issue is the broad consensus among proponents and opponents alike that violent crime victims have a deep, innate, and wholly legitimate interest in the cases that victims bring to the justice system for resolution. It is beyond serious question that for many or most crime victims the prosecution and punishment of their violators are the most important public proceedings of their lifetimes.

This, then, is the purpose of the Crime Victims' Rights Amendment: to acknowledge and honor the humanity and dignity of crime victims within our borders who entrust the Government to seek justice for them. In pursuit of this purpose, the Committee seeks to strengthen the great theme of the Bill of Rights—to ensure the rights of citizens against the deprecations and intrusions of government—and to advance the great theme of the later amendments, extending the participatory rights of American citizens in the affairs of government.

Background and Legislative History

For more than 15 years, a Federal Crime Victims' Rights Amendment has been under consideration in this country. The idea dates back to at least 1982, when the Presidential Task Force on Victims of Crime convened by President Reagan recommended, after hearings held around the country and careful consideration of the issue, that the only way to fully protect crime victims' rights was by adding such rights to the Constitution. The President's Task Force explained the need for a constitutional amendment in these terms:

In applying and interpreting the vital guarantees that protect all citizens, the criminal justice system has lost an essential balance. It should be clearly understood that this Task Force wishes in no way to vitiate the safeguards that shelter anyone accused of crime; but it must be urged with equal vigor that the system has deprived the innocent, the honest, and the helpless of its protection.

The guiding principle that provides the focus for constitutional liberties is that government must be restrained from trampling the rights of the individual citizen. The victims of crime have been transformed into a group oppressively burdened by a system designed to protect them. This oppression must be redressed. To that end it is the recommendation of this Task Force that the sixth amendment to the Constitution be augmented. (Office for Victims of Crime 1982), 114.

Following that recommendation, proponents of crime victims' rights decided to seek constitutional protection in the states initially before undertaking an effort to obtain a federal constitutional amendment (see Cassell 1994, recounting the history). As explained in testimony before the Committee, "[t]he 'states-first' approach drew the support of many victim advocates. Adopting state amendments for victim rights would make good use of the 'great laboratory of the states,' that is, it would test whether such constitutional provisions could truly reduce victims' alienation from their justice system while producing no negative, unintended consequences" (Senate Judiciary Committee Hearing, April 23, 1996, statement of Robert E. Preston, at 40). A total of 29 states, in widely differing versions, now have state victims' rights amendments. [Footnote 1 omitted].

With the passage of and experience with these State constitutional amendments came increasing recognition of both the national consensus supporting victims' rights and the difficulties of protecting these rights with anything other than a Federal amendment. As a result, the victims' advocates—including most prominently the National Victim Constitutional Amendment Network (NVCAN)—decided in 1995 to shift their focus towards passage of a Federal amendment. In 1997, the National Governors Association passed a resolution supporting a Federal constitutional amendment: "The rights of victims have always received secondary consideration within the U.S. judicial process, even though States and the American people by a wide plurality consider victims' rights to be fundamental. Protection of these basic rights is essential and can only come from a fundamental change in our basic law: the U.S. Constitution" (National Governors Association, Policy 23.1; effective winter 1997 to winter 1999).

In the 104th Congress, S.J. Res. 52, the first Federal constitutional amendment to protect the rights of crime victims, was introduced by Senators Jon Kyl and Dianne Feinstein on April 22, 1996. Twenty-seven other Senators cosponsored the resolution. A similar resolution (H.J. Res. 174) was introduced in the House by Representative Henry Hyde. On April 23, 1996, the Senate Committee on the Judiciary held a hearing on S.J. Res. 52. Representative Hyde testified in support of the amendment. Victims and representatives of victims' rights organizations also spoke in favor of the amendment: Katherine Prescott, the president of Mothers Against Drunk Driving (MADD); Ralph Hubbard, board member and State Coordinator of Parents of Murdered Children of New York State; John Walsh, the host of "America's Most Wanted"; Collene Campbell, a leader in the victims' rights movement in California; Rita Goldsmith, the national spokesperson of Parents of Murdered Children; and Robert E. Preston, co-chairman of the National Constitutional Amendment Network. Two legal experts testified in support of the amendment: Professor Paul Cassell and Steven J. Twist, a member of the board of the National Organization for Victim Assistance and the former Chief Assistant Attorney General of Arizona. Two legal experts testified against the amendment: Professor Jamin Raskin of Washington College of Law at American University and noted commentator Bruce Fein, former member of the Department of Justice.

With photos of herself and daughter in the foreground, Marsha Kight testifies on Capitol Hill before the Senate Judiciary Committee hearing on a proposed constitutional amendment to protect the rights of crime victims, April 16, 1997. Kight's daughter Frankie Merrill was killed in the Oklahoma City bombing. (AP Photo/Joe Marquette)

At the end of the 104th Congress, Senators Kyl and Feinstein introduced a modified version of the amendment (S.J. Res. 65). As first introduced, S.J. Res. 52 embodied eight core principles: notice of the proceedings; presence; right to be heard; notice of release or escape; restitution; speedy trial; victim safety; and notice of rights. To these core values another was added in S.J. Res. 65, the right of every victim to have independent standing to assert these rights.

In the 105th Congress, Senators Kyl and Feinstein introduced S.J. Res. 6 on January 21, 1997, the opening day of the Congress. Thirty-two Senators became cosponsors of the resolution. On April 16, 1997, the Senate Committee on the Judiciary held a hearing on S.J. Res. 6. Representative Robert C. Scott testified in opposition to the amendment and Representative Deborah Pryce testified in support of the amendment. U.S. Attorney General Janet Reno testified that "[b]ased on our personal experiences and the extensive review and analysis that has been conducted at our direction, the President and I have concluded that an amendment to the U.S. Constitution to protect victims' rights is warranted" (Senate Judiciary Committee Hearing, April 16, 1997, statement of Attorney General Reno, at 40–41).

Others testifying in support of the amendment included John Walsh, the host of 'America's Most Wanted'; Marsha Kight of Oklahoma City; Wisconsin attorney general Jim Doyle; Kansas attorney general Carla Stovall; Pima County attorney Barbara LaWall; and Prof. Paul Cassell of the University of Utah College of Law. The following people testified in opposition to the amendment: Lynne Henderson of Bloomington, IN; Donna F. Edwards, the executive director of the National Network to End Domestic Violence; and Virginia Beach Commonwealth Attorney Robert J. Humphreys.

S.J. Res. 44 was introduced by Senators Kyl and Feinstein on April 1, 1998. Thirty-nine Senators joined Senators Kyl and Feinstein as original cosponsors: Senators Biden, Lott, Thurmond, Torricelli, Breaux, Grassley, DeWine, Ford, Reid, Gramm, Mack, Landrieu, Cleland, Coverdell, Craig, Inouye, Bryan, Snowe, Thomas, Warner, Lieberman, Allard, Hutchison, D'Amato, Shelby, Campbell, Coats, Faircloth, Frist, Robert Smith, Gregg, Hagel, Helms, Gordon Smith, Hutchinson, Inhofe, Murkowski, Bond, and Grams. Senator Wyden subsequently joined as a cosponsor. The amendment included the core principles contained in the earlier versions. The scope of the amendment as originally proposed reached to crimes of violence and other crimes that may have been added by law. In the present text, the amendment is limited to crimes of violence.

On April 28, 1998, the Senate Committee on the Judiciary held a hearing on S.J. Res. 44. Raymond C. Fisher, the U.S. Associate Attorney General testified in support of an amendment. Additionally, the following witnesses testified in support of S.J. Res. 44: Prof. Paul Cassell; Steve Twist, a member of the National Victims' Constitutional Amendment Network and the former Chief Assistant Attorney General of Arizona; Norm Early, a former Denver district attorney and a board member of the National Organization for Victim Assistance; and Marlene Young, the executive director of the National Organization for Victim Assistance. The following witnesses testified in opposition to the amendment: Prof. Robert Mosteller of Duke Law School and Kathleen Kreneck, the executive director of the Wisconsin Coalition Against Domestic Violence.

On July 7, after debate at three executive business meetings, the Senate Committee on the Judiciary approved S.J. Res. 44, with a substitute amendment, by a vote of 11 to 6. The following Senators voted in favor of the amendment: Hatch, Thurmond, Grassley, Kyl, DeWine, Ashcroft, Abraham, Sessions, Biden, Feinstein, and Torricelli. The following Senators voted against the amendment: Thompson, Leahy, Kennedy, Kohl, Feingold, and Durbin. Senator Specter did not vote.

The Need for Constitutional Protection

After extensive testimony in hearings held over 3 different years, the Committee concludes that a Federal constitutional amendment will protect victims' rights in the Nation's criminal justice system. While a wide range of State constitutional amendments and other State and Federal statutory protections exist to extend rights to victims, that patchwork has not fully succeeded in ensuring comprehensive protection of victims' rights within the criminal justice system. A Federal amendment can better ensure that victims' rights are respected in the Nation's State and Federal courts.

The U.S. Supreme Court has held that "in the administration of criminal justice, courts may not ignore the concerns of victims" (*Morris v. Slappy*, 461 U.S. 1, 14 (1983)). Yet in today's world, without protection in our Nation's basic charter, crime victims are in fact often ignored. As one former prosecutor told the committee, "the process of detecting, prosecuting, and punishing criminals continues, in too many places in America, to ignore the rights of victims to fundamental justice" (Senate Judiciary Committee Hearing, April 23, 1996, statement of Steven J. Twist, at 88). In some cases victims are forced to view the process from literally outside the courtroom. Too often they are left uninformed about critical proceedings, such as bail hearings, plea hearings, and sentencings. Too often their safety is not considered by courts and parole boards determining whether to release dangerous offenders. Too often they are left with financial losses that should be repaid by criminal offenders. Too often they are denied any opportunity to make a statement that might provide vital information for a judge. Time and again victims testified before the Committee that being left out of the process of justice was extremely painful for them. One victim even found the process worse than the crime: "I will never forget being raped, kidnapped [sic], and robbed at gunpoint. However my disillusionment [with] the judicial system is many times more painful" (*President's Task Force on Victims of Crime* at 5).

It should be noted at the outset that a Federal amendment for victims' rights is intended to provide benefits to society as a whole, and not just individual victims. As Attorney General Reno has testified:

> [T]he President and I have concluded that a victims' rights amendment would benefit not only crime victims but also law enforcement. To operate effectively, the criminal justice system relies on victims to report crimes committed against them, to cooperate with law enforcement authorities investigating those crimes, and to provide evidence at trial. Victims will be that much more willing to participate in this process if they perceive that we are striving to treat them with respect and to recognize their central place in any prosecution. (Senate Judiciary Committee Hearing, April 16, 1997, statement of Attorney General Reno, at 41).

The Constitution Typically Protects Participatory Rights

The Committee has concluded that it is appropriate that victims' rights reform take the form of a Federal constitutional amendment. A common thread among many of the previous amendments to the Federal constitution is a desire to expand participatory rights in our democratic institutions. Indeed, the 15th amendment was added to ensure African-Americans could participate in electoral process, the 19th amendment to do the same for women, and the 26th amendment expanded such rights to young citizens. Other provisions of the Constitution guarantee the openness of civil institutions and proceedings, including the rights of free speech and assembly, the right to petition the Government for redress of grievances, and perhaps most relevant in this context, the right to a public trial. It is appropriate for this country to act to guarantee rights for victims to participate in proceedings of vital concern to them. These participatory rights serve an important function in a democracy. As the Justice Brandeis once stated, "[s]unlight is said to be the best of disinfectants" (Brandeis 1933, 62). Open governmental institutions, and the participation of the public, help ensure public confidence in those institutions. In the case of trials, a public trial is intended to preserve confidence in the judicial system, that no defendant is denied a fair and just trial. However, it is no less vital that the public—and victims themselves—have confidence that victims receive a fair trial.

In a Rose Garden ceremony on June 25, 1996, endorsing the amendment, President Clinton explained the need to constitutionally guarantee a right for victims to participate in the criminal justice process:

> Participation in all forms of government is the essence of democracy. Victims should be guaranteed the right to participate in proceedings related to crimes committed against them. People accused of crimes have explicit constitutional rights. Ordinary citizens have a constitutional right to participate in criminal trials by serving on a jury. The press has a constitutional right to attend trials. All of this is as it should be. It is only the victims of crime who have no constitutional right to participate, and that is not the way it should be.

Two leading constitutional law scholars recently reached similar conclusions:

> [The proposed Crime Victims' Rights Amendment] would protect basic rights
> of crime victims, including their rights to be notified of and present at all pro-
> ceedings in their case and to be heard at appropriate stages in the process.
> These are rights not to be victimized again through the process by which
> government officials prosecute, punish, and release accused or convicted
> offenders. These are the very kinds of rights with which our Constitution is
> typically and properly concerned—rights of individuals to participate in all
> those government process that strongly affect their lives. (Tribe and Cassell
> 1998 at B7).

Participation of victims is not only a value consistent with our constitutional
structure but something that can have valuable benefits in its own right. As experts
on the psychological effects of victimization have explained, there are valuable
therapeutic reasons to ensure victim participation in the criminal justice process:

> The criminal act places the victim in an inequitable, "one-down" position in
> relationship to the criminal, and the victims' trauma is thought to result
> directly from this inequity. Therefore, it follows that the victims' perceptions
> about the equity of their treatment and that of the defendants affects their
> crime-related psychological trauma. [F]ailure to * * * offer the right of [crimi-
> nal justice] participation should result in increased feelings of inequity on the
> part of the victims, with a corresponding increase in crime-related psychologi-
> cal harm. (Kilpatrick and Otto 1987).

For all these reasons, it is the view of the Committee that it is vital that victims
be guaranteed an appropriate opportunity to participate in our criminal justice
process.

Less Than Federal Constitutional Protection Has Been Inadequate

Most of the witnesses testifying before the Committee shared the view that victims' rights were inadequately protected today and that, without a Federal amendment, they would so remain. Attorney General Reno, for example, reported after
careful study that:

> Efforts to secure victims' rights through means other than a constitutional
> amendment have proved less than fully adequate. Victims' rights advocates
> have sought reforms at the State level for the past twenty years, and many
> States have responded with State statutes and constitutional provisions that
> seek to guarantee victims' rights. However, these efforts have failed to fully
> safeguard victims' rights. These significant State efforts simply are not suffi-
> ciently consistent, comprehensive, or authoritative to safeguard victims' rights.
> (Senate Judiciary Committee Hearing, April 16, 1997, statement of Attorney
> General Reno, at 64).

Similarly, a comprehensive report from those active in the field concluded that "[a] victims' rights constitutional amendment is the only legal measure strong enough to rectify the current inconsistencies in victims' rights laws that vary significantly from jurisdiction to jurisdiction on the state and federal level" (U.S. Department of Justice, Office for Victims of Crime 1998, 10). Indeed, Professors Tribe and Cassell have reached a similar conclusion: "Congress and the states already have passed a variety of measures to protect the rights of victims. Yet the reports from the field are that they have all too often been ineffective" (Tribe and Cassell 1998, B7).

Examples of Victims Denied the Opportunity to Participate

It is the view of the Committee that a Federal amendment can better ensure that victims' opportunity to participate in the criminal justice process is fully respected. The Committee heard significant testimony about how the existing patchwork fails to transform paper promises to victims into effective protections in the criminal justice system. At the Committee's 1998 hearing, Marlene Young, a representative of the National Organization for Victim Assistance (NOVA), gave some powerful examples to the Committee:

> Roberta Roper, who testified eloquently before the Committee in her capacity as the co-chair of the National Victims Constitutional Amendment Network, was denied the opportunity to sit in the courtroom at the trial of her daughter's murderer because it was thought she might, by her presence, influence the outcome.
>
> Sharon Christian, 20 years old, a young victim of rape reported the crime. After the offender was arrested, she was victimized by the system when, 2 weeks later she was walking down the street in her neighborhood and saw the young man hanging out on the corner. He had been released on personal recognizance with no notice to her and no opportunity to ask for a restraining order or for the court to consider the possibility of bond.
>
> Virginia Bell, a retired civil servant, was accosted and robbed in Washington, DC some five blocks from the Committee's hearing room, suffering a broken hip. Her medical expenses were over $11,000, and the resulting debilitation required her to live with her daughter in Texas. While her assailant pled guilty, Ms. Bell was not informed, and the impact of her victimization was never heard by the court. The court ultimately ordered restitution in the entirely arbitrary and utterly inadequate amount of $387.
>
> Ross and Betty Parks, parents of a murdered daughter Betsy, waited 7 years for a murder trial. The delay was caused, in part, by repeated motions that resulted in delay—thirty-one motions at one point.

The unfortunate and unfair treatment of these individuals was brought to the attention of the Committee by just one witness. But the reports from the field are that there are countless other victims that have been mistreated in similar ways. Yet sadly and all too often, the plight of crime victims will never come to the attention of the public or the appellate courts or this Committee. Few victims have the energy or resources to challenge violations of even clearly-established rights and, in those rare cases when they do so, they face a daunting array of obstacles. No doubt today many frustrated victims simply give up in despair, unable to participate meaningfully in the process.

Statistical Quantification of Violations of Victims' Rights

The statistical evidence presented to the Committee revealed that the current regime falls well short of giving universal respect to victims' rights. In the mid-1990's, the National Victim Center, under a grant from the National Institute of Justice, reviewed the implementation of victims' rights laws in four States. Two states were chosen because they had strong State statutory and State constitutional protection of victims' rights, and two were chosen because they had weaker protection. The study surveyed more than 1,300 crime victims and was the largest of its kind ever conducted. It found that many victims were still being denied their rights, even in States with what appeared to be strong legal protection. The study concluded that State protections alone are insufficient to guarantee victims' rights:

> The *Victims Rights Study* revealed that, while strong state statutes and state constitutional amendments protecting crime victims' rights are important, they have been insufficient to guarantee the rights of crime victims. While this sub-report focused on reports by crime victims regarding their personal experiences, the responses of local criminal justice and victim service providers to similar questions in the Victims' Rights Study corroborate the victim responses. Even in states with strong protection large numbers of victims are being denied their legal rights. (National Victim Center 1997, 7).

Important findings of the study included:

Nearly half of the victims (44 percent) in States with strong protections for victims and more than half of the victims (70 percent) in States with weak protections did not receive notice of the sentencing hearing—notice that is essential for victims to exercise their right to make a statement at sentencing.

While both of the States with strong statutes had laws requiring that victims be notified of plea negotiations, and neither of the weak protection States had such statutes, victims in both groups of States were equally unlikely to be informed of such negotiations. Laws requiring notification of plea negotiations were not enforced in nearly half of the violent crime cases included in the study.

Substantial numbers of victims in States with both strong and weak protection were not notified of various stages in the process, including bail hearings (37 percent not notified in strong protection states, 57 percent not notified in weak protection states); the pretrial release of perpetrators (62 percent not notified in strong protection states, 74 percent not notified in weak protection States); and sentencing hearings (45 percent not notified in strong protection States, 70 percent not notified in weak protection States).

A later report based on the same large data base found that racial minorities are most severely affected under the existing patchwork of victims' protections

(National Victim Center 1997, 5). Echoing these findings of disparate impact, another witness reported to the Committee, "There being no constitutional mandate to treat all of America's victims, white and non-white, with dignity and compassion . . . minority victims will continue to feel the sting of their victimization much longer than their white counterparts. Because of the large percentage of minority victims in the system, their neglect . . . continues to create disrespect for a process in the communities where such disrespect can be least afforded" (Senate Judiciary Committee Hearing, April 28, 1998, statement of Norm S. Early). A recent report concluded, after reviewing all of the evidence from the field, that "[w]hile victims' rights have been enacted in states and at the federal level, they are by no means consistent nationwide. All too often they are not enforced because they have not been incorporated into the daily functioning of all justice systems and are not practiced by all justice professionals" (U.S. Department of Justice, Office for Victims of Crime 1998, 9).

In sum, as Harvard Law Prof. Laurence H. Tribe has concluded, rules enacted to protect victims' rights "are likely, as experience to date sadly shows, to provide too little real protection whenever they come into conflict with bureaucratic habit, traditional indifference, sheer inertia, or any mention of an accused's rights regardless of whether those rights are genuinely threatened" (Tribe 1997, 3).

A Federal Amendment is Compatible with Important Federalism Principles

The proposed victims' rights constitutional amendment is fully compatible with the principles of federalism on which our republic is based. First, of course, the constitutionally specified process for amending the Constitution fully involves the States, requiring approval of three-quarters of them before any amendment will take effect. There is, moreover, substantial evidence that the States would like to see the Congress act and give them, through their State legislatures, the opportunity to approve an amendment. For example, the National Governors Association overwhelmingly endorsed a resolution calling for a Federal constitutional amendment.

The important values of federalism provide no good reason for avoiding action on the amendment. Already many aspects of State criminal justice systems are governed by Federal constitutional principles. For example, every State is required under the sixth amendment to the Federal constitution as applied to the States to provide legal counsel to indigent defendants and a trial by jury for serious offenses. Victims' advocates simply seek equal respect for victims' rights, to give the same permanence to victims' rights.

Adding protections into the U.S. Constitution, our fundamental law, will serve to ensure that victims' rights are fully protected. This same point was recognized by James Madison in considering whether to add to the Constitution a Bill of Rights. He concluded the Bill of Rights would acquire, by degrees, "the character of fundamental maxims" (Madison 1953, 254).

Amending the Constitution is, of course, a significant step—one which the Committee does not recommend lightly. But to protect victims, it is an appropriate one. As Thomas Jefferson once said: "I am not an advocate for frequent changes in laws and constitutions, but laws and institutions must go hand in hand with the progress of the human mind. As that becomes more developed, more enlightened, as new discoveries are made, new truths discovered and manners and opinions change, with the change of circumstances, institutions must advance also to keep pace with the times" (Jefferson 1816, 42-43). Throughout the country, there is a strong consensus that victims' rights deserve to be protected. But at the same time, as a country, we have failed to find a way to fully guarantee rights for victims in criminal justice processes of vital interest to them. It is time to extend Federal constitutional recognition to those who are too often forgotten by our criminal justice system—the innocent victims of crime.

The Need For Specific Rights in the Process

With this need for Federal constitutional protection of victims' rights in mind, the Committee finds that rights under eight general headings should be protected in an amendment to the Federal constitution. Each of these eight rights is discussed in turn.

Right to Notice of Proceedings

Rights for victims in the criminal justice process are of little use if victims are not aware of when criminal justice proceedings will be held. The Committee heard testimony about the devastating effects on crime victims when hearings about the crime are held without prior notice to them. For example, a witness from Parents of Murdered Children (POMC) testified:

> Each week at our national office, we receive more than 1,000 murder-related calls. Of these calls, about half involve homicide survivors who believe that they have been treated unfairly by some part of the criminal justice system. Some of our members even have as much anger about their unfair treatment by the criminal justice system as they do about the murder. . . .
>
> Many of the concerns arise from not being informed about the progress of the case. . . . [V]ictims are not informed about when a case is going to court or whether the defendant will receive a plea bargain. . . . [I]n many cases, the failure to provide information arises simply from indifference to the plight of the surviving family members or a feeling that they have no right to the information.
>
> Because they do not know what is going on, victims frequently must take it upon themselves to call . . . the prosecutor, or the courts for information about their case. All too often, such calls have to be made when victims' families are in a state of shock or are grieving from the loss of their loved ones. Victims' family should not have to bear the added burden of trying to obtain information. It should be their automatic right. (Senate Judiciary Committee Hearing, April 23, 1996, prepared statement of Rita Goldsmith, at 35–36).

No witness testified before the Committee that victims should not receive notice of important proceedings. The Committee concludes that victims deserve notice of important criminal justice proceedings relating to the crimes committed against them.

Based on a demonstrated need for victims to receive notice, as long ago as 1982 the President's Task Force on Victims of Crime recommended that legislation and policies to guarantee that victims receive case status information, prompt notice of scheduling changes of court proceedings, and prompt notice of a defendant's arrest and bond status. Reviewing this status of these recommendations, a recent Department of Justice Report found:

> Fifteen years later, many states, but not all, have adopted laws requiring such notice. While the majority of states mandate advance notice to crime victims of criminal proceedings and pretrial release, many have not implemented mechanisms to make such notice a reality. . . .
>
> Many states do not require notification to victims of the filing of an appeal, the date of an appellate proceeding, or the results of the appeal. Also, most do not require notification of release from a mental facility or of temporary or conditional releases such as furloughs or work programs.
>
> Some state laws require that notice be made "promptly" or within a specified period of time. . . . Victims also complain that prosecutors do not inform them of plea agreements, the method used for disposition in the overwhelming majority of cases in the United States criminal justice system. (U.S. Department of Justice, Office for Victims of Crime 1998, 13).

This recent report confirms the testimony that the Committee received that victims are too often not notified of important criminal justice proceedings. It is time to protect in the Constitution this fundamental interest of victims.

Right to Attend

The Committee concludes that victims deserve the right to attend important criminal justice proceedings related to crimes perpetrated against them. This is no new insight. In 1982, the President's Task Force on Victims of Crime concluded:

"The crime is often one of the most significant events in the lives of victims and their families. They, no less than the defendant, have a legitimate interest in the fair adjudication of the case, and should therefore, as an exception to the general rule provided for the exclusion of witnesses, be permitted to be present for the entire trial" (*President's Task Force on Victims of Crime*, 80).

Allowing victims to attend court proceedings may have important psychological benefits for victims. "The victim's presence during the trial may * * * facilitate healing of the debilitating psychological wounds suffered by a crime victim" (Eikenberry 1989). In addition, without a right to attend trials, victims suffer a further loss of dignity and control of their own lives. Applying witness sequestration rules in rape cases, for example, has proven to be harmful (see Madigan and Gamble 1989, 97).

The primary barrier to victims attending trial is witness sequestration rules that are unthinkingly extended to victims. Not infrequently defense attorneys manipulate these rules to exclude victims from courtrooms simply because the defendant would like the victim excluded. The Committee heard no convincing evidence that a general policy excluding victims from courtrooms is necessary to ensure a fair trial. As a Department of Justice report recently explained:

> There can be no meaningful attendance rights for victims unless they are generally exempt from [witness sequestration rules]. Just as defendants have a right to be present throughout the court proceedings whether or not they testify, so too should victims of crime. Moreover, the presence of victims in the courtroom can be a positive force in furthering the truth-finding process by alerting prosecutors to misrepresentations in the testimony of other witnesses. (U.S. Department of Justice, Office for Victims of Crime 1998, 15).

The Committee finds persuasive the experience of the growing number of States that have guaranteed victims an unequivocal right to attend a trial (see, e.g., Ariz. Const. Art. 2, Sec. 2.1(A)(3): victim right "[t]o be present . . . at all criminal proceedings where the defendant has the right to be present"; Mo. Const. Art. I, 32(1): victim has "[t]he right to be present at all criminal justice proceedings at which the defendant has such right"; Idaho Const. Art. I, 22(4): victim has the right "[t]o be present at all criminal justice proceedings"). An alternative approach is to give victims a right to attend a trial unless their testimony would be "materially affected" by their attendance. Congress has previously adopted such a standard, see 42 U.S.C. 10606(b)(4), but the results have proven to be unfortunate. In the Oklahoma City bombing case, for example, a district court concluded that testimony about the impact of their loss from family members of deceased victims of the bombing would be materially affected if the victims attended the trial. This perplexing ruling was the subject of unsuccessful emergency appeals (see Cassell 1997 testimony), and ultimately Congress was forced to act (see Victim Rights Clarifications Act of 1997, Pub. L. No 105-6, 111 Stat. 12 (codified as amended at 18 U.S.C. § 3510 (1997)). Even this action did not fully vindicate the victims' right to attend that trial. The Committee heard testimony from a mother who lost her daughter in the bombing that even this Act of Congress did not resolve the legal issues sufficiently to give the victims the legal assurances they need to attend all the proceedings (Senate Judiciary Committee Hearing, April 16, 1997, statement of Marsha Knight, at 73–74). Rather than create a possible pretext for denying victims the right to attend a trial or extended litigation about the speculative circumstances in victim testimony might somehow be affected, the Committee believes that such a victim's right to attend trial should be flatly recognized.

While a victim's right to attend is currently protected in some statutes or State constitutional amendments, only a Federal constitutional amendment will fully ensure such a right. The Committee was presented with a detailed legal analysis that convincingly demonstrated that there is no current federal constitutional right of criminal defendants to exclude generally victims from trials (see Senate Judiciary Committee Hearing, April 23, 1996, statement of Paul Cassell, at 26–34). While this appears to be an accurate assessment of constitutional legal principles, the fact remains that the law has not been authoritatively settled. In the wake of this uncertainty, State rights for victims to attend trials are not fully effective.

Confirmation of this point came when the Committee heard testimony that "even in some States which supposedly protect a victims' right to attend a trial, victims are often 'strongly advised' not to go in because of the possibility that it might create an issue for the defendant to appeal" (Senate Judiciary Committee Hearing, April 23, 1996, statement of Rita Goldsmith, at 36). Federal prosecutors in the Oklahoma City bombing case, for example, were forced to give victims less-than-clear-cut instructions on whether victims could attend proceedings (see Senate Judiciary Committee Hearing, April 16, 1997, statement of Marsh Knight, at 73–74).

Moreover, efforts to obtain clear-cut legal rulings have been unsuccessful. In Utah, for example, despite a strongly written amicus brief on behalf of a number of crime victims organizations requesting a clear statement upholding the right of victims to attend, the Utah Court of Appeals has left unsettled the precise standards for exclusion of crime victims (see Senate Judiciary Committee Hearing, April 16, 1997, statement of Paul Cassell, at 114–15, discussing *State v. Beltran-Felix*, No. 95-341-CA). The result has been that, in Utah and presumably many other States, crime victims must struggle with the issue of whether to attend trials of those accused of perpetrating crimes against them at the expense of creating a possible basis for the defendant to overturn his conviction. The issue of a victim's right to attend a trial should be authoritatively settled by Federal constitutional protection.

Right to Be Heard

Crime victims deserve the right to be heard at appropriate points in the criminal justice process. Giving victims a voice not only improves the quality of the process but can also be expected to often provide important benefits to victims. The Committee concludes that victims deserve the right to be heard at four points in the criminal justice process: plea bargains, bail or release hearing, sentencing, and parole hearings.

Victims have vital interests at stake when a court decides whether to accept a plea. One leading expert on victims' rights recently explained that:

> The victim's interest in participating in the plea bargaining process are many. The fact that they are consulted and listened to provides them with respect and an acknowledgment that they are the harmed individual. This in turn may contribute to the psychological healing of the victim. The victim may have financial interests in the form of restitution or compensatory fine.... [B]ecause judges act in the public interest when they decide to accept or reject a plea bargain, the victim is an additional source of information for the court. (Beloof 1998, 7–33).

Victim participation in bail hearings can also serve valuable functions, particularly in alerting courts to the dangers that defendants might present if released unconditionally. Without victim participation, courts may not be fully informed about the consequences of releasing a defendant. "It is difficult for a judge to evaluate the danger that a defendant presents to the community if the judge hears only from the defendant's counsel, who will present him in the best possible light, and from a prosecutor who does not know of the basis for the victim's fear. . . . The person best able to inform the court of [threatening] statements that may have been made by the defendant and the threat he poses is often the person he victimized" (*President's Task Force on Victims of Crime*, 65).

The Committee heard chilling testimony about the consequences of failing to provide victims with this opportunity from Katherine Prescott, the President of Mothers Against Drunk Driving (MADD):

> I sat with a victim of domestic violence in court one day and she was terrified. She told me she knew her ex-husband was going to kill her. The lawyers and the judge went into chambers and had some discussions and they came out and continued the case. The victim never had the opportunity to speak to the judge, so he didn't know how frightened she was. He might have tried to put some restrictions on the defendant if he had known more about her situation, but it was handled in chambers out of the presence of the victim.
>
> That night, as she was going to her car after her shift was over at the hospital where she was a registered nurse, she was murdered by her ex-husband, leaving four young children, and then he took his own life—four children left orphans. I will always believe that if the judge could have heard her and seen her as I did, maybe he could have done something to prevent her death. (Senate Judiciary Committee Hearing, April 23, 1996, statement of Katherine Prescott, at 25–26).

Victim statements at sentencing also serve valuable purposes. As the President's Task Force on Victims of Crime concluded:

> Victims of violent crime should be allowed to provide information at two levels. One, the victim should be permitted to inform the person preparing the presentence report of the circumstances and consequences of the crime. Any recommendation on sentencing that does not consider such information is simply one-sided and inadequate. Two, every victim must be allowed to speak at the time of sentencing. The victim, no less than the defendant, comes to court seeking justice. When the court hears, as it may, from the defendant, his lawyer, his family and friends, his minister, and others, simple fairness dictates that the person who has borne the brunt of the defendant's crime be allowed to speak. (*President's Task Force on Victims of Crime*, Final Report, 77).

Courts have found victim information helpful in crafting an appropriate sentence. For instance, in *United States v. Martinez*, the District Court for the District of New Mexico stated that it "has welcomed such [allocution] statements and finds them helpful in fashioning an appropriate sentence" (978 F. Supp. 1442, 1452 (D.N.M. 1997)). Likewise in *United States v. Smith*, 893 F. Supp. 187, 188 (E.D.N.Y. 1995), Judge Weinstein explained that the "sensible process [of victim allocution] helps the court gauge the effects of the defendant's crime not only on the victim but on relevant communities." Victim statements can also have important cathartic effects. For example, a daughter who spoke at the sentencing of her step-father for abusing her and her sister: "When I read [the impact statement], it healed a part of me—to speak to [the defendant] and tell him how much he hurt" (Senate Judiciary Committee Hearing, April 28, 1998, statement of Paul Cassell (quoting statement of victim)). The sister also explained: "I believe that I was helped by the victim impact statement. I got to tell my step-father what he did to me. Now I can get on with my life. I don't understand why victims don't have the same rights as criminals, to say the one thing that might help heal them" (Id.).

Victims deserve the right to be heard by parole boards deciding whether to release prisoners. Without victim testimony, the boards may be unaware of the true danger presented by an inmate seeking parole. An eloquent example of this point can be found that was provided by Patricia Pollard, who testified before the Committee in 1996. She was abducted, raped, brutally beaten, and had her throat slashed with the jagged edge of a beer can, and left to die in the Arizona desert. Miraculously she survived. In moving testimony, she described for the Committee what happened next:

> Eric Mageary, the man who attacked me, was caught and convicted. He was sentenced to 25 years to life in the Arizona State Prison. While he was still 10 years short of his minimum sentence he was released on parole, but no one ever told me or gave me a chance to say what I thought about it. The system had silenced me, just like Mageary did that night outside of Flagstaff . . .
>
> But my story does not end with Eric Mageary's first parole. Within less than a year he was back in prison, his parole [r]evoked for drug crimes. Then in 1990, the people of Arizona voted State constitutional rights for crime victims. In 1993, Mageary again applied for release from prison and, incredibly, he was again released without any notice to me. I was again denied any opportunity to tell the parole board about the horrible crime or the need to protect others in that community. They ignored my rights, but this time, I had a remedy.
>
> The county attorney in Flagstaff filed an action to stop the release and the court of appeals in Arizona forced the board, because they had denied me my constitutional rights, to hold another hearing and to hear from me. This time, after they heard from me directly and heard firsthand the horrible nature of the offense, they voted for public safety and Mageary's release was denied. (Senate Judiciary Committee Hearing, April 23, 1996, statement of Patricia Pollard, at 31–32).

Voices such as Patricia Pollard's must not be silenced by the system. Victims deserve the right to be heard at appropriate times in the process.

Right to Notice of Release or Escape

The Committee heard testimony about Sharon Christian, 20 years old, a young victim of rape who reported the crime and whose offender was arrested. She was doubly victimized when 2 weeks later she was walking down the street in her neighborhood and saw the young man hanging out on the corner. He had been released on personal recognizance with no notice to her and no opportunity to ask for a restraining order or for the court to consider the possibility of a bond (Senate Judiciary Committee Hearing, April 28, 1998, statement of Marlene Young).

Defendants who are released from confinement often pose grave dangers to those against whom they have committed crimes. In a number of cases, notice of release has been literally a matter of life and death. As the Justice Department recently explained:

"Around the country, there are a large number of documented cases of women and children being killed by defendants and convicted offenders recently released from jail or prison. In many of these cases, the victims were unable to take precautions to save their lives because they had not been notified of the release" (U.S. Department of Justice, Office for Victims of Crime 1998, 14).

The problem of lack of notice has been particularly pronounced in domestic violence and other acquaintance cases, in which the dynamics of the cycle of violence lead to tragic consequences. For example, on December 6, 1993, Mary Byron was shot to death as she left work. Authorities soon apprehended Donovan Harris, her former boyfriend, for the murder. Harris had been arrested 3 weeks earlier on charges of kidnaping [sic] Byron and raping her at gunpoint. A relative's payment of bond money allowed Harris to regain his freedom temporarily. No one thought to notify Byron or the police of her release (see Cross 1996 collecting this and other examples). The Committee concludes that victims deserve notice before violent offenders are released.

Recent technological changes have also simplified the ability to provide notice to crime victims. Today some jurisdictions use automated voice response technology to notify victims of when offenders are released. New York City, for example, recently implemented a system in which any victim with access to a telephone can register for notification simply by calling a number and providing an inmate's name, date of birth, and date or arrest. If an inmate is released, the victim receives periodic telephone calls for 4 days or until the victim confirms receiving the message by entering a personal code. Victim assistance providers and police have been trained to explain the system to victims. Other jurisdictions have developed other means of notification, including websites that allow victims to track the location of inmates at all times. While recent developments in these innovative jurisdictions are encouraging, notification needs to be made uniformly available for crime victims around the country.

Right to Consideration of the Victim's Interest in a Trial Free from Unreasonable Delay

Today in the United States, criminal defendants enjoy a constitutionally protected right in the sixth amendment to a "speedy trial." This is as it should be, for criminal charges should be resolved as quickly as is reasonably possible. Defendants, however, are not the only ones interested in a speedy disposition of the case. Victims, too, as well as society as a whole, have an interest in the prompt resolution of criminal cases. "Repeated continuances cause serious hardships and trauma for victims as they review and relive their victimization in preparation for trial, only to find the case has been postponed" (U.S. Department of Justice, Office for Victims of Crime 1998, 21). For victims, "[t]he healing process cannot truly begin until the case can be put behind them. This is especially so for children and victims of sexual assault or any other case involving violence" (*President's Task Force on Victims of Crime*, 75).

The Supreme Court has generally recognized such interests in explaining that "there is a societal interest in providing a speedy trial which exists separate from, and at times in opposition to, the interest of the accused" (*Barker v. Wingo*, 407 U.S. 514, 519 (1972)). However, as two leading scholars have explained, while the Supreme Court has acknowledged the "societal interest" in a speedy trial, "[i]t is rather misleading to say . . . that this 'societal interest' is somehow part of the [sixth amendment] right. The fact of the matter is that the Bill of Rights does not speak of the rights and interests of the government" (LaFave and Israel 1992, Sec. 18.1(b), at 787–88). Nor does the Bill of Rights currently speak, as it should, to the rights and interests of crime victims. Of course, victim's rights to consideration of her interest will not overcome a criminal defendant's right to adequate assistance of counsel.

Defendants have ample tactical reasons for seeking delays of criminal proceedings. Witnesses may forget details of the crime or move away, or the case may simply seem less important given the passage of time. Delays can also be used to place considerable pressure on victims to ask prosecutors to drop charges, particularly in cases where parents of children who have been sexually abused want to put matters behind them. Given natural human tendencies, efforts by defendants to unreasonably delay proceedings are frequently granted, even in the face of State constitutional amendments and statutes requiring otherwise.

Right to Order of Restitution

Crime imposes tremendous financial burdens on victims of crime. The Bureau of Justice Statistics reports that each year approximately two million people in America are injured as the result of violent crime. Approximately 51 percent of the injured will require some medical attention, with 23 percent requiring treatment at a hospital with an average stay of 9 days. While the true cost of crime to the victims is incalculable, the direct costs are simply staggering. In 1991, the direct economic costs of personal and household crime was estimated to be $19.1 billion, a figure that did not include costs associated with homicides.

The perpetrators of these crimes need to be held accountable to repay such costs to the extent possible. Victims deserve restitution from offenders who have been convicted of committing crimes against them. The Committee has twice previously explained that:

The principle of restitution is an integral part of virtually every formal system of criminal justice, or every culture and every time. It holds that, whatever else the sanctioning power of society does to punish its wrongdoers, it should also ensure that the wrongdoer is required to the degree possible to restore the victim to his or her prior state of well-being (S. Rep. 104-179, Senate Judiciary Committee, Victim Restitution Act of 1995, 104th Cong., 1st Sess. 12 (1995), quoting S. Rept. 97-532 at 30 (Judiciary Committee), Aug. 19, 1982 (to accompany S. 2420)).

Consistent with this principle, Federal and State courts have long had power to order restitution against criminal offenders. In practice, however, restitution orders are not entered as frequently as they should be. At the Federal level, for example, this Committee recently investigated Federal restitution procedures and found that restitution orders were often entered haphazardly and that "much progress remains to be made in the area of victim restitution" (S. Rep. 104-179, at 13). Similarly, a recent report from the U.S. Department of Justice concluded that "[w]hile restitution has always been available via statute or common law, it remains one of the most underutilized means of providing crime victims with a measurable degree of justice. Evidence of this is apparent both in decisions to order restitution and in efforts to monitor, collect, and disperse restitution payment to victims" (*New Directions From the Field*, 357).

The President's Task Force on Victims of Crime long ago recommended that "[a] restitution order should be imposed in every case in which a financial loss is suffered, whether or not the defendant is incarcerated" (*President's Task Force on Victims of Crime*, 79). As a step in this direction, in 1982 Congress passed the Victims Witness Protection Act, Pub. L. 97-291, codified at 18 U.S.C. Sec. 1501, 1503, 1505, 1510, 1512-1515, 3146, 3579, 3580. More recently, to respond to the problem of inadequate restitution at the Federal level, this Committee recently recommended, and Congress approved, the Mandatory Victim Restitution Act, codified at 18 U.S.C. 3663A and 3664. Valuable though this legislation may turn out to be, it applies only in Federal cases. To require restitution orders throughout the country, Federal constitutional protection of the victims' right to restitution is appropriate. Victims advocates in the field recently recommended that "restitution orders should be mandatory and consistent nationwide" (*New Directions From the Field*, 364). Of course, there will be many cases in which a convicted offender will not be able to pay a full order of restitution. In such cases, realistic payment schedules should be established and victims appraised of how much restitution can realistically be expected to be collected. But even nominal restitution payments can have important benefits for victims. And by having a full restitution order in place, the offender can be held fully accountable for his crime should his financial circumstances unexpectedly improve.

Right to Have Safety Considered

Victims are often placed at risk whenever an accused or convicted offender is released from custody. The offender may retaliate against or harass the victim for vindictive reasons or to eliminate the victim as a possible witness in future proceedings. Not only are victims threatened by offenders, but recent reports from across the country suggest that the intimidation of victims and other witnesses is a serious impediment to effective criminal prosecution.

Under current law, the safety of victims is not always appropriately considered by courts and parole boards making decisions about releasing offenders. Laws concerning whether victim safety is a factor in such decisions varies widely. The result, unsurprisingly, is that in too many cases offenders are released without due regard for victims. From witness after witness, the Committee heard testimony about the danger in which crime victims are placed when their attackers are released without any regard for their safety. Patricia Pollard, Dr. Marlene Young, and others each confirmed the real-life daily failures of the justice system.

The Committee concludes that, in considering whether to release an accused or convicted offender, courts and parole boards should give appropriate consideration to the safety of victims. Of course, victim safety is not the only interest that these entities will need to consider in making these important decisions. But the safety of victims can be literally a life and death matter that should be evaluated along with other relevant factors. In evaluating the safety of victims, decisionmakers should also take into account the full range of measures that might be employed to protect the safety of victims. For example, a defendant in a domestic violence case might be released, but subject to a "no contact" order with the victim. Or a prisoner might be paroled, on the condition that he remain within a certain specified area. If directed to consider victim safety, our Nation's courts and parole boards are up to the task of implementing appropriate means to protect that safety.

Notice of These Rights

Victims will be in a better position to exercise the foregoing rights if they are provided notice for them. As a recent analysis concluded:

Justice system and allied professions who come into contact with victims should provide an explanation of their rights and provide written information describing victims' rights and the services available to them. Furthermore, rights and services should be explained again at a later time if the victim initially is too traumatized to focus on the details of the information being provided. Explanations of rights and services should be reiterated by all justice personnel and victim service providers who interact with the victim (*New Directions From the Field*, 14).

In Patricia Pollard's case in Arizona, the State Court of Appeals found that her State constitutional right to notice was the lynchpin for her right to notice and for her right to be heard. Victims deserve appropriate notice of their rights in the process.

Section-by-Section Analysis

The Committee intends that the amendment guarantee the protection of and participation by crime victims in the criminal justice process.

The Committee rejected an amendment that would have required the courts to resolve any conflict between the constitutional rights of defendants and those of victims, in favor of defendants rights. As the chief justice of the Texas Court of Criminal Office has written, "[v]ictims' rights versus offenders[']" rights is not a "zero-sum-game." The adoption of rights for the victim need not come at the expense of the accused's rights (Barajas and Nelson 1997, internal citation omitted). The Crime Victims' Rights Amendment creates rights, not in opposition to those of defendants, but in parallel to them. The parallel goal in both instances is to erect protections from abuse by State actors. Thus, just as defendants have a sixth amendment right to a "speedy trial," the Crime Victims' Rights Amendment extends to victims the right to consideration of their interest "in a trial free from unreasonable delay." These rights cannot collide, since they are both designed to bring criminal proceedings to a close within a reasonable time. "[I]f any conflict were to emerge, courts would retain ultimate responsibility for harmonizing the rights at stake" (Tribe and Cassell 1998, B7).

In this respect, the Committee found unpersuasive the contention that the courts will woodenly interpret the later-adopted Crime Victims' Rights Amendment as superceded [sic] provisions in previously-adopted ones. Such a canon of construction can be useful when two measures address precisely the same subject. But no rigid rule of constitutional interpretation requires giving unblinking precedence to later enactments on separate subjects, and the Committee does not believe such a rule would—or should—be applied in this instance.

Instead, the Committee trusts the courts to harmonize the rights of victims and defendants to ensure that both are appropriately protected. The courts have, for example, long experience in accommodating the rights of the press and the public to attend a trial with the rights of a defendant to a fair trial. The same sort of accommodations can be arrived at to dissipate any tension between victims' and defendants' rights.

Section 1. "A victim of a crime of violence, as these terms may be defined by law. . . ."

The core provision of Senate Joint Resolution 44, as amended in Committee, is contained in section 1, which extends various enumerated rights to "a victim of a crime of violence, as these terms may be defined by law." The "law" which will define a "victim" (as well as "crime of violence") will come from the courts interpreting the elements of criminal statutes until definitional statutes are passed explicating the term. In this sense, the amendment should be regarded as "self executing"—that is, it will take effect even without a specific legislative definition. The Committee anticipates that Congress will quickly pass an implementing statute defining "victim" for Federal proceedings. Moreover, nothing removes from the States their plenary authority to enact definitional laws for purposes of their own criminal system. Such legislative definition is appropriate because criminal conduct depends on State and Federal law. Since the legislatures define what is criminal conduct, it makes equal sense for them to also have the ability to further refine the definition of "victim."

In determining how to structure a "victim" definition, ample precedents are available. To cite but one example, Congress has previously defined a "victim" of a crime for sentencing purposes as "any individual against whom an offense has been committed for which a sentence is to be imposed" (Fed. R. Crim. Pro. 32(f)). The Committee anticipates that a similar definition focusing on the criminal charges that have been filed in court will be added to the Federal implementing legislation and, in all likelihood, in State legislation as well.

In most cases, determining who is the victim of a crime will be straightforward. The victims of robbery, and sexual assault are, for example, not in doubt. The victim of a homicide is also not in doubt, but the victim's rights in such cases will be exercised by a surviving family member or other appropriate representative, as will be defined by law. Similarly, in the case of a minor or incapacitated victim, an appropriate representative (not accused of the crime or otherwise implicated in its commission) will exercise the rights of victims.

The amendment extends broadly to all victims of a "crime of violence." "Crimes of violence" likely will include all forms of homicide (including voluntary and involuntary manslaughter and vehicular homicide), sexual assault, kidnapping, robbery, assault, mayhem, battery, extortion accompanied by threats of violence, carjacking, vehicular offenses (including driving while intoxicated) which result in personal injury, domestic violence, and other similar crimes. A "crime of violence" can arise without regard to technical classification of the offense as a felony or a misdemeanor. It should also be obvious that a "crime of violence" can include not only acts of consummated violence but also of intended, threatened, or implied violence. The unlawful displaying of a firearm or firing of a bullet at a victim constitutes a "crime of violence" regardless of whether the victim is actually injured. Along the same lines, conspiracies, attempts, solicitations and other comparable crimes to commit a crime of violence could be considered "crimes of violence" for purposes of the amendment if identifiable victims exist. Similarly, some crimes are so inherently threatening of physical violence that they could be "crimes of violence" for purposes of the amendment. Burglary, for example, is frequently understood to be a "crime of violence" because of the potential for armed or other dangerous confrontation (see *United States v. Guadardo*, 40 F.3d 102 (5th Cir. 1994); *United States v. Flores*, 875 F.2d 1110 (5th Cir. 1989)). Similarly, sexual offenses against a child, such as child molestation, can be "crimes of violence" because of the fear of the potential for force which is inherent in the disparate status of the perpetrator and victim and also because evidence of severe and persistent emotional trauma in its victims gives testament to the molestation being unwanted and coercive (see *United States v. Reyes-Castro*, 13 F.3d 377 (10th Cir. 1993)). Sexual offenses against other vulnerable persons would similarly be treated as "crimes of violence," as would, for example, forcible sex offenses against adults and sex offenses against incapacitated adults. Finally, an act of violence exists where the victim is physically injured, is threatened with physical injury, or reasonably believes he or she is being physically threatened by criminal activity of the defendant. For example, a victim who is killed or injured by a driver who is under the influence of alcohol or drugs is the victim of a crime of violence, as is a victim of stalking or other threats who is reasonably put in fear of his or her safety. Also, crimes of arson involving threats to the safety of persons could be "crimes of violence."

Of course, not all crimes will be "violent" crimes covered by the amendment. For example, the amendment does not confer rights on victims of larceny, fraud, and other similar offenses. At the same time, many States have already extended rights to victims of such offenses and the amendment in no way restricts such rights. In other words, the amendment sets a national "floor" for the protecting of victims rights, not any sort of "ceiling." Legislatures, including Congress, are certainly free to give statutory rights to all victims of crime, and the amendment will in all likelihood be an occasion for victims' statutes to be re-examined and, in some cases, expanded.

Because of the formulation used in the amendment—"a victim of a crime of violence"—it is presumed that there must be an identifiable victim. Some crimes, such as drug or espionage offenses, do not ordinarily have such an identifiable victim and therefore would not ordinarily be covered by the amendment. However, in some unusual cases, a court or legislature might conclude that these offenses in fact "involved" violence against an identifiable victim. For example, treason or espionage against the United States resulting in death or injury to an American government official might produce an identifiable victim protected by the amendment.

"To reasonable notice of . . . any public proceedings relating to the crime"

To make victims aware of the proceedings at which their rights can be exercised, this provision requires that victims be notified of public proceedings relating to a crime. "Notice" can be provided in a variety of fashions. For example, the Committee was informed that some States have developed computer programs for mailing form notices to victims while other States have developed automated telephone notification systems. Any means that provides reasonable notice to victims is acceptable. "Reasonable" notice is any means likely to provide actual notice to a victim. Heroic measures need not be taken to inform victims, but due diligence is required by government actors. It would, of course, be reasonable to require victims to provide an address and keep that address updated in order to receive notices. "Reasonable" notice would be notice that permits a meaningful opportunity for victims to exercise their rights. In rare mass victim cases (i.e., those involving hundreds of victims), reasonable notice could be provided to mean tailored to those unusual circumstances, such as notification by newspaper or television announcement.

Victims are given the right to receive notice of "proceedings." Proceedings are official events that take place before, for example, trial and appellate courts (including magistrates and special masters) and parole boards. They include, for example, hearings of all types such as motion hearings, trials, and sentencings. They do not include, for example, informal meetings between prosecutors and defense attorneys. Thus, while victims are entitled to notice of a court hearing on whether to accept a negotiated plea, they are not entitled to notice of an office meeting between a prosecutor and a defense attorney to discuss such an arrangement.

Victims' rights under this provision are also limited to "public" proceedings. Some proceedings, such as grand jury investigations, are not open to the public and accordingly would not be open to the victim. Other proceedings, while generally open, may be closed in some circumstances. For example, while plea proceedings are generally open to the public, a court might decide to close a proceeding in which an organized crime underling would plead guilty and agree to testify against his bosses. Another example is provided by certain national security cases in which access to some proceedings can be restricted (see The Classified Information Procedures Act, 18 U.S.C. app). 3. A victim would have no special right to attend. The amendment works no change in the standards for closing hearings, but rather simply recognizes that such nonpublic hearings take place. Of course, nothing in the amendment would forbid the court, in its discretion, to allow a victim to attend even such a nonpublic hearing.

The public proceedings are those "relating to the crime." Typically these would be the criminal proceedings arising from the filed criminal charges, although other proceedings might also relate to the crime. Thus, the right applies not only to initial hearings on a case, but also rehearings, hearing at an appellate level, and any case on a subsequent remand. It also applies to multiple hearings, such as multiple bail hearings. In cases involving multiple defendants, notice would be given as to proceedings involving each defendant.

"... not to be excluded from ... any public proceedings relating to the crime"

Victims are given the right "not to be excluded" from public proceedings. This builds on the 1982 recommendation from the President's Task Force on Victims of Crime that victims "no less than the defendant, have a legitimate interest in the fair adjudication of the case, and should therefore, as an exception to the general rule providing for the exclusion of witnesses, be permitted to be present for the entire trial" (*President's Task Force on Victims of Crime*, 80).

The right conferred is a negative one—a right "not to be excluded"—to avoid the suggestion that an alternative formulation—a right "to attend"—might carry with it some government obligation to provide funding, to schedule the timing of a particular proceeding according to the victim's wishes, or otherwise assert affirmative efforts to make it possible for a victim to attend proceedings (*Accord* Ala. Code Sec. 15-14-54, right "not [to] be excluded from court or counsel table during the trial or hearing or any portion thereof ... which in any way pertains to such offense"). The amendment, for example, would not entitle a prisoner who was attacked in prison to a release from prison and plane ticket to enable him to attend the trial of his attacker. This example is important because there have been occasional suggestions that transporting prisoners who are the victims of prison violence to courthouses to exercise their rights as victims might create security risks. These suggestions are misplaced, because the Crime Victims' Rights Amendment does not confer on prisoners any such rights to travel outside prison gates. Of course, as discussed below, prisoners no less than other victims will have a right to be "heard, if present, and to submit a statement" at various points in the criminal justice process. Because prisoners ordinarily will not be "present," they will exercise their rights by submitting a "statement." This approach has been followed in the states (see, e.g., Utah Code Ann. 77-38-5(8); Ariz. Const. Art. II, Section 2.1).

A victim's right not to be excluded will parallel the right of a defendant to be present during criminal proceedings (see *Diaz v. United States*, 223 U.S. 442, 454-55 (1912)). It is understood that defendants have no license to engage in disruptive behavior during proceedings (see, e.g., *Illinois v. Allen*, 397 U.S. 337 (1977)); *Foster v. Wainwright*, 686 F.2d 1382, 1387 (11th Cir. 1982)). Likewise, crime victims will have no right to engage in disruptive behavior and, like defendants, will have to follow proper court rules, such as those forbidding excessive displays of emotion or visibly reacting to testimony of witnesses during a jury trial.

Right "to be heard, if present, and to submit a statement at all public proceedings to determine a conditional release from custody, an acceptance of a negotiated plea, or a sentence. ..."

The amendment confers on crime victims a right to be heard by the relevant decision makers at three critical points in the criminal justice process before the final decisions are made.

First, crime victims will have the right to be heard at proceedings "to determine a conditional release from custody." Under this provision, for example, a victim of domestic violence will have the opportunity to warn the court about possible violence if the defendant is released on bail, probation, or parole. A victim of gang violence will have the opportunity to warn about the possibility of witness intimidation. The court will then evaluate this information in the normal fashion in determining whether to release a defendant and, if so, under what conditions. Victims have no right to "veto" any release decision by a court, simply to provide relevant information that the court can consider in making its determination about release.

The amendment extends the right to be heard to proceedings determining a "conditional release" from custody. This phrase encompasses, for example, hearings to determine any pre-trial or post-trial release (including comparable releases during or after an appeal) on bail, personal recognizance, to the custody of a third person, or under any other conditions, including pre-trial diversion programs. Other examples of conditional release include work release and home detention. It also includes parole hearings or their functional equivalent, both because parole hearings have some discretion in releasing offenders and because releases from prison are typically subject to various conditions such as continued good behavior. It would also include a release from a secure mental facility for a criminal defendant or one acquitted on the grounds of insanity. A victim would not have a right to speak, by virtue of this amendment, at a hearing to determine "unconditional" release. For example, a victim could not claim a right to be heard at a hearing to determine the jurisdiction of the court or compliance with the governing statute of limitations, even though a finding in favor of the defendant on these points might indirectly and ultimately lead to the "release" of the defendant. Similarly, there is no right to be heard when a prisoner is released after serving the statutory maximum penalty, or the full term of his sentence. In such circumstances, there would be no proceeding to "determine" a release in such situations and the release would also be without condition if the court's authority over the prisoner had expired. The victim would, however, be notified of such a release, as explained in connection with the victims' right to notice of a release.

Second, crime victims have the right to be heard at any proceedings to determine "an acceptance of a negotiated plea." This gives victims the right to be heard before the court accepts a plea bargain entered into by the prosecution and the defense before it becomes final. The Committee expects that each State will determine for itself at what stage this right attaches. It may be that a State decides the right does not attach until sentencing if the plea can still be rejected by the court after the pre-sentence investigation is completed. As the language makes clear, the right involves being heard when the court holds its hearing on whether to accept a plea. Thus, victims do not have the right to be heard by prosecutors and defense attorneys negotiating a deal. Nonetheless, the Committee anticipates that prosecutors may decide, in their discretion, to consult with victims before arriving at a plea. Such an approach is already a legal requirement in many States (see National Victim Center 1996, 127–31), is followed by many prosecuting agencies (see, e.g., Senate Judiciary Committee Hearing, April 28, 1998, statement of Paul Cassell), and has been encouraged as sound prosecutorial practice (see *New Directions from the Field,*

15–16). This trend has also been encouraged by the interest of some courts in whether prosecutors have consulted with the victim before arriving at a plea. Once again, the victim is given no right of veto over any plea. No doubt, some victims may wish to see nothing less than the maximum possible penalty (or minimum possible) for a defendant. Under the amendment, the court will receive this information, along with that provided by prosecutors and defendants, and give it the weight it believes is appropriate in deciding whether to accept a plea. The decision to accept a plea is typically vested in the court and therefore the victims' right extends to these proceedings (see, e.g., Fed. R. Crim. Pro. 11(d)(3); see generally Beloof 1998, 7-30 to 7-63).

Third, crime victims have the right to be heard at any proceeding to determine a "sentence." This provision guarantees that victims will have the right to "allocute" at sentencing. Defendants have a constitutionally protected interest in personally addressing the court (see *Green v. United States*, 365 U.S. 301 (1961)). This provision would give the same rights to victims, for two independent reasons. First, such a right guarantees that the sentencing court or jury will have full information about the impact of a crime, along with other information, in crafting an appropriate sentence. The victim would be able to provide information about the nature of the offense, the harm inflicted, and the attitude of the offender. Second, the opportunity for victims to speak at sentencing can sometimes provide a powerful catharsis (see *United States v. Smith*, 893 F. Supp. 187, 188 (E.D.N.Y. 1995);*United States v. Hollman Cheung*, 952 F. Supp. 148, 151 (E.D.N.Y. 1997)). Because the right to speak is based on both of these grounds, a victim will have the right to be heard even when the judge has no discretion in imposing a mandatory prison sentence.

State and Federal statutes already frequently provide allocution rights to victims (see, e.g., Fed. R. Evid. 32(c), Ill. Const. Art. 1, Sec. 8.1(a)(4)). The Federal amendment would help to insure that these rights are fully protected. The result is to enshrine in the Constitution the Supreme Court's decision in *Payne v. Tennessee*, 501 U.S. 808 (1991), recognizing the propriety of victim testimony in capital proceedings. At the same time, the victim's right to be heard at sentencing will not be unlimited, just as the defendant's right to be heard at sentencing is not unlimited today. Congress and the States remain free to set certain limits on what is relevant victim impact testimony. For example, a jurisdiction might determine that a victims' views on the desirability or undesirability of a capital sentence is not relevant in a capital proceeding (Cf. *Robison v. Maynard*, 943 F.2d 1216 (10th Cir. 1991, concluding that victim opinion on death penalty not admissible)). The Committee does not intend to alter or comment on laws existing in some States allowing for victim opinion as to the proper sentence. Also, a right to have victim impact testimony heard at sentencing does not confer any right to have such testimony heard by a jury at trial (see *Sager v. Maass*, 907 F. Supp. 1412, 1420 (D. Or. 1995) (citing cases)). The victim's right to be heard does not extend to the guilt determination phase of trials, although victims may, of course, be called as a witness by either party (Cf. Fletcher 1995).

The victim's right is one to "be heard, if present, and to submit a statement." The right to make an oral statement is conditioned on the victim's presence in the courtroom. As discussed above, it does not confer on victims a right to have the

Government transport them to the relevant proceeding. Nor does it give victims any right to "filibuster" any hearing. As with defendants' existing rights to be heard, a court may set reasonable limits on the length and content of statements. At the same time, victims should always be given the power to determine the form of the statement. Simply because a decisionmaking body, such as the court or parole board, has a prior statement of some sort on file does not mean that the victim should not again be offered the opportunity to make a further statement.

Even if not present, the victim is entitled to submit a "statement" at the specified hearings for the consideration of the court. The Committee has not limited the word statement to "written" statements, because the victim may wish to communicate in other appropriate ways. For example, a victim might desire to present an impact statement through a videotape or via an Internet message over a system established by the courts. The term "statement" is sufficiently flexible to encompass such communications.

The right to be heard is also limited to "such proceedings," that is, to "such [public] proceedings." As discussed previously at greater length, a victim has no right to be heard at a proceeding that the court has properly closed under the existing standards governing court closures.

Right to "the foregoing rights at a parole proceeding that is not public, to the extent those rights are afforded to the convicted offender"

The right to be heard at public proceedings to determine a conditional release confers on victims the right to be heard at public parole proceedings. In some jurisdictions, however, parole decisions are not made in public proceedings, but rather in other ways. For such jurisdictions, the amendment places victims on equal footing with defendants. If defendants have the right to provide communications with the paroling or releasing authority, then victims do as well. For example, in some jurisdictions the parole board might review various folders on prisoners in making a parole decision. If the defendant is given an opportunity to provide information for inclusion in those folders, so will the victim. The phrase "the foregoing rights" encompasses all of the previously listed rights in the amendment, including the right to notice, to not be excluded, and to be heard, if present, and to submit a statement.

The term *parole* is intended to be interpreted broadly. Many jurisdictions are moving away from "parole" but still have a form of conditional release. The term also encompasses comparable hearings on conditional release from secure mental facilities.

Right to "reasonable notice of a release or escape from custody relating to the crime"

To ensure that the victim is not surprised or threatened by an escaped or released prisoner, the amendment gives victims a right to reasonable notice of such escape or release. As with other notice rights in the amendment, the requirement is not one of extraordinary measures, but instead of "reasonable" notice. As with the phrase used earlier in the amendment, "reasonable" notice is one likely to provide actual notice. New technologies are becoming more widely available that will simplify the process of providing this notice. For example, automated voice response technology exists that can be programmed to place repeated telephone calls to victims whenever a prisoner is released, which would be reasonable notice of the release. As technology improves in this area, what is "reasonable" may change as well. "Reasonable" notice would also need to be considered in light of the circumstances surrounding the case. While mailing a letter would be "reasonable" notice of an upcoming parole release date, it would not be reasonable notice of the escape of a dangerous prisoner bent on taking revenge on his accuser.

The requirement of notice is limited to a "release from custody." Thus, victims are not entitled to notice under this amendment if, for example, a prisoner is simply moved from one custodial facility to another, reclassified in terms of his security level, or allowed to participate in a supervised work detail outside the prison walls. Victims are, however, entitled to notice of any government decision to finally or conditionally release a prisoner, such as allowing a prisoner to enter a noncustodial work release program or to take a weekend furlough in his old home town.

The release must be one "relating to the crime." This includes not only a release after a criminal conviction but also, for example, a release of a defendant found not guilty of a crime by reason of insanity and then hospitalized in custody for further treatment, or a release pursuant to a habitual sex offender statute.

Right to "consideration of the interest of the victim that any trial be free from unreasonable delay"

Just as defendants currently have a right to a "speedy trial," this provision will give victims a protected right in having their interests to a reasonably prompt conclusion of a trial considered. The right here requires courts to give "consideration" to the victims' interest along with other relevant factors at all hearings involving the trial date, including the initial setting of a trial date and any subsequent motions or proceedings that result in delaying that date. This right also will allow the victim to ask the court to, for instance, set a trial date if the failure to do so is unreasonable. Of course, the victims' interests are not the only interests that the court will consider. Again, while a victim will have a right to be heard on the issue, the victim will have no right to force an immediate trial before the parties have had an opportunity to prepare. Similarly, in some complicated cases either prosecutors or defendants may have unforeseen and legitimate reasons for continuing a previously set trial or for delaying trial proceedings that have already commenced. But the Committee has heard ample testimony about delays that, by any measure, were "unreasonable" (see, e.g., Senate Judiciary Committee Hearing, April 16, 1997, statement of Paul Cassell, at 115–16). This right will give courts the clear constitutional mandate to avoid such delays.

In determining what delay is "unreasonable," the courts can look to the precedents that exist interpreting a defendant's right to a speedy trial. These cases focus on such issues as the length of the delay, the reason for the delay, any assertion of a right to a speedy trial, and any prejudice to the defendant (see *Barker v. Wingo*, 407 U.S. 514, 530-33 (1972)). Courts will no doubt develop a similar approach for evaluating victims' claims. In developing such an approach, courts will undoubtably recognize the purposes that the victim's right is designed to serve (Cf. *Barker v. Wingo*, 407 U.S. 514, 532 (1972, defendant's right to a speedy trial must be "assessed in the light of the interest of defendant which the speedy trial right was designed to protect")). The Committee intends for this right to allow victims to have the trial of the accused completed as quickly as is reasonable under all of the circumstances of the case, giving both the prosecution and the defense a reasonable period of time to prepare. The right would not require or permit a judge to proceed to trial if a criminal defendant is not adequately represented by counsel.

The Committee also anticipates that more content may be given to this right in implementing legislation. For example, the Speedy Trial Act of 1974 (Pub. L. 93-619 (amended by Pub. L. 96-43), codified at 18 U.S.C. Sec. 3152, 3161) already helps to protect a defendant's speedy trial right. Similar legislative protection could be extended to the victims' new parallel right.

Right to "an order of restitution from the convicted offender"

This provision recognizes that an offender should be held responsible for the harm his crime caused, through an order of restitution at sentencing. The Committee has previously explained this philosophy in some detail in connection with the Mandatory Victim Restitution Act, codified at 18 U.S.C. Sec. 3663A and 3664, and intends that this right operate in a similar fashion. The relevant details will be spelled out under the resulting case law or, more likely, statutes to implement the amendment. However, this amendment does not confer on victims any rights to a specific amount of restitution, leaving the court free to order nominal restitution if there is no hope of satisfying the order nor any rights with regard to a particular payment schedule.

The right conferred on victims is one to an "order" of restitution. With the order in hand, questions of enforcement of the order and its priority as against other judgments are left to the applicable Federal or State law. No doubt in a number of cases the defendant will lack the resources to satisfy the full order. In others, however, the defendant may have sufficient assets to do so and this right will place such an order in the victim's hands. The right is, of course, limited to "convicted" defendants, that is, those who pled guilty, are found guilty, or enter a plea of no contest. Even before a conviction, however, courts remain free to take appropriate steps to prevent a defendant's deliberate dissipation of his assets for the purpose of defeating a restitution order, as prescribed by current law.

A right to "consideration for the safety of the victim in determining any conditional release from custody relating to the crime"

This right requires judges, magistrates, parole boards, and other such officials to consider the safety of the victim in determining any conditional release. As with the right to be heard on conditional releases, this right will extend to hearings to determine any pre-trial or post-trial release on bail, personal recognizance, to the custody of a third person, on work release, to home detention, or under any other conditions as well as parole hearings or their functional equivalent. At such hearings, the decisionmaker must give consideration to the safety of the victim in determining whether to release a defendant and, if so, whether to impose various conditions on that release to help protect the victims' safety, such as requiring the posting of higher bail or forbidding the defendant to have contact with the victim. These conditions can then be enforced through the judicial processes currently in place.

This right does not require the decisionmaker to agree with any conditions that the victim might propose (or, for that matter, to agree with a victim that defendant should be released unconditionally). Nor does this right alter the Eighth Amendment's prohibition of "excessive bail" or any other due process guarantees to which a defendant or prisoner is entitled in having his release considered. The Supreme Court, however, has already rejected constitutional challenges to pretrial detention, in appropriate circumstances, to protect community safety, including the safety of victims (see *United States v. Salerno*, 481 U.S. 739 (1987)). This right simply guarantees victim input into a process that has been constitutionally validated.

Custody here includes mental health facilities. This is especially important as sex offenders are frequently placed in treatment facilities, following or in lieu of prison.

Right to "reasonable notice of the rights established by this article."

In the special context of the criminal justice system, victims particularly need knowledge of their rights. Victims are thrust into the vortex of complicated legal proceedings. Accordingly, the final right guaranteed by the amendment is the right to notice of victims rights. Various means have been devised for providing such notice in the States, and the Committee trusts that these means can be applied to the Federal amendment with little difficulty.

Once again, "reasonable" notice is one likely to provide actual notice. In cases involving victims with special needs, such as those who are hearing impaired or illiterate, officials may have to make special efforts in order for notice to be reasonable. Notice, whether of rights, proceedings, or events, should be given as soon as practicable to allow victims the greatest opportunity to exercise their rights.

Section 2. Only the victim or the victim's lawful representative shall have standing to assert the rights established by this article

This provision confers on victims and their lawful representatives standing to assert their rights. The term "standing" is used here in its conventional legal sense as giving victims the opportunity to be heard about their treatment, that is, to have the merits of their claims considered. For example, under this provision victims have the right to challenge their exclusion from the trial of the accused perpetrators of the crime. This overrules the approach adopted by some courts of denying victims an opportunity to raise claims about their treatment (see, e.g., *United States v. McVeigh*, 106 F.3d 325, 334-35 (10th Cir. 1997, finding victims of the Oklahoma City bombing lacked standing to challenge their exclusion from certain proceedings)). The provision is phrased in exclusive terms—"Only the victim or the victim's lawful representatives"—to avoid any suggestion that other, potentially intermeddling, persons have the right to be heard in criminal proceedings, and to avoid the suggestion that the accused or convicted offender has standing to assert the rights of the victim.

There will be circumstances in which victims find it desirable to have a representative assert their rights or make statements on their behalf. This provision recognizes the right of a competent victim to choose a representative to exercise his or her rights, as provided by law. Typically victims' rights statutes have provided a means through which victims can select their representatives without great difficulty.

Other "lawful representatives" will exist in the context of victims who are deceased, are children, or are otherwise incapacitated. In homicide cases, victim's rights can be asserted by surviving family members or other persons found to be appropriate by the court. This is the approach that has uniformly been adopted in victims' rights statutes applicable in homicide cases, thus insuring that in this most serious of crimes a voice for a victim continues to be heard. Of course, in such cases the "lawful representative" would not necessarily be someone who was the executor of the estate, but rather someone involved in issues pertaining to the criminal justice process. In cases involving child victims, a parent, guardian or other appropriate representative can do the same. For victims who are physically or mentally unable to assert their rights, an appropriate representative can assert the rights.

In all circumstances involving a "representative," care must be taken to ensure that the "representative" truly reflects the interests—and only the interests—of the victim. In particular, in no circumstances should the representative be criminally involved in the crime against the victim. The mechanics for dealing with such issues and, more generally, for the designation of "lawful" representatives will be provided by law—that is, by statute in relevant jurisdiction, or in its absence by court rule or decision.

"Nothing in this article shall provide grounds to stay or continue any trial, reopen any proceeding or invalidate any ruling, except with respect to conditional release or restitution or to provide rights guaranteed by this article in future proceedings, without staying or continuing a trial."

This provision is designed to protect completed criminal proceedings against judicially-created remedies that might interfere with finality. At the same time, the provision leaves open appropriate avenues for victims to challenge violations of their rights as well as the ability of Congress and the States to provide additional remedies.

In drafting the amendment, the Committee was faced with balancing the competing concerns of giving victims an effective means of enforcing their rights and of ensuring that court decisions retain a reasonable degree of finality. The Committee was concerned that, if victims could challenge and overturn all criminal justice proceedings at which their rights were violated, the goal of finality, and conceivably other goals, could be seriously frustrated. On the other hand, the Committee recognized that if victims were never given an opportunity to challenge previously-taken judicial actions, victims' rights might remain routinely ignored. The Committee's solution to the dilemma was to leave the issue of the most controversial remedies to the legislative branches. These branches have superior fact finding capabilities, as well as abilities to craft necessary exceptions and compromises. Thus, the provision provides that "Nothing in this article" shall provide grounds for victims to challenge and overturn certain previously taken judicial actions.

The provision prevents judicially-created remedies "to stay or continue any trial" because of the concern that a broad judicial remedy might allow victims to inappropriately interfere with trials already underway. The provision also prevents judicially-created remedies to "reopen any proceeding or invalidate any ruling" because of similar finality concerns. At the same time, however, the provision recognizes that victims can reopen earlier rulings "with respect to conditional release or restitution." In these particular areas, judicially created rules will allow victims to challenge, for example, a decision made to release a defendant on bail without consideration of the victim's safety. Similarly, victims are specifically allowed to challenge a ruling "to provide rights guaranteed by this article in future proceedings, without staying or continuing a trial." For example, in what will presumably be the rare case of a victim improperly excluded from a trial, a victim could seek an immediate expedited review of the decision under the existing rules allowing for expedited review, seeking admission to "future proceedings," that is, to upcoming days of the trial. Similarly, a victim who wishes to challenge a ruling that she is not entitled to notice of a release or escape of a prisoner can challenge that ruling until the release or escape takes place. Of course, limits on the ability of victims to "invalidate" a court ruling do not forbid a victim from asking a court to reconsider its own ruling or restrict a court from changing its own ruling.

"Nothing in this article shall give rise to or authorize the creation of a claim for damages against the United States, a State, a political subdivision, or a public officer or employee."

This provision imposes the conventional limitations on victims' rights, providing that the amendment does not give rise to any claim for money damages against governmental entities or their employees or agents. While some existing victims' rights provisions provide for the possibility of damage actions or fines as an enforcement mechanism in limited circumstances (see, e.g., Ariz. Rev. Stat. Ann. Sec. 13-4437(B), authorizing suit for "intentional, knowing, or grossly negligent violation" of victims rights), the Committee does not believe that consensus exists in support of such a provision in a Federal amendment. Similar limiting language barring damages actions is found in many state victims' rights amendments (see, e.g., Kan. Const. Art. 15, 15(b), "Nothing in this section shall be construed as creating a cause of action for money damages against the state. . . ."); Mo Const. Art. 1, 32(3), (5) (similar); Tex. Const. Art. I, 30(e), "The legislature may enact laws to provide that a judge, attorney for the State, peace officer, or law enforcement agency is not liable for a failure or inability to provide a right enumerated in this section"). The limiting language in the provision also prevents the possibility that the amendment might be construed by courts as requiring the appointment of counsel at State expense to assist victims (Cf. *Gideon v. Wainwright*, 372 U.S. 335 (1963), requiring counsel for indigent criminal defendants).

This provision in no way affects—by way of enlargement or contraction—any existing rights that may exist now or be created in the future independent of the amendment.

The Congress shall have the power to enforce this article by appropriate legislation

This provision is similar to existing language found in section 5 of the 14th amendment to the Constitution. This provision will be interpreted in similar fashion to allow Congress to "enforce" the rights, that is, to insure that the rights conveyed by the amendment are in fact respected. At the same time, consistent with the plain language of the provision, the Federal Government and the States will retain their power to implement the amendment. For example, the States will, subject to the Supremacy Clause, flesh out the contours of the amendment by providing definitions of "victims" of crime and "crimes of violence."

Exceptions to the rights established by this article may be created only when necessary to achieve a compelling interest

Constitutional rights are not absolute. There is no first amendment right, for example, to yell "Fire!" in a crowded theater. Courts interpreting the Crime Victims' Rights Amendment will no doubt give a similar, commonsense construction to its provisions.

To assist in providing necessary flexibility for handling unusual situations, the exceptions language in the amendment explicitly recognizes that in certain rare circumstances exceptions may need to be created to victims' rights. By way of example, the Committee expects the language will encompass the following situations.

First, in mass victim cases, there may be a need to provide certain limited exceptions to victims rights. For instance, for a crime perpetrated against hundreds of victims, it may be impractical or even impossible to give all victims the right to be physically present in the courtroom. In such circumstances, an exception to the right to be present may be made, while at the same time providing reasonable accommodation for the interest of victims. Congress, for example, has specified a close-circuit broadcasting arrangement that may be applicable to some such cases. Similar restrictions on the number of persons allowed to present oral statements might be appropriate in rare cases involving large numbers of victims.

Second, in some cases of domestic violence, the dynamics of victim–offender relationships may require some modification of otherwise typical victims' rights provisions. This provision offers the flexibility to do just that.

Third, situations may arise involving intergang violence, where notifying the member of a rival gang of an offenders' impending release may spawn retaliatory violence. Again, this provision provides flexibility for dealing with such situations.

While this exceptions clause adds some flexibility, the Committee-reported amendment provides that exceptions are permitted only for a "compelling" interest. In choosing this standard, formulated by the U.S. Supreme Court, the Committee seeks to ensure that the exception does not swallow the rights. The Committee rejected proposed language that would have lowered the required justification for an exception from the settled standard of "compelling interest" to the novel standard of "significant interest."

This article shall take effect on the 180th day after the ratification of this article. The right to an order of restitution established by this article shall not apply to crimes committed before the effective date of this article

The Committee has included a 180 day "grace period" for the amendment to allow all affected jurisdictions ample opportunity to prepare to implement the amendment. After the period has elapsed, the amendment will apply to all crimes and proceedings thereafter. The one exception that the Committee made was for orders of restitution. A few courts have held that retroactive application of changes in standards governing restitution violates the Constitution's prohibition of ex post facto laws (see, e.g., *United States v. Williams*, 128 F.3d 1239 (8th Cir. 1997)). The Committee agrees with those courts that have taken the contrary view that, because restitution is not intended to punish offenders but to compensate victims, ex post facto considerations are misplaced (see, e.g., *United States v. Newman*, No. 97-3246 (7th Cir. 1998)). However, to avoid slowing down the conclusion of cases pending at the time of the amendment's ratification, the language on restitution orders was added.

The rights and immunities established by this article shall apply in Federal and State proceedings, including military proceedings to the extent that the Congress may provide by law, juvenile justice proceedings, and proceedings in the District of Columbia and any commonwealth, territory, or possession of the United States.

This provision extends the amendment to all State and Federal criminal justice proceedings. Because of the complicated nature of military justice proceedings, including proceedings held in times of war, the extension of victims' rights to the military was left to Congress. The Committee intends to protect victims' rights in military justice proceedings while not adversely affecting military operations. This provision also extends victims' rights to all juvenile justice proceedings that are comparable to criminal proceedings, even though these proceedings might be given a noncriminal label. On this point, the Committee believes that "[t]he rights of victims of juvenile offenders should mirror the rights of victims of adult offenders" (*New Directions From the Field*, 22).

Vote of the Committee

The committee met on five occasions to consider S.J. Res. 44, on June 18, 24, 25, 1998 and twice on July 7, 1998. On July 7, 1998, Senator Kyl offered a substitute amendment, which was agreed to by unanimous consent. Two additional amendments were offered, but were defeated by rollcall votes. The Committee agreed to favorably report the S.J. Res. 44 to the full Senate, with an amendment in the nature of a substitute, on July 7, 1998, by a rollcall vote of 11 yeas to 6 nays....

* * *

Minority views of Senators Leahy, Kennedy, and Kohl

Introduction

Never before in the history of the Republic have we passed a constitutional amendment to guarantee rights to one group of citizens at the expense of a powerless minority. Never before in the history of the Republic have we passed a constitutional amendment to guarantee rights that every State is already scrambling to protect. Never before in the history of the Republic have we passed a constitutional amendment to guarantee rights that intrude so technically into such a wide area of law, and with such serious implications for the Bill of Rights.

This amendment is not, however, without precedent. There has been one instance in our history in which we amended the Constitution without carefully thinking through the consequences. Andrew Volstead led the Congress to passage of the 18th amendment, and opened a Pandora's box of unintended consequences. The 18th amendment was appealing and entirely well meaning. It also was an utter failure that the American people were required to undo with the 21st amendment.

The disaster of Prohibition should remind us that constitutional amendments based on sentiment are a dangerous business. It would be well for Congress to heed the words of James Madison, when he urged that amendments be reserved for "certain great and extraordinary occasions," and to heed the text of Article V, which reserves amendments for things that are "necessary."

The treatment of crime victims certainly is of central importance to a civilized society, and we must never simply "pass by on the other side." The question is not whether we should help victims, but how. It long has been and is now open to Congress immediately to pass a statute that would provide full victims' right throughout the Federal system, and at the same time provide the resources necessary to assist the States in giving force to their own, locally-tailored statutes and constitutional provisions. Instead, the proponents of S.J. Res. 44 invite Congress to delay relief for victims with a complex and convoluted amendment to our fundamental law that is less a remedy than another Pandora's box which, like the 18th amendment, will loose a host of unintended consequences and ultimately force the American people to elect a Congress to undo this mischief with another constitutional amendment.

The majority appears to believe that it can control some of the inevitable damage through explications in the Committee report about how the amendment will operate. We doubt that the courts will care much for such efforts. They will look first to the plain meaning of the text of the amendment. They will seek guidance in Supreme Court precedents interpreting provisions using similar language. They will not resort to the majority report to interpret wording that is clearly understood in current legal and political circles.

Any interpretative value of the majority report is further undermined by the inconsistency of the document, which in some situations narrows the impact of the amendment (e.g., by construing away the unpopular consequences for battered women and incarcerated victims) and in other circumstances expands the impact of the amendment (e.g., by devising a role for States in implementing the amendment and conjuring up a way for victims to sue for damages). Such inconsistency renders the majority report politically expedient, but legally meaningless. Weaknesses in the text of the amendment cannot with any confidence be cured by the majority's views, especially not when the majority's analysis is so directly at odds with the amendment's plain language and with settled constitutional doctrine.

It is not necessary to amend the constitution to protect victims' rights

Every proposal to amend our Federal Constitution bears a very heavy burden. Amendment is appropriate only when there is a pressing need that cannot be addressed by other means. No such need exists in order to protect the rights of crime victims. The proposed amendment therefore fails the standard contained in Article V of the Constitution: it is not "necessary."

Congress and the states have the power to protect victims' rights without a federal constitutional amendment

Nothing in our current Constitution inhibits the enactment of State or Federal laws that protect crime victims. On the contrary, the Constitution is generally supportive of efforts to give victims a greater voice in the criminal justice system. No Victims' Rights Amendment was necessary, for example, to secure a role for victims at pretrial detention and capital sentencing hearings (*United States v. Salerno*, 481 U.S. 739 (1987), due process and excessive bail clauses do not prohibit courts from considering safety of victims in making pretrial detention decision); *Payne v. Tennessee*, 501 U.S. 808 (1991), Eighth Amendment does not prohibit jury from considering victim impact statement at sentencing phase of capital trial).

A letter sent to Chairman Hatch by over 450 professors of constitutional and criminal law states that "[v]irtually every right contained in the proposed victims rights amendment can be safeguarded in federal and state laws" (Letter from Law Professors, reprinted in A Proposed Constitutional Amendment to Protect Victims of Crime, Hearing on S.J. Res. 6 before the Senate Comm. on the Judiciary, 105thCong., 1st Sess., at 140 (Apr. 16, 1997) [hereinafter "Hearing of Apr. 16, 1997"]).

* * *

We asked Professor Paul Cassell, another leading proponent of S.J. Res. 44, to list all the appellate cases in which a defendant's rights under the Federal Constitution were held to supersede a victim's rights under a Federal or State victims' rights provision. He failed to identify any. More recently, Professor Robert Mosteller challenged the pro-amendment participants in a symposium on victims' rights, including Professor Cassell, to provide such cases. They referred him to a single decision by an intermediate appellate court that would not be affected by passage of S.J. Res. 44 (see *Arizona ex rel. Romley v. Superior Court*, 836 P.2d 445 (Ariz. Ct. App. 1992)). Romley holds that a victim's right under the Arizona Constitution to refuse discovery requests by the defendant must yield to the defendant's due process right. Far from advancing the cause of constitutional amendment, however, the case illustrates the danger of empowering certain self-proclaimed victims at the expense of the unconvicted accused. . . .

Given our ability to proceed without amending the Constitution, one might reasonably wonder why so much time and effort has been expended on the project. We heard one explanation during the Committee markup. Quoting Professor Tribe, one of the amendment's sponsors told us that the "real problem" with existing statutes and State constitutional amendments is that they "provide too little real protection whenever they come into conflict with . . . bureaucratic habit, traditional indifference, sheer inertia, or any mention of an accused's rights, regardless of whether those rights are genuinely threatened" (Exec. Comm. Meeting, Senate Comm. on the Judiciary, 105th Cong., 2d Sess., at 23–24 (Jun. 25, 1998, statement of Sen. Jon L. Kyl). . . .

Have we so lost confidence in our ability to govern and to regulate the conduct of public officials sworn to follow the law that we now insist on amending our basic charter of government in order to overcome habit, indifference and inertia? Do we really believe that a constitutional amendment will accomplish this objective? Habit, indifference, inertia—none is automatically extinguished by the existence of a constitutional amendment. We are especially unlikely to defeat them with a constitutional amendment like S.J. Res. 44, which creates rights riddled with qualifications and exceptions and prohibits the award of damages for their violation.

Professor Lynne Henderson, herself a victim of a violent crime, told the Committee that what is needed are good training programs with adequate funding, not more empty promises (Statement of Lynne Henderson regarding S.J. Res. 6, prepared for the Senate Comm. on the Judiciary (Apr. 14, 1997)) . . .

Statutes are preferable to amending the federal constitution

We believe that ordinary legislation not only is sufficient to correct any deficiencies in the provision of victims' rights that currently exist, but also is vastly preferable to amending the Constitution. Indeed, the statutory approach is favored by a broad cross-section of the participants in the criminal justice system.

The U.S. Judicial Conference favors the statutory approach because it "would have the virtue of making any provisions in the bill which appeared mistaken by hindsight to be amended by a simple act of Congress" (Letter from William H. Rehnquist, Chief Justice, U.S. Supreme Court, to Judy Clarke, President, National Assn. of Criminal Defense Lawyers (Apr. 23, 1997))....

"Of critical importance, such an approach is significantly more flexible. It would more easily accommodate a measured approach, and allow for 'fine tuning' if deemed necessary or desirable by Congress after the various concepts in the Act are applied in actual cases across the country. At that point, Congress would have a much clearer picture of which concepts are effective, which are not, and which might actually be counterproductive" (Letter from George P. Kazen, Chief U.S. District Judge, Chair, Committee on Criminal Law of the Judicial Conference of the United States, to Sen. Edward M. Kennedy, Senate Comm on the Judiciary, at 2 (Apr. 17, 1997)).

The State courts also favor a statutory approach to protecting victims' rights. The Conference of Chief Justices has underscored "[t]he inherent prudence of a statutory approach," which could be refined as appropriate and "holds a more immediate advantage to victims who, under the proposed amendment approach, may wait years for relief during the lengthy and uncertain ratification process" (Statement of the Conference of Chief Justices regarding H.J. Res. 71 and H.R. 1322, prepared for the House Comm. on the Judiciary (June 25, 1997)).

Other major organizations, including several victims groups, concur. For example, the National Clearinghouse for the Defense of Battered Women says that statutory alternatives are "more suitable" to addressing the complex problems facing crime victims(Hearing of Apr. 16, 1997, at 161, 162, statement of National Clearinghouse for the Defense of Battered Women)....

The widespread support for enacting victims' rights by statute arises in part from evidence that statutes work—they can adequately ensure that victims of crimes are accorded important rights in the criminal justice process. We should not diminish the majesty of the Constitution of the United States when ordinary legislation is more easily enacted, more easily corrected or clarified, more directly applied and implemented, and more able to provide specific, effective remedies.

An extensive framework of victims' rights has already been created

In the past two decades, the victims' movement has made historic gains in addressing the needs of crime victims, on both the national and local level. An extensive framework of victims' rights has been created through Federal and State legislation and amendments to State constitutions. The majority report asserts, based on scant authority, that existing laws have not "fully succeeded" in ensuring "comprehensive" protection of victims' rights. But given the extraordinary political popularity of the victims' movement, there is every reason to believe that the legislative process will continue to be responsive to enhancing victims' interests, so that there is simply no need to amend the Constitution to accomplish this.

1. Federal crime victims initiatives

At the Federal level, Congress has enacted several major laws to grant broader protections and provide more extensive services for victims of crime. The first such legislation was the Victim and Witness Protection Act of 1982 (P.L. 97–291, Oct. 12, 1982, 96 Stat. 1248), which provided for victim restitution and the use of victim impact statements at sentencing in Federal cases, and the Victims of Crime Act of 1984 (P.L. 98–473, Title I, ch. XIV, Oct. 12, 1984, 99 Stat. 183), which encouraged the States to maintain programs that serve victims of crime. The Victims of Crime Act also established a Crime Victims' Fund, which matches 35 percent of the money paid by States for victim compensation awards.

In 1990, Congress enacted the Victims' Rights and Restitution Act (P.L. 101–647, Title V, Nov. 29, 1990, 104 Stat. 4789). This Act increased funding for victim compensation and assistance, and codified a victims' Bill of Rights in the Federal justice system. Federal law enforcement agencies must make their best efforts to accord crime victims with the following rights: (1) to be treated with fairness and respect; (2) to be protected from their accused offenders; (3) to be notified of court proceedings; (4) to be present at public court proceedings related to the offense under certain conditions; (5) to confer with the government attorney assigned to the case; (6) to receive restitution; and (7) to receive information about the conviction, sentencing, imprisonment, and release of the offender.

The Violence Against Women Act of 1994 (P.L. 103–322, Title IV, Sept. 13, 1994, 108 Stat. 179) made tens of millions of dollars available to the States through STOP (Services, Training, Officers, Prosecutors) grants for law enforcement, prosecution and victims services to prevent and respond to violence against women, including domestic violence. A recent study shows that STOP funds are being used for training of police and prosecutors, resulting in improved police handling of domestic violence incidents, interagency coordination, establishment of multi-disciplinary response teams, and higher conviction rates. Funds are also providing direct services to victims, resulting in increased victim cooperation and satisfaction (see 1998 Annual Report: Evaluation of the S.T.O.P. Formula Grants Under the Violence Against Women Act of 1994 (June 12, 1998)).

The Mandatory Victims Restitution Act of 1996 (P.L. 104–132, Title IIA, Apr. 24, 1996, 110 Stat. 121) required courts to order restitution when sentencing defendants for certain offenses. As part of the same crime bill, the Justice for Victims of Terrorism Act of 1996 (P.L. 104–132, Title IIC, Apr. 24, 1996, 110 Stat. 1214) appropriated funds to assist and compensate victims of terrorism and mass violence. The Act also filled a gap in our law for residents of the United States who are victims of terrorism and mass violence that occur outside the borders of the United States. In addition, Congress provided greater flexibility to our State and local victims' assistance programs and some greater certainty so they can know that our commitment to victims' programs will not wax and wane with current events. And we were able to raise the assessments on those convicted of Federal crimes in order to fund the needs of crime victims.

The Victim Rights Clarification Act of 1997 (P.L. 105–6, §2(a), Mar. 19, 1997, 111 Stat. 12) reversed a presumption against crime victims observing any part of the trial proceedings if they were likely to testify during the sentencing hearing. Specifically, this legislation prohibited courts from excluding victims from the trial on the ground that they might be called to provide a victim impact statement at the sentencing, and from excluding a victim impact statement on the ground that the victim had observed the trial. As a result of this legislation, victims of the Oklahoma City bombing were allowed both to observe the trial of Timothy McVeigh and to provide victim impact testimony.

Most recently, in this session, Congress passed the Crime Victims With Disabilities Awareness Act (S. 1976). This legislation will focus attention on the presently overlooked needs of crime victims with disabilities. It proposes to have the National Academy of Sciences conduct research so as to increase public awareness of victims of crimes with disabilities, to understand the nature and extent of such crimes, and to develop strategies to address the safety and needs of these peculiarly vulnerable victims.

Despite the gains that have been made through Federal statutes, some Members of Congress and some victims' rights groups continue to assert that statutes do not work to provide victims with certain participatory rights. For instance, during Committee deliberations on S.J. Res. 44 on June 25, 1998, two sponsors of the bill cited the Victim Rights Clarification Act as evidence that statutes cannot adequately protect a victim's rights. In particular, Senator Feinstein stated that the trial judge in the Oklahoma City bombing case "chose to ignore [the Act], just ignored it. . . . If the victim was present, the victim didn't have the right to make a statement. Senator Kyl made similar statements suggesting that Judge Matsch had refused to enforce the Act." Exec. Comm. Meeting, Senate Comm. on the Judiciary, 105th Cong., 2d Sess., at 16 (Jun. 25, 1998)

Given such assertions, we believe it important to look at how the Victim Right Clarification Act was actually applied in the Oklahoma City case. On June 26, 1996, Judge Matsch held that potential witnesses at any penalty hearing were excluded from pretrial proceedings and the trial to avoid any influence from that experience on their testimony. Congress proceeded to pass the Victim Rights Clarification Act, which the President signed into law on March 19, 1997. One week later, Judge Matsch reversed his exclusionary order and permitted observation of the trial proceedings by potential penalty phase victim impact witnesses (*United States v. McVeigh*, 958 F. Supp. 512, 515 (1997)). In other words, Judge Matsch did exactly what the statute told him to do. Not one victim was prevented from testifying at Timothy McVeigh's sentencing hearing on the ground that he or she had observed part of the trial.

So it is not accurate to assert that the Victim Rights Clarification Act did not work, or that statutes in general cannot adequately protect victims' rights. In fact, the Victim Rights Clarification Act is a paradigmatic example of how statutes, when properly crafted, can and do work. We are certain that additional clarifications would find judges equally receptive and willing to grant victims the rights Congress intends.

2. State crime victims initiatives

The individual States have also done their part in enhancing the role and protection of crime victims. Every State and the District of Columbia has some type of statutory provision providing for increased victims' rights, including some or all of the rights enumerated in S.J. Res. 44, as well as others. In addition, some 29 States have amended their State constitutions to provide a variety of protections and rights for crime victims.

While there may be room for improvement in the States' administration of their existing victims' rights laws, in general, victims and criminal justice personnel believe that these laws are sufficient to ensure victims' rights. For example, in 1989, the American Bar Association's Victim Witness Project analyzed the impact of State victims' rights laws on criminal justice practitioners and victims. The researchers found that prosecutors, judges, probation officers, and victim/witness advocates were almost universally satisfied with the State laws. They also found that those practitioners who had concerns about existing victims' rights provisions were generally dissatisfied with levels of funding for victims' services. With regard to victim satisfaction, the researchers concluded that "many victims in States with victims' rights legislation believe the criminal justice system is doing a satisfactory job of keeping them informed, providing them an opportunity to have a say in certain decisions and notifying them about case outcomes" (Hillenbrand and Smith 1989, 26).

Since 1989, States have continued to strengthen their victims' rights provisions and services. According to a 1997 report prepared by the National Criminal Justice Association with support from the Justice Department's Office for Victims of Crime ("OVC"): "It appears evident that the trend to expand the statutory rights of victims on the State level is continuing" (Office for Victims of Crime 1998)....

The majority report relies heavily on two recent studies that found current victims' rights laws inadequate. The first study was conducted by the National Victim Center ("NVC")—a strong proponent of a Victims' Rights Amendment (NVC 1997). Insofar as the NVC study can be read to have meaning, it suggests that it is money and additional State law provisions that are needed, not a Federal constitutional amendment. The "violations" it discusses are failures of enforcement, not instances of defendants' rights trumping the rights of victims.

The NVC study does not provide a clear picture of the impact of State victims' rights laws, however, because its methodology is seriously flawed. First, the researchers relied exclusively on uncorroborated reports by crime victims regarding their personal experiences; there was no attempt to verify that victims who claimed that they had been denied rights had, in fact, been denied rights. Second, the researchers surveyed victims in only four States—and they do not reveal which four States. Third, the researchers selected the four States based on a ranking of State statutory and constitutional victims rights provisions—but, again, they do not reveal what criteria they used for ranking the States. Fourth, the researchers concluded that State provisions are not enough because victims are not universally satisfied with the quality of treatment they receive. Yet the researchers did not appear to take into consideration important factors such as the structure of the various bureaucracies or the availability of financial resources or the levels of training among State criminal justice personnel, all of which may have a dramatic impact on the treatment of victims from State to State and may be significantly related to victim dissatisfaction. Such manifest flaws in the NVC's methodology led the OVC to conclude that "more research would be needed before any policy recommendations could be made based on the data" (Letter from Kathryn M. Turman, Acting Director, OVC, to Robert P. Mosteller, Professor, Duke University School of Law (Sept. 18, 1998)). An earlier intra-office memorandum memorializes the Justice Department's wish that the complete report not be published at all (Memorandum from Sam McQuade, Program Manager, National Institute of Justice, to Jeremy Travis, Director, National Institute of Justice (May 16, 1997), "OVC has requested that the complete report NOT be published because, in its view, the report contains contradictory information. * * *"; emphasis in original).

The second study cited in the majority report was compiled by the OVC based on anecdotal information from "the field"—that is, "crime victims themselves and representatives of the agencies and organizations that serve them" (*New Directions from the Field* vii). Once again, however, the deficiencies identified in the study—deficiencies in the implementation of State victims' rights laws and in the scope of some States' provisions—can be corrected without a Federal constitutional amendment.

There has been no impartial, comprehensive analysis done to indicate that victims' rights cannot adequately be protected by State and Federal laws. Before we take the grave step of amending the Constitution, we should know precisely how the Constitution fails to protect victims' rights. We should be certain that Federal statutes are not working and can not work, no matter how carefully crafted. We should have evidence that State constitutional provisions and statutes are not and can not do the job. Further study, we believe, will show that solutions short of amendment can provide effective and meaningful relief to crime victims.

The criminal justice system does not need to be "balanced"

The majority report subscribes to the popular canard that we need a Victims' Rights Amendment to correct an "imbalance" in our constitutional structure. According to this argument, the criminal justice system is improperly tilted in favor of criminal defendants and against victims' interests, as evidenced by the fact that the Constitution enumerates several rights for the accused and none, specifically, for the victim.

While aesthetically pleasing, however, the concept of "balance" makes little sense in this context. The paramount purpose of a criminal trial is to determine the guilt or innocence of the accused, not to make victims whole. The interests of the victim are protected by the right to bring a civil suit against the accused, by court-ordered restitution if the accused is convicted, by victim compensation programs, and, most importantly, by our well-considered tradition of the public prosecutor.

Of course, the public prosecutors of the United States represent "the people," not just the individual crime victim; they are required to seek justice for all, not individual justice or revenge. We have historically and proudly eschewed private criminal prosecutions based on our common sense of democracy. That the prosecutor's duty is to do justice may make the system appear unequal, but it is fundamentally sound: the interests of the people and the interests of the victim are often identical, but when they diverge, it is appropriate for the public prosecutor to pursue the interests of the people.

One crime victim who testified before the Committee against the proposed amendment made this point eloquently:

> Victims are citizens and people first. Unless one is defined solely and for all time by one's status as a victim, one has an interest in a free and democratic society that honors individual rights, including the rights of criminal defendants. We all, therefore, have an interest in the fairness of the criminal justice system and the manner in which the State treats its most disfavored citizens. (Statement of Lynne Henderson regarding S.J. Res. 6, prepared for the Senate Comm. on the Judiciary, at 19 (Apr. 14, 1997, emphases in original).

The majority report itself recognizes that "a public trial is intended to preserve confidence in the judicial system, that no defendant is denied a fair and just trial." This is as it should be. Victims' voices should be heard, but they should not be able to make judgments that would take from the rest of us our sense that justice is being served.

Beyond this, the "balance" argument mistakes the fundamental reason for elevating rights to the constitutional level. The rights enshrined in the United States Constitution are designed to protect politically weak and insular minorities against governmental overreaching or abuse (Cf. *United States v. Carolene Products Co.*, 304 U.S. 144, 152 n.4 (1938)), not to protect individuals from each other. When the government unleashes its prosecutorial power against an accused, it is the accused, not the victim, who faces the specter of losing his liberty, property, or even his life. The few and limited rights of the accused in the Constitution are there precisely because it will often be unpopular to enforce them so that even when we are afraid of a rising tide of crime, we will be protected against our own impulse to take shortcuts that will violate the essential dignity of the accused and increase the risk of wrongful conviction. In contrast, there is no need to grant constitutional protections to a class of citizens that commands virtually universal sympathy and substantial political power.

In the words of Bruce Fein, Deputy Attorney General during the Reagan Administration:

> [C]rime victims have no difficulty in making their voices heard in the corridors of power; they do not need protection from the majoritarian political process, in contrast to criminal defendants whose popularity characteristically ranks with that of General William Tecumseh Sherman in Atlanta, GA. (A Proposed Constitutional Amendment to Establish a Bill of Rights for Crime Victims, Hearing on S.J. Res. 52 before the Senate Comm. on the Judiciary, 104th Cong., 2d Sess. 100 (Apr. 23, 1996)).

The Proposed Amendment Would Have Dangerous and Uncertain Consequences for the Nation's Criminal Justice System

While the proposed amendment is at best unnecessary, at worst, it could help criminals more than it helps victims and cause the conviction of some who are innocent and wrongly accused. Passage of S.J. Res. 44 would enshrine new rights in the Constitution that would fundamentally realign this Nation's criminal justice system, opening a Pandora's box of dangerous unintended consequences.

The Amendment Would Impair the Ability of Prosecutors to Convict Violent Criminals

Since we first began holding hearings on a victims' rights amendment, prosecutors and other law enforcement authorities all across the country have cautioned that creating special constitutional rights for crime victims would have the perverse effect of impeding the effective prosecution of crime.

1. Restricting prosecutorial discretion

Most egregiously, the proposed amendment could compromise prosecutorial discretion and independence by allowing crime victims to second-guess and effectively dictate policy decisions made by prosecutors accountable to the public. As the National District Attorneys Association cautioned, it could afford victims the ability to place unknowing, and unacceptable, restrictions on prosecutors while strategic and tactical decisions are being made about how to proceed with a case (Letter from William L. Murphy, President, National District Attorneys Assn., to Sen. Patrick J. Leahy, Ranking Member, Senate Comm. on the Judiciary (May 27, 1998)). A constitutionally-empowered crime victim could override the professional judgment of the prosecutor concerning the investigation of the case, the timing of the proceedings, the disposition of the charges, and the recommendation as to sentence.

Prosecutorial discretion over plea bargaining is particularly at risk if S.J. Res. 44 passes, for it is here that the interests of the victim and the broader interests of the public most often diverge. Prosecutors enter into plea agreements for many reasons. A prosecutor may need to obtain the cooperation of a defendant who can bring down an entire organized crime ring; she may need to protect the identity of an informant-witness; she may think that the evidence against the defendant will not convince a jury beyond a reasonable doubt; she may just want to speed the processes of adjudication. In each instance, the prosecutor may be acting contrary to the wishes of the victim, or causing resentment on the part of one set of victims in order to do rough justice or provide immediate security to another set of victims.

How will this play out in the courts? A Miami defense lawyer tells of representing a murder defendant who accepted a plea offer from the prosecution. The judge refused to accept the offer after the victim's mother spoke out against it. His client went to trial and was acquitted (Fichenberg 1996). In California, relatives of a homicide victim complained to a judge that a plea bargain struck with the accused shooter was too lenient. They got what they wanted: withdrawal of the plea and prosecution of the man on murder charges. But at the close of the trial, the defendant was acquitted (see Wilson 1997). Defendant Loren Joost originally pleaded no contest to voluntary manslaughter, with the understanding that he would be sentenced to no more than 6 years in prison. The victim's family sabotaged the plea agreement by gathering more than 200 signatures denouncing the proposed settlement as too lenient.

Under the proposed amendment, well-meaning victims could obstruct plea proceedings, scuttling plea bargains, as in the Florida and California cases, or forcing prosecutors to disclose investigative strategies or weaknesses in their cases in order to persuade courts to accept victim-contested pleas. In this and other stages of the criminal process, prosecutors could be induced to make bad choices, or even to disregard their professional and ethical obligations, rather than risk violating a victim's constitutional rights.

There can be no doubt that prosecutors would feel personally constrained by the proposed amendment. S.J. Res. 44's express prohibition on claims for damages only increases the likelihood that courts would find other ways to vindicate its newly-minted rights. Just last year, the U.S. Supreme Court confirmed that the Federal civil rights laws permit criminal prosecutions in Federal court of any State official who willfully and under color of law deprived any person of any rights secured or protected under the Federal Constitution (*United States v. Lanier*, 520 U.S. 259 (1997)). At a minimum, prosecutors who made choices unpopular with victims would expose themselves to disciplinary action. Meanwhile, prosecutors who become adversaries to victims because of judicially-contested conflicts over a case could be required to recuse themselves from the case in order to defend themselves in the ancillary proceeding—another unintended consequence that could have significant adverse effects on the Nation's criminal justice system.

Even the Department of Justice, which supports amending the Constitution to provide for enhanced victims' rights, has acknowledged that in at least some situations, affording special constitutional rights to victims will "impact on the prosecutor's discretion and judgment" and "adversely affect the administration of justice" (Hearing of Apr. 16, 1997, at 48, 132, responses of Attorney General Janet Reno to questions from Sen. Patrick J. Leahy). We must not create entitlements for victims that will tie prosecutors' hands and cripple law enforcement.

2. Other Adverse Consequences

Creating an absolute right for crime victims to attend and participate in criminal proceedings could raise other serious problems for law enforcement. Consider the problem of the victim-witness. In many cases, the victim is the Government's key witness. If she insists on exercising her constitutional right to sit through the entire trial, there is a substantial danger that her testimony will be influenced by hearing and seeing other evidence concerning the same set of facts. Whether consciously or unconsciously, she could tailor her testimony to fit the other evidence.

Apart from the obvious fairness concerns implicated by this procedure, which facilitates and even encourages collusive and inaccurate testimony, there is also the danger that the victim's presence in the courtroom during the presentation of other evidence will cast doubt on her credibility as a witness. Defense attorneys will cross-examine victims at length on this point and argue, credibly, that the victims' testimony was irretrievably tainted. Inevitably, in some cases, this tactic will succeed: the jury will discredit or discount the victim's testimony. Whole cases, or important counts, may be lost in this way. Indeed, one proponent of the amendment, formerly a public defender, admitted during the Committee markup that the proposed amendment could inure to the benefit of defendants (Executive Comm. Meeting, Senate Comm. on the Judiciary, at 58 (July 7, 1998, statement of Sen. Joseph R. Biden, Jr.)).

As a practical matter, prosecutors may be able to shield victim testimony from the appearance of taint by putting the victim on the stand first. But what happens in the event that the victim is recalled for additional testimony? What happens in cases involving more than one victim-witness? A forced reshuffling of the witness list might not help, and could well compromise the coherence and effectiveness of the prosecution's presentation to the jury.

Constitutionalizing the right not to be excluded from public criminal proceedings could also give rise to actions by victims against decisions to conduct certain proceedings under seal. This could cause particular disruption in the context of juvenile justice proceedings, which are often closed to the public, and to which the proposed amendment expressly applies. Similarly, it could compromise courtroom closure laws designed to protect child witnesses (see, e.g., 18 U.S.C. § 3509(e)). A no-exclusion rule could also make it more difficult for prosecutors to do their jobs when, for example, they need secrecy at some stage of a proceeding in order to assure the safety of a witness.

Finally, S.J. Res. 44's creation of a victim's right to trial "free from unreasonable delay" raises another set of concerns for prosecutors. Suppose a prosecutor in a complex case needs more time to interview witnesses and prepare for trial. Could a victim sue to require the immediate commencement of trial? Forcing prosecutors to try cases before they are fully prepared plays into the hands of the defense and would undoubtedly result in many cases being dropped or lost.

* * *

The New Constitutional Rights for Victims Would Undermine Bedrock Constitutional Protections Afforded to the Accused by the Bill of Rights

The Department of Justice, the National District Attorneys Association, and the American Bar Association, among others, have underscored the urgent need to preserve the fundamental protections of those accused of crimes while giving appropriate protection to victims (see Mosteller 1998, concluding that a constitutional amendment supporting victims' rights should expressly guarantee that it will not diminish existing rights of the accused).

During the markup, we considered a proposed amendment to S.J. Res. 44 stating, "Nothing in this article shall be construed to deny or diminish the rights of the accused as guaranteed by this Constitution." The Committee rejected this amendment by a vote of 10 to 6 (Exec. Comm. Meeting, Senate Comm. on the Judiciary, 105th Cong., 2d Sess., at 109–11 (July 7, 1998)).

Courts may therefore conclude that S.J. Res. 44 was intended to override earlier-ratified provisions securing the accused's right to a fair trial. This would make it more likely that innocent people are convicted in cases involving irreconcilable conflict, where accommodation cannot protect the rights of both the victim and the accused.

Conflicts between the victims' rights created by S.J. Res. 44 and the protections accorded defendants by the Bill of Rights likely would be infrequent, but they would occur. Indeed, as currently drafted, S.J. Res. 44 practically invites conflict in several important areas.

Giving Victims' Rights at the Accusatory Stage of Criminal Proceedings Undercuts the Presumption of Innocence

Not all who claim to be victims are indeed victims and, more significantly, not all those charged are the actual perpetrators of the injuries that victims have suffered. By naming and protecting the victim as such before the accused's guilt has been determined, the proposed amendment would undercut one of the most basic components of a fair trial, the presumption of innocence.

Consider a simple assault case in which the accused claims that he was acting in self-defense. Absent some sort of corroborating evidence, the jury's verdict will likely turn on who it believes, the accused or his accuser. The amendment treats the accuser as a "victim," granting him broad participatory and other rights, before a criminal or even a crime has been established. Once charges have been brought—and the charges may be based on little more than the accuser's allegations—the accuser is entitled to attend all public proceedings and to have a say as to whether the accused should be released on bond, making it more likely that the accused will be imprisoned until the conclusion of the trial. While society certainly has an interest in preserving the safety of the victim, this fact alone cannot be said to overcome a defendant's liberty interest as afforded to him under the due process and excessive bail clauses.

A Victim's Right Not to Be Excluded Could Undermine the Accused's Right to a Fair Trial

The proposed amendment gives victims a constitutional right not to be excluded from public proceedings. Establishing such a preference for victims does not require a constitutional amendment, unless it is intended to create an absolute right that would be used to overcome a right currently afforded defendants. That is precisely what this provision would accomplish. But while crime victims have a legitimate interest in attending public proceedings involving matters that impacted their lives, this is not a limitless interest. At the point where the victims' presence threatens or interferes with the accuracy and fairness of the trial, restrictions should be imposed.

Accuracy and fairness concerns may arise, as we have already discussed, where the victim is a fact witness whose testimony may be influenced by the testimony of others. Another example is the case in which the victim or her family acts emotionally or disruptively in front of the jury. Whether done purposefully or unintentionally, a victim exhibiting such behavior may unfairly prejudice the defendant.

Indeed, by making the right of victims to be present very difficult, if not impossible, to forfeit, S.J. Res. 44 may encourage disruptive displays by victims—a manifestly illegitimate purpose for a constitutional amendment (see Mosteller 1997). Our Nation's jurisprudence explicitly warns against determinations of guilt and punishment based upon passion, prejudice or emotion, rather than reason or evidence (see, e.g., *Sheppard v. Maxwell*, 384 U.S. 333, 350 (1966).

Proponents of S.J. Res. 44 dismiss such concerns out-of-hand. The majority report declares that crime victims would have "no right" to engage in either disruptive behavior or excessive displays of emotion. The Attorney General claims that "common sense flexibility" would preserve judges' authority to keep courtrooms free from disruptive observers, even when those observers are victims (Hearing of Apr. 16, 1997, at 133, responses of Attorney General Janet Reno to questions from Sen. Patrick J. Leah But it is not at all clear how "common sense flexibility" could prevail over an inflexible constitutional right "not to be excluded.")

A Victim's Right to be Heard Could Undermine the Accused's Right to a Fair Trial

The proposed amendment gives victims a constitutional right to be heard, if present, and to submit a statement at all stages of the criminal proceeding. What happens when a victim's testimony is irrelevant, unduly or unnecessarily prolongs the proceedings, or is so inflammatory that justice would be undermined? Passage of the proposed amendment would make it much more difficult for judges to limit testimony by victims at trial and capital sentencing proceedings.

A Victim's Right to Expedite Trial Proceedings Could Undermine the Accused's Sixth Amendment Rights

S.J. Res. 44 gives victims of violent crimes a right to "trial free from unreasonable delay." Just as this provision risks forcing prosecutors to trial before they are fully prepared, it risks forcing defendants to do the same. Defendants may also seek to postpone the trial to let prejudicial publicity about the case dissipate. Under the proposed amendment, the defendant's need for more time could be outweighed by the victim's assertion of his right to have the matter expedited, seriously compromising the defendant's right to effective assistance of counsel and his ability to receive a fair trial.

Constitutionalizing Victims' Rights Raises Equal Protection Concerns

We should consider the question of equal protection and equality of treatment of our defendants. During one hearing, Representative Robert C. Scott asked what happens when a prosecutor routinely recommends a 1-year sentence for first-offense burglary, but the victim is unusually emotional or articulate: should that defendant get more time than a defendant whose victim is inarticulate or even absent? (Hearing of Apr. 16, 1997, at 34, 35, statement of Rep. Robert C. Scott). By the same token, should the amount of time that a defendant spends in jail turn on the effectiveness of the victim's attorney?

The United States is world renowned and admired for its system of public prosecutions. It bespeaks our leadership in the precepts of democracy that justice is mandated for all citizens. No individual or group is favored. Wealth does not determine whose case gets prosecuted, or how well. Crime victims themselves benefit from this system, as the majority report acknowledges. We should think long and hard before we revert to a system of private prosecutions based on wealth, power, and campaign contributions.

Construed to Avoid Any Conflicts with Defendants Rights, the Proposed Amendment Becomes Purely Hortatory

Attempting to divert attention from the foreseeable consequences of this proposal, some supporters of S.J. Res. 44 maintain that it would not, and was never intended to, denigrate the rights of the accused in any way. Indeed, one cosponsor has flatly asserted:

> There is no inconsistency between the rights of the accused and recognizing in a formal sense the victim's rights. . . . [T]here is not even a hypothetical case that has been put forward where there is a conflict between the rights guaranteed to the accused under our Constitution and the rights we are proposing . . . be enshrined in the Constitution for victims. There is no denigration, there is no choice required. This is not a matter of requiring anyone to say, in order to give a victim a right, we have to take away any right of the accused. If that were the case . . . I would not support this amendment. (Exec. Comm. Meeting, Senate Comm. on the Judiciary, 105th Cong., 2d Sess., at 19–20 (June 25, 1998, statement of Sen. Joseph R. Biden, Jr.).

The problem with this position, however, is that it proves too much. For if it were always possible to accommodate the constitutional rights of both the accused and the victim—a prospect that we, like the Department of Justice, find unlikely—then the proposed amendment would become purely hortatory. Professor Philip Heymann, a former Associate Deputy Attorney General, stated the matter succinctly:

> If it is not intended to free the States and Federal Government from restrictions found in the Bill of Rights—which would be a reckless tampering with provisions that have served us very well for more than 200 years—it is unclear what purpose the amendment serves. (Heymann 1997)

The Constitution of the United States is no place for symbolic decorations that fail to define real rights or to give real remedies.

Passage of the Proposed Amendment Could Actually Hurt the Victims of Crime

For all the reasons discussed above, passage of this well-meaning amendment could well prove counter-productive, accomplishing little while making the lives of crime victims more difficult. "We should never lose sight of the fact that the very best way that [we] . . . can serve victims of crime is to bring those responsible for crime to justice" (Hearing of Apr. 16, 1997, at 42, statement of Attorney General Janet Reno). Crime victims would be the first to suffer—and criminals the first to benefit—from a constitutional amendment that hindered prosecutors, forced law enforcement agencies to divert scarce resources from actual crime-fighting efforts, and clogged the courts with time-consuming, justice-delaying litigation. Moreover, few benefit if, in the end, the proposed amendment undermines core constitutional guarantees designed to protect all of us from wrongful convictions.

The Proposed Amendment Infringes on States' Rights

The proposed amendment constitutes a significant intrusion of Federal authority into a province traditionally left to State and local authorities. Many of our colleagues, in making their arguments in support of S.J. Res. 44, point out that nearly

95 percent of all crimes are prosecuted by the States. It is precisely that rationale that leads us to conclude that grants of rights to crime victims are—whenever possible—best left to the States to provide.

If the Federal Government had the general police power, then mandating a companion power to protect the rights of victims of crime would at least be consistent. But the Federal Government does not have this power. As the Supreme Court recently reminded us in *United States v. Lopez*, 514 U.S. 549 (1995), there is no general Federal police power. "Under our Federal system, the States possess primary authority for defining and enforcing the criminal law" (Id. at 561 n.3). S.J. Res. 44 would dramatically alter this framework by locking States into an absolutist national pattern regarding the participation of victims in the criminal justice system.

The majority report attempts to deflect the federalism concerns raised by S.J. Res. 44 by suggesting that the States will retain "plenary authority" to implement the amendment within their own criminal systems. We find this suggestion surprising given the plain language of the amendment's implementation clause (in section 3): "The Congress shall have the power to enforce this article by appropriate legislation." Identical language in earlier constitutional amendments has been read to vest enforcement authority exclusively in the Congress.

In the case of S.J. Res. 44, moreover, the text is illuminated by the legislative history. Earlier drafts of the amendment expressly extended enforcement authority to the states. [Footnote omitted]. These drafts drew fire from constitutional scholars, who expressed doubt that constitutionally-authorized State laws could be supreme over State constitutions or even over Federal laws, and concern that, for the first time, rights secured by the Federal Constitution would mean different things in different parts of the country. The Committee then amended the text to its current formulation. Faced with this history and text, courts will surely conclude that S.J. Res. 44 deprives States of any authority to legislate in the area of victims' rights.

This is troubling in three regards. First, S.J. Res. 44 would have an adverse effect on the many State and local governments which are already experimenting with a variety of innovative victims' rights initiatives. Second, it would create an enormous unfunded burden for State courts, prosecutors, law enforcement personnel, and corrections officials. Third, it would lead inevitably to Federal court supervision and micro-management of noncomplying State and local authorities.

* * *

Federal Court Supervision

Under S.J. Res. 44, a victim does not have the ability to sue for damages. A victim may, however, ask a Federal court for injunctive or declaratory relief against State officials, and possibly a writ of mandamus. The resulting interference with State criminal proceedings would be unprecedented and ill-advised.

Even more alarming is the specter of Federal class actions against noncomplying State authorities. When we asked the Department of Justice what sort of relief there might be when district attorney offices failed, as many now are failing, to provide full notice for victims, they said that the relief would be court orders like those in prison reform litigation. There is the potential for big costs to States, enormous expenditure of judicial resources, and undignified hauling into court of local prosecutors, judges, and corrections officers.

The States chief justices have expressed grave concerns that the proposed constitutional amendment would lead to "extensive lower Federal court surveillance of the day to day operations of State law enforcement operations" (see Letter from Joseph R. Weisberger, Chief Justice, Supreme Court of Rhode Island, Chairperson, Conference of Chief Justices Task Force on Victim Rights, to Sen. Orrin G. Hatch, Chairman, Senate Comm. on the Judiciary, at 1 (May 16, 1997)). We share these concerns. The laudable goal of making State and local law enforcement personnel more responsive to victims should not be achieved by establishing Federal court oversight of the criminal justice and correctional systems of the 50 States.

"[F]ederalism was the unique contribution of the Framers to political science and political theory," and it has served this country well for over 200 years (*Lopez*, 514 U.S. at 575 (Kennedy, J., concurring)). We do not need a constitutional amendment to turn this system on its head. We have no pressing reason to thwart the States' experimentation with innovative victims' rights initiatives and to displace State laws in an area of traditional State concern. We have no compelling evidence pointing to the need for another unfunded mandate. And we certainly do not need more Federal court supervision and micro-management of State and local affairs.

The Wording of the Proposed Amendment Is Problematic

As the preceding analysis has shown, any amendment to the Constitution to provide for victims rights would be fraught with problems, ranging from resource and training issues to a plethora of unintended consequences. But in addition to the general problems associated with a constitutional amendment, the specific language of S.J. Res. 44 is problematic.

Now in its 62nd draft, the proposed amendment remains decidedly vague, its key terms undefined. Far more work is needed before we can even debate its merits intelligently. As it stands, years of litigation would be necessary to flesh out the amendment's actual scope, enforcement mechanisms, and remedial nature.

* * *

Conclusion

We must not hamstring our prosecutors and sacrifice core protections guaranteed by the Bill of Rights to enact this unnecessary and problematic constitutional amendment on victims' rights.

Patrick Leahy
Ted Kennedy
Herb Kohl

Additional views of Senators Leahy and Kennedy [omitted]; additional views of Senator Biden [omitted]; additional views of Senators Russell D. Feingold and Richard J. Durbin [omitted].

* * *

Analysis

The United States Senate Report on Senate Joint Resolution 44 is the most developed document generated by the Congress concerning constitutional rights for victims. Like all political debates, it is difficult to separate the wheat from the chaff.

Majority report: The Constitution typically protects participatory rights.

Analysis: In criminal procedure, participatory rights of the accused are constitutionally based and supplemented with statutory rules. The defendant has many procedural rights rooted in the Constitution, such as due process, which form the backbone of defendants' participatory rights. To the extent that victims' rights are to be fundamental core values in criminal procedure, it would be conventional to constitutionalize them.

Minority Report: A constitutional amendment is unnecessary. The rights would have dangerous and uncertain consequences.

Analysis: Whether an amendment is necessary depends upon the value to be given the rights and interest of crime victims as well as whether there is to be a consistent set of rights for victims across the country. If victims' rights are as fundamental as defendant's rights, then they ought to be in the Constitution, which reflects the highest values the nation has.

Also, the only way to structurally create a consistent set of victims' rights nationwide is to put them in the federal constitution. This is because federal statutory victims' rights do not apply to the states. It is true that federal statutes are more readily modified than constitutional rights.

Majority Report: An amendment is compatible with federalism principles.

Analysis: Federalism is both a structure of government—that there is a federal government with somewhat independent state governments—and a political perspective—that certain decisions should be left to the states. As envisioned, a federal crime victims' rights constitutional amendment would be controlling on the states. In the latter half of the 1900s, the United States Supreme Court wrote a series of opinions that put the federal constitution in charge of minimal rights for criminal defendants in the states. For victims' rights to be consistently applicable throughout the country, the rights would have to be in the federal constitution.

Minority Report: Federalism is best protected by not having rights in the federal constitution.

Analysis: In the structural sense of federalism, the minority report has it right. A minimum set of victims' rights standards in the federal constitution would be imposed on the states. The argument is that each state should be free to experiment with victims' rights in a way that suits each state. Of course, it would take a three-quarters vote of states before the amendment could be part of the Constitution, so assuming the bare minimum of states voted for the Amendment, the Amendment would be imposed on only one-quarter of the states. Because of the states' ultimate authority over amendments, giving up their separate, independent authority over a basic level of victims' rights would be to a large extent their own choice.

Majority Report: Less than federal constitutional protection has been inadequate.

Analysis: The absence of a federal amendment means each state creates its own victims' rights. It is accurate to say that in many states, even those with state constitutional amendments, the laws are inadequate, because they are unenforceable as written or because state courts have minimized their enforceability. A federal amendment would create a baseline of victims' rights that would apply to the states.

Minority Report: There is an extensive framework of victims' rights in federal and state authority.

Analysis: This assertion is partly true, some type of "victims' rights" exist in all federal and state jurisdictions. As the *McVeigh* case after the Oklahoma City bombing (described in the preceding chapter) made apparent, the victims' rights existing when this Senate report was written were woefully inadequate because they were unenforceable. The Victim Rights Clarification Act passed after the bombing only applied to a very narrow subset of cases. Moreover, many of the states' rights were written in the early years of the movement and could be significantly improved by making them enforceable.

Majority Report: Denying victim participation is fundamentally unfair.

Analysis: This is perhaps the main fundamental difference between those who seek an amendment and those who oppose it: Are these fundamental rights that every American should have? Which view one holds is likely determinative of one's support or opposition to a victims' rights amendment.

Minority Report: Passage would hurt victims of crime; balance is not needed in the criminal process.

Analysis: The idea that rights would hurt crime victims is a very weak argument, particularly because, as victims' rights were constructed, individual victims could choose not to take advantage of the rights—to waive the rights—if they wanted. The Victims' Rights Movement has relied on the concept of balance to further the enactment of rights. The idea is that if there are only defendants' rights and state authority, the system becomes off balance because victims have no role. *Balance* is a rather imprecise term to describe what essentially is a fairness argument—it is unfair that victims do not have rights in the criminal process when others do. And victim harm means that victims should have a legitimate stake in the criminal process.

Majority Report: There is a need for specific rights versus minority report: Victims' rights would undermine defendants' rights.

Analysis: Modern victims' rights have not conflicted with the federal constitutional rights of criminal defendants. If a right did conflict, then federal constitutional rights would trump the victim's right. However, putting victims' rights in the Constitution means that if a conflict arose, the rights would be balanced, or reconciled, with each other. While the sides agree that conflict would be rare, the minority view is against victims' rights affecting defendants' existing rights in any way. The majority view is that on the rare occasions it would occur, the Supreme Court should find an appropriate accommodation for each right.

In History

The sponsors of constitutional rights for crime victims were Senator Jon Kyl of Arizona and Senator Diane Feinstein of California. Senator Feinstein was on the San Francisco city council when fellow councilman Harvey Milk was assassinated in part because he was gay. The killer used what became known as the "Twinkie" defense. This defense claimed that his body sugar was off balance. The murder deeply impacted councilwoman Feinstein, who became a strong advocate for victims' rights in the U.S. Senate. In the movie *Milk*, Sean Penn plays Harvey Milk.

The Scholarly Debate on the Constitutional Amendment

In addition to the United States Senate Report, which focused the debate over whether to constitutionalize victims' rights, the effort for an amendment brought out strong views among legal academics.

- **Document:** "Embed the Rights of Victims in the Constitution" by Laurence H. Tribe and Paul G. Cassell
- **Date:** July 6, 1998
- **Significance:** In this document, Professors Paul Cassell and Laurence Tribe argue in favor of embedding victim's rights in the federal constitution, thus balancing victims' and defendants' rights equally in the criminal process.
- **Source:** Tribe, Laurence H. and Paul G. Cassell. "Embed the Rights of Victims in the Constitution." *L.A. Times*, July 6, 1998. Reprinted with permission from Laurence H. Tribe.

---

* * *

The Supreme Court has instructed that "in the administration of criminal justice, courts may not ignore the concerns of victims." Sadly, those noble sentiments have yet to be translated into day-to-day realities in the administration of our nation's criminal justice system.

Fortunately, a remedy lies at hand. The Senate Judiciary Committee is expected to vote shortly on the Victims' Rights Amendment. The amendment enjoys unusually widespread, bipartisan support. We hope this Congress will approve it and send it to the states for consideration and ratification.

We take it to be common ground that the Constitution should never be amended merely to achieve short-term, partisan or purely policy objectives. Apart from a needed change in governmental structure, an amendment is appropriate only when the goal involves a basic human right that by consensus deserves permanent respect, is not and cannot adequately be protected through state or federal legislation, would not distort basic principles of the separation of powers among the federal branches or the division of powers between the national and state governments or the balance of powers between government and private citizens with respect to their basic rights.

The proposed Victims Rights' Amendment meets these demanding criteria. It would protect basic rights of crime victims, including their rights to be notified of and present at all proceedings in their case and to be heard at appropriate stages in the process. These are rights not to be victimized again through the process by which government officials prosecute, punish and release accused or convicted offenders.

These are the very kinds of rights with which our Constitution is typically and properly concerned—rights of individuals to participate in all those government processes that strongly affect their lives. "Participation in all forms of government is the essence of democracy," President Clinton concluded in endorsing the amendment.

Congress and the states already have passed a variety of measures to protect the rights of victims. Yet the reports from the field are that they have all too often been ineffective. Rules to assist victims frequently fail to provide meaningful protection whenever they come into conflict with bureaucratic habit, traditional indifference, sheer inertia or the mere mention of an accused's rights—even when those rights are not genuinely threatened.

Moreover, because we lack the resources to provide victims the guiding hand of appointed legal counsel in the criminal process, victims are largely left to stumble on their own through a "haphazard patchwork" of rules "not sufficiently consistent, comprehensive or authoritative to safeguard victims' rights," the Justice Department concluded after careful study. Empirical confirmation of this failure comes from a National Institute of Justice study reporting that today "large numbers of victims are being denied their legal rights." The same study found that victims' rights are more frequently denied to racial minorities and presumably other disfavored groups who are unable to assert their interests effectively. Only an unequivocal constitutional mandate will translate paper promises into real guarantees for all victims.

A Victims' Rights Amendment must, of course, be drafted so that the rights of victims will not furnish excuses for running roughshod over the rights of the accused. The current Senate resolution is such a carefully crafted measure, adding victims' rights that can coexist side by side with defendants'. For example, paralleling a defendant's constitutionally protected right to a "speedy" trial, the amendment would confer on victims the right to consideration of their interest "in a trial free from unreasonable delay." By definition, these rights could not collide, since they are both designed to bring matters to a close within a reasonable time. And if any conflict were to emerge, courts would retain ultimate responsibility for harmonizing the rights at stake.

The framers of the Constitution undoubtedly assumed the rights of victims would receive decent protection. Because experience has not vindicated this assumption, it is now necessary to add a corrective amendment. Doing so would neither extend the Constitution to an issue of mere policy, nor provide special benefits to a particular interest group, nor use the heavy artillery of constitutional amendment where a simpler solution is available. Nor would it put the Constitution to a merely symbolic use or enlist it for some narrow partisan purpose. Rather, the proposed amendment would help bridge a distinct and significant gap in our legal system's existing arrangements for the protection of basic human rights against an important category of government abuse.

* * *

Analysis

Laurence Tribe is among the most respected liberal constitutional legal scholars of our time. Paul Cassell is a conservative legal scholar who clerked for the United States Supreme Court. Despite their liberal and conservative approaches, they were able to come together to endorse the Crime Victims' Rights Amendment. This reveals that victims' rights cannot be readily labeled a conservative or liberal idea. Nevertheless, in supporting the amendment, they were in the minority of legal academics.

The next document is written by Professor Robert Mosteller, a distinguished professor from Duke Law School. He has been the leading academic writing in opposition to the victims' rights amendment.

Harvard Law professor Laurence Tribe urged Congress to pass a Crime Victims' Rights Amendment. (AP Photo/Susan Walsh)

- **Document:** "The Unnecessary Victims' Rights Amendment" by Robert P. Mosteller
- **Date:** 1999
- **Document Significance:** Professor Mosteller argues that the proponents of the victims' rights amendment have not met their burden of proof in establishing the need for a constitutional amendment.
- **Source:** Mosteller, Robert P. "The Unnecessary Victims' Rights Amendment." *Utah Law* Review(1999): 443. Reprinted with permission from Robert P. Mosteller.

* * *

No governmental bureaucracy operates perfectly, and the criminal justice system is hardly an exception. Given this context, it is preordained that existing victims' rights are not uniformly enforced. Nonenforcement of rights through various institutional failures may collectively be termed "official indifference."

In a recent commentary, conservative constitutional scholar Bruce Fein discussed this official indifference to victims' rights, noting that a federal constitutional right is both unnecessary and would provide no guarantee of effectiveness:

> Nothing in the Constitution or in any Supreme Court precedent inhibits the enactment of state or federal laws that protect crime victims. Indeed, victims' rights legislation is a staple of contemporary political life and seems destined to remain so. The beneficiaries command virtual universal sympathy, a failsafe formula for legislative success. Crime victims need no constitutional protection from political overreaching.
>
> It is said by amendment proponents, however, that state judges and prosecutors often short-change the scores of existing victims' rights statutes. If so, they would equally be inclined to flout the amendment. The judicial oath is no less violated in the first case as in the second.
>
> Furthermore, time will solve grudging bows to victims' rights. Most aging judges and prosecutors matured when victims' rights were stepchildren of the law. They instinctively resist any novelty or innovation in their work habits, such as requirements to notify and consult with crime victims in preparing and conducting a criminal prosecution and in sentencing the guilty.
>
> But the geriatric detractors of victims' rights will soon die or retire in favor of new judicial and prosecutorial officials inculcated with a victims' rights agenda and devoted to exacting enforcement standards.
>
> * * *
>
> The cresting of the amendment ironically comes when our constitutional system of federalism is addressing victims' rights exactly as the Founding Fathers hoped. Through statutes and state constitutional amendments, the 50 states are experimenting with varied approaches to blending the competing interests of victims, prosecutors, defendants and manageable judicial caseloads in search of an enlightened formula. The mix in one jurisdiction may exalt the cathartic needs of victims, while in another the interest in judicial dispatch reigns supreme (Fein 1998 at A14).

Fein's principal argument is simple and compelling-enacting a federal constitutional amendment will not cure the failures by judges and prosecutors to follow existing laws (see id., rejecting argument that judges and prosecutors will be more inclined to protect victims' rights under Amendment). Indeed, if such "bureaucrats" are willing to ignore the requirements of existing, binding law that they have sworn to uphold, adding another layer of law supporting the same right has no necessary impact (see id., stating that judges and prosecutors "would be equally inclined to flout the Amendment").

Significantly, the vast majority of the provisions in the proposed Victims' Rights Amendment that was approved by the Senate Judiciary Committee in July 1998 fall into this category of correcting official indifference (see S.J. Res. 44, 105th Cong. § 1 (1998, listing rights victims should have during official proceedings). The enforcement of these rights does not conflict with any constitutional right of defendants, and therefore, violations occur as a consequence of governmental officials' either purposefully or inadvertently ignoring their existing legal obligations. [Footnote 11 omitted]. The right to notice of all proceedings unequivocally falls into this category, as does the right of notice of release or escape of the defendant. Similarly, the right to be present and to be heard at many types of proceedings, such as hearings to determine conditional release from custody, acceptance of a negotiated plea, and parole, can also receive protection either by demanding compliance by state officials with established laws or by passing such laws and promulgating appropriate administrative procedures. The problem with enforcing these victims' rights does not and cannot result from judicial protection of defendants' constitutional rights, because such rights are nonexistent in these areas. Finally, as a matter of legal entitlement, the right to restitution may be granted as fully and effectively by statutory or state constitutional right as it can be by federal constitutional right, and the defendant convicted of an unlawful act against the victim has no basis for constitutional challenge to such an order. [Footnote 12 omitted].

Of course, one cannot know whether enshrining the right in a federal constitutional amendment would cause judges and prosecutors to take their oaths more seriously. Perhaps, but the impact is almost entirely speculative. [Footnote 13 omitted] The necessity of giving the additional dignity to these rights that a federal constitutional provision would entail is particularly questionable given the extraordinary popularity of victims' rights provisions. Normal political processes will, with time, effectively punish those administrative officials and even judges, many of whom are elected, who ignore the popular mandate to give victims greater notice and voice in the process.

Moreover, the existence of constitutional rights will not automatically eliminate official indifference to specific individual rights. For example, a recent ABC News report described how thousands of people arrested in New York City between 1996 and 1997 for minor offenses, such as driving with a suspended license or selling sneakers on the street without a vender's permit, were subjected to strip searches that federal courts had previously ruled illegal under the Fourth and Fourteenth Amendments to the Constitution (see Miller and Jennings 1998, discussing incidence of illegal strip searches, and stating that "between 1996 and 1997 New York City officials say because of a bureaucratic snafu, prison officials simply overlooked a requirement that an officer needed to have reasonable suspicion . . . before conducting a strip search"). The existence of a federal constitutional right did not prevent this huge "bureaucratic snafu," which is likely to cost the city millions of dollars (Id.).

This official indifference to the Fourth Amendment rights of arrested suspects serves as a good point of departure for evaluating the impact of enacting a constitutional amendment for victims. While I have used the term "official indifference" to describe the failure of officials to enforce fully existing victims' rights, that term is perhaps too negative in characterizing motivation. Most officials are not disdainful of victims or their rights, as is sometimes the case in the highly contentious and occa-sionally combative relationship between defendants and those in law enforcement. Indeed, malevolence, or even true indifference towards victims' rights, is largely unknown. Instead, I believe that officials fail to honor victims' rights largely as a result of inertia, past learning, insensitivity to the unfamiliar needs of victims, lack of train-ing, and inadequate or misdirected institutional incentives. However, the most impor-tant reason that existing victims' rights are not more fully enforced is the lack of resources and personnel needed to accomplish this new and additional set of tasks.

Fortunately, if nonrecognition of victims' rights results, as I contend, from the sys-tem's inability to find the time and personnel necessary to notify, consult, and pro-tect, this problem can be overcome by greater resources in most instances and by administrative sanctions for failure to comply in those rarer cases that approach actual indifference. A commitment of resources and administrative sanctions surely will exert a major impact in making victims' rights a reality for large numbers of vic-tims; to the contrary, the result of enacting a federal constitutional amendment, a largely symbolic act with respect to enforcing existing rights, is of speculative value by comparison. The Amendment's lack of direct effectiveness is particularly clear because it prohibits damage awards for violations of its provisions (see S.J. Res. 44, 105th Cong. § 2 (1998, stating that "nothing in this article shall give rise to or authorize the creation of a claim for damages against the United States, a State, a political subdivision, or a public officer or employee"), though damages are even available for violations of the Fourth Amendment rights of citizens, such as the improper strip searches cited earlier. [Footnote 17 omitted].

Although the amendment is not necessary to achieve enforcement of victims' participatory rights, such as notice and an opportunity to be heard, I want to acknowledge that a federal constitutional amendment could operate as a helpful mechanism for enforcing victims' rights against public officials through federal class action litigation that I doubt many of its political supporters would endorse. Damage actions are barred by Senate Joint Resolution 44, *See* S.J. Res. 44, 105th Cong. § 2 (1998), but suits for declaratory and injunctive relief are not. Class actions to enforce participatory rights against states also appear available. The Minority Report on Senate Joint Resolution 44 indicates that, in response to inquiry, the Justice Department acknowledged that federal court orders against states, like those in prison reform litigation, would be possible (see S. REP. NO. 105-409, at 71 (1998)). Indeed, this "specter of extensive lower federal court surveillance of the day to day operations of state law enforcement operations" has led the Conference of Chief Justices to oppose the Amendment.

* * *

Analysis

Professor Mosteller's central argument is that a statutory set of rights would adequately serve in the stead of a constitutional amendment. He is correct that stat-utes are far more readily modified than constitutional provisions. Few constitutional amendments have been eliminated or modified, the reversal of the prohibition amendment being one of the rare examples. The Victims' Rights Movement has strived for a constitutional amendment because it is far more likely to move the nation's criminal justice system toward meaningful consideration of victims' rights and interests. This too is likely an accurate assessment.

More law professors signed up in opposition to the amendment than in favor of it. The following letter was circulated among law schools to obtain as many signatures in opposition to the amendment as possible.

- **Document:** Letter from Law Professors Erwin Chemerinsky, Lynne Henderson, and Robert P. Mosteller
- **Date:** April 4, 1997
- **Significance:** This letter was circulated among law schools in an effort to obtain as many signatures in opposition to the victims' rights amendment as possible.
- **Source:** Letter from Law Professors Erwin Chemerinsky, Lynne Henderson, and Robert P. Mosteller. Reprinted in *A Proposed Constitutional Amendment to Protect Victims of Crime*, Hearing on S.J. Res. 6 before the Senate Comm. on the Judiciary, 105thCong., 1st Sess., at 140 (Apr. 16, 1997).

Letter from Law Professors Regarding the
Proposed Victim's Rights Constitutional Amendment
in A Proposed Constitutional Amendment to
Protect Victims of Crime: Hearings Before the
Senate Judiciary Committee, 105th Cong., 1st Sess. (1997)

Dear Senators Hatch and Leahy, and Representatives Hyde and Conyers,

We are law professors and practitioners who oppose the proposal to add a "Victims' Rights Amendment" to the United States Constitution (S.J. Res. 6). Although we commend and share the desire to help crime victims, amending the Constitution to do so is both unnecessary and dangerous. Indeed, ultimately the amendment is likely to be counter-productive in that it could hinder effective prosecution and put an enormous burden on state and federal law enforcement agencies.

The Constitution has been amended only 27 times in 210 years. Amendments should be added to our basic charter of government only when there is a pressing need that cannot be addressed in any other way. No such necessity exists in order to protect the rights of crime victims. Virtually every right contained in the proposed Victims' Rights Amendment can be safeguarded in federal and state laws.

Many of the rights contained in the Victims' Rights Amendment already are provided for in federal and state laws. For example, restitution for crime victims is required in federal court by the Antiterrorism and Effective Death Penalty Act of 1996 and in state courts by laws in virtually every state. Similarly, the right of victims to attend proceedings can be protected by statute as shown by laws that exist in many states and by the recent federal legislation that mandates that victims be allowed to attend even if they will be testifying during the sentencing phase of the proceedings. Victim impact statements are now a routine part of sentencing proceedings at both the federal and state levels.

Over 25 states have amended their state constitutions to protect victims' rights and most others have done this by statute. There is every reason to believe that the legislative process will continue to be responsive to protecting crime victims so that there is simply no need to amend the Constitution to accomplish this.

There are, however, grave dangers in amending the Constitution in this manner. The framers of the Constitution were aware of the enormous power of the government to deprive a person of liberty or even life in a criminal prosecution. The constitutional protections accorded criminal defendants are among the most precious and essential liberties provided in the Constitution. The Victims' Rights Amendment risks undermining these basic safeguards. For example, the proposed Amendment would give a crime victim the right "To a final disposition of the proceedings relating to the crime free from unreasonable delay." Any victim of a violent crime has standing under the Amendment to intervene and assert a constitutional right for a faster disposition of the matter. This could be used to deny defendants needed time to gather and present evidence essential in order to demonstrate their innocence.

The Amendment also would require "consideration for the safety of the victim in determining any release from custody." Pretrial release statutes already provide for consideration of dangerousness when courts decide whether to release criminal defendants before trial. The proposed Amendment, however, would go much further and allow a victim of a crime to argue that it is *unconstitutional* to release a person from prison even though the sentence had been completely served. The authorization for standing for crime victims, contained in section two of the proposed Amendment, would permit any victim of a violent crime to go to court and make such an argument any time any prisoner was about to be released.

Section three of the proposed Amendment authorizes Congress and the states to enact legislation to enforce the Amendment. This authority could be used to negate the rights of criminal defendants in an effort to protect crime victims. Courts would then face the enormously difficult task of determining the extent to which legislation to implement the new Amendment can undermine the rights of those accused of crimes. Also, the authorization for *states* to enact legislation to implement the Amendment is unique among constitutional amendments. It is unclear whether these constitutionally authorized state laws will be supreme over state constitutions or even over federal laws.

Moreover, the Amendment is likely to be counter-productive because it could hamper effective prosecutions and cripple law enforcement by placing enormous new burdens on state and federal law enforcement agencies. Prosecutions could be hindered by the creation of an absolute right for crime victims to attend and participate in criminal proceedings. In many instances, the testimony of a prosecutorial witness will be compromised if the person has heard the testimony of other witnesses. Yet, the proposed Amendment creates an absolute right for a victim to be present at criminal proceedings even over the prosecution's objections.

The right of crime victims to insist on a speedy resolution could force prosecutors to try cases before they were fully prepared. Prosecutorial efforts also could be hampered by the ability of crime victims to "submit a written statement ... to determine ... an acceptance of a negotiated plea or sentence." It is unclear how much weight judges will be required to give to a crime victim's objection to a plea bargain. Over 90 percent of all criminal cases are now resolved by plea bargaining. Even a small increase in the number of cases going to trial would unduly burden prosecutors' offices. Often prosecutors enter into plea agreements based on decisions about allocating scarce prosecutorial resources, or based on concerns about weaknesses in the evidence, or based on strategic choices to gain the cooperation of one defendant to enhance the likelihood of convicting others. Prosecutorial discretion would be seriously compromised if crime victims could effectively obstruct plea agreements or require that prosecutors disclose the weaknesses in their case in order to persuade a court to accept a plea.

The Amendment would impose a tremendous new burden on state and federal law enforcement agencies. These departments would be *constitutionally* required to make reasonable efforts to find and notify crime victims every time a case went to trial, every time a criminal case was resolved, and most significantly, every time a prisoner was released from custody. Additionally, the Amendment can be interpreted as creating a duty for the government to provide attorneys for crime victims. The right of victims "to be heard!" contained in section two of the proposed Amendment, might well be seen as requiring counsel in order to be heard effectively. This, too, would create a huge cost for government. How would these obligations be funded? In all likelihood, money would be diverted from other law enforcement efforts.

The Amendment also would create an enormous burden on state and federal courts. The Amendment grants crime victims standing and a right to participate in virtually every phase of trial and post-trial proceedings. The burden this imposes is magnified because the Amendment does not define who is a crime victim. Family members and even friends of those attacked in violent crimes can claim to be injured and invoke a constitutional right to intervene and be heard.

Protecting crime victims by federal and state statutes provides flexibility that is absent in a constitutional amendment. Moreover, amending the Constitution in this way changes basic principles that have been followed throughout American history. Principles of federalism always have allowed states to decide the nature of the protection of victims in state courts. The ability of states to decide for themselves is denied by this Amendment. Also, no longer would protecting the rights of a person accused of crime be a preeminent focus of a criminal trial.

Crime victims deserve protection, but this should be accomplished by statutes, not a constitutional amendment. As law professors and practitioners we urge the rejection of the proposed Victims' Rights Amendment as unnecessary and dangerous.

Sincerely,
Professor Erwin Chemerinsky
University of Southern California Law School

Professor Lynne Henderson
Indiana University, Bloomington

Professor Robert P. Mosteller
Duke University School of Law
[et al.]

* * *

Analysis

Professor Chemerinsky is a distinguished professor of constitutional law. Professor Lynne Henderson wrote an early critique of California's early version of its constitutional victims' bill of rights. Professor Robert Mosteller, the author of the document preceding this letter, is the leading academic writing against the amendment. The letter reveals the legal academy's resistance to victims' constitutional change in criminal procedure. This resistance is deeply entrenched. As Professor Erin O'Hara of Vanderbilt Law School observed: "Given that virtually all law professors were trained in criminal law classes that ignored victim involvement in the criminal process, it is perhaps not surprising that it is considered heretical to suggest that direct participation might be warranted" (13 J.L. & Pol'y 229, 229-30 (2005)).

The preceding document prompted separate responses from Professors Cassell and Tribe. These responses are the next documents.

- **Document:** "A Proposed Constitutional Amendment to Protect Victims of Crime" by Paul G. Cassell
- **Date:** 1997
- **Significance:** Professor Paul Cassell's statement provides a counterpoint to the law professor letter against the addition of the victim's rights amendment.
- **Source:** Cassell, Paul G. "A Proposed Constitutional Amendment to Protect Victims of Crime." Statement at hearings on S.J. Res. 6, 105th Congress (1997).

---

* * *

Statement of Professor Paul Cassell

in A Proposed Constitutional Amendment to
Protect Victims of Crime: Hearings Before the Senate
Judiciary Committee, 105th Cong., 1st Sess. (1997)

The law professors' 1997 letter is filled with dubious claims.

Assertion: "[T]he right of victims to attend proceedings can be protected by statute as shown by . . . the recent federal legislation that mandates that victims be allowed to attend if they will be testifying during the sentencing phase of the proceedings!"

Response: In fact, the converse is shown. The rights of the Oklahoma City bombing victims have not been protected by the newly passed federal legislation.

Assertion: The victim's right to a final disposition free from unreasonable delay "could be used to deny defendant needed time to gather and present evidence essential in order to demonstrate their innocence."

Response: Interestingly, in the 1996 letter [from professors opposing the Amendment], the Committee was told exactly the opposite—that his right would somehow be used "to force prosecutors to try cases before they have adequate evidence?" Neither of these conflicting claims is true. Victims only seek a final resolution of cases free from "unreasonable" delay. The citation-free letter from the law professors fails to provide any evidence that comparable provisions in state constitutions and statutes are creating problems for criminal defendants (or prosecutors, for that matter).

Assertion: "Prosecution efforts also could be hampered by the ability of crime victims to submit [statements on plea bargains]."

Response: A victim's right to be heard before plea is already the law in many states, yet the law professors provide no reports of prosecutors being hampered. This is likely because this "hypothetical" problem, while perhaps interesting as a classroom discussion point, has not manifested itself in the real world. For example, it is the unqualified conclusion of the Maricopa County prosecutor—who prosecutes in a large metropolitan area (Phoenix) under one of the most expansive victims' rights amendments in the country (which specifically includes a right of the victim to be heard before a plea is accepted)—that "[c]onstitutional rights for victims will not obstruct prosecutors." Problems do not frequently arise from giving victims a right to be heard because most plea bargains reflect a reasonable resolution of the case. In the unusual instance where plea bargaining authority is being abused, the victim's right to be heard serves as a valuable safety valve. It is also important to remember that even in those cases where the victim's views are heard but not accepted by the judge, the victim may still leave the process more satisfied than if there was no opportunity for victim participation at all.

Assertion: The amendment creates enforcement authority that "could be used to negate the right of criminal defendants in an effort to protect crime victims."

Response: Enforcement authority is a rather standard feature of state victims' rights amendments, yet the professors provide no examples of enforcement authority being employed in this fashion. This is no doubt because the right to "enforce" a right for a crime victim does not create a right to "negate" rights for criminal defendants. The weakness [in] the professors' claim is demonstrated by the fact that they choose not to offer any specific illustrations of the hypothesized dangers. It is also interesting that in their 1996 letter, the professors appeared to make the opposite claim: that victims would be left with "few, if any, remedies for violations of . . . [the] rights enumerated."

Assertion: "The proposed Amendment . . . would . . . allow a victim of a crime to argue that it is *unconstitutional* to release a person from prison even though the sentence had been completed served?"

Response: A victim could possibly, as the law professors carefully put it, "argue" this far-fetched point, but the argument would plainly fail. The right conferred by the proposed Amendment is to have the victim's safety considered at the time a decisionmaker is "determining" a release from custody. If the sentence has already been determined and served, there is nothing further to be considered.

Assertion: "The ability of the states to decide for themselves is denied by this Amendment."

Response: This concern for federalism will strike some as equivalent to "confirmation conversion," given that many of the signatories to the letter have lauded, for example, Supreme Court decisions by the Warren Court federalizing a whole host of criminal procedure questions (*e.g.*, the exclusionary rule and *Miranda* warnings). The victims' movement has consistently maintained that it merely seeks equal treatment. If defendants' rights are constitutionalized and applied throughout the country, then victims' rights should be too. It is also important to remember that a super-majority of the states will have to ratify any proposed amendment before it takes effect.

These are some of the more obvious problems with the letter. The careful reader familiar with the proposed Victims' Rights Amendment will no doubt see many more. In its deliberations, Congress should, of course, weigh all points of view and all competing concerns. The right of the law professors, no less than other citizens, to provide information to Congress deserves our full respect. But Congress should not give any special weight to misinformed, inaccurate, or inflammatory criticism—such as that unfortunately found in the "law professors" letters.

Conclusion

The United States Supreme Court has recognized that "in the administration of criminal justice, courts may not ignore the concerns of victims:" Yet to crime victims, it has appeared in recent years that courts and others in the criminal justice system have been doing just that. Some level of victim frustration with the system is inevitable. But the examples of victims' problems reported to this Committee, both here and in other testimony, suggest substantial justification for frustration with the current patchwork of protections outside the Constitution.

Something more simply must be done. Congress should approve the Victims' Rights Amendment and send it on its way to the states for ratification. Our criminal justice system already provides ample rights for the accused and the guilty; it can— and should—do the same for the innocent.

* * *

- **Document:** "A Proposed Constitutional Amendment to Protect Victims of Crime" by Laurence Tribe
- **Date:** 1997
- **Significance:** Professor Laurence H. Tribe's statement provides a counterpoint to the law professor letter against the victims' rights amendment.

- **Source:** Tribe, Laurence. "A Proposed Constitutional Amendment to Protect Victims of Crime." Statement at hearings on S.J. Res. 6, 105th Congress (1997).

---

* * *

Statement of Professor Laurence H. Tribe

Harvard University Law School, *in* A Proposed Constitutional Amendment to Protect Victims of Crime: Hearings Before the Senate Judiciary Committee, 105th Cong., 1st Sess. (1997)

Beginning with the premise that the Constitution should not be amended lightly and should never be amended to achieve short-term, partisan, or purely policy objections, I would argue that a constitutional amendment is appropriate only when the goal involves (1) a needed change in government structure, or (2) a needed recognition of a basic human right, where (a) the right is one that people widely agree deserves serious and permanent respect, (b) the right is one that is insufficiently protected under existing law, (c) the right is one that cannot be adequately protected through purely political action such as state or federal legislation and/or regulation, (d) the right is one whose inclusion in the U.S. Constitution would not distort or endanger basic principles of the separation of powers among the federal branches, or the division of powers between the national and state governments, and (e) the right would be judicially enforceable without creating open-ended or otherwise unacceptable funding obligations.

I believe that S.J. Res. 6 meets these criteria. The rights in question—rights of crime victims not to be victimized yet again through the processes by which government bodies and officials prosecute, punish, and release the accused or convicted offender—are indisputably basic human rights against government, rights that any civilized system of justice would aspire to protect and strive never to violate. To protect these rights of victims does not entail constitutionalizing the rights of private citizens against other private citizens; for it is not the private citizen accused of crime by state or federal authorities who is the source of the violations that victims' rights advocates hope to address with a constitutional amendment in this area. Rather, it is the government authorities themselves, those who pursue (or release) the accused or convicted criminal with insufficient attention to the concerns of the victim, who are sometimes guilty of the kinds of violations that a properly drawn amendment would prohibit.

Pursuing and punishing criminals makes little sense unless society does so in a manner that fully respects the rights of their victims to be accorded dignity and respect, to be treated fairly in all relevant proceedings, and to be assured a meaningful opportunity; to observe, and take part in, all such proceedings. These are the very kinds of rights with which our Constitution is typically and properly concerned. Specifically, our Constitution's central concerns involve protecting the rights of individuals to participate in all those government processes that directly and immediately involve those individuals and affect their lives in some focused and particular way. Such rights include the right to vote on an equal basis whenever a matter is put to the electorate for resolution by voting; the right to be heard as a matter of procedural due process when government deprives one of life, liberty, or property; and various rights of the criminally accused to a speedy and public trial, with the assistance of counsel, and with various other participatory safeguards including the right to compulsory process and to confrontation of adverse witnesses. The parallel rights of victims to participate in these proceedings are no less basic, even though they find no parallel recognition in the explicit text of the U.S. Constitution.

I have read the letter from law professors, dated April 4, 1997, attacking the proposed Victims' Rights Constitutional Amendment. Although I share many of the broad views set forth in the letter—including the views that the Constitution should not be amended without a strong need and that the constitutional rights of persons accused of crime should not be sacrificed in order to serve other values—I do not believe the letter makes a convincing case for its ultimate conclusions. The case for the proposed amendment need not rest on some nebulous notion that the playing field must be balanced as between criminal defendants and crime victims. It rests on the twin propositions (1) that victims have important human rights that can and should be guaranteed protection without endangering the genuine rights of those accused or convicted, but (2) that attempts to protect these rights of victims at the state level, or through congressional legislation, have proven insufficient (although helpful) in light of the concern—recurring even if misguided—that taking victims' rights seriously, even when state or federal statutes or state constitutions appear to require doing so, will somehow be unfair to the accused or to others *even when no actual constitutional rights of the accused or of anyone else would be violated by respecting the rights of victims in the manner requested.* The proposed amendment would, in essence, counteract this problem.

Courts have sometimes recognized that the Constitution's failure to say anything explicit about the right of the victim or the victim's family to observe the trial of the accused should not be construed to deny the existence of such a right—provided, of course, that it can be respected consistent with the fair-trial rights of the accused. In *Richmond Newspapers v. Virginia*, 448 U.S. 555 (1980), for example, the plurality opinion, written by Chief Justice Burger, noted the way in which protecting the right of the press and the public to attend a criminal trial—even where, as in that case, the accused and the prosecution and the trial judge all preferred a closed proceeding—serves to protect not only random members of the public but those with a more specific interest in observing, and right to observe—namely, the dead victim's close relatives (see 448 U.S. at 571, "Civilized societies withdraw both from the victim and the vigilante the enforcement of criminal laws, but they cannot erase from people's consciousness the fundamental, natural yearning to see justice done— or even the urge for retribution."). Although the Sixth Amendment right to a public trial was held inapplicable in *Richmond Newspapers* on the basis that the Sixth Amendment secures that right only to the accused, and although the First Amendment right to free speech was thought by some (see, e.g., 448 U.S. at 604–06, Rehnquist, J., dissenting) to have no direct bearing in the absence of anything like government censorship, the plurality took note of the Ninth Amendment, whose reminder that the Constitution's enumeration of explicit rights is not to be deemed exclusive furnished an additional ground for the plurality's conclusion that the Constitution presupposed, even though it nowhere enumerated, a presumptive right of openness and participation in trial proceedings (see 448 U.S. at 579–80 & n.15, "Madison's efforts, culminating in the Ninth Amendment, served to allay the fears of those who were concerned that expressing certain guarantees could be read as excluding others").

I discuss *Richmond Newspapers* in some detail here not just because I argued that case but because it illustrates so forcefully the way in which victims' rights to observe and to participate, subject only to such exclusions and regulations as are genuinely essential to the protection of the rights of the accused, may be trampled upon in the course of law enforcement simply out of a concern with administrative convenience or out of an unthinking assumption that, because the Constitution nowhere refers to the rights of victims in so many words, such rights may and perhaps even should be ignored or at least downgraded. The happy coincidence that the rights of the victims in the *Richmond Newspapers* case overlapped with the First Amendment rights of the press prevented the victims in that case—the relatives of a hotel manager who had been found stabbed to death—from being altogether ignored on that occasion. But many victims have no such luck, and there appears to be a considerable body of evidence showing that, even where statutory or regulatory or judge-made rules exist to protect the participatory rights of victims, such rights often tend to be honored in the breach, *not* on the entirely understandable basis of a particularized determination that affording the victim the specific right claimed would demonstrably violate some constitutional right of the accused or convicted offender, but on the very different basis of a barely-considered reflex that protecting a victim's rights would represent either a luxury we cannot afford or a compromise with an ignoble desire for vengeance.

As long as we do so in a manner that respects the separation and division of powers and does not invite judges to interfere with law enforcement resource allocation decisions properly belonging to the political branches, we should not hesitate to make explicit in our Constitution the premise that I believe is implicit in that document but that is unlikely to receive full and effective recognition unless it is brought to the fore and chiseled in constitutional stone—the premise that the processes for enforcing state and federal criminal law must, to the extent possible, be conducted in a manner that respects not only the rights of those accused of having committed a crime but also the rights of those they are accused of having victimized.

The fact that the States and Congress, within their respective jurisdictions, already have ample affirmative authority to enact rules protecting these rights is a reason for not including new *enabling* or *empowering* language in a constitutional amendment on this subject, but is not a reason for opposing an amendment altogether. For the problem with rules enacted in the absence of such a constitutional amendment is not that such rules, assuming they are enacted with care, would be struck down as falling outside the affirmative authority of the relevant jurisdiction. The problem, rather, is that such rules are likely, as experience to date sadly shows, to provide too little real protection whenever they come into conflict with bureaucratic habit, traditional indifference, sheer inertia, or any mention of an accused's rights regardless of whether those rights are genuinely threatened.

Of course any new constitutional language in this area must be drafted so that the rights of victims will not become an excuse for running roughshod over the rights of the accused. This amendment has been written so that courts will retain ultimate responsibility for harmonizing, or balancing, the potentially conflicting rights of all participants in any given case. Assuring that this fine-tuning of conflicting rights remains a task for the judiciary is not too difficult. What is difficult, and perhaps impossible, is assuring that, under the existing system of rights and rules, the constitutional rights of victims—rights that the Framers of the Constitution undoubtedly assumed would receive fuller protection than has proven to be the case—will not instead receive short shrift.

To redress this imbalance, and to do so without distorting the Constitution's essential design, it may well be necessary to add a corrective amendment on this subject. Doing so would neither extend the Constitution to a purely policy issue, nor provide special benefits to a particular interest group, nor use the heavy artillery of constitutional amendment where a less radical solution is available. Nor would it put the Constitution to a merely symbolic use, or enlist it for some narrow or partisan purpose. It would instead, help solve a distinct and significant gap in our existing legal system's arrangements for the protection of basic human rights against an important category of governmental abuse.

* * *

Analysis

Ultimately, the argument to experiment with a statutory set of rights before turning to a constitutional amendment prevailed. The Senate has 100 members, but to move an amendment forward requires a supermajority of the Senate. In 2002, the proposed amendment went to the floor of the Senate for a debate. But the supermajority needed would not be obtained. In the next session of Congress, it was decided that the Amendment would be offered and then "flipped" or turned into a statute because there were not 60 votes for cloture for Amendment. The resulting statute was part of the Justice For All Act. The provisions relating to victims' rights were called the Crime Victims Rights' Act, or CVRA, and were codified as 18 U.S.C. 3771. This statute, and the federal victims' statutes that preceded it, are the subject of the next chapter.

REFERENCES

Ala. Code Sec. 15-14-54.
Ariz. Const. Art. 2, Sec. 2.1.
Arizona ex rel. Romley v. Superior Court, 836 P.2d 445 (Ariz. Ct. App. 1992).
Ariz. Rev. Stat. Ann. Sec. 13-4437(B).
Barajas, Richard, and Scott Alexander Nelson. *The Proposed Crime Victims' Federal Constitutional Amendment: Working Toward a Proper Balance.* 49 Baylor L. Rev. 1, 17 (1997).
Barker v. Wingo, 407 U.S. 514 (1972).
Beloof, Douglas E. *Victims in Criminal Procedure: A Casebook.* Durham, NC: Carolina University Press, 1998.

Brandeis, Louis. *Other People's Money*. Washington, DC: National Home Library Foundation, 1933.

Burt, Martha, Lisa C. Newmark, Lisa K. Jacobs, and Adele V. Harrell. *Report: Evaluation of the STOP Formula Grants Under the Violence Against Women Act of 1994*. Washington, DC: Urban Institute, 1998.

Cassell, Paul G. "A Proposed Constitutional Amendment to Protect Victims of Crime," statement at hearings on S.J. Res. 6, 105th Congress, 1997.

Cassell, Paul G. *Balancing the Scales of Justice: The Case for and the Effects of Utah's Victims' Rights Amendment*. 1994 Utah L. Rev. 1373 (1994).

Classified Information Procedures Act. CIPA, Pub.L. 96-456, 94 Stat. 2025, enacted October 15, 1980 through S. 1482 (codified at 18 U.S.C. App. III. Sections 1–161980).

Cross, Jeffrey A. *The Repeated Sufferings of Domestic Violence Victims Not Notified of Their Assailant's Pre-Trial Release from Custody: A Call for Mandatory Domestic Violence Victim Notification Legislation*. 34 J. Family L. 915 (1996).

Diaz v. United States, 223 U.S. 442 (1912).

Eikenberry, Ken. *The Elevation of Victims' Rights in Washington State: Constitutional Status*. 17 Pepperdine L. Rev. 19, 41 (1989).

Exec. Comm. Meeting, Senate Comm. on the Judiciary, 105th Cong., 2d Sess., at 23–24 (Jun. 25, 1998).

Exec. Comm. Meeting, Senate Comm. on the Judiciary, 105th Cong., 2d Sess., at 109–11 (July 7, 1998).

Fein, Bruce. "Deforming the Constitution." *Washington Times*, July 6, 1998.

Fichenberg, Robert. *The Controversial Victims' Rights Amendment*, 30–Oct Prosecutor 38 (1996).

Fletcher, George P. *With Justice for Some: Protecting Victims' Rights in Criminal Trials*. Massachusetts: Addison Wesley, 1995.

Foster v. Wainwright, 686 F.2d 1382 (11th Cir. 1982).

Gideon v. Wainwright, 372 U.S. 335 (1963).

Green v. United States, 365 U.S. 301 (1961).

Heymann, Philip B. *A Proposed Victims' Rights Constitutional Amendment: Against an Amendment*. 14 State-Federal Judicial Observer, 1 (Apr. 1997).

Hillenbrand, Susan and Barbara E. Smith. *Victims' Rights Legislation: An Assessment of Its Impact on Criminal Justice Practitioners and Victims*, American Bar Assn. Criminal Justice Section Victim Witness Program. Washington, DC: American Bar Association, May 1989.

Idaho Const. Art. I, 22(4).

Illinois v. Allen, 397 U.S. 337 (1977).

Jefferson, Thomas. Letter to Samuel Kercheval, July 12, 1816. In *The Writings of Thomas Jefferson*, edited by Paul L. Ford, vol. 10. New York and London: GP Putnam's Sons, 1899.

Kan. Const. Art. 15, 15(b).

Kazen, George P. Chief U.S. District Judge, Chair, Committee on Criminal Law of the Judicial Conference of the United States, letter to Sen. Edward M. Kennedy, Senate Comm on the Judiciary, at 2 (Apr. 17, 1997).

Kilpatrick, Dean G. and Randy K. Otto. *Constitutionally Guaranteed Participation in Criminal Proceedings for Victims: Potential Effects on Psychological Functioning*. 34 Wayne L. Rev. 7, 19 (1987).

Knight, Marsha. "A Proposed Constitutional Amendment to Protect Victims of Crime," statement at hearings on S.J. Res. 6, 105th Congress, 1997.

LaFave, Wayne R. and Jerold H. Israel. *Criminal Procedure*. 2nd Ed. New York: West Group, 1992.

Letter from Law Professors. Reprinted in *A Proposed Constitutional Amendment to Protect Victims of Crime*, Hearing on S.J. Res. 6 before the Senate Comm. on the Judiciary, 105th Cong., 1st Sess., at 140 (Apr. 16, 1997).

Madigan, Lee, and Nancy C. Gamble. *The Second Rape: Society's Continued Betrayal of the Victim.* New York: Lexington Books, 1989.

Madison, James. *The Complete Madison.* Edited by Saul K. Padover. New York: Harper, 1953.

Mandatory Victims Restitution Act of 1996. Pub. L. No. 104-132, tit. IIA, 110 Stat. 1227 (codified as amended at 18 U.S.C.§ 3663(a) (1996)).

Memorandum from Sam McQuade, Program Manager, National Institute of Justice, to Jeremy Travis, Director, National Institute of Justice (May 16, 1997).

Miller, John and Peter Jennings. "A Closer Look: Why People Were Strip Searched for Minor Crimes." *World News Tonight,* April 23, 1998, *available in* 1998 WL 7292306.

Mo. Const. Art. I, 32(1).

Morris v. Slappy, 461 U.S. 1 (1983).

Mosteller, Robert. *Victims' Rights and the Constitution: Moving from Guaranteeing Participatory Rights to Benefiting the Prosecution.* 29 St. Mary's L.J. 1053 (1998).

Mosteller, Robert. *Victims' Rights and the United States Constitution: An Effort to Recast the Battle in Criminal Litigation,* 85 Geo. L.J. 1691 (1997).

Mosteller, Robert. *The Unnecessary Victims' Rights Amendment.* 1999 Utah L. Rev. 443.

Murphy, William. President, National District Attorneys Assn., Letter to Sen. Patrick J. Leahy, Ranking Member, Senate Comm. on the Judiciary (May 27, 1998).

National Governors Association. Policy 23.1 (effective winter 1997 to winter 1999).

National Victim Center. *Victims' Rights Sourcebook.* Washington, DC: Victim Rights Center, 1996.

National Victim Center. *Statutory and Constitutional Protection of Victims' Rights: Implementation and Impact on Crime Victims—Sub-Report: Crime Victim Responses Regarding Victims' Rights.* Washington, DC: National Victim Center, April 15, 1997.

National Victim Center. *Statutory and Constitutional Protection of Victims' Rights: Implementation and Impact on Crime Victims—Sub-Report: Comparison of White and Non-White Crime Victim Responses Regarding Victims' Rights.* Washington, DC: National Victim Center, 1997.

Office for Victims of Crime, *Victims' Rights Compliance Efforts: Experiences in Three States.* Washington, DC: United States Office of Justice Programs, 1998.

Office for Victims of Crime. *President's Task Force on Victims of Crime: Final Report.* Washington DC: U.S. Government Printing Press, 1982.

O'Hara, Erin. *Victim Participation in the Criminal Process.* 13 J.L. & Pol'y 229 (2005).

Payne v. Tennessee, 501 U.S. 808 (1991).

President Clinton, statement of. Rose Garden Ceremony, June 25th 1996.

Proposed Constitutional Amendment to Establish a Bill of Rights for Crime Victims, A. Hearing on S.J. Res. 52 before the Senate Comm. on the Judiciary, 104th Cong., 2d Sess. 100 (Apr. 23, 1996).

Rehnquist, William. Chief Justice, U.S. Supreme Court, letter to Judy Clarke, President, National Assn. of Criminal Defense Lawyers (Apr. 23, 1997).

Richmond Newspapers v. Virginia, 448 U.S. 555 (1980).

Robison v. Maynard, 943 F.2d 1216 (10th Cir. 1991).

Sager v. Maass, 907 F. Supp. 1412 (D. Or. 1995).

Senate Judiciary Committee Hearing, April 23, 1996.

Senate Judiciary Committee Hearing, April 16, 1997.

Senate Judiciary Committee Hearing, April 28, 1998.

Senate Report. *United States Senate Report on Senate Joint Resolution 44.* S.J. Res. 44, 69–010, Calendar No. 455, 105TH Congress, Report, Senate, 2d Session, 105–409. Washington, DC: United States Senate, 1998.

Sheppard v. Maxwell, 384 U.S. 333, 350 (1966).

S.J. Res. 44, 105th Cong. (1998).

Speedy Trial Act, The. 18 U.S.C.§§3161–3174 (2008).

S. Rep. 104–179, Senate Judiciary Committee, Victim Restitution Act of 1995, 104th Cong., 1st Sess. 12 (1995).

Statement of the Conference of Chief Justices regarding H.J. Res. 71 and H.R. 1322, prepared for the House Comm. on the Judiciary (June 25, 1997).

Tex. Const. Art. I, 30(e).

Tribe, Laurence H. & Paul G. Cassell. "Embed the Rights of Victims in the Constitution." *L.A. Times*, July 6, 1998.

Tribe, Laurence. "A Proposed Constitutional Amendment to Protect Victims of Crime," statement at hearings on S.J. Res. 6, 105th Congress, 1997.

Turman, Kathryn. Acting Director, OVC. Letter to Robert P. Mosteller, Professor, Duke University School of Law (Sept. 18, 1998).

United States v. Carolene Products Co., 304 U.S. 144 (1938).

United States v. Flores, 875 F.2d 1110 (5th Cir. 1989).

United States v. Guadardo, 40 F.3d 102 (5th Cir. 1994).

United States v. Hollman Cheung, 952 F. Supp. 148 (E.D.N.Y. 1997).

United States v. Lanier, 520 U.S. 259 (1997).

United States v. Lopez, 514 U.S. 549 (1995).

United States v. Martinez, 978 F. Supp. 1442 (D.N.M. 1997).

United States v. McVeigh, 106 F.3d 325 (10th Cir. 1997).

United States v. McVeigh, 958 F. Supp. 512 (1997).

United States v. Newman, No. 97-3246 (7th Cir. 1998).

United States v. Reyes-Castro, 13 F.3d 377 (10th Cir. 1993).

United States v. Salerno, 481 U.S. 739 (1987).

United States v. Smith, 893 F. Supp. 187(E.D.N.Y. 1995).

United States v. Williams, 128 F.3d 1239 (8th Cir. 1997).

U.S. Department of Justice, Office for Victims of Crime. *New Directions From the Field: Victims' Rights and Services for the 21st Century*. Washington, DC: U.S. Government Printing Press, 1998.

Utah Code Ann. 77-38-5(8).

Victims of Crime Act of 1984. Pub. L. No. 98-473, 98 Stat. 2170 (codified as amended at 42 U.S.C. § 10601) (1984)).

Victim Rights Clarification Act of 1997. Pub. L. No 105-6, 111 Stat. 12 (codified as amended at 18 U.S.C. § 3510 (1997)).

Victims' Rights and Restitution Act of 1990. Pub. L. No. 101-647, 104 Stat. 4820 (codified as amended at 42 U.S.C. § 10606 (1990)).

Victims Witness Protection Act. Pub. L. 97-291 (codified at 18 U.S.C. Sec. 1501, 1503, 1505, 1510, 1512–1515, 3146, 3579, 3580 (1982)).

Violence Against Women Act of 1994, The. P.L. 103–322, Title IV, Sept. 13, 1994, 108 Stat. 179 (codified as amended at scattered sections of 18 U.S.C. and 42 U.S.C. (1994)).

Weisberger, Joseph R. Chief Justice, Supreme Court of Rhode Island, Chairperson, Conference of Chief Justices Task Force on Victim Rights, Letter to Sen. Orrin G. Hatch, Chairman, Senate Comm. on the Judiciary, at 1 (May 16, 1997).

Wilson, Wayne. "Man acquitted in killing after protest by victim's kin torpedoed plea deal." *The Sacramento Bee*, July 2, 1997.

Young, Marlene. National Organization for Victim Assistance (NOVA) committee meeting, 1998.

Additional Reading

Bandes, Susan. *Victim Standing*. 1999 Utah Law Review 331 (1999).

Cassell, Paul G. *Barbarians at the Gates? A Reply to the Critics of the Victims' Rights Amendment*. 1999 Utah L. Rev. 479 (1999).

7

THE CRIME VICTIMS' RIGHTS ACT

THE CRIME VICTIMS' RIGHTS ACT

The Crime Victims' Rights Act (CVRA) was passed by Congress and enacted into law in 2004. As explained in the previous chapter, the CVRA was a compromise to ascertain if a statute would suffice in lieu of a constitutional amendment. The CVRA only provides victims' rights in federal prosecutions, which make up a very small percentage of all criminal cases. The vast majority are state prosecutions. It would take a federal constitutional amendment to provide consistent and uniform rights nationwide to all victims.

The CVRA was a product of the attempt to enact federal constitutional rights for victims of crime. The following letter from Steve Twist, Chief Counsel and lobbyist for the constitutional amendment effort, to the leaders of the Crime Victims' Rights Movement explains the reasons for moving from an amendment to the CVRA.

- **Document:** Letter to Supporters of Senate Joint Resolution 1, the Crime Victims' Rights Amendment by Steve Twist
- **Date:** April 28, 2004
- **Significance:** This letter from Steve Twist provides insight behind the reasons for the concession from a Constitutional Amendment to the CVRA.
- **Source:** Twist, Steve. Letter to Supporters of Senate Joint Resolution 1, the Crime Victims' Rights Amendment. National Victims Constitutional Amendment Project, 2004.

* * *

To: Supporters of Senate Joint Resolution 1, the Crime Victims'
Rights Amendment
From: Steve Twist, Chief Counsel, National Victims Constitutional
Amendment Project
Date: April 28, 2004.

As I am certain that you know, on the afternoon of Thursday, April 22, Senators Jon Kyl (R-AZ) and Dianne Feinstein (D-CA), the primary sponsors of the S. J. Res. 1, proposed a statutory substitute for their amendment proposal. The bill had no one to speak against it, and when the roll was called, is passed ninety-six to one. I want to give you the reasoning that caused our two champions and me, as the lead representative of the victims' movement in the discussions, first, to explore and, in the end, to support a statutory alternative.

In all this, I believe we acted honorably and with the best interests of crime victims at heart—and I hope this memo will lead you to the same conclusions. . . .

What I did do was to bring Mothers Against Drunk Driving, Parents of Murdered Children, National Organization for Victim Assistance, Force 100, and all of our supporters present in Washington in on the statutory alternative, as I did by phone to a number of our prominent leaders around the country, including Roberta Roper and Bob Preston, the National Victim Constitutional Amendment Passage's co-chairs. That I didn't circulate the plan more widely was at the request of our sponsors as they were building the extraordinary bipartisan support that greeted the proposal.

While all of us deeply regretted the failure to get 67 votes for S. J. Res. 1, we all accepted the idea that Federal legislation which establishes real and enforceable rights would advance our cause in the long run. . . .

Let me review how the statutory alternative came into play and why its provisions make it a very strong victim rights statute.

The genesis of the bill was simply this: we came to the sober realization that despite our best efforts, we didn't have the 67 needed votes for final passage. Senator Kyl elaborated on that on the Senate floor.

After eight years of work on the Federal constitutional amendment, supported by President Bush and the Attorney General, we were able to schedule . . . the constitutional amendment for floor action today. [But] knowing we would not have the 67 votes to pass it, we decided it was time to get something tangible in a statute to protect the rights of victims, and accompanying it could be a modest appropriation of money to help actually support these victims in court when that was necessary and called for. We believed despite the potential that it would not serve adequately, it was time to try something, to be successful, and to at least move the ball forward.

As Senator Leahy said in a press conference we had earlier, the Judiciary Committee of the Senate will provide very strong oversight of implementation of this statute, so we will know if it is not working. If it does not work, we will be able to come back and pursue the constitutional remedy. But we consulted with the victims' rights groups that have been most active in support of this.

They concurred it was time to pursue the statutory remedy, if we could get some assurance we would be successful in that pursuit and that it would not be simply a fool's errand.

. . . Consensus was reached that it was time for us to convert the constitutional proposal into a statute. This occurred within the last 48 hours. Through the cooperation of Senator Leahy, Senator Hatch, staff, and several other Senators, but most importantly because of the very hard work done by Senator Feinstein's staff and mine, they were able to literally convert these rights in the constitutional proposal into the statutory proposal for submission. That is what is before us today and what we will be voting on.

Senator Feinstein's comments were much the same:

* * *

". . . Will it work? I hope so. The bill before us is a new and bolder approach than has ever been tried before in our Federal system."

In the lead-up to the bill, Senators Kyl and Feinstein—along with Senator Patrick Leahy (D-VT), who had proposed a different statutory alternative—agreed that the bill should encompass three principles:

- the rights listed must be drawn directly from the amendment;
- the enforcement mechanisms must be tough;
- and the bill must authorize financial support of victims' law clinics so that victims could assert their rights not only under the Federal law but state laws as well.

The bill meets every one of those tests.

For all of us in the nine-year Constitutional Amendment campaign this moment is both bitter and sweet. We bent every intellectual and emotional muscle we could muster to put victim justice into our national charter. While we did not succeed, the Senate has overwhelmingly passed a statute that will put the arguments of our opponents to the final test. If this statute in particular will not work (and we will fight hard to make it work for the victims we serve) we will have proven that no statutes alone will work except as tools to implement a Constitutional amendment.

Be assured, we will fight hard to make it work. And even as we work to have these rights implemented in the Federal courts, we will redouble our efforts to get states to better comply with their bills of victims' rights. As Senator Feinstein observed:

"This act, of course, binds only the federal system, but is designed to affect the states also. First it is hoped that states will look to this law as a model and incorporate it into their own systems. This law encourages that by allowing both types of grants—legal assistance and victim notification—to be provided to state entities, and for use in state systems, where the state has in place laws substantially equivalent to this act."

Note that last phrase. After the Justice Department issues regulations defining "substantially equivalent" victim rights laws, we will all have a benchmark to see how our state statutes measure up—and a ready plan to have them meet that test.

Here are the basic features of the bill, the rights established are clear and unequivocal, taken from S. J. Res. 1 and current law; the victim (or the prosecutor) has standing to assert the victim's rights in the Federal District court with jurisdiction in the case; further, the enforcement mechanisms require the court which denies a victim's petition to uphold a specified right must explain its denial on the record; at that stage, the victim may seek a review by a Federal Appeals court, which must not only hear the appeal but act on it promptly, and order the District Court to make whatever redress is required.

To help the victim learn of and enforce these rights, funding is authorized for a Federal notification system (so that the administrative dimension of the law is advanced) and for legal clinics to help victims to assert and protect their rights. States that have victim rights laws substantially equivalent to the Federal may also receive grants. A separate funding provision allows states and localities to construct their own compliance systems, with or without lawyers. These too are unprecedented features of any victim rights law.

Finally, the bill requires the Administrative Office of the Courts to report annually every assertion of a victim's right in a criminal case that was not honored by the court and the result of every mandamus action in the Court of Appeals which challenged a lower court's denial of a right.

I encourage you to read the bill in full (go to http://www.nvcap.org). The basic features are plain to see. But some are more subtle. For example, as a colloquy during the debate between Senators Kyl and Feinstein indicates, if a court that finds that a plea bargain was accepted under circumstances where the victim's rights were ignored, such a plea may be voided. The same is true of sentences handed down improperly.

* * *

I again want to thank all of you for your support for our movement for victims' rights; when [the bill] passes the House and is signed by the President, we will have moved our cause forward in a dramatic way.

* * *

Analysis

The inability to achieve a constitutional amendment providing victims' rights was a tremendous disappointment for the Victims' Rights Movement. Faced with the imminent appointment of Senator Leahy, an opponent of the Victims' Rights Amendment, to the chair of the Senate Judiciary Committee, the choice to switch to a statute was a pragmatic one. The hope was that enforcement would be routine in federal courts, and the statute might serve as a model for the states. If it did not succeed, the Amendment effort would return. At a minimum, if it turned out that the statute was flawed, the awareness of its weaknesses could be used to improve a subsequent amendment.

In History

The National Crime Victim Amendment Network (NVCAN) is the collection of victim groups and prominent leaders who lead the amendment effort. Steve Twist is its general counsel. NVCAN has worked for an amendment since the mid-1990s and continues to be active.

On October 30, 2004, President Bush signed into law the Scott Campbell, Stephanie Roper, Wendy Preston, Louarna Gillis, and Nila Lynn Crime Victims' Rights Act (CVRA). This Act is designed to strengthen the federal statutes protecting crime victims' rights, particularly the victims' bill of rights laid out in *United States v. McVeigh* in Chapter 5. For federal crimes, the statute provides a list of victims' rights and enhanced enforcement.

The Text of the Crime Victims' Right Act

- **Document:** *The Crime Victims' Rights Act (CVRA)*, Scott Campbell, Stephanie Roper, Wendy Preston, Louarna Gillis, and Nila Lynn
- **Date:** Effective December 1, 2009
- **Significance:** The CVRA encodes the rights of victims of crime in all federal prosecutions and may serve as model legislation for states to adopt.
- **Source:** Campbell, Scott, Stephanie Roper, Wendy Preston, Louarna Gillis, and Nila Lynn. *The Crime Victims' Rights Act (CVRA)*. Pub. L. No. 108–405, §§ 101–104, 118 Stat. 2260, 2261–65 (2004) (codified at 18 U.S.C. § 3771).

Attorney Steve Twist is legal counsel for the National Victims Constitutional Amendment Network. He worked to pass a victims' rights amendment; this work led to enactment of the Crime Victims' Rights Act (CVRA). (Courtesy Steve Twist)

* * *

18 U.S.C. § 3771.

Crime victims' rights

(a) Rights of crime victims.—A crime victim has the following rights:

    (1) The right to be reasonably protected from the accused.

    (2) The right to reasonable, accurate, and timely notice of any public court proceeding, or any parole proceeding, involving the crime or of any release or escape of the accused.

    (3) The right not to be excluded from any such public court proceeding, unless the court, after receiving clear and convincing evidence, determines that testimony by the victim would be materially altered if the victim heard other testimony at that proceeding.

    (4) The right to be reasonably heard at any public proceeding in the district court involving release, plea, sentencing, or any parole proceeding.

    (5) The reasonable right to confer with the attorney for the Government in the case.

    (6) The right to full and timely restitution as provided in law.

    (7) The right to proceedings free from unreasonable delay.

    (8) The right to be treated with fairness and with respect for the victim's dignity and privacy.

(b) Rights afforded.—

    (1) In general.—In any court proceeding involving an offense against a crime victim, the court shall ensure that the crime victim is afforded the rights described in subsection (a). Before making a determination described in subsection (a)(3), the court shall make every effort to permit the fullest attendance possible by the victim and shall consider reasonable alternatives to the exclusion of the victim from the criminal proceeding. The reasons for any decision denying relief under this chapter shall be clearly stated on the record.

    (2) Habeas corpus proceedings.—

        (A) In general.—In a Federal habeas corpus proceeding arising out of a State conviction, the court shall ensure that a crime victim is afforded the rights described in paragraphs (3), (4), (7), and (8) of subsection (a).

        (B) Enforcement.—

            (i) In general.—These rights may be enforced by the crime victim or the crime victim's lawful representative in the manner described in paragraphs (1) and (3) of subsection (d).

           (ii) Multiple victims.—In a case involving multiple victims, subsection (d)(2) shall also apply.

        (C) Limitation.—This paragraph relates to the duties of a court in relation to the rights of a crime victim in Federal habeas corpus proceedings arising out of a State conviction, and does not give rise to any obligation or requirement applicable to personnel of any agency of the Executive Branch of the Federal Government.

        (D) Definition.—For purposes of this paragraph, the term "crime victim" means the person against whom the State offense is committed or, if that person is killed or incapacitated, that person's family member or other lawful representative.

(c) Best efforts to accord rights.—

    (1) Government.—Officers and employees of the Department of Justice and other departments and agencies of the United States engaged in the detection, investigation, or prosecution of crime shall make their best efforts to see that crime victims are notified of, and accorded, the rights described in subsection (a).

(2) Advice of attorney.—The prosecutor shall advise the crime victim that the crime victim can seek the advice of an attorney with respect to the rights described in subsection (a).

(3) Notice.—Notice of release otherwise required pursuant to this chapter shall not be given if such notice may endanger the safety of any person.

(d) Enforcement and limitations.—

(1) Rights.—The crime victim or the crime victim's lawful representative, and the attorney for the Government may assert the rights described in subsection (a). A person accused of the crime may not obtain any form of relief under this chapter.

(2) Multiple crime victims.—In a case where the court finds that the number of crime victims makes it impracticable to accord all of the crime victims the rights described in subsection (a), the court shall fashion a reasonable procedure to give effect to this chapter that does not unduly complicate or prolong the proceedings.

(3) Motion for relief and writ of mandamus.—The rights described in sub-section (a) shall be asserted in the district court in which a defendant is being prosecuted for the crime or, if no prosecution is underway, in the district court in the district in which the crime occurred. The district court shall take up and decide any motion asserting a victim's right forth-with. If the district court denies the relief sought, the movant may peti-tion the court of appeals for a writ of mandamus. The court of appeals may issue the writ on the order of a single judge pursuant to circuit rule or the Federal Rules of Appellate Procedure. The court of appeals shall take up and decide such application forthwith within 72 hours after the petition has been filed. In no event shall proceedings be stayed or subject to a continuance of more than five days for purposes of enforcing this chapter. If the court of appeals denies the relief sought, the reasons for the denial shall be clearly stated on the record in a written opinion.

(4) Error.—In any appeal in a criminal case, the Government may assert as error the district court's denial of any crime victim's right in the proceed-ing to which the appeal relates.

(5) Limitation on relief.—In no case shall a failure to afford a right under this chapter provide grounds for a new trial. A victim may make a motion to re-open a plea or sentence only if—

(A) the victim has asserted the right to be heard before or during the proceeding at issue and such right was denied;

(B) the victim petitions the court of appeals for a writ of mandamus within 14 days; and

(C) in the case of a plea, the accused has not pled to the highest offense charged. This paragraph does not affect the victim's right to restitu-tion as provided in title 18, United States Code.

(6) No cause of action.—Nothing in this chapter shall be construed to authorize a cause of action for damages or to create, to enlarge, or to

imply any duty or obligation to any victim or other person for the breach of which the United States or any of its officers or employees could be held liable in damages. Nothing in this chapter shall be construed to impair the prosecutorial discretion of the Attorney General or any officer under his direction.

(e) Definitions.—For the purposes of this chapter, the term "crime victim" means a person directly and proximately harmed as a result of the commission of a Federal offense or an offense in the District of Columbia. In the case of a crime victim who is under 18 years of age, incompetent, incapacitated, or deceased, the legal guardians of the crime victim or the representatives of the crime victim's estate, family members, or any other persons appointed as suitable by the court, may assume the crime victim's rights under this chapter, but in no event shall the defendant be named as such guardian or representative.

(f) Procedures to promote compliance.—

(1) Regulations.—Not later than 1 year after the date of enactment of this chapter, the Attorney General of the United States shall promulgate regulations to enforce the rights of crime victims and to ensure compliance by responsible officials with the obligations described in law respecting crime victims.

(2) Contents.—The regulations promulgated under paragraph (1) shall—

(A) designate an administrative authority within the Department of Justice to receive and investigate complaints relating to the provision or violation of the rights of a crime victim;

(B) require a course of training for employees and offices of the Department of Justice that fail to comply with provisions of Federal law pertaining to the treatment of crime victims, and otherwise assist such employees and offices in responding more effectively to the needs of crime victims;

(C) contain disciplinary sanctions, including suspension or termination from employment, for employees of the Department of Justice who willfully or wantonly fail to comply with provisions of Federal law pertaining to the treatment of crime victims; and

(D) provide that the Attorney General, or the designee of the Attorney General, shall be the final arbiter of the complaint, and that there shall be no judicial review of the final decision of the Attorney General by a complainant.

* * *

Document Analysis of the CVRA

- **Document:** "New Rights and Remedies: The Federal Crime Victims' Rights Act of 2004" by David E. Aaronson

- **Date:** Summer 2008
- **Significance:** In this article, Aaronson reviews the development, evolution, and implications of the CVRA.
- **Source:** Aaronson, David E. "New Rights and Remedies: The Federal Crime Victims' Rights Act of 2004." *Pace Law Review* 28 (2008): 623, 646–671. Reprinted with permission.

---

* * *

Victims' Rights at Different Stages of the Criminal Process

The rights provided by the CVRA vary according to the nature of the right and the stage of the proceeding. The rights to reasonable notice and not to be excluded are expansive, applying to "any public court proceeding, or any parole proceeding, involving the crime or of any release or escape of the accused" (18 U.S.C. § 3771 (b)). The right to be reasonably heard, however, only applies at public proceedings involving release, plea, sentencing, or parole and not at the actual trial. The other five rights afforded to victims under the Act make no mention of the different stages of criminal proceedings (see Cassell 2005, hereinafter Cassell, Recognizing Victims, arguing that the legislative history of the CVRA indicates Congress intended it as a remedial statute, and therefore any general provision should be interpreted "generously so as to effectuate the important congressional goals."); Cassell 2007, hereinafter Cassell, Treating Crime Victims Fairly). In determining what is "reasonable" in relation to five of the eight crime victims' rights set forth in the CVRA, courts are likely to take into consideration the different stages of the criminal process in balancing the needs and interests of the prosecutors, defendants, and crime victims. Defendants' interest in pretrial and trial proceedings are greater than in post-trial proceedings. The presumption of innocence and the right to prepare a defense are protected by the due process clause prior to adjudication of guilt. At sentencing and post-trial proceedings, such as parole hearings, defendants have a diminished liberty interest.

Pretrial Rights: Right to be Reasonably Protected from the Accused and to be Present and Reasonably Heard at Pretrial Release Hearings

The crime victim's right to notice of, to be present at, and to be heard at the pretrial release hearing or the defendant's initial appearance potentially juxtaposes a crime victim's rights against a jailed suspect's liberty interest in a prompt judicial determination of pretrial release (see 18 U.S.C. § 3771(a)(2)–(4)). The first right of crime victims set forth in the CVRA is "[t]he right to be reasonably protected from the accused" (Id. § 3771(a)(1)). A crime victim may have relevant information to provide the judge, for example, facts unknown to the prosecutor that relate to the future dangerousness of the defendant.

There is a potential conflict between the defendant's statutory rights under Rule 5(a) and the victim's rights under the CVRA, section 3771(a)(2). Under Rule 5(a) of the Federal Rules of Criminal Procedure, a person making an arrest within the United States must take the defendant without unnecessary delay before a judicial officer (Fed. R. Crim. P. 5(a)). Is it "necessary" within the meaning of Rule 5(a) to delay the defendant's initial appearance to ensure that crime victims receive reasonable, accurate, and timely notice of this proceeding? Also, section 3771(a)(2) of the CVRA only requires "reasonable" notice (see 18 U.S.C. § 3771(a)(2)). Is it reasonable for the judge to delay the initial appearance if the accused is in jail in order to allow time for all alleged victims to be notified?

There may be little time to notify alleged crime victims and inquire whether they wish to be present and heard. The judge's duty to insure that the crime victim's rights are protected may impose an obligation to ask the prosecutor if victims of the alleged offenses have been properly informed of their right to be present and heard at a pretrial release hearing. In addition, initial appearances may be conducted by video teleconferencing, with the defendants' consent (Fed. R. Crim. P. 5(f)). Procedures need to be developed to clarify how to provide accurate and timely notice of the initial appearance to crime victims, including who should notify them, which persons should be notified, whether these persons desire to be present and heard, and where they should go (see *United States v. Turner*, 367 F.Supp.2d 319, 323-38 (E.D.N.Y. 2005)).

In *United States v. Turner*, the judge discovered, at the defendant's bail hearing, that the victims in the case had not received adequate notice of either the initial hearing or the bail hearing. The judge, sua sponte, ordered the prosecutor to provide all alleged victims with a written summary of the proceedings to that point and notification of their rights under the CVRA to attend and be heard at future proceedings (Id. at 324). The judge determined, however, that under the Bail Reform Act, no conditions of release would reasonably assure the defendant's appearance and entered an order of detention pending trial, with defendant's consent, subject to reconsideration (Id. at 321, citing 18 U.S.C. § 3142(e) (1984)). In a carefully crafted opinion Judge Orenstein observed that the defendant is entitled to a presumption of innocence and suggested that an accused should not be subjected to further incarceration without a substantive ruling on whether conditions of release exist that satisfy the requirements of the Bail Reform Act (Bail Reform Act, 18 U.S.C. §§ 3141–50 (1984); see also *United States v. Salerno*, 481 U.S. 739, 750 (1987; "The Bail Reform Act . . . narrowly focuses on a particularly acute problem in which the Government interests are overwhelming. The Act operates only on individuals who have been arrested for a specific category of extremely serious offenses. Congress specifically found that these individuals are far more likely to be responsible for dangerous acts in the community after arrest. . . . In a full blown adversary hearing, the Government must convince a neutral decision maker by clear and convincing evidence that no conditions of release can reasonably assure the safety of the community or any person. While the Government's general interest in preventing crime is compelling, even this interest is heightened when the Government musters convincing proof that the arrestee, already indicted or held to answer for a serious crime, presents a demonstrable danger to the community. Under these narrow circumstances, society's interest in crime prevention is at its greatest. . . . On the other side of the scale, of course, is the individual's strong interest in liberty. We do not minimize the importance and fundamental nature of this right. But . . . this right may, in circumstances where the government's interest is sufficiently weighty, be subordinated to the greater needs of society.").

Other courts have interpreted the right to be present inconsistently. In *United States v. Marcello*, the court held that the victim's right to be heard at a pretrial release hearing could be accommodated through written statements, and the victim was not entitled to appear in person before the court (*United States v. Marcello*, 370 F.Supp.2d 745, 746-50 (N.D. Ill. 2005); *Cf. United States v. Blumhagen*, no. 03-CR-56S, 2006 U.S. Dist. LEXIS 15380, at 4–5 (W.D.N.Y. 2006; ordering government to provide notice allowing a reasonable time for victims to attend a hearing for dismissal of the indictment).) On the other hand, in *United States v. Degenhardt*, the court held that a crime victim's right to "be reasonably heard" at sentencing gives the victim the right to speak directly to the judge at sentencing (*United States v. Degenhardt*, 405 F.Supp.2d 1341, 1345 (D. Utah 2005); see also *Kenna v. United States Dist. Court* (*In Re Kenna*), 435 F.3d 1011, 1016 (9th Cir. 2006; "The statements of the sponsors of the CVRA and the committee report for the proposed constitutional amendment disclose a clear congressional intent to give crime victims the right to speak at proceedings covered by the CVRA. Our interpretation advances the purposes of the CVRA. The statute was enacted to make crime victims full participants in the criminal justice system. Prosecutors and defendants already have the right to speak at sentencing. . . .")).

Rights during Trial Proceedings: Right Not to Be Excluded, Emotional Displays, and Victims' Seating

Right Not to Be Excluded from the Courtroom

Suppose there is a case involving several eyewitness victims, and the defendant is concerned that the testimony of some victim-witnesses will be influenced by their presence in the courtroom during the testimony of other victim-witnesses. Should each of these witnesses have the right to be present in the courtroom during the testimony of the other witnesses? (see Mosteller 1997). More generally, what should the legal standard be when the victim is scheduled to testify and his or her testimony would be susceptible to alteration if he or she observed the proceedings?

The CVRA states that a crime victim has "the right not to be excluded from any . . . public court proceedings, unless the court, after receiving clear and convincing evidence, determines that testimony by the victim would be materially altered if the victim heard other testimony at that proceeding" (18 U.S.C. § 3771(a)(3) (2004)).

The above provision effectively amends Rule 615 of the Federal Rules of Evidence to allow victims to attend trial proceedings prior to their testimony when they are serving as witnesses, unless the stringent standard of proof set forth above is met by the defendant (see in re *Mikhel*, 453 F.3d 1137, 1139–40 (9th Cir. 2006, ordering trial court to make specific findings of whether there was "clear and convincing evidence" of material alteration of the victim's prospective testimony to support exclusion of victim from trial)). In the Ninth Circuit, the trial judge must find by clear and convincing evidence that it is highly likely, and not merely possible, that the victim's testimony would be materially altered if allowed to observe the proceedings prior to testifying (Id.). The provision also applies to the right to attend other public court proceedings, such as pretrial release hearings and preliminary hearings to determine probable cause.

Recent amendments to the Federal Rules of Criminal Procedure to implement the CVRA, effective December 1, 2008, include a new Rule 60(a)2, "Attending the Proceeding," which states:

> The court must not exclude a victim from a public court proceeding involving the crime, unless the court determines by clear and convincing evidence that the victim's testimony would be materially altered if the victim heard other testimony at that proceeding. In determining whether to exclude a victim, the court must make every effort to permit the fullest attendance possible by the victim and must consider reasonable alternatives to exclusion. The reasons for any exclusion must be clearly stated on the record. (Amendments to the Federal Rules of Criminal Procedure, April 23, 2008, available at http://www.supremecourtus.gov/orders/courtorders/frcr08p.pdf (Washington, D.C., 2008)).

The presence of a victim during a criminal trial prior to the victim testifying has not been held to be a violation of the Fifth Amendment right to due process (see Beloof and Cassell 2005, discussing the broad rejection of any constitutional right to victim exclusion; see also *State v. Beltran-Felix*, 922 P.2d 30, 33–34 (Utah Ct. App. 1996, quoting various federal and state cases in which it was determined that permitting a witness to remain in the courtroom was not a facial violation of a defendant's Fifth Amendment Rights); id. at 33). However, as the Utah Court of Appeals noted in *State v. Beltran-Felix*, 922 P.2d 30 (Utah Ct. App. 1996), victim attendance may violate the Fifth Amendment, as applied, in cases where the defendant manages to successfully prove both that the victim's attendance allowed the victim to conform his or her testimony, and that the tainted testimony affected the outcome of the trial (Id. at 33–35).

Traditionally, courts considered it presumptively prejudicial to the defendant if a witness were permitted to remain in the courtroom prior to testifying after a formal removal request. State victims' rights constitutional amendments, legislation, and witness sequestration rules have altered that presumption (see *State v. Fulimante*, 975 P.2d 75, 92 (Ariz. 1999); see also Beloof and Cassell at 524–27).

The CVRA requires a showing of "clear and convincing evidence" that the victim's testimony will be materially altered and places this burden on the defendant (see Garner 2004, 256, defining clear and convincing evidence as "evidence indicating that the thing to be proved is highly probable or reasonably certain. This is a greater burden than preponderance of the evidence, the standard applied in most civil trials, but less than evidence beyond a reasonable doubt, the norm for criminal trials."). The Act imposes a higher burden of proof than most state constitutions and statutes require in order to exclude a victim-witness from the courtroom (see *United States v. Johnson*, 362 F.Supp.2d 1043, 1055–56 (N.D. Iowa 2005)). In Delaware, Nevada, and Wyoming, the victim is permitted to attend trial unless "good cause" can be shown to exclude the victim (see Del. Code Ann. tot. 11 § 9407 (1993, "A victim or an individual designated by the victim may be present whenever a defendant has a right to be present during a court proceeding concerning the crime charged other than a grand jury proceeding, unless good cause can be shown by the defendant to exclude the victim."); Nev. Rev. Stat. § 171.204 (1997, The magistrate may, if good cause is shown and upon the request of any party or on his own motion, exclude from the examination every person except: . . . the victim, after he has testified as a prosecuting witness and his cross-examination has been completed"); Wyo. Stat. Ann.§ 1-40-206 (1991, "Unless the court for good cause shown shall find to the contrary, the victim, the victim's designee or both shall have the right to be present at all trial proceedings which may be attended by the defendant")). The Nevada statute exempts victims from exclusion based on "good cause" only if victims have completed both direct and cross-examination testimony (Nev. Rev. Stat. § 171.204 (1997)). Other states such as Arkansas, North Carolina, Virginia, and Wisconsin qualify the victim's right to attend public proceedings based on possible interference with the operation of a fair trial (see Ark. Code. Ann. § 16-90-1103 (1997, "The victim or a representative of the victim may be present whenever the defendant has a right to be present during a court proceeding concerning the crime charged, other than a grand jury proceeding, unless the court determines that exclusion of the victim or the victim's representative is necessary to protect the defendant's right to a fair trial or the confidentiality or fairness of a juvenile proceeding."); N.C. Gen. Stat. § 15A-832 (1998, "When the victim is to be called as a witness in a court proceeding, the court shall make every effort to permit the fullest attendance possible by the victim in the proceedings. This subsection shall not be construed to interfere with the defendant's right to a fair trial."); Va. Code. Ann. § 19.2-265.01 (1995, "Any victim . . . may remain in the courtroom and shall not be excluded unless the court determines, in its discretion, the presence of the victim would impair the conduct of a fair trial."); Wis. Stat. § 906.15 (1997, "Unless the judge or circuit court commissioner finds that exclusion of the victim is necessary to provide a fair trial for the defendant or a fair fact-finding hearing for the juvenile")). The California statute provides several situations—the defendant's right to a fair trial among them—in which it is appropriate to exclude the victim from the proceedings (see Cal. Penal Code § 1102.6 (1995, "A victim may be excluded from a criminal proceeding only if each of the following criteria are met: any movant, including the defendant, who seeks to exclude the victim from any criminal proceeding demonstrates that there is a substantial probability that overriding interests will be prejudiced by the presence of the victim. 'Overriding interests' may include, but are not limited to, the following: . . . the defendant's right to a fair trial . . ."')).

The CVRA's focus is to preserve and strengthen the victim's right to attend trials, as opposed to emphasizing the policies underlying a defendant's right to a fair trial (see, e.g., *United States v. Grace*, 408 F.Supp.2d 998, 1020, 1021 (D. Mont. 2006, denying defendant's motions for a change of venue based on prejudicial pretrial publicity, noting that the CVRA required courts to make "every effort" to afford victims' full attendance, and this requirement was integrated into the consideration of the interest of the community as a whole in a local trial)). Some prosecutors prefer, when the order of witnesses permits, to have the victim testify first or early in the trial to minimize the possibility of altered testimony. This also prevents defense counsel from impeaching the victim on cross-examination by attempting to show that the victim's testimony may have been influenced by observing other witnesses. Another remedy might be to require formal pretrial statements or depositions designed to freeze victim testimony before the trial begins.

Emotional Displays in the Courtroom

The CVRA does not provide guidance when a victim's behavior in the courtroom involves overt displays of emotion, unless such emotional displays are somehow connected to the material alteration of the victim's testimony (see Mosteller at 1699–1700; *Lanham v. Commonwealth*, 171 S.W.3d 14, 32 (Ky. 2005, upholding trial court decision refusing to move victims attending the trial out of the sight of the jury when they began to cry during a photo presentation)). It may be argued, however, that courts have the inherent power to exclude disruptive victims (see 150 Cong. Rec. S4260, 4264 (Statement of Sen. Kyl, "Obviously, everyone in the courtroom has to behave. The judge can throw anybody out if they do not behave or if they express emotions or try to communicate w/ the jury. That is not the issue.")). Because courts have exercised their power to exclude disruptive defendants, although defendants have a constitutional right under the Confrontation and Due Process Clauses to be present during court proceedings, they may have the same power to exclude disruptive victims.

How emotionally disruptive would a victim's conduct have to be before a court would hold that the victim's conduct interfered enough to deny a defendant a fair trial? Suppose in a murder trial members of the victim's family sat in the front row of the spectators' gallery throughout the trial wearing large buttons with a picture of the deceased victim. Is this conduct so inherently prejudicial that it deprives a defendant of a fair trial? In *Musladin v. Lamarque*, 427 F.3d 653, 656–58 (2005), the Ninth Circuit reversed the defendant's conviction on the above facts, concluding that the spectators' courtroom conduct was inherently prejudicial to the defendant. Yet, the next year in *Carey v. Musladin*, 549 U.S. 70 (2006), the Supreme Court reversed the Ninth Circuit's decision (Id.). In a concurring opinion, Justice Kennedy stated that there was insufficient showing that the defendant's conviction was obtained in a trial tainted by an atmosphere of coercion or intimidation (Id. See also *Ducote v. State*, 873 A.2d 1099 (Del. 2005, victim hugging victim support counselor after her testimony in view of the jury was inappropriate, but cured by the judge's cautionary instruction); *State v. Boone*, 820 P.2d 930 (Utah Ct. App. 1991, victim's wife making exclamations such as "that's not true!" in the courtroom did not interfere enough to deny defendant a fair trial)).

Where Should Victims Sit in the Courtroom?

Where the victim sits in the courtroom requires a consideration of whether crime victims should be treated more like witnesses or parties. Should a crime victim sit in the spectator gallery unless called to testify, at the prosecutor's table, or should a third table be added in the courtroom along with prosecution and defense tables? If crime victims were treated more like parties, would that be more likely to influence the jury prejudicially in violation of the defendant's right to a fair trial? The CVRA is silent concerning the preferred or appropriate location for the victim to sit during those proceedings in which the victim is permitted to attend. Of the eight rights provided in the CVRA, the victim's right to be reasonably heard and to confer with the government's attorney is central to the question of where the victim should sit in the courtroom. As discussed earlier, the victim's right to be heard in the district court is limited to proceedings involving release, plea, sentencing, or parole (see 18 U.S.C. § 3771 (a)(4) (2004)). The answers to these questions probably will vary depending on the proceeding.

While the majority of states do not permit the victim to sit at counsel table, a few states have determined that it is permissible. An Alabama statute provides victims the right to sit at counsel table with the prosecutor (see Ala. Code § 15-14-53 (1983, "The victim of a criminal offense shall be entitled to be present in any court exercising any jurisdiction over such offense and therein to be seated at counsel table of any prosecutor prosecuting such offense . . .")). In an Alabama case, a victim was permitted to sit at counsel table where she began to cry during testimony describing the autopsy of her murdered husband (*Crowe v. State*, 485 So. 2d 351, 362–63 (Ala. Crim. App. 1984)). The court found that the victim's crying did not constitute behavior that would violate the defendant's constitutional right to a fair trial (Id. at 363). In a California case, the California Court of Appeals permitted a victim to sit at counsel table, but qualified its decision in order to retain a clear dividing line between witness and party status and to prevent prejudicial trial practices (*State v. Ramer*, 21 Cal. Rptr. 2d 480, 484 (Ct. App. 1993, "We do not wish this opinion to be viewed as approving of the practice of permitting a victim to sit with a prosecutor at the counsel table. At a criminal trial at which the victim testifies, the victim is a witness and not a party to the case. . . . The court should not, in our view, allow a seating arrangement which treats a witness, even a key witness, as if the witness were a party to the case. . . . We do recognize, that the presence of the victim at the counsel table does increase the possibility of both emotional and jury focus on factors which may not be consistent with the jury trial process involved in assessing criminal guilt")). On the other hand, Louisiana expressly prohibits victims from sitting at counsel table (see La. Code Evid. Ann. art. 615 (2000, "The court shall also enter such other order as may appear reasonably necessary to preserve decorum and insure a fair trial, provided that the victim shall not be allowed to sit at the counsel table")).

Other practical issues might arise when there are multiple victims. How should the court determine which victims deserve a seat in the well of the court? With multiple victims, there is also a risk of creating dissention among victims who might feel excluded or neglected if one victim or group of victims is given special treatment.

Plea Agreements, Guilty Pleas, and Sentencing Proceedings

Plea agreements have been a source of victim dissatisfaction, complaint, and litigation. Victims' rights advocates believe that plea agreements reached between prosecutors and defendants are sometimes inappropriate and that an injustice occurs when cases are resolved without the victims' knowledge or participation. Defense attorneys complain that plea agreements are violated when victims recommend a sentence greater than the one the prosecutor has agreed to recommend to the court, sometimes with the prosecutor's full knowledge and encouragement.

Under the CVRA, victims have the right to reasonably confer with the prosecutor concerning plea agreements (see 18 U.S.C. § 3771(a)(5) (2004)). A limitation of this right is the CVRA's provision that "[n]othing in this chapter shall be construed to impair the prosecutorial discretion of the Attorney General or any officer under his direction" (18 U.S.C. § 3771(d)(6)). In *In re W.R. Huff Asset Management Co.*, a group of crime victims petitioned for a writ of mandamus, seeking to vacate a settlement agreement in a forfeiture action (409 F.3d 555, 560–61 (2d Cir. 2005)). One of the victims' arguments was that the government did not adequately consult with them before entering into the settlement agreement as required by the CVRA, section 3771(a)(5) (Id. at 561). In rejecting this claim, the Second Circuit stated: "Nothing in the CVRA requires the Government to seek approval from crime victims before negotiating or entering into a settlement agreement" (Id. at 564).

The CVRA also provides that victims have a right to be heard at any public proceeding involving pleas and sentencing. The CVRA does not address the question of when the victim must be heard. However, Kyl, Twist, and Higgins argue that, to be effective, the right to be heard must allow the victim to address the judge before the judge exercises discretion to accept or reject a plea (see Kyl et al., at 603).

When there are multiple defendants sentenced at the same trial, does the crime victim have a right to be heard at the sentencing of each defendant? *Kenna v. U.S. Dist. Court* (*In re Kenna*) arose out of a dispute over the right of a victim to be heard when the judge had already heard from that victim regarding a different defendant (435 F.3d 1011, 1013 (9th Cir. 2006)). The defendants, a father and son, defrauded numerous victims in an investment scheme and several victims spoke at the father's sentencing (435 F.3d at 1012–13). When the son was sentenced three months later, the court denied the victims the opportunity to speak, ruling that the victims had been heard at the previous sentencing, and there was nothing the victims could say that would impact the court's sentence (Id.). The Ninth Circuit granted the petition for mandamus filed by one of the victims (Id. at 1018). Determining that the statute "is ambiguous as to what it means for crime victims to be heard," the Ninth Circuit, after reviewing the legislative history and finding a congressional intent to give crime victims the right to speak at proceedings covered by the CVRA, held that the right to be heard at any public proceeding involving sentencing "means that the district court must hear from the victims, if they choose to speak, at more than one criminal sentencing" (Id. at 1015, 1016). The Ninth Circuit left it to the district court to decide whether it should conduct a new sentencing hearing (see id. at 1017–18).

Under what circumstances is the crime victims' right to be heard at plea and sentencing hearings satisfied by submission of written statements rather than being heard in person? (*Cf. United States v. Marcello*, 370 F. Supp. 2d 745, 746–50 (N.D. Ill. 2005, holding that the victim's right to be heard at a pretrial release hearing could be accommodated through written statements, and the victim was not entitled to appear in person before the court)). Cassell argues that the term "reasonably" should be narrowly interpreted to allow for alternative methods of communicating a victim's views to the court when the victim is unable to attend the proceedings (see Cassell, Recognizing Victims, at 890). Other situations, however, may justify the receipt of written statements. For example, in cases involving a very large number of crime victims, courts have leeway to fashion reasonable procedures in a way that does not unduly complicate or prolong the proceedings (see 18 U.S.C. § 3771 (d)(2) (2004)).

In *United States v. Degenhardt*, the court concluded that while the phrase "to be reasonably heard" is ambiguous, the legislative history "makes it clear that the CVRA created a right to be heard in person" (405 F.Supp.2d 1341, 1346 (D. Utah 2005)). The court also stated that the victim's right to speak is mandatory and not subject to the discretion of the court, unless such a large number of victims are involved that the effective functioning of the court would be impaired (Id. at 1343–45).

A controversial issue is whether crime victims are entitled to have access to the presentence report, including statements in the report made by the defendant. Crime victims' rights advocates argue that because the CVRA provides for the right of crime victims to make sentencing impact statements, there is a need for victims to view the defendants' pre-sentencing report statements in order to be adequately prepared. The crime victim may be the only person with first-hand knowledge of the circumstances of the crime who may be able to refute the defendant's allegations. Also, victim rights' advocates may argue that the overarching right to be treated with "fairness" and with respect for the victim's "dignity" justify victim access to the presentence report (see 18 U.S.C. § 3771 (a)(8)).

Defense advocates may argue that defendants have a right under the Sixth Amendment's Confrontation Clause, and as a matter of fundamental fairness under the Due Process Clause, to view and challenge crime victims' written or oral sentencing statements (see *Crawford v. Washington*, 541 U.S. 36 (2004)). If defendants have a Confrontation Clause right, this may also include the right of cross-examination (Wood 2008, 8). In response, similar to a defendant's right to allocute at sentencing, crime victims' advocates may argue that crime victims are not functioning as "witnesses" testifying against defendants, and therefore defendants have no confrontation rights in this context. If a crime victim is provided access to a defendant's presentence report statements, defense counsel could argue that a defendant is entitled to similar access to the crime victim's statements, absent compelling privacy interests.

In *In re Kenna*, the Ninth Circuit found that the victim in a fraud case did not demonstrate that his reasons for requesting the presentence report outweighed the confidentiality that should be given to the report (453 F.3d 1136, 1137 (9th Cir. 2006, per curiam)). The victim filed a petition for writ of mandamus under the CVRA seeking an order requiring the district court to release to the victim the entire presentence report (Id.). The Ninth Circuit held that there is no support "in either the language of the statute or the legislative history" for the proposition that the CVRA conferred a general right for crime victims to have access to presentence reports (Id. See also *In re Brock*, No. 08-1086, 2008 U.S. App. LEXIS 2104 (4th Cir. Jan. 31, 2008, per curiam); *United States v. Citgo Petroleum Corp.*, No. C-06-563, 2007 U.S. Dist. LEXIS 57686 (S.D. Tex. Aug. 8, 2007); *United States v. Sacane*, No. 3:05-cr-325, 2007 U.S. Dist. LEXIS 22178 (D. Conn. March 28, 2007)).

The CVRA provides that crime victims have "(t)he right to full and timely restitution as provided in law" (18 U.S.C. § 3771(a)(6) (2004)). This provision interacts with existing restitution statutes. Does the CVRA provide an additional right that restitution be "full" and "timely"? In *United States v. Sacane*, the victims, a group of investment funds, moved for an order requiring more detailed financial disclosures from the defendant in advance of a restitution hearing (2007 U.S. Dist. LEXIS 22178, at 2). They claimed that they needed to inspect the presentence report in order to enforce their CVRA right to full and timely restitution (Id. at 2–3). The district court denied the request, holding that the CVRA does not provide a right to disclosure of the presentence report (Id. at 4, 8). The Court stated that if the victims believed that additional financial disclosure was necessary, they may pursue their CVRA right to enlist the assistance of the government (Id. at 6). [Footnote 162 omitted].

Right to Be Present and Heard at Parole Hearings

The CVRA specifically provides crime victims the right to reasonable, accurate, and timely notice of any parole proceeding (18 U.S.C. § 3771(a)(2)). Additionally, they have the right to attend and be reasonably heard at any parole proceeding (Id. at § 3771(a)(4)). In a recent federal case applying Michigan's version of the CVRA, the district court denied the defendant's due process claim that the parole board's reliance on victim statements violated the defendant's constitutional rights *Palmer v. Granholm*, No. 1:06-cv-301, 2006 U.S. Dist. LEXIS 45333, at 29 (W.D. Mich. July 5, 2006)). Because Michigan's provision protects victim privacy, the victim's statements were kept confidential, and the defendant had no knowledge of what was asserted and consequently had no opportunity to rebut the claims in front of the parole board (Id. at 4). The court reasoned that because the defendant had no liberty interest in parole, the defendant's rights had not been violated (Id. at 10–13). If this case had been decided under the CVRA, the result likely would have been the same, since the basis of the decision was the defendant's diminished rights after conviction.

Overarching Rights: Right to Be Treated with Fairness and Respect for Dignity and Privacy

The CVRA provides crime victims with "[t]he right to be treated with fairness and with respect for the victim's dignity and privacy" (18 U.S.C. § 3771(a)(8)). This right is not easily classified into discrete stages of the criminal proceeding, and to a greater extent than the other enumerated rights in the CVRA, the applicability of this general right will likely be defined by courts as they interpret the statute in specific situations. However, this right has already influenced the Rules Committee responsible for proposing amendments to the United States Supreme Court.

In a recent set of proposed amendments to the Federal Rules, crime victims' right to fairness, dignity, and privacy was, in part, a basis for recommendations that victims' personal information not be disclosed in the case of an alibi defense, victims be notified and given an opportunity to quash subpoenas issued on third parties seeking information about crime victims, and the convenience of victims be considered in determining the place of the trial (see Committee on Rules of Practice and Procedure of the Judicial Conference of the United States 2006, 349–75; Cassell, Treating Crime Victims Fairly; see 18 U.S.C. § 3771 (a)(3)). In proposing these changes, the Committee stated that it "sought to incorporate, but not go beyond, the rights created by the statute" (Committee on Rules of Practice and Procedure at 350). These changes were adopted by the Supreme Court and submitted to Congress on April 23, 2008, effective December 1, 2008 (see Amendments to the Federal Rules of Criminal Procedure).

Proponents of these broad rights for victims equate them with due process rights and seek to import the due process framework of fundamental fairness (see Cassell, Recognizing Victims, at 858–59). Senator Kyl, one of the primary legislative sponsors of the CVRA, stated: "The broad rights articulated in this section are meant to be rights themselves and are not intended to just be aspirational. One of these rights is the right to be treated with fairness. Of course, fairness includes the notion of due process" (Id. at 859, quoting 150 Cong. Rec. S4269 (statement of Sen. Kyl)).

It remains unclear if courts will accept this characterization. While defendants' due process rights are predicated on potential deprivation of life, liberty, or property, victims have none of these at stake in the criminal process. There is no obvious limit to the circumstances that could trigger a victim's right to be treated with fairness and dignity and, likewise, little limit on the interpretations different courts may embrace.

In *United States v. Heaton*, the prosecutor charged the defendant with attempting to entice a minor into unlawful sexual activity. The prosecutor then sought leave to dismiss the charge without prejudice (*United States v. Heaton*, 458 F. Supp. 2d 1271, 1271 (D. Utah 2006); see also *United States v. Patkar*, No. 06-00250, 2008 U.S. Dist. LEXIS 6055 (D. Haw. Jan. 28, 2008); *United States v. Kaufman*, No. 04-40141-01, 2005 U.S. Dist. LEXIS 21006 (D. Kan. Oct. 17, 2005)). The district judge stated that it would make its own determination whether dismissal is warranted, that the victim's right to be treated with fairness and dignity extends to the court's decision of whether to dismiss an indictment, and that, unlike other rights in the CVRA, this right is not limited to "public proceedings" (Heaton, 458 F. Supp. 2d at 1272). The judge then ordered the government to consult with the victim and inform the court "that the victim has been consulted on the dismissal and what the victim's views were on the matter" (Id. at 1272–73).

Enforcement of Victims' Rights

CVRA's Enforcement Remedies: Standing, Fast-Track Appeal, Mandatory Appellate Review, Authorized Stay of Proceedings, and Written Record, if Relief Denied

A principal goal of the victims' rights movement, reflected in the drafting of the CVRA, is to develop an effective judicial enforcement regime so that victims' rights can be meaningfully exercised. The enactment of the CVRA's remedies granting crime victims standing along with an expedited right of appeal and the resulting nascent development of appellate case law are the CVRA's most important contributions to the advancement of crime victims' rights.

What has been most lacking in state constitutional amendments and federal and state legislation are meaningful enforcement mechanisms. [Footnote 178 omitted]. Without adequate remedies, victims cannot exercise their rights when prosecutors or trial judges deny them. In the legislative history of the CVRA, Senators Feinstein and Kyl make clear that providing victims with an enforcement mechanism to initiate review of alleged violations of victims' rights is an essential component of the legislation (see 150 Cong. Rec. S4270 (Apr. 22, 2004, statement of Sen. Feinstein: "This provision is critical for a couple of reasons. First, it gives the victim standing to appear before the appellate courts of this country and ask for review of a possible error below. Second, while mandamus is generally discretionary, this provision means that courts must review these cases. Appellate review of denials of victims' rights is just as important as the initial assertion of a victim's right. This provision ensures review and encourages courts to broadly defend the victims' rights"; see also id. (statement of Sen. Kyl, "For a victim's right to truly be honored, a victim must be able to assert the rights in trial courts, to then be able to have denials of those rights reviewed at the appellate level, and to have the appellate court take the appeal and order relief. By providing for all of this, this bill ensures that victims' rights will have meaning").

According to Professor Beloof, there are three main obstacles to turning victims' illusory rights into real rights: "(1) government discretion to deny rights, (2) lack of a meaningful remedy to enforce rights, and (3) appellate court discretion to deny review" (see Beloof, *The Third Wave*, at 258). Only eight states provide standing to crime victims to seek legal redress for a violation of their rights. Arizona, Indiana, Maryland, Michigan, Nevada, South Carolina, Texas, and Utah. Review by traditional writ of mandamus is discretionary with federal and state appellate courts and is an unlikely avenue for routine review of violations of crime victims' rights (see *Black's Law Dictionary* at 712, A writ of mandamus is typically discretionary and usually reserved for extraordinary situations when a "superior court must compel a lower court or government officer to perform mandatory or purely ministerial duties correctly").

The CVRA establishes a new statutory review mechanism—although the CVRA uses the traditional label of a writ of mandamus—that includes: (1) standing for crime victims to appeal a violation of their rights immediately after the violation occurs to federal appellate courts; (2) a mandatory review by an appellate court; (3) a fast track time schedule, requiring that the appellate court take up and decide the case within seventy-two hours after a petition has been filed; (4) a stay or continuance of the proceedings below for up to five days while the appeal is being heard; and (5) a written opinion clearly stating the reasons for denial, if the court of appeals denies the relief sought (18 U.S.C. § 3771(d)(3) (2004)).

The CVRA states:

Motion for Relief and Writ of Mandamus. The rights described . . . shall be asserted in the district court in which a defendant is being prosecuted for the crime or, if no prosecution is underway, in the district court in the district in which the crime occurred. The district court shall take up and decide any motion asserting a victim's right forthwith. If the district court denies the relief sought, the movant may petition the court of appeals for a writ of mandamus. The court of appeals may issue the writ on the order of a single judge pursuant to circuit rule of the Federal Rules of Appellate Procedure. The court of appeals shall take up and decide such application within 72 hours after the petition has been filed. In no event shall proceedings be stayed or subject to a continuance of more than five days for purposes of enforcing this chapter. If the court of appeals denies the relief sought, the reasons for the denial shall be clearly stated on the record in a written opinion. (Id.)

Thus, the CVRA authorizes crime victims to independently assert their rights granted by the CVRA and to be represented by an attorney (see id. § 3771(d)(1), "Rights: the crime victim or the crime victim's lawful representative and the attorney for the Government may assert the rights described in subsection (a)"). The Government may also independently assert these rights on behalf of the crime victims (see id.). In addition, the federal district judges are directed to ensure that crime victims are afforded these rights "[i]n any court proceeding involving an offense against a crime victim" (Id. § 3771(b)).

There are some instances when staying proceedings for up to five days may infringe upon the defendant's constitutional or statutory rights. For example, suppose a crime victim believes that his or her rights were violated by a trial judge's denial of the right to be reasonably heard at a pretrial release hearing (see *United States v. Turner*, 367 F. Supp. 2d 319 (E.D.N.Y. 2005)). The victim files an appeal to the appellate court, which grants a stay of a few days. If the defendant can show that this stay affected his or her liberty interests or ability to prepare a defense, there may be a basis for a due process claim. Also, a delay may violate the defendant's right, under Rule 5(a) of the Federal Rules of Criminal Procedure, to be taken before a judicial officer without unnecessary delay and may also affect the computation of the defendant's rights under the Speedy Trial Act (The Speedy Trial Act, 18 U.S.C. §§ 3161–3174 (2008)).

Limitations of CVRA's Enforcement Remedies

The CVRA prohibits the award of damages. The CVRA states:

No Cause of Action. Nothing in this chapter shall be construed to authorize a cause of action for damages or to create, to enlarge, or to imply any duty or obligation to any victim or other person for the breach of which the United States or any of its officers or employees could be held liable in damages. (18 U.S.C. § 3771(d)(6))

However, during the floor debate on the CVRA, Senator Leahy expressed a preference for a damages remedy over the use of a mandamus mechanism, fearing that victims' assertions of a denial of fairness or respect in the criminal process could "be difficult claims to adjudicate" (150 Cong. Rec. S4260, 4271 (2004, statement of Senator Leahy, "I note with some regret that S. 2329 [CVRA] picks up language from S.J. Res. 1 [proposed constitutional amendment] denying victims any cause of action for damages in the event that their rights are violated. Allowing victims to vindicate their rights through separate proceedings for damages instead of through mandamus actions in the criminal case could well be a more efficient as well as a more effective way of ensuring that victims' rights are honored").

Another limitation of the CVRA enforcement mechanism is the statutory language limiting remedies that may affect the independent role of the public prosecutor: "Nothing in this chapter shall be construed to impair the prosecutorial discretion of the Attorney General or any officer under his direction" (18 U.S.C. § 3771(d)(6)).

In addition, there are limitations on voiding or vacating certain hearings or procedures and redoing or reopening them (Beloof, *The Third Wave*, at 304, The right to reopen or redo a particular proceeding has been referred to as "the superior remedy"). The CVRA states:

> Limitation on Relief. In no case shall a failure to afford a right under this chapter provide grounds for a new trial. A victim may make a motion to re-open a plea or sentence only if—(A) the victim has asserted the right to be heard before or during the proceeding at issue and such right was denied; (B) the victim petitions the court of appeals for a writ of mandamus within 10 days; and (C) in the case of a plea, the accused has not pled to the highest offense charged. (18 U.S.C. § 3771(d)(5))

The CVRA's limitation that crime victims and prosecutors may not seek a new trial as a remedy for a violation of victims' rights is buttressed by federal—and state—constitutional protections for defendants under the Double Jeopardy Clause. The Double Jeopardy Clause insures that the Federal government and the states may not undertake multiple prosecutions against a defendant for the same offense. Double jeopardy attaches at trial when the jury is selected and sworn or when the first witness is sworn in a non-jury trial. Thus, the Double Jeopardy Clause prevents the voiding of trials and re-prosecution.

There are limited exceptions when the Double Jeopardy Clause does not bar a retrial or a reconsideration of the verdict, such as when the defendant seeks and obtains a mistrial or when the defendant appeals and the court orders a retrial. The only way for the state to get a retrial after a mistrial is "manifest necessity" (*Illinois v. Somerville*, 410 U.S. 458, 462-463 (1973, manifest necessity requires prejudice either to the defendant or the state). Beloof observes that "the denial of a trial attendance right does not necessarily result in prejudice to victims or the state in the crucial sense that the absence of a victim is likely to alter the result of the trial" (Beloof, *The Third Wave*, at 308). He concludes that "presently it is unlikely that manifest necessity can be the basis for voiding a trial when a victim's right to attend is violated" (Id. at 309). While a retrial is unlikely, a victim does have the right to pursue an expedited interlocutory appeal—included in the CVRA's definition of a "writ of mandamus"—until the trial is over (see *Kenna v. United States*, 435 F.3d 1011, 1015-16 (9th Cir. 2006)).

Double jeopardy does not bar voiding and reconsidering certain pretrial and post-trial proceedings as a remedy for a violation of victims' rights. For example, the Double Jeopardy Clause does not bar reconsideration of the victims' rights to notice and to be heard at pretrial release hearings, or of a release order as a remedy for failure to notify a crime victim of the scheduling of a parole or release hearing.

What are the consequences when a motion to reconsider a plea or sentence is granted? The procedure is unclear. Does the defendant have a right to withdraw the plea and seek to renegotiate a plea agreement? Does the prosecutor have a right to renegotiate a plea agreement? Voiding an entire proceeding may result in rejecting all evidence presented in that proceeding and starting anew. An alternative is to vacate the result without voiding the original proceeding. At the reconsideration hearing, a crime victim can exercise his or her right to be heard and the judge will then void, modify, or affirm the prior ruling or order (see Beloof, *The Third Wave*, at 305). After the victim(s) is given the opportunity to be heard, the defendant and government arguably should be allowed to respond.

Conflict among the Federal Circuits of the Standard for Review to Issue a Writ of Mandamus

Although a crime victim has standing to immediately appeal an alleged violation of the crime victim's CVRA rights along with the mandatory right to have the appeal heard on an expedited basis by a federal appellate court, a conflict exists among the appellate courts as to whether the applicable legal standard for granting a requested writ of mandamus should be discretionary or mandatory when the trial court's order reflects an abuse of discretion or legal error. Congress may have created the uncertainty by naming the appellate remedy a "writ of mandamus," the name of a common law, discretionary judicial remedy (see *In re Antrobus*, 519 F.3d 1123 (10th Cir. 2008, discussing the appellate standard of review under the CVRA).

In a Fifth Circuit case, *In re Dean*, 527 F.3d 391 (5th Cir. 2008) (per curiam) an explosion at a refinery operated by the defendant, BP Products North America Inc., killed fifteen and injured more than 170 persons (*United States v. BP Prods. N. Am. Inc.*, No. H-07-434, 2008 U.S. Dist. LEXIS12893, at 3 (S.D. Tex. Feb. 21, 2008)). The Department of Justice filed a sealed ex parte motion, prior to bringing any criminal charges, seeking an order from the district court excusing the government from the requirement of notifying crime victims until after a plea agreement had been signed (*In re Dean*, 527 F.3d at 392). The government argued that: (1) notification to victims in advance of the public announcement of a plea was impractical because of the large number of victims, and (2) media coverage of a potential criminal disposition could impair the plea negotiation process and might prejudice the case if no plea were reached (Id.). The district court, on the same day, signed an ex parte order granting the government's motion (Id. at 395). After the defendant signed the plea agreement and pled guilty, all victims who wished to be heard, either personally or through counsel, were permitted to speak at a plea hearing (Id. at 393).

Twelve of the victims asked the district court to reject the plea agreement, alleging, inter alia, that the ex parte proceedings violated the CVRA and that they were denied the "reasonable right to confer with the attorney for the Government in the case" (Id. at 392). While the district court acknowledged that CVRA rights may apply before any prosecution is underway, it denied the request (*In re Dean*, 527 F.3d at 393). The victims then petitioned the Fifth Circuit for a writ of mandamus, seeking a reversal and a remand with "instructions that the plea agreement not be accepted and the parties are permitted to proceed as they determine—so long as it is in a way that respects crime victims' rights" (Id. at 392). Within seventy-two hours, a Fifth Circuit panel granted the mandamus petition in part, directing the district court to "take no further action to effect the plea agreement, pending further order and awaiting additional briefing" (Id. at 393).

On appeal, the parties disputed the standard of review. The victims argued that ordinary appeal standards apply rather than the stricter standards for obtaining a writ of mandamus (Id. at 393–94). The Fifth Circuit recognized that decisions of the Second and Ninth Circuits supported the victims' position (Id. at 394 [quotation omitted]). In *Kenna*, Judge Kozinski observed: "The CVRA creates a unique regime that does, in fact, contemplate routine interlocutory review of district court decisions denying rights asserted under the statute. . . . [W]e must issue the writ whenever we find that the district court's order reflects an abuse of discretion or legal error" (*Kenna*, 435 F.3d at 1017). The Third Circuit, in an unpublished decision, also agreed with the Second and Ninth Circuits (see *In re Walsh*, No. 06-4792, 2007 U.S. App. LEXIS 9071 (3rd Cir. Apr. 19, 2007)).

The Fifth Circuit, however, disagreed with this standard, holding that a writ of mandamus may issue only if: "(1) the petitioner has 'no other adequate means' to attain the desired relief; (2) the petitioner has demonstrated a right to the issuance of the writ that is 'clear and indisputable;' and (3) the issuing court, in the exercise of its discretion, is satisfied that the writ is 'appropriate under the circumstances'" (*In re Dean*, 527 F.3d at 394 [quotation omitted]). The court found support from the Tenth Circuit, which recently held that the discretionary standard for mandamus applied: "[M]andamus is a well worn term of art in our common law tradition" (Id. at 394 [quotation omitted]).

Applying this three-prong standard, the Fifth Circuit held that the third-prong— a writ of mandamus must be "appropriate under the circumstances"—was not met, despite finding that the district court, with the best of intentions, misapplied the law (Id. at 394–5). The district court's use of ex parte proceedings had no precedent and was contrary to the provisions of the CVRA (Id.). Yet, the court found that, despite the trial judge's error, the victims were notified, although much too late in the process, and were allowed "substantial and meaningful participation" at the plea hearing (Id. at 395). The court concluded:

> We are confident, however, that the conscientious district court will fully consider the victims' objections and concerns in deciding whether the plea agreement should be accepted. The decision whether to grant mandamus is largely prudential. We conclude that the better course is to deny relief, confident that the district court will take heed that the victims have not been accorded their full rights under the CVRA and will carefully consider their objections and briefs as this matter proceeds. (Id.)

Subsequently, the U.S. Supreme Court denied an application for stay of enforcement of the judgment of the Fifth Circuit (*Dean v. U.S. Dist. Court*, 128 S. Ct. 2996 (2008)).

Accordingly, the Second, Third, and Ninth Circuits have adopted a pro-victim standard of review to determine when a writ of mandamus should be issued. Their view is that the CVRA contemplates routine review of trial court decisions denying victims' rights when a court's order reflects an abuse of discretion or legal error. The Fifth and Tenth Circuits, however, have viewed the writ of mandamus in the common law tradition that allows appellate courts broad discretion whether to issue a writ of mandamus when crime victims' rights have been violated. This conflict among the circuit courts on such an important issue merits consideration either by the U.S. Supreme Court or Congress.

* * *

Analysis

The CVRA authorized spending to implement the Act, but authorization is not the same as actually providing funds. In fact, Congress has failed to significantly fund the Crime Victims' Rights Act since it was enacted. Due to lack of funding, the CVRA experiment has largely failed. Without funding to determine if the laws work, litigation has been episodic and infrequent. Victims do not have the legal assistance that the CVRA intended to provide.

Nevertheless, the CVRA has impacted a sufficient number of cases to reveal two significant trends. First, the United States Justice Department is actively working to narrow the potential scope and significance of rights and the remedy under the CVRA. Second, the courts are split as to whether to side with the Justice Department or not. Ultimately, these issues, which will be discussed further below, will be resolved by the United States Supreme Court. And, if the Court votes to narrow the scope of the CVRA's rights and remedy, the Crime Victims' Rights Movement will likely revive the quest for a constitutional amendment.

The CVRA applies only in federal criminal cases, unlike the proposed constitutional amendment, which would have applied to the states as well. The CVRA sets out a list of rights both specific and general. Where the CVRA has provided rights, victims generally have standing to enforce those rights. As law professor Aaronson explained in his analysis of the CVRA, the federal circuit courts are presently split on what is called the "standard of review." Some federal appellate courts have held that the CVRA means that federal appellate courts must address victim rights violations. Other appellate federal courts have held that the proper standard of review is much more difficult to meet and that violations of victims' rights do not require correction. This latter interpretation means that victims' rights will only be enforced in exceptional circumstances. Such an interpretation would represent a failed CVRA. What follows are two federal court opinions: the *Kenna* case, which requires courts to enforce victims' rights, and the *Antrobus* case saga, which does not. These cases are from different circuits. Each circuit has independent authority to interpret the law, subject only to the final authority of the Supreme Court.

- **Document:** *Kenna v. United States District Court for the Central District of California*
- **Date:** January 11, 2006
- **Significance:** Determining that the statute "is ambiguous as to what it means for crime victims to be heard," the Ninth Circuit in *Kenna* held that the right to be heard at any public proceeding involving sentencing "means that the district court must hear from the victims, if they choose to speak, at more than one criminal sentencing." Furthermore, it held that the standard of review requires courts to address denials of victims' rights.
- **Source:** *Kenna v. United States District Court for the Central District of California*, 435 F.3d 1011 (9th Cir. 2006).

---

* * *

Opinion

Kozinski, Circuit Judge.

We consider whether the Crime Victims' Rights Act, 18 U.S.C. § 3771, gives victims the right to allocute at sentencing.

Moshe and Zvi Leichner, father and son, swindled scores of victims out of almost $100 million. While purporting to make investments in foreign currency, they spent or concealed the funds entrusted to them. Each defendant pleaded guilty to two counts of wire fraud and one count of money laundering. More than sixty of the Leichners' victims submitted written victim impact statements. At Moshe's sentencing, several, including petitioner W. Patrick Kenna, spoke about the effects of the Leichners' crimes—retirement savings lost, businesses bankrupted and lives ruined. The district court sentenced Moshe to 240 months in prison.

Three months later, at Zvi's sentencing, the district court heard from the prosecutor and the defendant, as required by Federal Rule of Criminal Procedure 32(i)(4). But the court denied the victims the opportunity to speak. It explained:

> I listened to the victims the last time. I can say for the record I've rereviewed all the investor victim statements. I have listened at Mr. Leichner's father's sentencing to the victims and, quite frankly, I don't think there's anything that any victim could say that would have any impact whatsoever. I—what can you say when people have lost their life savings and what can you say when the individual who testified last time put his client's [sic] into this investment and millions and millions of dollars and ended up losing his business? There just isn't anything else that could possibly be said.

One victim protested that "[t]here are many things that are going on with the residual and second and third impacts in this case that have unfolded over the last

90 days since we were last in this courtroom." But the
district judge told the victims that the prosecutor could
bring those developments to his attention, and continued to refuse to let the victims speak. Zvi was sentenced
to 135 months in prison.

Kenna filed a timely petition for writ of mandamus
pursuant to the Crime Victims' Right Act (CVRA), 18
U.S.C. § 3771(d)(3). He seeks an order vacating Zvi's
sentence, and commanding the district court to allow
the victims to speak at the resentencing.

The criminal justice system has long functioned on the
assumption that crime victims should behave like good
Victorian children—seen but not heard. The Crime Victims' Rights Act sought to change this by making victims
independent participants in the criminal justice process
(see Scott Campbell, Stephanie Roper, Wendy Preston,
Louarna Gillis, and Nila Lynn Crime Victims' Rights
Act, Pub. L. No. 108–405,§§ 101–104, 118 Stat. 2260,
2261–65 (2004) (codified at 18 U.S.C. § 3771)). The
CVRA guarantees crime victims eight different rights,
and unlike the prior crime victims' rights statute, allows
both the government and the victims to enforce them
(see 18 U.S.C. § 3771(a), (d)(1); *United States v. McVeigh*,
106 F.3d 325, 335 (10th Cir.1997) (per curiam)).

John Gillis, a powerful advocate for enforceable rights, was
director of the Office for Victims of Crime. He pioneered
grant funding of legal advocates for victims. (Courtesy John
Gillis)

Kenna and the district court disagree over the scope of
one of the rights guaranteed by the CVRA: "The right to be reasonably heard at any
public proceeding in the district court involving release, plea, sentencing, or any
parole proceeding" (18 U.S.C. § 3771(a)(4)). Kenna contends that his right to be
"reasonably heard" means that he is entitled to speak in open court at Zvi's sentencing, if that is how he chooses to express himself. The district court argues that the
words "reasonably heard" vest the judge with discretion about how to receive the
views of the victims, and that the judge is entitled to limit Kenna to written victim
statements or his prior statements at Moshe's sentencing. No court of appeals has
considered the scope of this CVRA right, and the two district courts that have
closely considered it have reached opposite conclusions (compare *United States v.
Degenhardt*, 405 F.Supp.2d 1341, 1345-49 (D.Utah 2005, CVRA grants victims a
right to speak) with *United States v. Marcello*, 370 F.Supp.2d 745, 748 (N.D.Ill.
2005, no it doesn't)).

Kenna would have us interpret the phrase "reasonably heard" as guaranteeing his
right to speak. For support, he points to the dictionary definition of "hear"—"to perceive (sound) by the ear"(American Heritage Dictionary Eds. 2000). Kenna con-
cedes that the district court may place reasonable constraints on the duration and
content of victims' speech, such as avoiding undue delay, repetition or the use of
profanity. However, in Kenna's view, the district court may not prohibit victims
from speaking in court altogether or limit them to making written statements. This
is the interpretation adopted by the district court in *Degenhardt*.

But this isn't the only plausible interpretation of the phrase "reasonably heard." According to the district court, to be "heard" is commonly understood as meaning to bring one's position to the attention of the decisionmaker orally or in writing (see, e.g., *Fernandez v. Leonard*, 963 F.2d 459, 463 (1st Cir.1992, "Where the parties have had a 'fair opportunity to present relevant facts and argument to the court,' a matter may be ' "heard" on the papers' alone," quoting *Aoude v. Mobil Oil Corp.*, 862 F.2d 890, 894 (1st Cir.1988)). The district court urges us to follow *Marcello* and hold that the CVRA guarantees victims only a right to make their position known by whatever means the court reasonably determines (see *Marcello*, 370 F.Supp.2d at 748). Even though "heard" has been held to include submission on the papers in some contexts, it does not follow that the CVRA calls for an equally broad construction. It merely shows that the district court's interpretation of the term is also plausible. [Footnote 2 reads: "We do not read *Paladin Associates, Inc. v. Montana Power Co.*, 328 F.3d 1145, 1164–65 (9th Cir. 2003), as compelling a contrary result. In *Paladin*, a party seeking to avoid discovery sanctions argued that its right to be heard under Federal Rule of Civil Procedure 37(c)(1) entitled it to an evidentiary hearing. We held that 'under the facts and circumstances of the present case, the opportunity to submit briefs was an "opportunity to be heard" within the meaning of Rule 37(c)(1).' *Paladin*, 328 F.3d at 1164–65. Kenna does not claim the right to present evidence or testify under oath; he seeks the right of allocution, much like that traditionally guaranteed a criminal defendant before sentence is imposed. Paladin thus not only construed the term 'heard' in a different context, but also dealt with the right to present evidence, which is not at issue here."].

The district court also argues that, had Congress meant to give victims a right to speak at sentencing hearings, it could easily have done so by using the word "speak" which clearly connotes only oral communications, not written ones. This is the term used in Federal Rule of Criminal Procedure 32(i)(4)(B), which gives the victims of certain types of crimes the right "to speak or submit any information about the sentence." The district court would have us infer from the fact that Congress used the more ambiguous term "heard" that it meant to give victims of crimes not covered by Rule 32 a more circumscribed right to present their views. However, the term "heard" does not appear in isolation in the CVRA. The full phrase we are construing is "[t]he right to be reasonably heard at any public proceeding in the district court involving . . . sentencing." Virtually all proceedings in district court are public in the sense that the papers and other materials may be viewed by anyone on request to the clerk's office. When Congress used the word "public" in this portion of the CVRA, however, it most likely meant to refer to proceedings in open court—much as the word is used in the common phrase "public hearing." So read, the right to be "heard" at a "public proceeding" becomes synonymous with "speak" and we can draw no negative inference from the congressional choice of one term over the other.

In the end, we find none of these textual arguments dispositive and conclude, as did *Degenhardt*, that both readings of the statute are plausible. The statute is therefore ambiguous as to what it means for crime victims to be heard. To resolve this ambiguity, we turn to the legislative history of the CVRA (see *Toibb v. Radloff*, 501 U.S. 157, 162 (1991, "[A] court appropriately may refer to a statute's legislative history to resolve statutory ambiguity . . . ")). The Senate considered the CVRA in

April 2004, and at that time the primary sponsors of the bill, Senators Jon Kyl and Dianne Feinstein, discussed this very issue:

> It is not the intent of the term "reasonably" in the phrase "to be reasonably heard" to provide any excuse for denying a victim the right to appear in person and directly address the court. Indeed, the very purpose of this section is to allow the victim to appear personally and directly address the court. (150 Cong. Rec. S4268 (daily ed. April 22, 2004, statement of Sen. Kyl); see also id. (statement of Sen. Feinstein, "That is my understanding as well.")

Six months later, the CVRA was attached to a House bill, and Senator Kyl reiterated his understanding of the CVRA language.

> It is important that the "reasonably be heard" language not be an excuse for minimizing the victim's opportunity to be heard. Only if it is not practical for the victim to speak in person or if the victim wishes to be heard by the court in a different fashion should this provision mean anything other than an in-person right to be heard. (150 Cong. Rec. S10911 (daily ed. Oct. 9, 2004, statement of Sen. Kyl.)

Floor statements are not given the same weight as some other types of legislative history, such as committee reports, because they generally represent only the view of the speaker and not necessarily that of the entire body. However, floor statements by the sponsors of the legislation are given considerably more weight than floor statements by other members (see *NLRB v. St. Francis Hosp. of Lynwood*, 601 F.2d 404, 415 n. 12 (9th Cir.1979)), and they are given even more weight where, as here, other legislators did not offer any contrary views. Silence, the maxim goes, connotes assent (see Bolt 1962, 88) and so we can draw from the fact that no one registered disagreement with Senators Kyl and Feinstein on this point the reasonable inference that the views they expressed reflected a consensus, at least in the Senate.

We also note that the CVRA passed as a compromise measure after a lengthy effort to amend the Constitution to protect victims' rights. The proposed constitutional amendment used language almost identical to that ultimately enacted in the CVRA; it guaranteed victims the right "reasonably to be heard" (S.J. Res. 1, 108th Cong. (2003)). But the legislative history of the proposed amendment is more substantial than that of the CVRA. The Senate Report on the amendment notes that:

> The victim's right is to "be heard." The right to make an oral statement is conditioned on the victim's presence in the courtroom. . . . [V]ictims should always be given the power to determine the form of the statement. Simply because a decision making body, such as the court . . . has a prior statement of some sort on file does not mean that the victim should not again be offered the opportunity to make a further statement. . . . The Committee does not intend that the right to be heard be limited to "written" statements, because the victim may wish to communicate in other appropriate ways. (S.Rep. No. 108–191, at 38 (2003)).

The statements of the sponsors of the CVRA and the committee report for the proposed constitutional amendment disclose a clear congressional intent to give crime victims the right to speak at proceedings covered by the CVRA.

Our interpretation advances the purposes of the CVRA. The statute was enacted to make crime victims full participants in the criminal justice system. Prosecutors and defendants already have the right to speak at sentencing (see Fed.R.Crim.P. 32(i)(4)(A)); our interpretation puts crime victims on the same footing. Our interpretation also serves to effectuate other statutory aims: (1) To ensure that the district court doesn't discount the impact of the crime on the victims; (2) to force the defendant to confront the human cost of his crime; and (3) to allow the victim "to regain a sense of dignity and respect rather than feeling powerless and ashamed" (Barnard 2001). Limiting victims to written impact statements, while allowing the prosecutor and the defendant the opportunity to address the court, would treat victims as secondary participants in the sentencing process. The CVRA clearly meant to make victims full participants.

Nor was Kenna's statutory right vindicated because he had the opportunity to speak at Moshe's sentencing three months earlier. The statute gives victims a "right to be reasonably heard at any public proceeding in the district court involving release, plea, sentencing, or any parole proceeding" (18 U.S.C. § 3771(a)(4)). This language means that the district court must hear from the victims, if they choose to speak, at more than one criminal sentencing. The court can't deny the defendant allocution because it thinks "[t]here just isn't anything else that could possibly be said." Victims now have an indefeasible right to speak, similar to that of the defendant, and for good reason: The effects of a crime aren't fixed forever once the crime is committed—physical injuries sometimes worsen; victims' feelings change; secondary and tertiary effects such as broken families and lost jobs may not manifest themselves until much time has passed. The district court must consider the effects of the crime on the victims at the time it makes its decision with respect to punishment, not as they were at some point in the past. Moreover, the CVRA gives victims the right to confront every defendant who has wronged them; speaking at a codefendant's sentencing does not vindicate the right of the victims to look this defendant in the eye and let him know the suffering his misconduct has caused.

We normally apply strict standards in reviewing petitions for a writ of mandamus, in large part to ensure that they not become vehicles for interlocutory review in routine cases. To this end, we grant the writ only when there is something truly extraordinary about the case—for example, clear or oft-repeated legal error by the district court, no other means for the petitioner to obtain review or an issue of first impression. This may well be such a case: The petitioner raises an issue of first impression, the district court clearly erred in its interpretation and Kenna has no other means of vindicating his rights. This case may thus merit review even under the strict standard announced in *Bauman v. United States District Court*, 557 F.2d 650, 654–55 (9th Cir.1977).

However, we need not balance the usual *Bauman* factors because the CVRA contemplates active review of orders denying victims' rights claims even in routine cases. The CVRA explicitly gives victims aggrieved by a district court's order the right to petition for review by writ of mandamus, provides for expedited review of such a petition, allows a single judge to make a decision thereon, and requires a reasoned decision in case the writ is denied. The CVRA creates a unique regime that does, in fact, contemplate routine interlocutory review of district court decisions denying rights asserted under the statute. We thus need not balance the Bauman factors in ruling on mandamus petitions brought under the CVRA; rather, we must issue the writ whenever we find that the district court's order reflects an abuse of discretion or legal error. The Second Circuit has come to the same conclusion (see *United States v. Rigas (In re W.R. Huff Asset Mgmt. Co.)*, 409 F.3d 555, 562 (2d Cir. 2005, holding that "a petitioner seeking relief pursuant to the mandamus provision set forth in § 3771(d)(3) need not overcome the hurdles typically faced by a petitioner seeking review of a district court determination through a writ of mandamus")). We are aware of no court of appeals that has held to the contrary.

As we explained above, the district court here committed an error of law by refusing to allow petitioner to allocute at Zvi's sentencing and we must therefore issue the writ. We turn now to the scope of the remedy. Kenna asks us to vacate Zvi's sentence, and order the district court to resentence him after allowing the victims to speak. The problem is that the CVRA gives district courts, not courts of appeals, the authority to decide a motion to reopen in the first instance (see 18 U.S.C. § 3771(d)(5)). Moreover, defendant Zvi Leichner is not a party to this mandamus action, and reopening his sentence in a proceeding where he did not participate may well violate his right to due process. It would therefore be imprudent and perhaps unconstitutional for us to vacate Zvi's sentence without giving him an opportunity to respond.

We could delay further our consideration of the petition and order briefing from the defendant, but we think it more advisable to let the district court consider the motion to reopen in the first instance. In ruling on the motion, the district court must avoid upsetting constitutionally protected rights, but it must also be cognizant that the only way to give effect to Kenna's right to speak as guaranteed to him by the CVRA is to vacate the sentence and hold a new sentencing hearing. We note that if the district court chooses not to reopen the sentence, Kenna will have another opportunity to petition this court for mandamus pursuant to the CVRA. Likewise, defendant will be able to contest any change in his sentence through the normal avenue for appeal (assuming he has not waived such rights as part of the plea bargain).

Finally, we recognize that under 18 U.S.C. § 3771(d)(3), we were required to "take up and decide [this] application forthwith within 72 hours after the petition [had] been filed" (Id.). We acknowledge our regrettable failure to consider the petition within the time limits of the statute, and apologize to the petitioner for this inexcusable delay. It may serve as a small comfort for petitioner to know that, largely because of this case, we are in the process of promulgating procedures for expeditious handling of CVRA mandamus petitions to ensure that we comply with the statute's strict time limits in future cases. As victim participation in the criminal justice system becomes more common, we expect CVRA claims to become more frequent, and thus encourage district courts to modify their own procedures so as to give full effect to the CVRA.

Conclusion

We grant the petition for writ of mandamus and hold that the district court erred in refusing to allow Kenna and other victims to speak at Zvi Leichner's sentencing hearing. The district court shall deem timely a motion pursuant to 18 U.S.C. § 3771(d)(5) filed by Kenna or any other of Zvi's victims within 14 days of the date of our opinion. If the district court grants the motion, it shall conduct a new sentencing hearing, according Kenna and the other victims the right to speak as described above.

Petition Granted

The panel retains jurisdiction over any future mandamus petitions arising from the Zvi Leichner criminal case.

* * *

Analysis

From the perspective of the Victims' Rights Movement, Judge Kozinski got it right in the *Kenna* case. Interpreting the legislative history to require a remedy, the case was sent back to the trial court to determine what that remedy would be. The trial court voided the sentence and set a new sentencing hearing at which the victims were allowed to speak. There was quiet celebration in the Crime Victims' Rights Movement after *Kenna* because crime victims had finally achieved enforceable rights, the type of rights the Oklahoma City Bombing victims never had.

The United States Justice Department vs. Victims' Rights

The initial optimism sown by the *Kenna* case was short lived as some other federal circuit courts came to the opposite conclusion. These courts have required victims to show that their need for relief was "clear and undisputable." These decisions were largely influenced by the position of the Justice Department—an agency that has significant influence in federal appellate courts. The *Antrobus* case, from the 10th Circuit Court of Appeals, represents a failure of victims' rights under the CVRA. This failure results, in no small measure, from the United States Justice Department's determination to narrow the scope and remedy of the CVRA. Professor Paul Cassell litigated the case and tells the story in the following document.

- **Document:** "Protecting Crime Victims in Federal Appellate Courts: The Need to Broadly Construe the Crime Victims' Rights Act's Mandamus Provision" by Paul G. Cassell
- **Date:** 2010
- **Significance:** Paul Cassell's article explores the weakening of the CVRA after *Antrobus* and the ways in which it must be strengthened. It also demonstrates how the U.S. Justice Department obstructed the victims' efforts to assert their rights.

- **Source:** Cassell, Paul G. "Protecting Crime Victims in Federal Appellate Courts: The Need to Broadly Construe the Crime Victims' Rights
Act's Mandamus Provision." *Denver University Law Review* 87 (2010):
599. Reprinted with permission.

---

* * *

Introduction

In 2004, Congress passed the Crime Victims' Rights Act ("CVRA" or "Act"),
Pub. L. No. 108-405, § 102(a), 118 Stat. 2260, 2261–62 (2004) (codified as
amended at 18 U.S.C. § 3771 (2006)) to dramatically reshape the federal criminal
justice system and ensure that crime victims are treated fairly in the criminal process. The Act created a "broad and encompassing" victims' bill of rights, guaranteeing victims (among other things) the rights to notice of court hearings, to attend
those hearings, and to be heard at particular hearings, such as plea and sentencing
hearings (150 Cong. Rec. S4261 (daily ed. Apr. 22, 2004, statement of Sen. Feinstein)). Congress intended for these rights to give victims the opportunity to participate in criminal justice proceedings, protect their interests, and shape the outcome
of those proceedings (Id. at S4263).

An important feature of the CVRA is its provisions allowing victims to enforce
their rights not only in trial courts, but also in appellate courts. Among the enforcement provisions is one guaranteeing a crime victim expedited access to appellate
review. The CVRA provides that if the district court denies any relief sought by a
crime victim, the victim "may petition the court of appeals for a writ of mandamus.
The court of appeals shall take up and decide such application forthwith within
72 hours after the petition has been filed" (18 U.S.C. § 3771 (d)(3)). In enacting
this provision, Congress sought to give crime victims genuine rights at all stages in
the criminal justice process. As one of the CVRA's co-sponsors explained, "[W]ith-
out the ability to enforce the [victims'] rights in the criminal trial and appellate
courts of this country any rights afforded are, at best, rhetoric" (150 Cong. Rec.
S10, 912 (daily ed. Oct. 9, 2004, statement of Sen. Kyl)).

The CVRA's appellate review provision appeared to provide crime victims the
same sort of appellate protections as all other litigants—as several courts of appeals
have held in reviewing crime victims' petitions. Unfortunately, in a recent decision
the Tenth Circuit parted company with those other circuits and eviscerated the
appellate protections promised to crime victims. In *In re Antrobus*, 519 F.3d 1123
(10th Cir. 2008), the Tenth Circuit rejected carefully reasoned decisions from the
Second and Ninth Circuits and held that crime victims could only obtain appellate
relief if they show that the district court had made a "clear and indisputable" error
(Id. at 1130–31). The Tenth Circuit believed that, when Congress used the term
"mandamus" in the CVRA, it meant to drastically restrict the ability of appellate
courts to give crime victims relief (Id. at 1130–31). The Tenth Circuit's demanding
standard means that, as a practical matter, it will be very difficult (if not impossible)
for many crime victims to overturn erroneous decisions of district courts, particularly

given that crime victims' rights law is a new and evolving field in which "indisputable" errors may be hard to prove.

This Article critiques the Tenth Circuit's *Antrobus* decision, arguing that the Second and Ninth Circuits got it right and the Tenth Circuit simply got it wrong. When victims of crime are denied relief in the district court, they should receive the same sort of appellate protections as other litigants. This increased protection is what the language of the CVRA clearly provides and what Congress plainly intended.

* * *

The Antrobuses' Quest to Give a Victim Impact Statement

The Antrobuses' efforts to give a victim impact statement at the sentencing of the man who sold the gun used to murder their daughter produced long and complicated litigation. The history of the litigation is worth recounting, however, because it shows both the importance of victims having effective appellate review of their claims and the difficulties that have arisen in the Tenth Circuit in providing such review. Remarkably, despite four different trips to the Tenth Circuit, the Antrobuses were unable to have the circuit review a district court ruling against them.

The Issue: Was Vanessa Quinn a "Crime Victim" Protected by the CVRA?

The underlying issue in the Antrobus litigation was whether Vanessa Quinn was a protected "crime victim" pursuant to the CVRA. Mackenzie Hunter committed a crime in the summer of 2006, when he illegally sold a handgun to Sulejman Talovic, a juvenile (Id. at 1124). As Hunter well knew, Talovic could not lawfully possess a handgun because he was a juvenile. In fact, it appears Talovic asked Hunter to obtain the gun for him because he (Talovic) was blocked from buying one. About six months later, on February 12, 2007, Talovic entered the Trolley Square Shopping Center in Salt Lake City, Utah. In the largest mass murder in recent Utah history, Talovic used the handgun and a 12-gauge shotgun to kill five people and seriously injure four others. A bullet from the handgun Hunter had illegally sold to Talovic killed Vanessa Quinn, daughter of Kenny and Sue Antrobus (*United States v. Hunter*, No. 2:07 CR307DAK, 2008 WL 53125, at 1 (D.Utah Jan. 3, 2008)).

On May 16, 2007, a federal grand jury returned a two-count felony indictment against Hunter: Count I charged him with being a drug user in possession of a firearm, and Count II charged him with unlawful transfer of a firearm to a juvenile with knowledge or reason to know that it would be used in a violent crime (see 18 U.S.C. § 922(g)(3) (2006); id. §§ 922(x)(1)(A), 924(a)(6)(B)(ii)). Plea negotiations ensued, and on November 5, 2007, Hunter entered guilty pleas pursuant to a plea agreement. Hunter pled guilty to Count I (drug user in possession of a firearm) and a newly filed misdemeanor criminal charge, alleging unlawful transfer of a firearm to a juvenile (without any allegation about knowledge that the gun would be used in a crime of violence; see id. §§ 922(x)(1), 924(a)(6)(B)(i)). Under the plea agreement, the Justice Department agreed to move to dismiss the original Count II at the time of sentencing. After entry of the pleas, the district court set sentencing for January 14, 2008.

About a month later, on December 13, 2007, having secured pro bono legal counsel, the Antrobuses filed a motion requesting that the district court recognize their daughter, Vanessa Quinn, as a "crime victim" and the Antrobuses as her representatives under the CVRA. Their motion noted that the indictment charged Hunter with illegal sale of a firearm with knowledge that it would be used to commit a crime of violence. The motion further alleged that, based on an article in the Salt Lake Tribune newspaper, Talovic told Hunter that he wanted the handgun to rob a bank. Based on the indictment and the bank robbery discussion, the Antrobuses asked that their daughter be recognized as a "crime victim" under the CVRA.

The CVRA defines a "crime victim" as "a person directly and proximately harmed as a result of the commission of a Federal offense" (18 U.S.C. § 3771(e) (2006)). The Antrobuses argued that there could be no doubt that Vanessa was "directly" harmed when a bullet from the gun Hunter illegally sold to Talovic killed her. The Antrobuses also argued it was clear that this harm was "proximately" caused by Hunter's crime. Not only did Hunter make his illegal sale directly to Talovic, but he specifically foresaw Talovic using the gun to commit a violent crime. That the foreseen crime was a bank robbery, rather than a mass murder, was of no consequence. The Antrobuses explained that the tragic death of Vanessa Quinn (among others) was precisely what Congress intended to prevent by prohibiting illegal trafficking of guns. The Antrobuses, therefore, urged the district court to recognize Vanessa as a "victim" of the defendant's crime under the CVRA. As her representatives under the CVRA, they sought to deliver a victim impact statement at sentencing, receive restitution for unreimbursed funeral expenses, and express their objections to the dismissal of Count II. Neither Hunter nor the United States filed objections to these motions.

Nonetheless, on January 3, 2008, the district court denied the Antrobuses' CVRA motion, holding that Hunter's crime was "too factually and temporally attenuated" from the death of Vanessa Quinn to recognize her as a "victim" of the crime (*Hunter*, 2008 WL 53125, at 4). The district court acknowledged that the Antrobuses had referred to a discussion between Hunter and Talovic about a bank robbery, but deemed this statement "general speculation" (Id.). "This type of speculation," the court concluded, "does not demonstrate the type of knowledge or foreseeability necessary to finding Hunter's sale of the firearm to a minor to be the proximate cause of Quinn's death" (Id. at 5). Accordingly, the district court held that Vanessa Quinn was not a "victim" of Hunter's illegal sale of the handgun used to murder her and, therefore, that Vanessa had no rights under the CVRA for the Antrobuses to assert. The district court also denied the Antrobuses' motion to gain access to information (including an ATF Report) about what Hunter and Talovic had discussed during the sale of the gun.

In one last rebuff of the Antrobuses, the district court further declined to exercise its discretion at sentencing to briefly hear the Antrobuses for even a few minutes. The Antrobuses made the alternative argument that, even if their daughter did not technically fall within the protections of the CVRA, the district court should nonetheless allow them to present a brief victim impact statement at sentencing (see generally Cassell 2009). The district court, however, while conceding it had authority to hear from the Antrobuses about the murder of their daughter, declined

242 of their views (*Hunter*, 2008 WL 53125, at 6).

to use its discretionary authority to hear from them because it had "an adequate understanding" of their views (*Hunter*, 2008 WL 53125, at 6).

The Tenth Circuit Erects a Barrier to Review of Victims' Claims that Fall Short of a "Clear and Indisputable" Error

Having been stymied by the district court, the Antrobuses sought appellate review of the "crime victim" decision by the district court. They did so by filing a writ of mandamus, the procedural device spelled out in the CVRA (18 U.S.C. § 3771(d)(3) (2006)). Once again, the Justice Department did not object to the Antrobuses' petition. Defendant Hunter objected, but only on the ground that the Antrobuses' factual representations below were not sufficiently substantiated.

The Tenth Circuit denied the Antrobuses' petition (*Antrobus*, 519 F.3d, at 1126). The court began by stating that it would not follow decisions from the Second and Ninth Circuits, which held that a CVRA mandamus petition provides crime victims with ordinary appellate review (Id. at 1124 [internal citations omitted]). Instead, the court held that the Antrobuses would have to meet a very demanding standard of showing "that their right to the writ is 'clear and indisputable' " (Id. at 1124 [internal citations omitted]). The court reasoned that Congress had only authorized crime victims to file a "writ of mandamus," thereby importing with that phrase "traditional mandamus standards" that permit relief "only in extraordinary situations" (Id. at 1124–25 [internal citations omitted]). Even proceeding on that basis, the court conceded that the case was a "difficult" one (Id. at 1125). Nonetheless, the court could not "say that the Antrobuses' right to the writ is clear and indisputable" (Id. at 1126 [internal citations omitted]), because it was not "clear and indisputable" that Vanessa Quinn was a foreseeable victim of Hunter's criminal firearms sale (see id. at 1125 n.1, 1126).

The majority opinion for the court noted that "[o]ne might question whether, with additional discovery, the Antrobuses might have been able to determine whether, in fact, Mr. Hunter knew about Talovic's intentions and what such knowledge might mean for the foreseeability to Mr. Hunter of Talovic's crimes" (Id. at 1125 n.1). The concurring opinion from Judge Tymkovich went even further, adding: "In my view, the district court and the government erred in failing to permit the Antrobuses reasonable access to evidence which could support their claim" [34]. The court, however, declined to address the discovery issues, finding that those issues were not raised in the immediate proceeding.

On January 25, 2008, the Antrobuses filed a petition for panel rehearing with suggestion of rehearing en banc. On March 14, 2008, the panel denied the petition, adhering to the "clear and indisputable" standard for conventional mandamus review (see id. at 1130). In doing so, the panel added additional explanation for its holding. The panel began by stating that the term "[m]andamus is a well worn term of art in our common law tradition" (Id. at 1127). The panel then reasoned that:

> [W]here Congress borrows terms of art in which are accumulated the legal tra-
> dition and meaning of centuries of practice, it presumably knows and adopts
> the cluster of ideas that were attached to each borrowed word in the body of
> learning from which it was taken and the meaning its use will convey to the

judicial mind unless otherwise instructed. (Id. at 1127–28 [internal citations omitted])

In view of the fact that the conventional standard of review for mandamus petitions is "clear and disputable" error, the panel concluded that the same standard of review was appropriate for CVRA petitions. The panel also decided that it had properly applied the standard in rejecting the Antrobuses' petition. Accordingly, the panel declined to grant a rehearing. The panel also rejected the Antrobuses' motion to consolidate the mandamus petition with a parallel appeal that the Antrobuses had filed (discussed in the next section) (see *United States v. Hunter*, No. 2:07 CR307DAK, 2008 WL 53125, at 5 (D. Utah Jan. 3, 2008)). The petition for rehearing en banc was denied at the same time.

The Sentencing of Hunter and the Antrobuses' Efforts to Obtain Information About Plans for a Bank Robbery

While their petition for rehearing was pending with the Tenth Circuit, the Antrobuses renewed their efforts in the district court to obtain proof of the bank robbery discussion between Hunter and Talovic. On the morning set for sentencing, January 14, 2008, the Antrobuses filed a motion for reconsideration of the district court's earlier denial of their motion for production of the ATF Report. On that afternoon, however, the district court denied their motion in a written order, on the basis that the Justice Department had already certified that it had no such information. The district court stated:

> The government previously informed the court that it did not possess any information relevant to Hunter's forseeability of Talovic's subsequent crime. There remains no basis for this court to question the government's position, and this court will not entertain repeated motions on the same issues, when the effect of those motions [is to] delay a sentencing that is set to proceed. (*United States v. Hunter*, No. 2:07 CR307DAK, 2008 WL 153798, at 1 (D. Utah Jan. 14, 2008))

Later that afternoon, having concluded that the Justice Department possessed no information "relevant" to Hunter foreseeing any crime committed by Talovic, the district court held a sentencing hearing for Hunter. At the hearing, counsel for the Antrobuses first requested that the Justice Department clarify whether the district court's written order was correct in stating that the Department "did not possess any information relevant to Hunter's foreseeability" of misuse of the gun in any violent crime—not just the Trolley Square massacre (*Hunter*, 2008 WL 153798, at 5). The following exchange ensued:

Antrobuses' counsel:	"The sentence in the Court's order seems to suggest that the government has indicated it has no information regarding the use of the gun in any subsequent crime of violence. If that's correct, we need to know that. If it's not—"

Court:	"That's my understanding. That's my understanding. Do you want to say anything about that or not?"
Assistant United States Attorney:	"Judge, I'd rather not. I think we have built a record. We have made representations."
Court:	"The record is the record" (Id. at 5–6).

The court then adhered to its position. Thus, based on its understanding that the Justice Department had no information that Hunter knew that Talovic would use the gun in any subsequent violent crime, the district court rejected the Antrobuses' efforts to have Vanessa Quinn recognized as a "victim" of Hunter's crime under the CVRA. The district court then proceeded to sentence Hunter without giving the Antrobuses a chance to make a victim impact statement, as would be their right had Vanessa been a "victim" under the CVRA.

On January 25, 2008, the Antrobuses filed a mandamus petition with the Tenth Circuit to compel the Justice Department to turn over documents, including the ATF Report, that would prove Talovic and Hunter had discussed a bank robbery. After ordering responses, the Tenth Circuit denied the petition—again noting that it had previously established a demanding standard of "clear and indisputable" error review (*In re Antrobus*, No. 08-4013, slip op. at 3, 10 (10th Cir. Feb. 1, 2008)). The basis for the denial appeared to be that the Department had promised to file relevant portions of the ATF Report under seal with the district court and would have no objection to release of the document to the Antrobuses, thereby rendering the Antrobuses' mandamus petition moot (Id. at 9 n.2).

Back in the district court, on February 7, 2008, the Justice Department gave notice that it had "filed" the ATF Report under seal. [Footnote 44 omitted]. The next day, the Antrobuses filed an unopposed motion for release of the redacted ATF Report with the district court. Remarkably, however, even without opposition, on March 17, 2008, the district court tersely denied the motion. The district court stated that although the motion was unopposed, it had not been stipulated to by the Government. The court further stated: "While the court recognizes that it may have discretion to disclose the ATF Report, the court is unwilling to create such a precedent to individuals who are attempting to establish their status as victims of a given offense" (*United States v. Hunter*, No. 2:07CRE307DAK, slip op. at 2 (D. Utah Mar. 17, 2008)).

On March 28, 2008, the Antrobuses filed a motion for reconsideration of the district court's denial of their unopposed motion for release of the ATF Report. The Antrobuses contended that because the Justice Department had filed the documents under seal, it was obligated to provide "good cause" for the sealing under the court's local rules, which strictly limit what documents can be filed under seal (D. Utah Civ. R. 49-2(b)). The Antrobuses further argued that release of the document was required to correct the record in the case because the district court had previously ruled based on the belief that the Justice Department had no information in its files regarding a bank robbery discussion between Talovic and Hunter, when in fact there had been such a discussion—a fact that the Justice Department well knew.

On April 21, 2008, the district court denied the motion for reconsideration. The court stated briefly that the Government "did not file the documents" but merely provided them for in camera review (*United States v. Hunter*, No. 2: o7CR307DAK, slip op. at 1 (D. Utah Apr. 21, 2008)). Accordingly, the requirements of the local rules were "inapplicable" and nothing in the Antrobuses' motion persuaded the court to alter its previous ruling (Id.).

The Antrobuses' Unsuccessful Parallel Appeal

Meanwhile, the Antrobuses continued to press for appellate vindication of their right to give a victim impact statement by a separate procedural vehicle—an appeal to the Tenth Circuit of the district court's decision denying their motion to be recognized as the victim's representatives. After the Antrobuses' timely notice of appeal, the Justice Department filed a motion to dismiss for lack of jurisdiction. The Tenth Circuit ordered full briefing on the jurisdictional question and the merits, and the Antrobuses filed their opening brief on May 29, 2008. Two months later, the Justice Department filed its response brief (see Brief for the United States, *United States v. Hunter*, 548 F.3d 1308 (10th Cir. 2008, No. 08-4010)). For the first time, the Justice Department admitted, in a public record, that Talovic had told Hunter while the sale was being negotiated that he wanted the gun to rob a bank. The Justice Department's Statement of the Facts recounted that "Hunter asked Talovic why he wanted a gun, and Talovic said something to the effect that he wanted a gun to use to rob a bank" (Id. at 13). The underlying basis for that particular recounting of the facts was apparently the ATF Report the Antrobuses had long been seeking, as that specific recitation of the facts did not appear anywhere else in the public record of the case. Curiously, the Justice Department did not include a citation for that sentence in its brief, in contrast to other parts of its statement of facts, and declined to provide the Antrobuses' counsel with any further information about the source of the statement.

Simultaneously with filing its brief in the Tenth Circuit, the Justice Department filed a motion to lodge the ATF report under seal, attaching the ATF Report. [Footnote 51 omitted]. The motion stated that the Justice Department was lodging the ATF Report with the Tenth Circuit "in the interest of completeness." The Antrobuses promptly filed an objection to the filing of a sealed document, noting that the Justice Department had failed "to provide any justification for [the] sealing." The Justice Department filed a reply to this objection, stating that until the Tenth Circuit determined that it had jurisdiction, it could not act on the Antrobuses' objection. In any event, the Justice Department argued that the Privacy Act provided a basis for sealing the document—apparently concluding that the privacy interests of a deceased mass murderer came ahead of the Antrobuses' interests in learning everything they could about how their daughter was killed.

On September 2, 2008, the Antrobuses filed a motion for remand in light of newly revealed evidence in the government's files. The Antrobuses explained that the Government's admission in its response brief was the first public disclosure of the bank robbery conversation between Talovic and Hunter. Because this critical and potentially dispositive fact had been previously concealed, the

Antrobuses argued, a remand to permit the district court to consider the evidence was appropriate.

Following oral argument, on December 2, 2008, the Tenth Circuit dismissed the Antrobuses' appeal (*Hunter*, 548 F.3d, at 1317). The court concluded that "neither our case law nor the CVRA provide for non-parties like the Antrobuses to bring a post-judgment direct appeal in a criminal case" (Id. at 1316). The court noted that the CVRA provides for mandamus review of denials of crime victims' rights, but does not explicitly provide crime victims a right to appeal. Based on this fact, the court reasoned "[t]hat the [fact the] CVRA does not provide for victim appeals is consistent with the well-established precept that 'only parties to a lawsuit, or those that properly become parties, may appeal an adverse judgment' " (Id. at 1311 [internal quotation omitted]). The court acknowledged that the Antrobuses had cited a series of cases in which various circuits (including the Tenth Circuit itself) had allowed non-parties to take appeals, including appeals in criminal cases. The court found those cases unpersuasive, stating, "There is a common thread in those criminal cases in which courts have permitted non-party appeals: the appeals all related to specific trial issues and did not disturb a final judgment" (Id. at 1314). The court did not explain why the Antrobuses' challenge to the "victim" ruling was a specific issue apart from the final judgment. Nor did it explain why it would not reach a final conclusion on that issue, which would affect issues apart from the final judgment in the case (such as whether the Antrobuses would receive notice of any parole or other release for Hunter at some later point in time). The court also relied on the fact that the Antrobuses could seek mandamus review as a basis for rejecting their appeal. "To hold otherwise," the court reasoned, "would effectively grant victims two opportunities to appeal" (Id. at 1315 n.5)—although, in its earlier ruling, it took great pains to emphasize that it was not giving the Antrobuses the equivalent of an ordinary appeal.

The court then turned to the Antrobuses' motion for remand for rehearing in light of the newly-revealed evidence and the Government's motion to seal the ATF report. On the remand motion, the Tenth Circuit declined to reach the merits "because at this stage a motion for a rehearing should be filed in the district court" (Id. at 1316). The court noted that it was proper for the Antrobuses to have first sought a remand in the Court of Appeals. "But now that the appeal is no longer pending, the district court is free to grant the relief the Antrobuses seek, and therefore the district court is the proper venue for the motion for a new hearing" (Id. at 1317 n.8). The Circuit concluded that "[b]ecause we are now dismissing the Antrobuses' appeal, they can—and should—file their motion for a new hearing in light of newly discovered evidence in the district court" (Id. at 1316–17).

The Antrobuses' Final Attempt to Secure a Hearing in Light of the Justice Department's Newly Revealed Evidence

Following the Tenth Circuit's direct suggestion, the Antrobuses returned to the district court and filed a motion for a new hearing. The Antrobuses explained to the district court that the Justice Department's newly-revealed information placed the initial ruling—that Hunter could not foresee the use of the gun in a violent crime—in an entirely new light. Once again, however, the Antrobuses were rebuffed by the district court.

On February 10, 2009, in a brief order, the district court denied the Antrobuses' motion for a new hearing (*United States v. Hunter*, No. 2:07 CR307DAK, 2009 U.S. Dist. LEXIS 90822, at 4 (D. Utah Feb. 10, 2009)). The district court assumed that it had the authority to grant the motion but declined to do so for two reasons. First, the district court concluded that "the reference in the government's brief to the conversation between Hunter and Talovic does not constitute newly revealed evidence" (Id. at 3). Second, the district court concluded that its ruling a year earlier denying the Antrobuses unopposed motion for release of the ATF Report constituted a ruling on the merits of whether the report would change its conclusion (Id. at 3–4). The district court did not explain why its earlier ruling did not even mention (much less discuss) the merits of this issue. Nor did the district court explain how it was fair to the Antrobuses to have ruled a year earlier on the merits of a claim that had not been presented by the parties and on which they had not been heard. Nor did the district court explain how it could have possibly had jurisdiction to rule on the merits of the Antrobuses' claim, as the matter was on appeal to the Tenth Circuit at that time, thereby stripping the district court of the ability to rule on the matter (see *In re Antrobus*, 519 F.3d 1123, 1127 (10th Cir. 2008)).

On February 20, 2009, the Antrobuses filed another mandamus petition with the Tenth Circuit challenging the district court's ruling. In their fourth trip to the Tenth Circuit in just over a year, the Antrobuses explained that the Justice Department's newly revealed evidence placed the central issue of whether Hunter could foresee his gun being used in a crime of violence before the court. The new evidence showed that Hunter was not "surmis[ing] that Talovic might" rob a bank, as the district court had initially ruled, but rather was told directly by Talovic that this was his plan for the gun during the course of Hunter's sale (see *United States v. Hunter*, No. 2:07 CR307DAK, 2008 WL 53125, at 5 (D. Utah Jan. 3, 2008)). The Antrobuses also argued, in the alternative, that if the Tenth Circuit was unable to conclude that any district court error was clear and indisputable, then they objected to being forced to satisfy that demanding standard of review. They therefore asserted an objection to this standard to preserve their right to seek further review of the issue.

The Tenth Circuit, however, appeared to want to close the case once and for all, and rebuffed all the Antrobuses' efforts. The court began by reaffirming its "clear and indisputable error" standard of review for mandamus petitions (*In re Antrobus*, 563 F.3d 1092, 1097 (10th Cir. 2009)). Moreover, the court gratuitously preempted the Antrobuses' effort to preserve the issue for review in the Supreme Court. The court first noted that the holding was now the "law of the case" because the Antrobuses had not sought certiorari to review the issue earlier (Id.). The court did not acknowledge that it had effectively prevented the Antrobuses from seeking Supreme Court review earlier by denying their motion to consolidate their parallel appeal with the mandamus petition (see *In re Antrobus*, No. 08-4013, 2008 U.S. App. LEXIS 27527, at 13 (10th Cir. Feb. 1, 2008)). The Circuit also stated, in dicta, that it would reach the same conclusion on the petition under either standard of review.

Turning to the merits of the Antrobuses' arguments, the Tenth Circuit did not repeat—or even acknowledge—its earlier statement that the Antrobuses "should" pursue the issue of discovery in the district court. Instead, the court stated that the Antrobuses had failed to articulate a specific legal standard that the district court failed to properly apply (*Antrobus*, 563 F.3d at 1097). Even if they had provided such a standard, the court continued, the Antrobuses failed to show that the information about the bank robbery was "newly discovered." The Circuit stated: "The difficulty is that the Antrobuses have not demonstrated that they were unable to present evidence along these very same lines over a year ago, when this litigation began" (Id. at 1099). Without recounting all of the litigation that the Antrobuses had pursued in an attempt to obtain the ATF Report, the court stated: "Had they made a record showing diligent but stymied efforts on this front, we might have a different case" (Id.).

To put the final nail in the coffin, the Tenth Circuit then went on to hold that the Antrobuses did not have any important new evidence. The court stated: "Most generously, then, the Antrobuses' 'new evidence' demonstrates only that Hunter knew—rather than just 'surmised'—that Talovic intended to rob a bank. But that is not so substantial a difference as the Antrobuses insist" (Id. at 1100 [quotation omitted]).

At this point, then, the Antrobuses' litigation efforts came to an end. To add one last insult to injury, however, the Justice Department (which for more than a year had steadfastly refused to turn over the ATF documents to the Antrobuses because of the Privacy Act and other purported impediments), decided to act on a long-pending Freedom of Information Act request from the Salt Lake Tribune for the same documents. The Justice Department released the documents, which lead to a newspaper article headlined "Notes Confirm Suspicions of Trolley Square Victim's Family" (Carlisle 2009). The article explained:

> Newly released FBI documents say that Sulejman Talovic told a coworker he wanted a gun to commit a bank robbery.
>
> The statement corroborates an argument made by the parents of a Trolley Square victim Vanessa Quinn. Sue and Ken Antrobus have said one of the people who sold Talovic a .38-caliber pistol knew Talovic was going to use it to commit a crime. (Id.)

The Justice Department released these documents to the media—without first providing them to the Antrobuses, whose daughter was murdered at Trolley Square—and in contravention of its previous representations to the Tenth Circuit that it could not release the documents due to Privacy Act concerns. Conveniently, all of this happened after the Antrobuses' opportunity to provide the documents to the Tenth Circuit had evaporated because their appeal had come to an end.

In summary, it is worth briefly highlighting the net result of the Antrobuses' tortuous journey through the courts. After the district court denied their motion to have their daughter recognized as a "crime victim," they were unable to have the merits of that decision reviewed by the Tenth Circuit, despite four separate attempts. In the first trip, the Tenth Circuit rejected the holdings of (at least) two other circuit courts to erect a demanding "clear and indisputable error" standard of review. Having imposed that barrier, the court then stated that the case was a "close" one but that they would not grant relief—with one concurring judge noting that sufficient proof of the Antrobuses' claim might rest in the Justice Department's files. The Antrobuses then returned to the district court, where the Justice Department refused to clarify the district court's misunderstanding of what information rested in its files. The Antrobuses then sought mandamus review of the question of discovering that information in the Justice Department files, which the Department "mooted" by agreeing to file that information with the district court and not opposing any release to the Antrobuses. But the district court stymied the Antrobuses' attempt by refusing to grant their unopposed motion for release of the documents.

The Antrobuses then sought appellate review of the district court's initial "victim" ruling, only to have the Tenth Circuit conclude that they were barred from taking an appeal. The Tenth Circuit, however, said that they "should" pursue the issue of release of the material in the Justice Department's files in the district court. So they did—only to lose again in the district court. And on a final mandamus petition to the Tenth Circuit, the court ruled (among other things) that the Antrobuses had not been diligent enough in seeking the release of the information. With their appeals at an end, the Justice Department chose to release discovery information about the case—not to the Antrobuses, but to the media.

* * *

Analysis

The ordeal of the *Antrobus* saga is reminiscent of the poor treatment accorded the Oklahoma City Bombing victims. The main difference however, is that in *Antrobus*, it is the U.S. Justice Department's actions, rather than a federal judge's actions, that are prominently on display.

A relevant and interesting question springs from the disappointing result of *Antrobus*: Why is the Justice Department intent on narrowing the scope of victims' rights and/or directly violating them? Traditionally, the Justice Department has defended convictions. For example, if a criminal defendant is convicted but argues his rights were violated, the Justice Department will defend the conviction and, in doing so, assert that the defendant's rights were not violated. In the *Antrobus* case, the Justice Department violates victims' rights and then secures a conviction. Once the conviction occurs, the Justice Department defends it. Thus, the Justice Department has chosen to oppose victims' rights when those rights conflict with the defense of a conviction.

However, the Department of Justice has conflicting obligations that could readily necessitate its support of victims' rights. First, it is obligated to defend statutes passed by Congress, such as the CVRA. Additionally, the Justice Department has a specific statutory obligation to victims' rights in the CVRA. The CVRA requires the Justice Department to use its "best efforts" to ensure victims' rights are complied with: "Officers and employees of the Department of Justice and other departments and agencies of the United States engaged in the detection, investigation, or prosecution of crime shall make their best efforts to see that crime victims are notified of, and accorded, the rights ..." The "best efforts" requirement creates a statutory requirement different from the traditional value of defending convictions. The *Antrobus* case arguably reveals that the Justice Department is not in compliance with its statutory obligation to the CVRA requirement of "best efforts" to ensure that crime victims are accorded their rights.

The *Antrobus* case is not an isolated example of the Justice Department's hostility to victims' rights in the CVRA. Even outside of the CVRA, the Justice Department has taken stances against victims. In *In re Amy*, 636 F.3d 190 (5th Cir. 2011), the 5th Circuit rejected the Department of Justice's narrow construction of a child pornography restitution statute.

In the *In re Stewart* case, the Justice Department took the position that victims of a white-collar crime involving mortgage fraud were not crime victims under the CVRA (552 F.3d 1285 (2008)). In a rare admonishment of the Justice Department, the court held that the defrauded people were victims under the CVRA and wrote, "Although the [victim's] petition does not seek relief against the Assistant United States Attorney prosecuting the case, we expect that attorney to be mindful of the [best efforts] obligations imposed by section 3771(c) of the statute."

Even having been admonished by the court, the Justice Department continued to deny victims their rights. This is recounted in a subsequent motion by the victims' attorney seeking to get the Justice Department to comply with the victims' right to confer provided for by the CVRA (*In re Stewart*. Motion For An Order Directing The Government To Afford Crime Victims Their Rights To Confer And To Timely Notice Under The Crime Victims' Rights Act And For Sanctions For Failure To Comply With The Act. No. 10-12344-E, United States Court of Appeals for the Eleventh Circuit (2002)).

The following case involves the Defendant BP Petroleum. This is the same BP responsible for the infamous Gulf of Mexico oil spill. As you will see in the court's opinion, the Justice Department worked to intentionally deny victims their rights by seeking a secret court order denying the victims consultation about a plea deal the victims likely would have opposed. The facts involve criminal liability for an explosion at a BP plant that killed the workers there.

- **Document:** *In re Dean*
- **Date:** May 7, 2008
- **Significance:** *In re Dean* provides yet another example of the Department of Justice's intentional attempt to deny victims' rights.
- **Source:** *In re Dean*, 527 F.3d 391 (5th Cir. 2008).

---

* * *

Per Curiam:

In the related criminal proceeding, twelve of the victims asked the district court to reject the plea agreement, alleging violations of the Crime Victims' Rights Act ("CVRA"), 18 U.S.C. § 3771. The district court denied the request (see *United*

States v. BP Prods. N. Am. Inc., No. H-07-434, 2008 WL 501321, 2008 U.S. Dist. LEXIS 12893 (S.D.Tex. Feb. 21, 2008)). The victims petition for writ of mandamus with the prayer that "[t]he decision of the district court should be reversed and the case remanded with instructions that the plea agreement [not be] accepted and the parties are permitted to proceed as they determine—so long as it is in a way that respects crime victims' rights." We find a statutory violation but, for reasons we explain, we deny relief.

I.

The factual background and the judicial events that led to the mandamus petition are cogently set forth in the district court's Memorandum and Order, id. 2008 WL 501321, at 1-6, 2008 U.S. Dist. LEXIS 12893, at 3–18, in the criminal case. As there explained, an explosion at a refinery operated by the criminal defendant, BP Products North America Inc. ("BP"), killed fifteen and injured more than 170. Extensive civil litigation ensued.

The Department of Justice investigated the possibility of federal criminal violations. Before bringing any charges, the government, on October 18, 2007, filed a sealed ex parte motion for "an order outlining the procedures to be followed under the [CVRA]." The government announced that a plea agreement was expected to be signed in about a week and that because of the number of victims, "consulting the victims prior to reaching a plea agreement would not be practicable" and that notifying the victims would result in media coverage that "could impair the plea negotiation process and may prejudice the case in the event that no plea is reached."

As explained in the district court's order, the government, in its sealed ex parte motion, made specific recommendations for how the court should fashion a "reasonable procedure" under the CVRA's multiple crime victim exception. The district court, per an order signed by a district judge who had been assigned to the case in its status as a miscellaneous matter (see id. 2008 WL 501321, at 1 n. 1, 2008 U.S. Dist. LEXIS 12893, at 4 n. 1), responded with impressive speed, issuing on that same day a sealed order finding that notification to victims in advance of the public announcement of a plea agreement was impracticable because of the "large number of victims" and because, on account of the extensive media coverage, "any public notification of a potential criminal disposition resulting from the government's investigation [of the] explosion would prejudice [BP] and could impair the plea negotiation process and may prejudice the case in the event that no plea is reached." The ex parte order prohibited the government from notifying victims of a potential plea agreement until one had been executed; it directed that once an agreement had been signed, the government "shall provide reasonable notice to all identifiable victims and afford the victims the rights set forth [in the CVRA] prior to actual entry of the guilty plea. . . ."

The government filed the criminal information under seal on October 22. Two days later, the government and BP signed the plea agreement. The next day, the information was unsealed, and the plea agreement was announced. The government mailed three notices to the victims, in November and January, advising of scheduled proceedings and of their right to be heard. On November 20 and 23, various victims moved to appear and asked that the plea agreement be rejected or at least that the court handling the criminal matter require a presentence report.

After two district judges had declared themselves recused, the matter was permanently assigned, as a criminal matter, to the judge who entered the February 21 order that is the subject of this mandamus petition. Some victims appeared through counsel at a status conference on November 28 and presented their opposition to the plea agreement; 134 of them filed victim impact statements.

BP pleaded guilty at a hearing on February 4. All victims who wished to be heard, personally or through counsel, were permitted to speak. The attorneys reiterated the victims' request that the court reject the plea agreement on the basis of the CVRA violations alone; the district court reserved decision on the victims' other challenges to the plea agreement. As the district court describes it, "the victims focused on three challenges: the fine was too low; the probation conditions were too lenient; and certain CVRA requirements had been violated" (*BP Prods.*, 2008 WL 501321 at 5, 2008 U.S. Dist. LEXIS 12893, at 15). The victims and their attorneys supplemented their appearances at the hearing with substantial post-hearing submissions.

On February 21, the district court entered the above-cited order, denying the victims' request that the court reject the plea agreement. Feeling aggrieved by the order, the victims filed the instant mandamus petition on February 28. Also on that date, a panel of this court, in compliance with the requirement of 18 U.S.C. § 3771 (d)(3) that we act within seventy-two hours, entered an order granting the mandamus petition in part: It directed the district court to take no further action to effect the plea agreement, pending further order and awaiting additional briefing.

II.

The parties dispute the standard of review. The victims assert that despite the fact that the CVRA states that "[i]f the district court denies the relief sought [by a victim], the movant may petition the court of appeals for a writ of mandamus" (18 U.S.C. § 3771(d)(3)), the ordinary appeal standards (instead of the stricter standards for obtaining a writ of mandamus) apply. Two circuits agree with the victims (see *Kenna v. United States Dist. Court*, 435 F.3d 1011, 1017 (9th Cir.2006); *In re W.R. Huff Asset Mgmt. Co.*, 409 F.3d 555, 563 (2d Cir. 2005)).

The Tenth Circuit, however, taking the view that "[m]andamus is a well worn term of art in our common law tradition," most recently has held that mandamus standards apply (*In re Antrobus*, 519 F.3d 1123, 1127 (10th Cir. 2008) (per curiam) (on petition for rehearing and rehearing en banc)). We are in accord with the Tenth Circuit for the reasons stated in its opinion.

III.

A.

We have carefully examined the pleadings, the thorough order of the district court, and the applicable law. We conclude that although the district court, with the best of intentions, misapplied the law and failed to accord the victims the rights conferred by the CVRA, the mandamus standard is not satisfied.

A writ of mandamus may issue only if (1) the petitioner has "no other adequate means" to attain the desired relief; (2) the petitioner has demonstrated a right to the issuance of a writ that is "clear and indisputable;" and (3) the issuing court, in the exercise of its discretion, is satisfied that the writ is "appropriate under the circumstances" (*In re United States*, 397 F.3d 274, 282 (5th Cir.2005) (quoting *Cheney v. United States Dist. Court*, 542 U.S. 367, 380-81, 124 S.Ct. 2576, 159 L.Ed.2d 459 (2004)). We need not decide whether the first two prongs are met because, for prudential reasons, a writ of mandamus is not "appropriate under the circumstances."

B.

With due respect for the district court's diligent efforts to do justice, we conclude that, under the specific facts and circumstances of this case, it was contrary to the provisions of the CVRA for the court to permit and employ the ex parte proceedings that have taken place—proceedings that have no precedent, as far as we can determine. To obtain the order, the government filed only a brief ex parte statement, apparently with a proposed order. The fact of the ex parte motion and order was compounded by the intentional delay of three months before the victims were notified that the ex parte proceeding had occurred.

The district court acknowledged that "[t]here are clearly rights under the CVRA that apply before any prosecution is underway" (*BP Prods.*, 2008 WL 501321 at 11, 2008 U.S. Dist. LEXIS 12893, at 36). Logically, this includes the CVRA's establishment of victims' "reasonable right to confer with the attorney for the Government" (18 U.S.C. § 3771(a)(5)). At least in the posture of this case (and we do not speculate on the applicability to other situations), the government should have fashioned a reasonable way to inform the victims of the likelihood of criminal charges and to ascertain the victims' views on the possible details of a plea bargain.

The district court's reasons for its ex parte order do not pass muster. The first consideration is the number of victims. The government and the district court relied on the provision of the CVRA that states that "[i]n a case where the court finds that the number of crime victims makes it impracticable to accord all of the crime victims the rights described in subsection (a), the court shall fashion a reasonable procedure to give effect to this chapter that does not unduly complicate or prolong the proceedings" (18 U.S.C. § 3771(d)(2)). Here, however, where there were fewer than two hundred victims, all of whom could be easily reached, it is not reasonable to say that notification and inclusion were "impracticable." There was never a claim that notification itself would have been too cumbersome, time-consuming, or expensive or that not all victims could be identified and located; the government itself suggested a procedure whereby the victims would be given prompt notice of their rights under the CVRA after the plea agreement was signed.

The real rub for the government and the district court was that, as the district judge who handled the ex parte proceeding as a miscellaneous matter reasoned, "'[d]ue to extensive media coverage of the . . . explosion, . . . any public notification of a potential criminal disposition resulting from the government's investigation . . . would prejudice BP . . . and could impair the plea negotiation process and may prejudice the case in the event that no plea is reached'" (*BP Prods.*, 2008 WL 501321 at 2, 2008 U.S. Dist. LEXIS 12893, at 6–7). In making that observation, the court missed the purpose of the CVRA's right to confer. In passing the Act, Congress made the policy decision—which we are bound to enforce—that the victims have a right to inform the plea negotiation process by conferring with prosecutors before a plea agreement is reached. That is not an infringement, as the district court believed, on the government's independent prosecutorial discretion (see id. 2008 WL 501321, at 11–12, 2008 U.S. Dist. LEXIS 12893, at 37–38); instead, it is only a requirement that the government confer in some reasonable way with the victims before ultimately exercising its broad discretion.

It is true that communication between the victims and the government could, in the district court's words, "impair the plea negotiation process" (id. 2008 WL 501321, at 2–3, 2008 U.S. Dist. LEXIS 12893, at 7), if, by using the word "impair," the court meant that the views of the victims might possibly influence or affect the result of that process. It is also true (and we cannot know whether the court considered) that resourceful input from victims and their attorneys could facilitate the reaching of an agreement. The point is that it does not matter: The Act gives the right to confer. The number of victims here did not render notice to, or conferring with, the victims to be impracticable, so the victims should have been notified of the ongoing plea discussions and should have been allowed to communicate meaningfully with the government, personally or through counsel, before a deal was struck.

C.

As announced above, we decline to issue a writ of mandamus in this specific situation, because a writ is not "appropriate under the circumstances" (*In re United States*, 397 F.3d at 282). The unfortunate fact is that the plea agreement was reached without the victims' being able to participate by conferring in advance. On the other hand, as we have explained, the victims were notified—albeit much too late in the process—and were allowed substantial and meaningful participation at the February 4 hearing. As the district court recounted,

> the court heard from all those present who wanted to speak, whether represented by counsel or not and whether they had previously indicated an intent to appear or not. Ten individuals spoke in open court. The lawyers representing the victims presented arguments on the asserted grounds for asking the court to reject the proposed plea agreement. . . .
>
> At the conclusion of the . . . hearing, the victims' counsel asked for, and were granted, an opportunity to submit additional briefing focused on specific legal issues. . . . The court also granted the victims' request to delay filing their brief until the transcript was prepared and allowed the government and BP . . . to file responsive briefing. (*BP Prods.*, 2008 WL 501321 at 4–5, 2008 U.S. Dist. LEXIS 12893, at 13–16, footnote omitted)

The district court, therefore, has the benefit of the views of the victims who chose to participate at the hearing or by their various filings. The victims do have reason to believe that their impact on the eventual sentence is substantially less where, as here, their input is received after the parties have reached a tentative deal. As we have explained, that is why we conclude that these victims should have been heard at an earlier stage. We are confident, however, that the conscientious district court will fully consider the victims' objections and concerns in deciding whether the plea agreement should be accepted.

The decision whether to grant mandamus is largely prudential. We conclude that the better course is to deny relief, confident that the district court will take heed that the victims have not been accorded their full rights under the CVRA and will carefully consider their objections and briefs as this matter proceeds.

The petition for writ of mandamus, to the extent that it has not already been granted in part, is Denied.

* * *

Analysis

After the case was remanded, the district court did not void the sentence, instead choosing to leave it in place. The *In re Dean* case is another example of the Justice Department seeking to skirt around victims' rights under the CVRA. Whether the Justice Department's legal position on victims' rights will ever be grounded in the CVRA requirement that it exercise "best efforts" is probably dependent on whether the United States Attorney General or the courts direct the U.S. Justice Department to do so. If not, it will take additional efforts by the Victims' Rights Movement to achieve meaningful enforceable rights that the government will comply with.

The position of the United States Justice Department in the *Dean* case appears to be that they can operate with impunity in not notifying crime victims of plea dispositions. Moreover, the actions of the Justice Department in the *Dean* case are plainly intentional, even going to the trouble of obtaining a court order to avoid complying with the CVRA. The actions of the U.S. Justice Department reveal the fundamental opposition the Justice Department has to victims' rights. It provides a new sense of understanding about why victims need rights against government and dramatically demonstrates how the Justice Department does not represent the interests of crime victims.

The Justice Department has also taken the view that remedy for violation of the CVRA rights is optional for the federal appellate courts. Justice's position is that only in extraordinary circumstances should appellate courts correct lower court violations of victims' rights. If the Supreme Court agrees, this will increase the ability of the government to ignore victims' rights with impunity, because few cases will result in remedy. The problem posed after the McVeigh case, that rights are not remediable, will remain. As of November 2011, this Supreme Court has before it a petition for certiorari directly presenting this issue. *Fisher et al. v. U.S. Dist. Ct. for N.D. Texas, 11-1518* (2011). The Supreme Court has discretion whether to review the issue.

The Justice Department has also taken the position that the CVRA does not provide victims' rights before charging. A federal court of appeals has held otherwise, holding that the Justice Department's view contradicts the plain language of the CVRA. *In re Dean*, 527 F.3d 391 (5th Cir. 2008).

The choices of the Justice Department in seeking to curtail victims' rights in the CVRA provide a prime example of why the Victims' Movement came to be.

The movement developed largely because of the callous indifference and dismissiveness of government officials toward victims of crime. The government's opposition also means that victims will need to effectively defend their rights in court if the rights are to be meaningful.

REFERENCES

Aaronson, David E. *New Rights And Remedies: The Federal Crime Victims' Rights Act Of 2004*, 28 Pace L. Rev. 623 (2008).

Ala. Code § 15-14-53 (1983).

Amendments to the Federal Rules of Criminal Procedure, April 23, 2008, available at http://www.supremecourtus.gov/orders/courtorders/frcr08p.pdf. Washington, DC, 2008.

American Heritage Dictionary Eds., *The American Heritage Dictionary of the English Language*, 4th Edition. Boston: Houghton Mifflin Harcourt, 2000.

Arizona v. Fulminante, 499 U.S. 279 (1991).

Arkansas Code. Ann. § 16-90-1103 (1997).

Bail Reform Act, 18 U.S.C.§§ 3141-50 (1984).

Barnard, Jayne W. *Allocution for Victims of Economic Crimes*. 77 Notre Dame L. Rev. 39, 41 (2001).

Bauman v. United States District Court, 557 F.2d 650 (9th Cir.1977).

Beloof, Douglas E. and Paul G. Cassell, *The Crime Victim's Right to Attend the Trial: The Reascendent National Consensus*, 9 Lewis & Clark L. Rev. 481, 527–34 (2005).

Beloof, Douglas E. *The Third Wave of Crime Victims' Rights: Standing, Remedy, and Review*, 2005 BYU L.Rev. 255 (2005).

Beloof, Douglas E., Paul G. Cassell, and Steven J. Twist. *Victims in Criminal Procedure*. Durham, NC: North Carolina Academic Press, 2006.

Bolt, Robert. *A Man for All Seasons*, Act 2. New York: Samuel French, 1962.

Brief for the United States, *United States v. Hunter*, 548 F.3d 1308 (10th Cir. 2008) (No. 08-4010).

Cal. Penal Code § 1102.6 (1995).

Carey v. Musladin, 549 U.S. 70 (2006).

Carlisle, Nate. "Notes Confirm Suspicions of Trolley Square Victim's Family," in *The Salt Lake Tribune*, June 25, 2009.

Cassell, Paul. *In Defense of Victim Impact Statements*. 6 Ohio St. J. Crim. L. 611 (2009).

Cassell, Paul G. *Protecting Crime Victims in Federal Appellate Courts: The Need to Broadly Construe the Crime Victims' Rights Act's Mandamus Provision*. 87 Denv. Univ. L. Rev. 599 (2010).

Cassell, Paul G. *Recognizing Victims in the Federal Rules of Criminal Procedure: Proposed Amendments in Light of the Crime Victims' Rights Act*, 2005 B.Y.U. L. Rev. 835, 855 (2005).

Cassell, Paul G. *Treating Crime Victims Fairly: Integrating Victims into the Federal Rules of Criminal Procedure*, 2007 Utah L. Rev. 861 (2007).

Committee on Rules of Practice and Procedure of the Judicial Conference of the United States. *Proposed Amendments to the Federal Rules of Bankruptcy and Criminal Procedure, and the Federal Rules of Evidence*. Washington, DC: U.S. Government Printing Press, 2006.

Crawford v. Washington, 541 U.S. 36 (2004).

Crime Control Act of 1990, The. Pub. L. No. 101-647, 104 Stat. 4789 (codified as amended at 18 U.S.C. § 922(q) (1990))

Crime Victims' Rights Act, The. Scott Campbell, Stephanie Roper, Wendy Preston, Louarna Gillis, and Nila Lynn Crime Victims' Rights Act (CVRA). Pub. L. No. 108–405, §§ 101–104, 118 Stat. 2260, 2261–65 (2004) (codified at 18 U.S.C. § 3771).

Crime Victims' Rights Act Congressional Record. 150 Cong. Rec. S4268, Apr. 22, 2004, 150 Cong. Rec. S10912 Oct. 9, 2004, 150 Cong. Rec. S4261, Apr. 22, 2004.

Crowe v. State, 485 So. 2d 351 (Ala. Crim. App. 1984).

Dean v. U.S. Dist. Court, 128 S. Ct. 2996 (2008).

Delaware Code Annotated tot. 11 § 9407 (1993).

Ducote v. State, 873 A.2d 1099 (Del. 2005).

D. Utah Civ. R. 49-2(b).

Exhibit 9 *In re Stewart*. Letter from U.S. Department of Justice dated March 4, 2009.

Fernandez v. Leonard, 963 F.2d 459 (1st Cir.1992).

Garner, Bryan A. ed., *Black's Law Dictionary*, 8th Edition. New York: Thompson West, 2004.

Garvin, Margaret. Email to David Aaronson, dated Sept. 5, 2005. On file with Aaronson.

Garvin, Margaret. Telephone interview with David Aaronson, Apr. 28, 2008.

Illinois Coalition Against Sexual Assault. http://www.icasa.org/home.aspx?pageID=500& (last visited July 15, 2011).

Illinois v. Somerville, 410 U.S. 458 (1973).

In re Amy, 636 F.3d 190 (5th Cir. 2011).

In re Antrobus, 519 F.3d 1123 (10th Cir. 2008).

In re Antrobus, No. 08-4013, slip op. (10th Cir. Feb. 1, 2008).

In re Antrobus, 563 F.3d 1092, 1097 (10th Cir. 2009).

In re Brock, No. 08-1086, 2008 U.S. App. LEXIS 2104 (4th Cir. Jan. 31, 2008) (per curiam).

In re Dean, 527 F.3d 391 (5th Cir. 2008).

In re Kenna, 453 F.3d 1136 (9th Cir. 2006) (per curiam).

In re Mikhel, 453 F.3d 1137 (9th Cir. 2006).

In re Stewart, 552 F.3d 1285 (2008).

In re United States, 397 F.3d 274 (5th Cir.2005).

In re Walsh, No. 06-4792, 2007 U.S. App. LEXIS 9071 (3rd Cir. Apr. 19, 2007).

In re W.R. Huff Asset Management Co., 409 F.3d 555, 560-61 (2d Cir. 2005).

Iowa Coalition Against Sexual Assault, http://www.iowacasa.org/ (last visited July 14, 2011).

Justice League of Ohio, The. http://www.thejusticeleagueohio.org/ (last visited July 14, 2011).

Justice For All Act, Pub. L. No. 108-405 (codified as amended in 42 U.S.C. § 10603d) (2004)).

Kenna v. United States Dist. Court (*In Re Kenna*), 435 F.3d 1011 (9th Cir. 2006).

Kyl, Jon, Steven J. Twist, & Stephen Higgins. *On the Wings of Their Angels: The Scott Campbell, Stephanie Roper, Wendy Preston, Louarna Gillis, Nila Lynn Crime Victims' Rights Act.* 9 Lewis & Clark L. Rev. 581 (2005).

La. Code Evid. Ann. art. 615 (2000).

Lanham v. Commonwealth, 171 S.W.3d 14 (Ky. 2005).

Leonard, Pamela B. "All But Death, Can Be Adjusted." In *Champion Magazine*, Dec. 2006.

Mandatory Victims Restitution Act of 1996. Pub. L. No. 104-132, tit. IIA, 110 Stat. 1227 (codified as amended at 18 U.S.C.§ 3663(a) (1996)).

Mosteller, Robert P. *Victims' Rights and the United States Constitution: An Effort to Recast the Battle in Criminal Litigation.* 85 Geo. L.J. 1691 (1997).

Mothers Against Drunk Driving, http://www.madd.org/ (last visited July 14, 2011)

Musladin v. Lamarque, 427 F.3d 653 (2005).

National Organization of Parents of Murdered Children. http://www.pomc.org/ (last visited July 14, 2011).

National Sexual Violence Resource Center. http://www.nsvrc.org/ (last visited July 14, 2011.

National Victims' Constitutional Amendment Passage. http://www.nvcap.org (last visited July 5, 2011).

N.C. Gen. Stat. § 15A-832 (1998).

Nev. Revised Stat. § 171.204 (1997).

NLRB v. St. Francis Hosp. of Lynwood, 601 F.2d 404 (9th Cir.1979)

Office for Victims of Crime, *President's Task Force on Victims of Crime: Final Report*. Washington DC: U.S. Government Printing Office, 1982.

Owens v. Samkle Automotive, Inc., 425 F.3d 1318 (11th Cir. 2005).

Paladin Associates, Inc. v. Montana Power Co., 328 F.3d 1145 (9th Cir. 2003).

Palmer v. Granholm, No. 1:06-cv-301, 2006 U.S. Dist. LEXIS 45333 (W.D. Mich. July 5, 2006).

Pennsylvania Coalition Against Rape. http://www.pcar.org/ (last visited July 14, 2011).

Petitioners, *In re Stewart*. Motion For An Order Directing The Government To Afford Crime Victims Their Rights To Confer And To Timely Notice Under The Crime Victims' Rights Act And For Sanctions For Failure To Comply With The Act. No. 10-12344-E.

Scott Campbell, Stephanie Rober, Wendy Preston, Lourna Gillis, and Nila Lynn. Crime Victims' Rights Act. 150 Cong. Rec. S4260-01, 2004 WL 867940 (2004).

Scott Campbell, Stephanie Roper, Wendy Preston, Louarna Gillis, Nila Lynn. Crime Victims Rights Act: Hearing on HR. 4342 Before the H.R. Comm. on the Judiciary. 109th Cong. (June 21, 2006).

S.J. Res. 1, 108th Cong. (2003).

Speedy Trial Act, The. 18 U.S.C.§§ 3161–3174 (2008).

S.Rep. No. 108–191(2003).

State v. Beltran-Felix, 922 P.2d 30 (Utah Ct. App. 1996).

State v. Boone, 820 P.2d 930 (Utah Ct. App. 1991).

State v. Fulimante, 975 P.2d 75 (Ariz. 1999).

State v. Ramer, 21 Cal. Rptr. 2d 480 (Ct. App. 1993).

Toibb v. Radloff, 501 U.S. 157 (1991).

Twist, Steven J. *Letter to Supporters of Senate Joint Resolution 1, the Crime Victims' Rights Amendment*. National Victims Constitutional Amendment Project, 2004.

Unlawful Acts. 18 U.S.C. § 922.

United States v. Blumhagen, no. 03-CR-56S, 2006 U.S. Dist. LEXIS 15380 (W.D.N.Y. 2006).

United States v. BP Prods. N. Am. Inc., No. H-07-434, 2008 U.S. Dist. LEXIS12893 (S.D. Tex. Feb. 21, 2008).

United States v. Citgo Petroleum Corp., No. C-06-563, 2007 U.S. Dist. LEXIS 57686 (S.D. Tex. Aug. 8, 2007).

United States v. Cronic, 466 U.S. 648 (1984).

United States v. Degenhardt, 405 F.Supp.2d 1341 (D. Utah 2005).

United States v. Dominguez Benitez, 542 U.S. 74 (2004).

United States v. Grace, 408 F.Supp.2d 998 (D. Mont. 2006).

United States v. Heaton, 458 F. Supp. 2d 1271 (D. Utah 2006).

United States v. Hunter, No. 2:07 CR307DAK, 2008 WL 53125 (D. Utah Jan. 3, 2008).

United States v. Hunter, No. 2:07CRE307DAK, slip op. (D. Utah Mar. 17, 2008).

United States v. Hunter, No. 2:07 CR307DAK, 2009 U.S. Dist. LEXIS 90822 (D. Utah Feb. 10, 2009).

United States v. Johnson, 362 F.Supp.2d 1043 (N.D. Iowa 2005).

United States v. Kaufman, No. 04-40141-01, 2005 U.S. Dist. LEXIS 21006 (D. Kan. Oct. 17, 2005).

United States v. Marcello, 370 F.Supp.2d 745 (N.D. Ill. 2005).

United States v. McVeigh, 106 F.3d 325 (10th Cir. 1997).

United States v. Reyna, 358 F.3d 344 (5th Cir. 2004) (en banc).

United States v. Rigas (In re W.R. Huff Asset Mgmt. Co.), 409 F.3d 555 (2d Cir.2005).

United States v. Patkar, No. 06-00250, 2008 U.S. Dist. LEXIS 6055 (D. Haw. Jan. 28, 2008).

United States v. Sacane, No. 3:05-cr-325, 2007 U.S. Dist. LEXIS 22178 (D. Conn. March 28, 2007).

United States v. Salerno, 481 U.S. 739 (1987).

United States v. Turner, 367 F.Supp.2d 319 (E.D.N.Y. 2005).

U.S. Dep't of Justice. *Attorney General Guidelines for Victim and Witness Assistance*. Washington, DC: U.S. Government Printing Office, 2005.

Vasquez v. Hillary, 474 U.S. 254 (1986).

Va. Code. Ann. § 19.2–265.01 (1995).

Victim and Witness Protection Act of 1982. Pub. L. No. 97-291, 96 Stat. 1248 (codified as amended at 18 U.S.C.§§ 1512–1514, 3679–3580 (1982)).

Victims of Crime Act of 1984. Pub. L. No. 98-473, 98 Stat. 2170 (codified as amended at 42 U.S.C. § 10601) (1984)).

Victims' Rights and Restitution Act of 1990. Pub. L. No. 101-647, 104 Stat. 4820 (codified as amended at 42 U.S.C. § 10606 (1990)).

Victim Rights Clarifications Act of 1997. Pub. L. No 105-6, 111 Stat. 12 (codified as amended at 18 U.S.C. § 3510 (1997)).

Violent Crime Control and Law Enforcement Act of 1994. Pub. L. No. 103-322, 108 Stat. 1796 (codified as amended at 42 U.S.C.§§ 13701–14223 (1994)).

Wis. Stat. § 906.15 (1997).

Wood, Jefri. *The Crime Victims' Rights Act of 2004 and the Federal Courts*. Washington, DC: Federal Judicial Center: 2008.

Wyoming Stat. Ann. § 1-40-206 (1991).

Additional Reading

Doyle, Charles. *The Crime Victims' Rights Act*. New York: Nova Science Publishers Inc., 2008.

Federal Sentencing Reporter, Vol. 19, No. 1 & 2 (October 2006).

Zitter, Jay M. *Validity, Construction and Application of State Constitutional or Statutory Victims' Bill of Rights*, 91 A.L.R. 5th 343 (2001).

8

PRESENT STATUS AND THE FUTURE OF VICTIMS' RIGHTS

PRESENT STATUS

The sources of victims' rights, first discussed in the introductory material in Chapter 1, consist of common law rights, modern broad and specific state constitutional rights, state and federal statutes, third-party rights, limits on the courts' jurisdiction over victims, and those accommodations granted or withheld by the government's discretion.

Common Law Rights

The end of the era of private prosecution left a variety of enduring citizen participation rights that vary between jurisdictions. These common law rights exist in various procedural contexts. In the investigative phase, citizens can conduct a private investigation. They can request grand jury and judicial investigations, and, in some contexts, citizens can finance public investigations. Citizens can arrest without a warrant for felonies, breaches of the peace, and, in some jurisdictions, misdemeanors committed in the citizen's presence. Citizens can access grand juries and seek judicial charging, and, in the case of misdemeanors, subject to the public prosecutor's authority to *nolle prosequi*, victims can initiate judicial charging and privately prosecute the case. Citizens can obtain assistance of counsel at their own expense to defend their historic rights. Moreover, citizen participation rights are judicially cognizable, as citizens can seek review of and remedy for rights violations.

Broad State Constitutional Rights

Victims' state constitutional rights can be either broad or specific rights. Broad rights include the victims' rights to fairness, respect, dignity, privacy, freedom from abuse, due process, and reasonable protection (see generally Beloof 2005, outlining victims' state constitutional rights). Nineteen state constitutions provide for "fairness" and/or "due process" to victims (Beloof 1999). One or more of the rights to "respect," "dignity," and "freedom from abuse" appear in 21 state constitutions (Id.). Six constitutions include the express right to victim "privacy" (Id.). Eight constitutions provide for a victim's right to "reasonable protection" (see generally Beloof 2005).

With only one exception, state courts have interpreted these broad victims' rights to have substantive meaning (but see *Bandoni v. State*, 715 A.2d 580, 587 (R.I. 1998, providing exception to broad victims' rights as having substantive meaning). For example, in the New Jersey case *State v. Timmendequas*, 737 A.2d 55, 64 (1999), the state prosecuted Timmendequas for kidnapping, sexually assaulting, and murdering Megan Kanga. The New Jersey Constitution provides the broad guarantee that "a victim of crime shall be treated with fairness, compassion and respect by the criminal justice system" (N.J. Const. art. I, 22). The New Jersey Supreme Court held that this broad language, coupled with a victim's right to be present at public judicial proceedings, could be the lawful basis to deny a defendant's motion to change venue (*Timmendequas*, 737 A.2d, at 76). The court held that the victim possessed standing in the trial court to seek and obtain the empanelling of a foreign jury in preference to a change of venue (Id. at 76). In Arizona, intermediate appellate courts have held that victims' broad rights to fairness, respect, dignity, freedom from abuse, and due process, coupled with more particular rights, rendered unlawful orders requiring victims to submit to fingerprinting or requiring state interviews of victims to be electronically recorded and made available to the defense (*State v. O'Neil*, 836 P.2d 393, 394 (Ariz. Ct. App. 1991)).

Several state courts have recognized victims' broad constitutional rights only to find that the scope of the rights did not extend to the factual context of the cases. The Illinois Supreme Court held broad language providing that "[c]rime victims... shall have the following rights as provided by law... [including] the right to be treated with fairness and respect for their dignity and privacy throughout the criminal justice process" did not alter the rule that a defendant's death before final appeal abated the judgment below (*People v. Robinson*, 187 Ill.2d 461, 463 (Ill. 1999; see also Ill. Const. art. I, 8.1(a)(8)). In *State v. Broberg*, the Maryland Supreme Court acknowledged that "victim[s] of crime shall be treated by agents of the State with dignity, respect, and sensitivity during all phases of the criminal justice process," but nevertheless granted a trial court discretion to admit into evidence in-life photographs of a homicide victim (677 A.2d 602, 612 (Md. 1996)). In a New Mexico case, the court refused to extend a crime victim's constitutional "right to be treated with fairness and respect for the victim's dignity and privacy throughout the criminal justice process" to alter a law concerning waiver of evidentiary privileges (*State v. Gonzales*, 912 P.2d 297, 300 (Az. 1996)). In Wisconsin, the court declined to rely on broad provisions to give the victim an interest in the change of venue proceeding (*State v. Rymer*, 2001 WI Ct. App. 31U, P 16, 622 N.W.2d 770, cert. denied, 2001 WI 15, 626 N.W.2d 807 (2001)). The broad constitutional rights reviewed in these opinions plainly have substantive meaning or the courts would not have bothered to assess the scope of the right.

Specific State Constitutional Rights

In contrast to broad rights, specific victims' rights provide rights more focused than general "fairness." They can be parsed into the categories of due process and protection. Due process rights include rights to be notified, present, and heard at particular stages of the criminal process. Typically, a victim's right to be present is limited to critical stages of the criminal process or stages in which a defendant also has a right to be present (see generally Beloof 2005). Victims have rights to receive notice of their rights and notice of criminal proceedings. While the most common victims' right allows the victim to speak at the defendant's sentencing, some constitutions provide for the right to speak at pretrial release or bail hearings and to be heard concerning a negotiated plea (see, e.g., *People v. Stringham*, 253 Cal. Rptr. 484, 492 (Cal. Ct. App. 1988)). Constitutions in certain states give victims a right to confer with the prosecution concerning charging or disposition. This is not a right to control the prosecution but, rather, to gather information, to express concerns and preferences. Some constitutions grant victims the right to be heard at postconviction release hearings, such as parole hearings. Victims have rights to a speedy trial or prompt disposition, and the right to attend the trial in many jurisdictions. Finally, rights of protection include notice of pretrial release, imprisonment, and postsentence release or escape (see generally Beloof 2005).

While victims have these specific rights, some courts have been reluctant to give specific rights an expansive interpretation in certain contexts. For example, under the Texas Constitution, the specific right to confer with the prosecutor coupled with the broad right to "fairness" did not grant the victim the right to discover evidence in the prosecutor's file to facilitate a civil suit (*State ex rel. Hilbig v. McDonald*, 839 S.W.2d 854, 855-56 (Tex. App. 1992)). Additionally, the Illinois appellate court held that "the [victims' rights] Act and the [victims' rights] amendment" did not alter the "fundamental principle" that a conviction based on illegally obtained, inadmissible evidence could not stand (*People v. Nestrock*, 735 N.E.2d 1101, 1109 (Ill. App. ct. 2000), appeal denied, 747 N.E.2d 332 (Ill. 2000)). In Arizona, a state constitutional right allows victims to refuse pretrial interviews but does not implicitly include a right not to testify in a pretrial hearing or refuse to testify at presentence hearings (*State ex rel. Dean v. City of Tucson*, 844 P.2d 1165, 1167 (Ariz. Ct. App. 1992); *A.H. ex rel Weiss v. Superior Court*, 911 P.2d 633, 636 (Ariz. Ct. App. 1996)). Concerning victims' rights to attend trial, a Florida appellate court ruled that a victim's right "to be present at all crucial stages of criminal proceedings" did not create a right for victims to sit at counsel table (Fla. Const. art. I, 16(b); *Hall v. State*, 579 So. 2d 329, 331 (Fla. Dist. Ct. App. 1991)). Under California law, victims' right to speak at sentencing does not mean that a victim alone can alter the terms of the sentence (*Dix v. Superior Court*, 807 P.2d 1063, 1067 (Cal. 1991)). In these jurisdictions, these specific rights have substantive meaning, although the scope of the rights did not encompass the facts of the cases.

On the other hand, some courts have held that specific constitutional provisions have enough substantive force to alter lesser laws in certain contexts. For example, in Michigan, a victim's constitutional right to restitution precludes abatement of a restitution order based on a criminal judgment. A Michigan constitutional amendment provides that "[c]rime victims . . . shall have . . . [t]he right to restitution" (Mich. Const. art. I, 24(1)). The Michigan Supreme Court held that rules of abatement, which once voided defendants' conviction and judgment upon death if death occurs before appeals are exhausted, were now modified by the victims' constitutional rights (*People v. Peters*, 537 N.W.2d 160, 164 (Mich. 1995)). In an Arizona case, it was held proper to balance a victim's right to a speedy trial with the defendant's due process right to prepare for trial. The result was denial of a defense continuance when the defendant had fired his lawyer and desired to represent himself (*State v. Lamar*, 72 P.3d 831, 836-37 (Ariz. 2003)). As reviewed above, courts have coupled specific rights with broad rights and determined that these rights are powerful enough to alter procedural choices in favor of the victim.

Specifically, victims' constitutional rights are superior to and, where a conflict exists, trump statutes or court rules (see *State v. Roscoe*, 912 P.2d 1297, 1299–1302 (Ariz. 1996); *State v. O'Neil*, 836 P.2d 393 (Ariz. Ct. App. 1991)). For example, under the Arizona Constitution, " '[v]ictim' means a person against whom the criminal offense has been committed" (Ariz. Const. art. II, 2.1(C)). In *State v. Roscoe*, the Arizona Supreme Court held that an enabling statute narrowly defining the term *crime victim* to exclude police officers was unconstitutional because it conflicted with the broader meaning of *victim* set forth in the Victims' Bill of Rights (912 P.2d, at 1302).

When victims are exercising either their broad or specific rights, they are no longer merely witnesses or third parties in the criminal process. Rather, victims are "participants" in the criminal process. Being a participant means the "crime victim [has] rights of intermittent participation in the criminal [trial] process" (Beloof 2003). Victims are participants because they possess independent rights to participate at certain stages of the criminal process. For example, victims have an independent right to give impact statements at sentencing, typically including the right to give a sentencing recommendation (Id.). Victims may address the court at sentencing regardless of whether they are called as witnesses by either party and despite the objection of either party (Id.). Thus, victims at sentencing are not witnesses called by parties to give victim impact testimony but, rather, are independent participants at sentencing hearings with a right to present impact information and sentencing recommendations (Id.).

The personal nature of victims' rights is revealed by the plain language of the various constitutional provisions as well as relevant court opinions. The titles of the constitutional sections clearly delineate the rights as "Victims' Rights" or "Rights of Crime Victims." The texts of the amendments also make apparent that the rights are personal to the victim by expressly stating that "victims have the right to" or "victims have the following rights," or similar language. Moreover, the rights are lodged in states' bills of rights, revealing that the rights are individual rights against government.

State court opinions confirm that victims' rights are personal to the victim and that only the victims may waive their own rights. For example, an Arizona appellate court held that a victim's failure to assert a right to restitution within a reasonable time constituted a waiver (*In re Alton D.*, 994 P.2d 402, 406 (Ariz. 2000)). On the other hand, victims' rights are not susceptible to waiver by the prosecutor (see, e.g., *State v. Robinson*, No. C1-02-1957 2003 WL 21694412, at 3 (Minn. Ct. App. Jul. 22, 2003)). The state has no authority to waive victims' right to restitution, and, additionally, prosecutors cannot waive victims' right to make a separate sentencing recommendation (*People v. Valdez*, 30 Cal. Rptr. 2d 4, 8 (Cal. Ct. App. 1994); *Robinson* at 3). Thus, a victim did not waive the right to restitution when the probation officer failed in his statutory duty to contact the victim about monetary loss (*State v. Contreras*, 885 P.2d 138, 142 (Ariz. Ct. App. 1994)).

Victims' rights are protected against waiver by the state even when the state has authority to enforce the rights. Most victims cannot readily afford counsel, do not have a right to appointed counsel, or may not be able to be present at every proceeding. As a result, some jurisdictions allow prosecutors to enforce victims' rights. But even when the state may enforce victims' rights, the state has no authority to waive victims' rights. In an action that consolidated three Arizona cases, the defendants sought to interview the victim (*State v. Warner*, 812 P.2d 1079, 1081–82 (Ariz. Ct. App. 1990)). In two of the cases, the prosecutor's paralegal made representations that an interview of the victim would occur (Id. at 1081). In the third case, the victim appeared at the motion to compel hearing and invoked her right not to be interviewed (Id.). In all three cases, the trial court ordered the victim interview (Id.). The appellate court overturned the orders, holding that the state did not have authority to waive victims' rights and the defendants did not have a right to rely on the paralegal's representations as to the effect of the amendment on the cases (Id.). The personally held nature of victims' rights is further evidenced by the exclusion of defendants from the benefits of victims' rights amendments.

In sum, the plain language and location of victims' constitutional rights amendments establish that victims' rights are personal to the victim. Furthermore, court opinions holding that victims can exercise or waive victims' rights and that the state or nonvictims cannot waive such rights confirm that the rights are personal to the victim. Victims' rights consist of broad rights to fairness, dignity, privacy, freedom from abuse, due process, and reasonable protection. Specific rights include rights of participation, privacy, and protection. Victims exercising their rights are participants in the criminal process, and victims enforcing rights violations are full parties to the rights enforcement action.

Third-Party Rights

Due to legal tradition, witnesses, including crime victims, have standing to object to unlawful invasions of privacy. Privacy laws, such as protection of school records and evidentiary privileges (e.g., privacy of counseling records) are typically defended directly by the third party and/or victim when such records are sought by defendants or prosecutors. For example, victims have crisis counseling privileges in many state jurisdictions. Crime victims may directly defend against disclosure of those counseling records. Some state courts strongly uphold such privileges. Others have denigrated the privileges, rationalizing that state due process for criminal defendants prohibits absolute privileges for victims' counseling records.

Jurisdictional Issues

Crime victims are not formal parties to criminal proceedings. Instead, they are participants with intermittent rights of participation, privacy, and protection in the criminal process. Because they are not formal parties, the courts have limited control over compelling victims to do certain things. Particularly controversial are court efforts to get sexual assault victims to submit to a medical or psychiatric examination sought by the defense or prosecution. Another hot topic is whether courts may allow defendants into the home of a surviving victim. The expansion of victims' rights argues against such incursions, although some courts have held that defendants' evolving due process rights require such incursions.

Judicial and Prosecutorial Discretion in the Public Interest

In many contexts, judges and prosecutors have discretion to make decisions in the public interest. Examples of these are plea bargains proposed by prosecutors and sentencing decisions offered by judges. The potential for the judges and prosecutors to seek the input of crime victims is always within such public-interest discretion. Before the advent of victims' rights, this was rarely done. It is still not routine. Today, it is appropriate for victims to ask a prosecutor or court for such an accommodation even if no specific right exists. For example, a state may not have a right for the victim to consult with the prosecutor about a plea bargain. However, the prosecutor is within his discretion to consult with the victim. A judge may not be required to hear from a victim concerning the pretrial release of a suspect but certainly has the discretion to do so.

THE HAVE-NOT JURISDICTIONS

When rights are unenforceable, government may ignore them with impunity. The *McVeigh* case in Chapter 5 illustrated how unenforceable rights fail victims. Unfortunately, the problem is not confined to federal law before the CVRA. The state jurisdictions are divided into "haves" and "have nots"—the states with enforceable rights (the haves) and the states without (the have nots). Moreover, it remains to be determined by the United States Supreme Court whether the federal criminal process, under the Crime Victims' Rights Act (CVRA), provides meaningful enforcement.

The following two documents are in regard to a case in Massachusetts, which confirmed that Massachusetts was a "have-not" state. The first document is an op-ed piece by constitutional law professor Laurence Tribe, expressing his view that the victim has enforceable rights. The second document is the opinion by the Massachusetts court denying enforcement.

- **Document:** "A Black Hole for Victims' Rights" by Laurence H. Tribe
- **Date:** Fall, 2005

- **Significance:** Professor Tribe's piece reviews *Hagen v. Commonwealth*, pointing out what he believes to be glaring faults in the United States justice system regarding the treatment of victims of crime and reinforcing his view that the victim has enforceable rights.
- **Source:** Tribe, Laurence H. "A Black Hole for Victims' Rights." 9 *Lewis and Clark Law Review* 9 (2005): 665. Originally printed as an op-ed in the *Boston Globe*, March 29, 2002. Reprinted with permission.

---

* * *

A case set for argument on Monday before the Massachusetts Supreme Judicial Court dramatizes the need to take victims' rights more seriously than we do now—and the fallacy of the argument that victims' rights must come at the expense of defendants' rights or of prosecutorial flexibility.

Over 16 years ago, James Kelly brutally raped Debra Hagen in Leominster.

A jury convicted Kelly on two counts of rape and one count of indecent assault and battery, and in April 1988 the trial judge sentenced him to serve two 10-year jail terms and one five-year term, to run concurrently.

Fourteen years have passed; we've lived through recession and boom, two Bush presidencies, the rise of the Internet, and Sept. 11. Through all that time Kelly has yet to serve a single day in jail.

First the court granted him a stay for health reasons. Later in 1988, Kelly filed a new trial motion. The state claims it simply forgot to respond, apparently losing some of the trial transcripts along the way. The case lay dormant until 1992, when Hagen wrote to ask the trial judge for an explanation.

The district attorney's office responded by urging that she be satisfied with a deal that would revoke Kelly's prison sentence and put him on probation. The odds were good that he would receive a new trial, she was told. Kelly was aging rapidly and in poor health. Wouldn't she prefer not to relive the attack by having to take the witness stand? Wouldn't she prefer closure?

In fact, the new trial motion was denied, but the state still did nothing to take Kelly into custody. Hagen—who finally left Massachusetts to avoid crossing paths with her attacker—desperately wanted to put the attack behind her. But consenting to a "get out of jail free" card for a rapist who had served not one day of his sentence provided anything but comfort. And escorting Kelly to prison to begin serving his term while appealing the denial of his new trial motion would have violated none of his rights and imposed no undue burden on the state.

After nine more years of state resistance, Hagen sought relief under the Massachusetts victims' rights statute. One provision said victims "shall be afforded . . . a prompt disposition of the case in which they are involved." But Worcester County District Attorney John Conte calls that nothing more than a suggestive guide and claims that because he represents the people, his word on what constitutes a prompt disposition is final and unreviewable.

In legal jargon, the district attorney's argument is that—despite what the victims' rights statute calls "basic and fundamental rights"—victims lack "standing." They have no power to enforce their rights in the courts. In fact, they have no right to be heard at all. Besides, he adds, the "disposition" in this case occurred more than promptly enough: It was disposed of, as far as he's concerned, when the rapist was sentenced back in 1988.

To put it bluntly, no disinterested reader of the Commonwealth's statutes, which say the victim's rights last "until the final disposition of the charges, including . . . all postconviction . . . (and) appellate proceedings," could possibly find Conte's argument convincing. It's an argument more worthy of Franz Kafka or George Orwell than of a self-respecting law enforcement officer.

One can only hope that the SJC, guided by the light of reason, will let Debra Hagen's voice be heard through her own lawyer, not through her supposed surrogate in the person of the district attorney.

Indeed, this 14-year-long procedural black hole by itself demonstrates a compelling need to empower victims with a meaningful voice in the criminal justice system—through an amendment to the federal Constitution if necessary.

Some questions in this field are doubtless difficult. Exactly what remedy to order for the inexcusable delay in this case remains to be debated. Other questions are painfully simple: "Justice should be denied or delayed to no one," the Magna Charta proclaimed many centuries ago. The SJC should heed those words.

Ours is the Commonwealth that proclaimed, long before our nation's Constitution was written, that its government was one of laws, not men. When its laws assure all citizens that their fundamental rights as victims of crime to a prompt disposition shall be secure, let no man tell them they lack standing to redeem that guarantee. Otherwise, that guarantee will, to quote Justice Jackson, be but "a promise to the ear to be broken to the hope, like a munificent bequest in a pauper's will."

* * *

Analysis

Tribe is a preeminent Harvard Law professor. However, the highest Massachusetts court did not agree. *Hagen v. Commonwealth*, 722 N.E.2d 32 (Ma. 2002), clearly exemplified Massachusetts as a "have not" state—a state that does not have enforceable rights for victims of crime.

In *Hagen*, the Massachusetts Supreme court denied the victim standing and remedy in the appellate courts. Without standing, the remedy of voiding, and nondiscretionary review, crime victims' rights are illusory. This was the problem in the *McVeigh* case discussed in Chapter 5. Illusory rights are problematic because crime victims cannot enforce their rights in a way that ensures they will be able to exercise those rights. Victims' rights were created to be enforced against the government, but the government is instead free to ignore and even intentionally violate those rights. Without victim standing to enforce victims' rights, numerous problems arise. Judicial hierarchy is turned upside down because the trial courts are allowed to usurp appellate courts' traditional authority, thus disturbing the hierarchy of laws; adversity is corrupted, rights enforcement is crippled, victims' advocacy in favor of defendants is constrained, and constitutional rights are degraded.

Given that victims' rights are routinely exercised at the trial court level, considerable dysfunctions arise when victims are denied appellate standing. With true rights (like defendants' rights), appellate courts are the ultimate arbiters of the meaning of constitutional rights. On the other hand, illusory victims' rights—with trial-level standing and no appellate court standing—invert judicial hierarchy. In this inverted process, trial courts are the ultimate arbiters of victims' constitutional rights. Each trial court can arrive at a unique conclusion about the meaning and scope of victims' rights. Moreover, these trial courts can apply their inconsistent interpretations of victims' constitutional rights without fear of reversal. The result is disparate treatment: different rights for different victims based on which trial judge presides over the case.

In our legal hierarchy, statutes are lesser laws than constitutions. Providing victims' standing to enforce statutes but not constitutional rights contradicts this hierarchy of laws. Without victim standing, victims' rights can only be contested on review by parties that have no personal stake in the right (i.e., a prosecutor). Yet only victims can predictably be truly adverse to those infringing upon their rights. In *Doe*, a context analogous to victims' rights, the Fourth Circuit Court granted a rape victim an appeal from an adverse ruling under federal rape shield laws and opined that "[n]o other party in the evidentiary proceeding shares these interests to the extent that they might be viewed as a champion of the victim's rights" (*Doe v. U.S.*, 666 F.2d 43, 46 (4th Cir. 1981)). Victims are the only ones personally interested in their rights. As a result, the adversarial system will never work properly unless victims are granted standing, remedy, and review to enforce those rights.

Denying victims standing to enforce their rights means that only the state can litigate rights violations. However, the state is far from a consistent advocate for crime victims' rights.

Absent victim standing and with the state in control of rights enforcement, victims' rights are artificially framed as rights conflicting with defendants' rights, even though victims' rights are centrally rights against the government. To be sure, in many cases, victims speak against defendants' positions. Nevertheless, a victims' rights process that precludes appellate court scrutiny when victims intend to speak for defendants and are denied the right is fundamentally corrupt and exemplifies why the government should never be exclusively in charge of individual constitutional rights. Legal rights without standing are destructive to the conventional model of constitutional civil liberties. The seminal case of *Marbury v. Madison* reasoned:

> The very essence of civil liberty certainly consists in the right of every individual to claim the protection of the laws, whenever he receives an injury. . . . The government of the United States has been emphatically termed a government of laws, and not of men. It will certainly cease to deserve this high appellation, if the laws furnish no remedy for the violation of a vested legal right. (5 U.S. 137, 163 (1803))

THE FUTURE OF VICTIMS' RIGHTS
AND THE THIRD WAVE

- **Document:** "The Third Wave of Crime Victims' Rights: Standing, Remedy, and Review" by Douglas E. Beloof
- **Date:** 2005
- **Significance:** In this article, Professor Beloof argues for provision of standing, remedy, and review in order for victims of crime to effectively enforce their rights.
- **Source:** Beloof, Douglas E. "The Third Wave of Crime Victims' Rights: Standing, Remedy, and Review." *Brigham Young University Law Review* (2005): 225.

* * *

The crime victims' rights movement worked to enact rights in two waves. The first wave provided victims with statutory rights (Siegleman and Tarver 1988). Unsatisfied with the response of the legal culture to statutory rights, the crime victims' movement began to work to enact state constitutional rights (see, e.g., Office for Victims of Crime 1982, 114). The achievements of these victims' rights pioneers are nothing short of astonishing. The second wave resulted in thirty-three state constitutional amendments that contain some kind of victims' rights provision (see Beloof 1999). In the mid-1900s, before the advent of victims' rights, victims were lawfully exiled from criminal processes and rarely notified of important events. Against an entrenched legal culture that completely excluded victims from the criminal process, [Footnote 12 reads: Except, of course, as witnesses] these pioneers established critical beachheads for the victims' rights movement. As impressive a feat as securing these beachheads was, the first and second wave of statutory and constitutional victims' rights have not been consistently successful in establishing real crime victims' rights. Present victim rights' laws (or courts' interpretation of those laws) often severely curtail victim standing, remedy, or review. Thus, it is time to move inland.

In this context, standing is the ability of victims to defend a denial of their rights in appellate courts. Differences in standing law appear among jurisdictions, but this Article does not examine various standing doctrines in all fifty-one jurisdictions. Right now, as illustrated by the stories in the introduction, victims are often without standing to vindicate the rights that the first and second waves of the victims' rights movement secured for them. The third wave of victims' standing, remedy, and review will transform these illusory rights into real rights.

There are three main obstacles in the way of turning victims' illusory rights into real rights: (1) government discretion to deny rights, (2) lack of a meaningful remedy to enforce rights, and (3) appellate court discretion to deny review.

The language in some state constitutions permits state governments to exercise their discretion to infringe severely on or completely eliminate victims' rights guaranteed by those state constitutions. Governments have the discretion to ignore constitutional rights that are not mandatory and, when constitutionally required, not reinforced with enabling legislation. Some victims' constitutional rights are cast in discretionary language, and, with limited exceptions, victims have no standing to obtain review of these discretionary rights when the government disregards them. Also, broad victims' constitutional rights provisions are vague. The vagueness of these provisions gives courts the discretion to narrowly apply them.

Victims' rights are also illusory when there is no adequate remedy. Without adequate remedy, victims cannot exercise their rights when prosecutors or trial courts deny them. In certain constitutions, voiding and reconsideration remedies for violations of victims' rights are prohibited or unduly restricted. Because a prerequisite to standing is remedy, the absence of remedy precludes standing. Even in jurisdictions where such remedies are available, problems of mootness or lack of ripeness prevent remedy. Furthermore, some state constitutional victims' rights deny the courts any authority to stay proceedings while a rights violation is on review. The unavailability of stays aggravates the mootness problem.

Finally, victims' rights are illusory unless there is a nondiscretionary review mechanism. When remedy is available and the violation fits within the scope of the rights, review by writ is expressly or implicitly available under all state constitutional victims' rights provisions. But writ review is discretionary. Because review by writ is discretionary, it is improbable that courts will routinely review individual victims' rights violations.

Troubling too are appellate court deviations from conventional constitutional analyses that result in denials of victim standing. In states where courts should affirm victim standing, emerging judicial opinions deny standing. For example, constitutional rights must be mandatory before there can be standing, remedy, and review. Despite the existence of plain mandatory language in some states' respective bills of rights, however, courts label constitutional rights "directory," thus rendering them discretionary and eliminating potential enforcement. [Footnote 14 omitted]. Additionally, constitutional rights must be enabled before there can be standing and remedy. And, even when strong evidence exists that victims' rights are self-enabled, courts have sometimes held that victims' rights amendments are merely advisory and not binding. This reasoning is particularly unpersuasive when compared to courts' vigorous enforcement of defendants' constitutional rights.

There are three legal mechanisms for bringing about victims' standing, adequate remedy, and review. A federal constitutional amendment to the Bill of Rights providing victims' rights, accompanied by standing, meaningful remedy, and review is, from the perspective of providing consistent national rights, the best option. It is also the best option from the perspective of ensuring that courts will conclude that victims' rights are mandatory and enabled. Moreover, a federal constitutional amendment improves the chances that state courts will interpret and enforce the rights in a consistent manner, because the Supreme Court will be the ultimate arbiter of rights. But, as a practical matter, a federal constitutional amendment is the solution most difficult to attain. A second and considerably easier solution is to amend state constitutions to provide explicit protection of victims' rights. Ultimately, a vote of the people of the state is required to approve the amendment, and voters have been historically very receptive to such victim amendments. Third and perhaps the most easily achieved solution is for states to enact legislation that would enable the victims' rights already provided in their state constitutions. Where victims' amendments presently permit, enabling legislation should be rapidly enacted to provide for or clarify victims' standing, meaningful remedy, and review. Unfortunately, some states' constitutional amendments will themselves need amendment before enabling legislation will succeed. In these circumstances legislatures could act to provide independent statutory victims' rights with standing, remedy, and review provisions completely independent of the state constitution. Such statutes would be an interim measure until the state constitution was amended.

Constitutional rights that do not grant people the standing to enforce them are so contrary to our legal traditions that they create a host of dysfunctions. These dysfunctions include: (1) turning judicial hierarchy upside down, (2) upsetting the hierarchy of laws, (3) corrupting the adversary process, (4) crippling rights enforcement, (5) constraining victims' ability to advocate for defendants, and (6) diluting constitutional rights. Providing victims with standing to enforce rights violations along with voiding and reconsideration remedies and appellate review as a matter of right will resolve all of these dysfunctions. Providing for standing, remedy, and review makes victims' rights directly enforceable by victims, brings victims' rights into conformance with the conventional model of individual rights, signals courts' intent to follow conventional constitutional analyses in interpreting victims' rights, and enhances government compliance with these rights.

* * *

Analysis

The foundations of the rights in the CVRA and the drafted federal constitutional victims' amendment that preceded it are the state constitutional rights that exist in two-thirds of the states. The Victims' Rights Movement determined that placing constitutional rights in state constitutions would provide a credible platform for federal constitutional victims' rights. The effort to create new state constitutional rights began in the late 1970s. The first amendments were enacted in the early 1980s. The state constitutional amendments themselves were preceded by statutory versions of rights.

These stages, first statute and then state constitution, are the first two waves of victims' rights. The third wave is the effort to take these statutes and constitutions and provide enforceability of the rights where it doesn't already exist. Some state constitutions were enacted as real rights, with a remedy explicitly or implicitly provided. Other laws were significantly flawed and either did not contain enough rights or failed to provide a remedy. Since 2008, a few states have amended their constitutions to provide enforceable rights.

The next document describes Oregon's successful effort to become part of the third wave of victims' rights.

- **Document:** "Oregon Surprises Activists, Victims' Rights Movement Moving Again" by John H. Stein
- **Date:** September/October 2007
- **Significance:** The following article, penned by John Stein, documents Oregon's successful effort to become a part of the third wave of victims' rights.
- **Source:** Stein, John H. "Oregon Surprises Activists, Victims' Rights Movement Moving Again," in *The Crime Victims Report*. New York: Civic Research Institute, 2007. Reprinted with permission.

---

* * *

At their annual meeting August 20, 2006, at the NOVA conference, board members of the National Victims' Constitutional Amendment Passage (NVCAP) urged one another to rekindle efforts to bring the 17 states without such amendments on board. Equally important, the participants agreed, was to return to those states whose amendments were less than adequate to repair the flaws.

At this point, Steve Twist, NVCAP's general counsel, reported that California Governor Arnold Schwarzenegger was in discussions with Democratic legislators, who are in the majority in both houses in California, over just such a proposal. This was received warmly, since activists in the field had often squirmed when putting California on the list of 33. Its "Victims' Bill of Rights," enacted by a statewide initiative in 1982 was the first of its kind, and thus a landmark. But the one section affecting victims specifically reads, "Restitution shall be ordered from the convicted persons in every case, regardless of the sentence or disposition imposed, in which a crime victim suffers a loss," which predates all other "mandatory restitution" enactments in the U.S. However, even that bold policy commitment was tempered with, "unless compelling and extraordinary reasons exist to the contrary." Bedrock rights, to be informed, present, and heard, remain absent.

NVCAP board members who stayed in touch with Twist and colleagues in California in the months that followed were all disappointed that the proposed "re-amendment" was put on the shelf for the 2007 session.

Oregon's Voluntary Code

Then, unexpectedly, out stepped Connie Gallagher, the administrator of victim compensation and services in Oregon's Department of Justice. She was well regarded among service providers in the state and her colleagues in the two national VOCA administrators' organizations. Moreover, she walked the walk: A trained member of the state's crisis response team, she joined on the two teams Oregon sent to New York after the terrorist attacks of September 11, 2011. The service programs administered by her Crime Victims Assistance Section grew by six during her tenure, and her budget rose from $19 to $35 million.

But victim services were not her sole passion. After she heard Steve Twist speak at a national gathering, her concern over the state of victims' rights in Oregon rose to a new level.

She, like others, knew that Oregon's 1999 victims' rights amendment was a very strong in its core precepts—its prescriptions on how the justice system must accord victims' rights to be informed, present, heard, and restituted—were unambiguous. But embedded in the language was this caveat:

> . . . nor may this section be used *to invalidate an accusatory instrument, ruling of a court, conviction, or adjudication or otherwise suspend or terminate any criminal or juvenile delinquency proceedings at any point* after the case is commenced or on appeal.

Oregon's amendment, in short, is a voluntary code which justice officials may freely ignore. (Only Virginia has the same unenforceability built into its amendment.) Gallaher had already taken steps to strengthen its effect by obtaining a three-year "victims' rights compliance project" grant from the federal Office for Victims of Crime, assembling victim advocates and justice officials to spell out those rights in detail with specific procedures and best practices for all actors in the system. That project has been fruitful; for example, a great many victims now receive a rights card from the responding law enforcement officer (see www.OregonCrime VictimsRights.org).

But Gallaher never envisioned goodwill, even at the highest level, as a substitute for authentic victims' rights. Somewhere in her routine interactions with Oregon's elected prosecutors, she sensed that perhaps they just might be open to reconsidering this roadblock to the enforcement of rights which, as it happens, had been added to the amendment at their urging seven years earlier. In the early months of 2006, she raised with her boss, Attorney General Hardy Myers, the idea of broaching the district attorneys to get a hearing on the issue. He was very supportive, having already been a backer of a federal amendment for victims' rights. She then received a polite reception from the president of the Oregon District Attorneys association, Benton County District Attorney Scott Heiser. Her suggestion was that the association invite NVCAP's counsel, Steve Twist, to address the district attorneys' summer conference. Heiser and his executive committee were open to that request.

Twist's Presentation

Thus, on July 19, 2006, Twist gave a half-hour talk, both lawyerly and passionate, to over 100 prosecutors. He reminded them that, in law, a "right" without a remedy in law is meaningless, a nullity. He then drew on his unique experience in Arizona, having written the initiative that was adopted by the voters in 1990, and having since been its chief appellate litigator and founder of the crime victims' law clinic at the Arizona State University law school—all pro bono, it should be noted. The sky, he asserted, had not fallen down upon the justice system as victims and their lawyers brought legal actions to repair matters when the victims' rights had been denied (or, most often, overlooked). The courts were comfortable righting the wrongs, however infrequent, that were uncovered in this litigation. And this was the kicker for this audience: The officials from whom the courts are requiring remedial action are, in the large majority of cases, themselves trial court judges. Prosecutors, rather than being the respondents in these cases, are typically the very ones who referred the victims to the free services of the law clinic.

In the judgment of this biased observer at the conference, the Twist argument was persuasive, but hardly received as a call to action. As one very pro-victim district attorney told me, "it's a good idea but let's let this compliance project take on the problem first." Others saw the two approaches in the same light, as either/or propositions—the compliance project's impending guidelines or an enforceable amendment.

Amendment to the Amendment

Some, however, saw the issue as a matter of "both/and," not "either/or," none more so than the president of the Oregon District Attorneys' Association, Scott Heiser. He later approached Attorney General Myers and Twist to help frame an amendment-to-the-amendment and, after a number of private discussions with his colleagues, took that proposal to his next executive committee meeting, whereupon the association decided to join with Myers to present that reform to the legislature. That resolution was adopted without dissent.

This was "Surprise Number One" to Twist and other veterans of the movement. The very same reservations Oregon prosecutors once held about constitutional rights for crime victims were in evidence in virtually every state in which an amendment campaign had been launched. True, formal support had been cajoled, in time, in some of those campaigns, but rarely with real enthusiasm—and certainly never unanimously.

Resolution Submitted

Thereafter, Attorney General Myers with help from his deputy, Pete Shepherd, and Professor Douglas Beloof of the Lewis and Clark Law School, prepared the resolution which he formally submitted in partnership with Steve Doell, president of Crime Victims United, a statewide advocacy group and the sponsor of the original package of amendments.

On April 9, 2007, the House Judiciary Committee took testimony on the resolutions. Supportive testimony was offered by the attorney general, a representative of the district attorneys' association, Mary Elledge of Parents of Murdered Children, Steve Doell, and Professor Beloof. For Beloof, this was a moment of special satisfaction. As the author of the first law school casebook on victims' rights and the founding director of the National Crime Victim Law Institute, he was distressed that his Institute has been midwife to any number of free law clinics for victims around the country, but not in his home state, where victims and their lawyers had no standing to challenge rights violations.

Painful Denial of Victims' Rights

Also speaking was Kimberly Larson, director of the local victim-witness program, who said:

I've worked with many victims who have chosen to make statements to the judge at sentencing. They do so because they want the judge to know exactly what impact the crime has had on them. So often victims feel as though the crimes themselves don't provide the full picture of the impact. They stand and bare their souls about sleepless nights, lack of trust, continual fear, and an endless roller coaster of emotions. They talk about marriages that have dissolved because of the stress and impact of the crime; they talk about children who have turned to drugs and alcohol, and sometimes suicide, because of an inability to cope with what's happened. In the end, these same victims, regardless of the sentence imposed, felt that they had a voice in the process and were heard. For some it is a step in their healing process. For others it is an opportunity to be heard in a system where they felt no one was listening.

Unfortunately, I have also worked with victims who wanted to make a statement at sentencing and were not afforded the opportunity to do so. I have had to have those difficult, and sometimes gut-wrenching, conversations that always state with "I'm sorry . . . " It is impossible to make sense of the fact that victims have rights, but when those rights are not recognized, there's nothing they can do about it. These conversations are often, justifiably so, met with anger, frustration, hostility, hurt, disappointment, and a deep sense of injustice. In the end the question is always asked, "What about my rights?"

Measure of Status, Dignity

This writer was the last of the invited proponents, representing both the National and International Organizations for Victim Assistance. My testimony ended with this challenge to the most consistent opponents of victims' rights—whose representatives, as luck would have it, followed me to the witness table:

A final comment: In the 30-some years of the victims' movement, many in the civil liberties and criminal defense bars have opposed all manner of victim rights. That saddens me because I believe victim rights and defendant rights advocates share a common core tenet—that in our constitutional democracy, every citizen should be given tools to keep the government from bullying them—the accuser no less than the accused.

I have also grown impatient with their posture of wanting to protect defendants' rights against the corrosive effects of testing crime victims with dignity. I encourage this committee to ask any who express that view to review all the cases that have been prosecuted since victim rights have been enacted over 30-plus years—surely the cases where all the victims' rights were honored now number in the many hundreds of thousands nationwide—and then to bring to your attention the most appalling cases where appellate courts have found the assertion of victim rights had trammeled on the rights of the accused.

This challenge has been made repeatedly in the U.S. Congress and state legislatures over the past decade or more, and we patiently await the naming of a single case describing the injustices they so darkly predict. Theirs is a fear that harkens to the one Franklin Delano Roosevelt railed against—"nameless, unreasoning, and unjustified." I urge you to put it gently aside and get on with the task of finally restoring to crime victims in America a measure of status and dignity they enjoyed at the founding of the United States.

Next up, the witness representing criminal defense lawyers began with a lawyer-like critique of the phrasing of the text—and then said no more. In contract, the representative of the state's civil liberties union expressed substantial policy differences with the proposal. Enforceability of rights, he argued, should not be extended to crime victims alone but to all other classes of citizens protected in the state's bill of rights. That ended the hearing.

Surprises Two and Three

In the interests of full disclosure, I should note that your correspondent drove home in a state of surreal euphoria.

The rest is all in keeping with this turn of events, with no more shocks. The resolutions were voted out of the House committee, adopted by the full House, then by the Senate Judiciary Committee and the full Senate with the date changed as to when it would appear on the ballot (May 20, 2008), so finally back to the full House where it was accepted as revised. Each of these five votes was unanimous.

At the next meeting of the National Victims' Constitutional Amendment Passage, scheduled for July 12, 2007, at NOVA's annual conference in Reno, the Oregon delegation plans to lecture colleagues on the simplicity of upgrading victims' rights: Assemble your state's Connie Gallagher, Scott Heiser, and Hardy Myers, bring in Steve Twist, and then watch the justice system, the bar, and the legislature fall neatly in line. We may even be able to recruit for you three of our stars as volunteers: Scott is now a senior attorney with the Animal Legal Defense Fund, while Connie and husband Terry have expatriated themselves to the Turks and Caicos Islands—and Steve has never been known to refuse to help compatriots in the cause.

The more serious lesson is that advocates who support fundamental rights for crime victims—and who are sick of telling twice-violated crime victims, "I'm sorry"—should periodically go back to their allies in the public policy arena with the message that victim rights have proven to be deeply gratifying for victims, they deserve the status of fundamental rights, and they need to be expressed in our state constitutions in a way that is both meaningful and enforceable.

Sadly, the list of states who do not meet this standard goes beyond the 17 with no provision at all, and far beyond the two states mentioned here, California and Virginia, whose amendments are as much in need of amending as Oregon's.

* * *

Analysis

In 2008, California and Oregon amended their constitutional victims' rights to provide enforceable victims' rights. The Illinois legislature is currently (as of 2011) working on a similar reform. The California and Oregon laws were enacted in very different ways. Oregon's law was changed in a collaborative development led by state attorney general Hardy Myers. The process ultimately included legislative counsel and various stakeholders. The California legislature was resistant to bringing its constitution into the third wave of victims' rights. Dr. Henry Nicholas spearheaded an initiative, which the people of California approved, granting crime victims enforceable rights. He authored the law with the help of a number of leading scholars, built the organization, and financed the campaign. Dr. Nicholas' only sibling, Marsy, was murdered by her former boyfriend. The California initiative was named after his sister—Marsy's Law. Dr. Nicholas and his mother, Marcella, endured substantial secondary victimization in the criminal justice system, which ultimately led them to pursue victims' rights advocacy. Their commitment to the Movement is unwavering.

Henry Nicholas, cofounder of chip maker Broadcom, led the effort to amend the California Constitution with the nation's most comprehensive crime victims' bill of rights. Seventeen rights are codified under Marsy's Law, named after his sister, also pictured, who was murdered by her former boyfriend in 1983. (Marsy's Law For All)

The California Victims' Bill of Rights is a very robust constitutional amendment. For the first time in California, it provides for a host of rights, all of which are enforceable in court. California is home to one out of eight people in the United States; thus, this amendment benefits far more crime victims then the Federal CVRA. The Oregon Constitution already had rights set out, but the rights were unenforceable. The 2008 amendment made it possible for victims to enforce their rights in court.

THE PROBLEM OF LACK OF LEGAL REPRESENTATION FOR VICTIMS

- **Document:** "The Next Step for a Maturing Victim Rights Movement: Enforcing Crime Victim Rights in the Courts" by John Gillis and Douglas Beloof
- **Date:** Summer, 2002
- **Significance:** Gillis and Beloof's article summarizes the need for victim representation in the current climate of victims' rights enforcement.

- **Source:** Gillis, John and Douglas Beloof. "The Next Step for a Maturing Victim Rights Movement: Enforcing Crime Victim Rights in the Courts." *McGeorge Law Review* 33 (2002): 689.

---

* * *

To be successful, any rights movement must mature to the point where the promulgated civil rights are defended by lawyers and ultimately interpreted and enforced in appellate court rulings. Enacted civil liberties for crime victims are only as meaningful as the ability to enforce these rights in court. In the formative years of our country, Justice Marshall recognized that, "[w]here a specific duty is assigned by law, and individual rights depend upon performance of that duty, it seems equally clear, that the individual who considers himself injured, has a right to resort to the laws of his country for a remedy" (*Marbury v. Madison*, 5 U.S. 137, 166 (1803)). A victim's right is meaningless if there is no remedy for a violation of it.

Even after the successful enactment of victims' rights laws, those rights remain at a critical developmental stage. Meaningful development of victims' rights in the United States requires that both the victims' statutory and state constitutional rights be tested for viability in the courts. Before the civil rights of victims in the criminal process can effectively be enforced by litigation, several barriers to judicial enforcement must be removed. The two most significant barriers to victims' rights compliance addressed in this essay are: (1) the structural procedural problems that prevent challenges to rights violations; and (2) the lack of legal advocates for crime victims. . . .

* * *

. . . As a result of the dearth of lawyers trained in this field, few victims' rights cases are litigated at the trial level, and even fewer cases make it to the appellate courts. Consequently, only educated guesses can be made about the meaning and enforceability of victims' rights. Moreover, without appellate court opinions, there is no meaningful opportunity to amend and thereby perfect legislation. Naturally, only a few cases have been litigated. These cases have been scattered throughout the country. As a result, there are remarkably few significant opinions involving victims' rights.

The lack of victims' rights attorneys results not only in limited enforcement of victims' rights, it is also results in a lack of adequate victim advocacy. In the few victims' rights cases that do make it to the appellate court, there is typically no legal advocate for the victim. The only parties to the appeal are the defendants and the state, who do not usually adequately defend the rights of victims. The lack of legal advocates significantly reduces the chance that a victim's position will be sufficiently briefed or that the law supporting the right will be fully developed. . . .

* * *

Typically, the only way to meaningfully enforce victims' rights is in the criminal case. There are barriers to rights enforcement in the procedures of the criminal courts. Several challenges arise in enforcing victims' rights because of the pre-existing structure of the criminal process. One such challenge is temporal because the criminal process moves rapidly. A rights violation may take place in a pretrial,

trial, or sentencing hearing, and the opportunity to enforce the right in that hearing may be brief. Because the victim does not have an attorney, the opportunity to enforce the right may be missed. Furthermore, timely enforcement is needed because the defendant's right not to be exposed to double jeopardy may eliminate any future remedy. Because a victim is not typically represented at the time the violation occurs, the victim often will not know what the right is, when or how to exercise the right, or that an attorney can represent them. If the victim's right conflicts with the position of the public prosecutor, the unwillingness of the prosecutor to defend the right leaves the victim as a pro se person in a complex and intimidating procedural system. Even if the victim were comfortable enough to pursue the right pro se, it is unlikely that he or she would be as effective as an attorney.

* * *

In History

The National Crime Victim Law Institute was founded as a non-profit at the turn of the millennium. It serves as a national resource for crime victim lawyers and files amicus briefs in the U.S. Supreme Court and other courts. [NCVLI.org].

Attorney Margaret Garvin is the executive director of the National Crime Victim Law Institute, which supports victims' attorneys in criminal cases throughout the United States. (Chris F. Wilson)

Victims' Rights under International Standards

The next document in this chapter, and the last in the book, is the 2008 Report on Victims' Rights in America prepared by the highly respected non-governmental organization, Human Rights Watch. The Report is important is several respects. First, it is the pioneer review of victims' rights in America by an international human rights organization. Second, it compares American instruments on victims' rights to international instruments on victims' rights, created by organizations such as the United Nations. Third, with the exception of some important negative criticism, the Report is generally quite favorable to victims' rights.

- **Document:** "Mixed Results: US Adherence to International Standards on the Rights and Interests of Crime Victims" by Human Rights Watch
- **Date:** September 23, 2008
- **Significance:** Human Rights Watch puts together a comprehensive survey of victims'

rights and interests in America, comparing and contrasting American instruments to International instruments created by organizations like the U.N.

- **Source:** Human Rights Watch. "Mixed Results: US Adherence to International Standards on the Rights and Interests of Crime Victims." Author, 2008. Available at http://www.hrw.org/en/reports/2008/09/23/mixed-results. Reprinted with permission.

---

* * *

Definition of a Crime Victim

Under the Basic Principles for Victims, "victims of crime" are defined as:

Persons who, individually or collectively, have suffered harm, including physical or mental injury, emotional suffering, economic loss or substantial impairment of their fundamental rights, through acts or omissions that are in violation of criminal laws operative within Member States.... (UN General Assembly, Declaration of Basic Principles of Justice for Victims of Crime and Abuse of Power, General Assembly Resolution 40/34, November 29, 1985, para. 1 [hereinafter "Basic Principles for Victims"])

The term *victim* includes "where appropriate, the immediate family or dependants of the direct victim" (Id., paras. 2 and 3). By contrast, under most US state laws, family members are afforded victim status only if the direct victim of the crime is a minor, incapacitated, or deceased (see, for example, Alaska Statutes, sec. 12.55.185(19); Arizona Constitution, art. II, sec. 2.1(C); Colorado Revised Statutes, sec. 18-1.3-602(4)(a)(V); Florida Constitution, Art. I, sec. 16; Georgia Code Annotated, sec. 17-17-3(11); Illinois Compiled Statutes 120/3 sec. 725 (a); Indiana Code, sec. 35-40-12-1; Maine Revised Statutes Annotated, title 17-A, sec. 1171; Michigan Compiled Laws, sec. 780.752, subsec. 2(1)(l); Mississippi Code Annotated, sec. 99-36-3; New Hampshire Revised Statutes Annotated, sec. 21-M:8-k; Ohio Revised Code Annotated, sec. 2930.02; South Dakota Codified Laws, sec. 23A-28C-4; Vermont Statutes Annotated, title 13, sec. 5301(4).... Iowa Code, sec. 915.10(3)).

In addition, in practice some state laws may fail to be as inclusive as the Basic Principles for Victims' definition because the designation of victim status is left up to individual prosecutors or police officers, or the status is only recognized once a suspect is arrested and charged. For example, Delaware's statutory definition of a victim is the person or entity "identified as the victim of a crime *in a police report*" (emphasis added; Delaware Code, title 11, sec. 9410(5)). In Utah, the victim is "any natural person against whom the charged crime or conduct is alleged to have been perpetrated or attempted by the defendant or minor..." (Utah Code Annotated, sec. 77-38-2(9)(a)). In some states, there are more restrictive definitions when the crime has allegedly been perpetrated by a person below the age of 18. For example, in Oregon, " 'victim' means any person determined by the district attorney or juvenile department to have suffered direct financial, psychological or physical harm as a result of an act that has brought the youth or youth offender before the juvenile court" (Oregon Revised Statutes, sec. 419A.004(31)).

Even in states without these restrictive definitions, victims who disagree with the prosecution's decision to seek the most severe punishment available—often the death penalty—have sometimes not been communicated with or afforded basic information about the progress of the investigation or prosecution of their cases. One advocate said:

> Prosecutors get to, for the most part, decide who the victim is. . . . Certain crime victims' family members, and I can name cases, have been excluded from the courtroom and from the inside circle of prosecutors' offices because the prosecutor would pick and choose who would get to be [considered as victims'] family members based on whether or not they supported the harshest penalties possible. (Human Rights Watch interview with Jennifer Bishop Jenkins, August 28, 2007)

Also contrary to the Basic Principles for Victims, in certain states incarcerated individuals, persons accused of crimes, and some police officers have been denied victim status or the ability to enjoy all the same rights afforded to other types of victims. Police officers harmed in the course of their duties are not considered victims under Ohio's victims' rights statute (*In re Walling*, 91 Ohio Misc. 2d 181, 698 N.E. 2d 154, 1997 Ohio Misc. LEXIS 335 (Ct. Cl. 1997)). In Arizona, the definition of "victim" excludes any person who is "in custody for an offense or is the accused" (Arizona Constitution art. 2, section 2.1(C)). Incarcerated victims are not granted the right to be heard and must instead submit evidence in writing (Arizona Rules of Criminal Procedure 39 (2007)). In Alabama, a person may be considered a victim "except if the person is in custody for an offense or is the accused" (Alabama Code, sec. 15-23-60(19)). In Michigan, "an individual who is incarcerated is not eligible to exercise the privileges and rights established for victims under this article except that he or she may submit a written statement to the court for consideration at sentencing" (Michigan Compiled Laws, sec. 780.752, subsec. 2(1)(l)). The federal Victims of Crime Act restricts the use of funds under the act to prohibit offering rehabilitative or "support services to incarcerated individuals, even when the service pertains to the victimization of that individual" (US Department of Justice 1996). In addition, some states accord rights to victims of only certain categories of crime (New Mexico Statutes Annotated, sec. 31-26-3(F), victim rights are provided to any victim against whom a "specified criminal offense" is committed. Victim also means a family member or a victim's representative when the individual against whom a criminal offense was committed is a minor, is incompetent or a homicide victim. The specified criminal offenses for this purpose include: negligent arson resulting in death or bodily injury, aggravated arson, aggravated assault, aggravated battery, dangerous use of explosives, negligent use of a deadly weapon, murder, voluntary and involuntary manslaughter, kidnapping, criminal sexual penetration, criminal contact with a minor, armed robbery, homicide by a vehicle, great bodily injury by vehicle, abandonment or abuse of a child, stalking or aggravated stalking, aggravated assault against a household member, assault against a household member with intent to commit a violent felony, battery against a household member, or aggravated battery against a household member.); Louisiana Revised Statutes, sec. 46:1842(9), "'Victim' means a person against whom any of the following offenses have been committed: (a) any homicide, or any felony offense defined or enumerated in R.S. 14:2(B); (b) any sexual offense; (c) the offenses of vehicular negligent injuring and first degree vehicular negligent injuring; (d) Any offense against the person as defined in the Criminal Code committed against a family or household member as defined in R.S. 46:2132(4) or dating partner as defined in R.S. 46:2151(B)").

According to the Basic Principles for Victims, a person may be considered a victim irrespective of whether the perpetrator is identified. While this is technically also true in the United States, as discussed below, some victims' rights advocates raise concerns that the systems in place to support victims become effective only after a suspect is identified (see Human Rights Watch 2008).

Also under international standards, victim status should be determined "regardless of the familial relationship between the perpetrator and the victim" (see Basic Principles for Victims). The United States tends to adhere to this standard; however, some victims' rights advocates explain that systems set up to assist victims can break down when the victim and offender have family relationships. Victims' assistance programs can sometimes disregard the prevalence of murders in which the deceased victim and the offender knew one another, rendering the surviving family's allegiances less distinct than the system presumes. Nowhere is this more vivid than in cases of intrafamilial murder, where the relatives of the victim and the relatives of the offender are one and the same. (Murder Victims' Families for Reconciliation 2002, 13)

A sub-component of this definitional problem arises in the context of crime victims who are children. For example, definitions of crime victims under state and federal law have failed to adequately address the problems arising from child abuse. One victims' rights advocate explained:

> The challenge in defining victims is ensuring that the persons harmed are the persons with the rights. This is relatively easy when the victim is an adult with mental capacity. But there remain challenges with minor victims. If a parent is protective and nurturing, it is one thing to have them involved in the process. But in cases of child abuse, it is not uncommon for parents to join in unity against the child victim. That definitional problem has not been tackled. (Human Rights Watch interview with Professor Doug Beloof, October 2, 2007)

Finally, victim status can be temporal and blurred. For example, sometimes individuals who perpetrate crimes against others were themselves once victims of crime. Spouses who are victims of domestic violence and then commit crimes against their abusers, or children who are abused by parents and then commit violent crimes against them, are just two examples (Human Rights Watch 2005, 85). An individual's prior victimization never justifies subsequent criminal acts, but it is important to note the complexities of victim status. Similarly, definitional problems arise when persons who are engaging in criminal acts are simultaneously victims of crime; examples include "a teenage girl who is drinking but is also a victim of sexual assault, or a prostitute who is violently sexually assaulted and beaten" (Human Rights Watch interview with Professor Doug Beloof, October 2, 2007).

Access to Prompt Redress

According to the Basic Principles for Victims, victims "are entitled to access to the mechanisms of justice and to prompt redress, as provided for by national legislation" (see Basic Principles for Victims). The purpose of redress is for the state and the offender to offset some of the harm done to the victim (to make the victim as whole as possible) and to provide a "socially constructive way for the offender to be held accountable, while offering the greatest possible scope for rehabilitation" (UN Office for Drug Control and Crime Prevention 1999, 47, hereinafter "Handbook for Victims").

It includes redress provided by the offender to the victim (commonly referred to as "restitution"); but it also embraces compensation by the state, including in cases in which an alleged offender is never identified or prosecuted.

Many courts worldwide order restitution as a part of sentencing (UN Economic and Social Council 1996). It means payment by an offender to the victim for out-of-pocket losses caused by the offender's wrongful acts. Since international standards on victims of crime embrace restorative justice principles, restitution may also include some of the activities an offender may engage in during alternative or restorative justice processes, such as admission of responsibility and apology to the victim (*Handbook for Victims*, at 43).

Compensation refers to payments or assistance offered by the state according to state law in addition to or in lieu of restitution paid by the offender (see Basic Principles for Victims). Victims often need to follow specific steps required by law in order to obtain compensation, such as filing their claims within a set time frame. In cases in which an offender is not convicted or cannot pay restitution, the state can fill the gap by paying compensation to the victim (see Human Rights Watch 2008). Compensation can include access to social, health, or other public insurance systems. As with restitution, because international standards embrace restorative or alternative justice processes, compensation may involve providing state funding for public art installations, victim impact panels presented to the community, or other forms of commemoration of victims' experiences (*Handbook for Victims*, at 43).

The redress provisions of the Basic Principles for Victims make clear that victims are entitled to claim some form of restitution and compensation for the harm they have suffered. However, that does not necessarily mean that they are entitled to see an offender tried by a court. National authorities, such as criminal prosecutors, may decide not to prosecute a particular crime without infringing on a victim's entitlement to redress, as long as that decision is not made in a discriminatory manner. In the United States, as well as elsewhere in the world, this reality can cause conflicts between victims and prosecutors. As one prosecutor told Human Rights Watch:

While the victim's input is very important, it may not decide the outcome of the case. The prosecutor will explain to the victim that he or she can only bring to trial a case that can be proved beyond a reasonable doubt. So sometimes, if for example a victim can't pick out someone from a line-up, a prosecutor may not be able to make a charge. (Human Rights Watch telephone interview with Maria Bee, chief of victim services and former assistant district attorney, San Francisco District Attorney's Office, San Francisco, California, September 14, 2007)

One victims' rights advocate explained her views on the role of victims in prosecutorial decision-making:

Our system is quite correct to keep the victims as much a part of it as possible in order to respect their feelings and their journey, but you can't make them the prosecutors. The dispassionate blindfolded woman that holds the scales of justice is supposed to be blind. You can't have a dispassionate objective system that is based on the passion and grief of victims seeking vengeance. (Human Rights Watch interview with Jennifer Bishop Jenkins, August 28, 2007)

However, according to international standards, in specific instances redress may embrace more than simple restitution and compensation. For certain crimes, a judicial remedy may be necessary. The Human Rights Committee, which supervises compliance with the ICCPR, to which the US is bound, has recognized that "purely disciplinary and administrative remedies" cannot be deemed to constitute effective remedies when a victim has suffered "a particularly serious violation of human rights, notably in the event of an alleged violation of the right to life" (*Bautista v. Colombia*, communication No. 563/1993, para. 8.2, CCPR/C/55/D/563/1993 (1995)). The Basic Principles for Victims also emphasize the importance of "informal mechanisms for the resolution of disputes, including mediation, arbitration and customary justice" (Basic Principles for Victims, para. 7).

In addition, Article 2 of the ICCPR provides that the rights recognized by the treaty must be respected "without distinction of any kind, such as race, colour, sex, language, religion, political or other opinion, national or social origin, property, birth or other status." Therefore, if victims of a particular race or gender are provided access to state compensation programs but others are not, that would violate the treaty's prohibition on discrimination. In fact, if any of the standards on victims' rights and interests discussed in this report are not observed on an equal basis, Article 2 would be implicated. In addition, Article 2 provides that persons who suffer violation of their rights under the ICCPR are entitled to an "effective remedy," and that any person:

claiming such a remedy shall have his right thereto determined by competent judicial, administrative or legislative authorities . . . [and] the competent authorities shall enforce such remedies when granted. (International Covenant on Civil and Political Rights (ICCPR), adopted December 16, 1966, G.A. Res. 2200A (XXI), 21 U.N. GAOR Supp. (No. 16) at 52, U.N.

Doc. A/6316 (1966), 999 U.N.T.S. 171, entered into force March 23, 1976 [hereinafter "ICCPR"])

Access to Information

During criminal proceedings or trials, human rights standards recognize that victims may prefer to be centrally involved (to the extent that this does not prejudice the rights of the accused) or to remain as anonymous and uninvolved as possible. The Basic Principles for Victims establish that victims should have a choice about their access to information and participation, stating that victims should be:

- Informed of the role, scope, timing, and progress of proceedings and dispositions, especially in the case of serious crimes and when victims have asked for such information;
- Allowed to present their views and concerns at appropriate stages of the proceedings and without prejudice to the accused; and
- Provided with assistance throughout the legal process. (Basic Principles for Victims, paras. 6(a)-(c))

There is consensus in international standards and domestic law on the importance of providing victims with information about developments in the criminal case. This may be because victims themselves view access to information as one of the most powerful needs they have:

You cannot imagine how important it is for most victims to know what is going on with their case. Information is more important than almost anything. Victims will say this is so even if they have worked through restorative justice with an offender who has apologized for murdering their loved one and they have forgiven them. Even in those cases, the one thing that victims seem to need is information: "Why did you do it? What happened? What were the details? What were her last words?" That's what victims seem to need more than anything else is information. And that is so often what they don't get. (Human Rights Watch interview with Jennifer Bishop Jenkins, August 28, 2007)

In accordance with the Basic Principles for Victims, the vast majority of jurisdictions in the United States give victims notice of court proceedings, sentencing hearings, final dispositions, and pardon or parole hearings. Fewer provide notice of arraignments, plea negotiations, schedule changes, or post-conviction proceedings or appeals (National Conference of State Legislatures 2004). Some advocates are concerned about the lack of information provided to victims about these latter stages in the criminal process:

We're doing better and better in guaranteeing that victims have notice about formal stages in the trial, but we're doing less well in providing information to victims about how the case is proceeding outside of the court. Victims should be informed about plea negotiations, and victims should have the chance to consult with the prosecutor about what the court should know before a bail decision is made. Victims often have legitimate safety concerns that should be heard during bail, plea, and sentencing hearings, but we are not doing a good job of ensuring that they are heard. (Human Rights Watch interview with Hon. Paul Cassell, September 25, 2007)

Although most laws in the US make notice mandatory, the Basic Principles for Victims make clear that victims should not be informed of developments in a case if they do not want that information. Some victims' rights advocates strongly believe that mandatory notice should remain the practice in the US, irrespective of what the Basic Principles for Victims state (Human Rights Watch interview with a victims' rights advocate who chose to remain anonymous, Portland, Oregon, June 3, 2008). Other victims' rights advocates told Human Rights Watch that they understand why victims must specifically request information and updates:

There is actually good psychological evidence for the fact that some victims are re-traumatized just by hearing about the ongoing proceeding. Everybody deals with their grief in a different way, but some people have chosen to deal with their grief and trauma simply by blotting it out and not wanting to hear about it. And for those people, there was enough thinking in the writing of these policies that policymakers said "Well, the only way to give them choice is to ask them to request whether they want notification or not." (Human Rights Watch interview with Jennifer Bishop Jenkins, August 28, 2007)

Yet victims' rights advocates emphasize that in giving victims choice over access to information, they should all be informed of their right to ask for information, and unfortunately this does not consistently happen in the United States. One advocate said:

What has happened is that people have been massively re-traumatized because they aren't told of the need to ask for information. When they find out later that something was happening with their case and they weren't notified, then they are told "well, you have to ask to be notified" and they say, "well, you never told us we had to ask to be notified." There are people's lives who are in re-traumatization because of this. I have seen very sad examples. (Id.)

As noted above, all states in the US keep victims informed of various stages in the criminal proceedings, but there is less clarity about giving victims an opportunity to "opt out" of information. However, as one prosecutors' office in San Francisco explained, "as a practical matter, a [prosecutor] wouldn't force that information on a victim if it wasn't wanted" (Human Rights Watch interview with Maria Bee, September 14, 2007). Another victims' rights advocate explained to a Human Rights Watch researcher that in some states, the decision must be made early in the process, which is often the moment when victims are most acutely suffering from trauma:

Some states, for example Oregon, require victims to opt in to notification at the beginning of the process, which is often right in the middle of the victim's trauma. These states treat a failure to opt in as a waiver of all subsequent notice rights, but that's problematic because victims cannot make a knowing and voluntary waiver in the middle of trauma. (Human Rights Watch interview with Meg Garvin, October 2, 2007)

Despite these failings, in other ways the United States has gone far beyond international standards in giving victims information about offenders. In many jurisdictions victims are informed about parole hearings and when an offender is released from prison. Many victims in the United States receive information through a computer system called "Victims' Information and Notification Everyday" (VINE). Thirty-one states and one or more large counties in an additional 12 states plus the District of Columbia use VINE to provide crime victims and the general public with information about an offender's location through a toll-free number or a website. [Footnote 80 omitted]. Through VINE:

> Victims can inquire whether an offender is held in jail as well as the facility's location; users can register to be notified immediately of a change in the offender's status, such as release, transfer, or escape; when a notification is triggered, VINE automatically calls the number or numbers the victim has provided; calls continue for a designated period of time, or until the victim enters a four-digit PIN. (Appriss, Inc., "VINE Fact Sheet," http://www .appriss.com/sitedocs/VINECutSheet.pdf)

Some victims' rights advocates explain that resource constraints prevent some jurisdictions from providing this kind of information to victims. In addition, problems remain even in jurisdictions that have implemented VINE. For example, victims of crimes that pre-date the institution of the computer system are not able to be retroactively included. Therefore, if a parole hearing comes up 20 years after the crime, but the offense occurred prior to VINE, victims may not receive information about the hearing.

Ability to Participate

The Basic Principles for Victims require that victims should be able to present their "views and concerns" at appropriate stages of the criminal proceedings "without prejudice to the accused" (Basic Principles for Victims, para. 6). The precise timetables and procedures under which this occurs are up to each jurisdiction. These issues are controversial because of concerns that victim participation can result in inequality of treatment and punishment among criminal offenders since "if victims are allowed to present claims or to address the court, it is asserted that only some victims would do so and that the defendants in these cases may be subjected to harsher punishment" (Handbook for Victims, 36). Others have argued that opportunities for victim participation should occur in each and every stage in the process-charging decisions, bail, plea bargaining, trial, sentencing, appeal, parole, and probation (Human Rights Watch interviews with Hon. Paul Cassell, September 25, 2007, and Professor Doug Beloof, October 2, 2007; Beloof and Cassell 2005). Still others emphasize that victims should be notified of and participate in legislation that might retroactively change the outcomes in their cases, although there is no such requirement under applicable international human rights laws (Human Rights Watch interview with Jennifer Bishop Jenkins, August 28, 2007).

In the United States, most states provide for victims' participation during sentencing, although Delaware only allows victims to present impact statements if they have "cooperated with the court and with Investigative Services officers," Texas only allows statements to be made after the sentence is pronounced, and Virginia only allows for a victim to testify if the prosecutor agrees (Delaware Code Annotated, Title 11, sec. 4331(g), Texas Code of Criminal Procedure Annotated article 42.03, Virginia Code Annotated, sec. 19.2-295.3). The majority of states provide for victims' participation at all "critical" or "crucial" states of proceedings; these states allow victims to confer with prosecutors, including during plea negotiations, and they allow victims to be present at parole hearings. Far fewer states allow victims to be present at any stage at which the defendant is allowed to appear; allow victims to sit at the prosecutor's table; or allow victims to have an advocate or family member present with them (National Conference of State Legislatures 2004).

Even if they are not required to participate as a principal witness in criminal proceedings, there are many reasons why victims or their family members may seek to participate in criminal prosecutions. In some cases, it is simply to ensure that justice is done. In others, relatives of direct victims seek to demonstrate the love and respect they have for the individual who was injured or killed. In still other cases, victims may wish to ensure that others are not victimized by the same offender in the future. Or victims may seek to participate because they oppose the type of punishment—such as the death penalty—that the accused may face. This was the case for one family member of a person killed in the 1995 Oklahoma City bombing in the United States. In that case, the victim's family member wanted to testify about her own opposition to the death penalty at the sentencing of convicted bomber Timothy McVeigh, but she was not allowed to do so (Knight 1997, 70–71).

In a similar case in Arizona, Duane Lynn, whose wife had been murdered, wished to testify to the jury in order to express his preference for a life sentence (as opposed to the death penalty). The state prosecutor opposed the victim's petition to the court to make such a statement. The Supreme Court of Arizona ruled in favor of the prosecution and against Mr. Lynn's desire to participate. It held that the US Constitution only allowed for statements from victims relating to the harm they have suffered, and that

> statements regarding sentencing exceed those bounds and violate the Eighth Amendment, and therefore are prohibited. Victims' recommendations to the jury regarding the appropriate sentence a capital defendant should receive are not constitutionally relevant to the harm caused by the defendant's criminal acts or to the defendant's blameworthiness or culpability. (*Lynn v. Reinstein*, 68 P.3d 412, 417 (Ariz. 2003))

In other jurisdictions the practice is different. For example, one prosecutor in California said, "Victims have a right to speak at the sentencing. That is their right" (Human Rights Watch interview with Maria Bee, September 14, 2007).

Some authors have interpreted the provisions in the Basic Principles for Victims relating to participation to require states to provide legal counsel for victims, separate from the state prosecutor in the case. Italy and India appear to provide separate counsel for victims, although eligibility is based on a strict means test, which makes it "relevant for only a minority of victims in practice" (Van Dijk 2006, referring to the experience in Italy; see also *Handbook for Victims*, 38, referring to the experience in India). Many other jurisdictions, including the United States, do not consider it necessary for victims to receive legal assistance other than that provided by police and prosecutorial professionals. However, some victims' advocates in the United States commend states that have put in place an independent victims' rights ombudsman (a public official with power to assist victims who are seeking rights protection) who is separate from the prosecutor or defense attorneys in the case. In addition, some states in the United States are experimenting with defense attorneys playing a role with victims of crime, as a means of reducing the adversarial nature (which is perceived by some as harmful) of the criminal justice system (Email communication from Jennifer Bishop Jenkins to Human Rights Watch, November 3, 2007).

Participation through the Presentation of Evidence

While victims may have different levels of interest and capacity to participate in criminal trials, one area in which they have less autonomy is in the presentation of evidence. For many crime victims, presentation of evidence of the harm they have suffered, including any forensic evidence relating to the identity of the offender, is an important part of their participation in criminal proceedings. Of course, analysis and presentation of this evidence (for example, forensic evidence relating to the identity of a perpetrator of a rape, discussed below), can be equally important to protect the rights of the accused.

Some victims may prefer not to give testimony or other evidence, but this preference is not protected under human rights standards or US law. In fact, under international standards, the accused has a right "to examine, or have examined, the witnesses against him and to obtain the attendance and examination of witnesses on his behalf under the same conditions as the witnesses against him" (ICCPR, Article 14.3(e)). The Sixth Amendment to the US Constitution similarly provides that the accused must be "confronted with the witnesses against him; [and] have compulsory process for obtaining witnesses in his favor..."

One prosecutor described the balance her office tries to strike when dealing with a victim who does not want to participate:

> Typically we need the victim to testify in court...a lot of times it's very difficult to prosecute without the victim coming forward. We hope that the victim will cooperate and come in to work with us. Prosecutors do have the option of issuing a subpoena and issuing a body attachment to make sure that they do, but that should be a last resort because it is re-traumatizing to the victim. (Human Rights Watch interview with Maria Bee, September 14, 2007)

While no states have granted victims a right to refuse to give evidence to the prosecution, nine states (Alabama, Alaska, Arizona, Idaho, Louisiana, Oregon,

Pennsylvania, Tennessee, and Wyoming) have granted victims a right to refuse an interview with the defense. Out of sensitivity to victims' concerns over safety and privacy, "several jurisdictions [outside the United States] allow the taking of evidence with video or closed-circuit television;" yet these forms of testimony are not generally accepted in the United States as they are perceived as prejudicing the constitutional rights of the accused to confront the witnesses against him or her (*Handbook for Victims*, 36).

While some victims may be reluctant to present evidence, many others see this as a very important part of their participation in criminal proceedings. With advances in forensic technology, evidence from crime scenes has become an increasingly reliable way for investigators to identify potential suspects and exclude others. In particular, DNA testing of biological evidence (for example, blood, semen, skin cells) is one of the most accurate ways to both eliminate suspects and identify perpetrators (Riley 2005). Unfortunately, states' failures to preserve or process evidence have frustrated law enforcement's ability to hold offenders accountable.

One issue at the heart of the problem is that state crime lab personnel have sometimes destroyed crime scene evidence before testing it. In July of 2007, the *Denver Post* conducted an investigation of evidence purges in 10 states (Moffeit and Greene 2007). The *Post* discovered that law enforcement authorities destroyed biological evidence in nearly 6,000 rape and murder cases during the past decade (Moffeit and Greene 2007). For example, in 2002, the Los Angeles police and sheriff departments threw away at least 3,000 rape kits to clear space in a crowded evidence locker (Id.).

The destruction of untested rape kits is an illustrative and important example of how flawed evidentiary policies can thwart justice for victims of sexual violence, and violates international standards. The destruction of such rape kit evidence in particular contravenes the "Model Strategies and Practical Measures on the Elimination of Violence against Women in the Field of Crime Prevention and Criminal Justice," which urges in Article 3 that state police forces "develop investigative techniques that do not degrade women subjected to violence . . . *while maintaining standards for the collection of the best evidence*" (emphasis added; UN General Assembly 1997).

In the United States there are no national, uniform regulations that mandate how police agencies preserve evidence, which leaves agencies with broad discretion. Twenty-two states have statutes that compel police agencies to preserve evidence. [The states are: Arkansas, California, Connecticut, Florida, Georgia, Illinois, Kentucky, Louisiana, Maine, Maryland, Michigan, Montana, Nebraska, New Hampshire, New Mexico, North Carolina, Oklahoma, Rhode Island, Texas, Virginia, Washington, and Wisconsin]. However, flaws in some state preservation statutes result in the continued destruction of evidence. For example, in most states, there are no penalties for those responsible for destroying evidence, a consequence that might deter improper evidence disposal (Innocence Project).

Provision of Restitution and Compensation

The Basic Principles for Victims make clear that victims of crime should receive restitution and compensation. According to the Basic Principles for Victims, restitution should include "the return of property or payment for the harm or loss suffered, [and] reimbursement of expenses incurred as a result of the victimization" (Basic Principles for Victims, paras. 8 and 12). When offenders cannot provide restitution, under international standards, states should endeavor to provide compensation, especially to victims who have sustained significant bodily injury or impairment of physical or mental health as a result of serious crimes and to their families, especially dependents of persons who have died (Id., para. 12(a) and (b)).

In the United States, offenders are typically ordered by the court to pay restitution to their victims. Many offenders do not have the funds to pay these costs upon conviction and if they are incarcerated, it may be nearly impossible for the garnishing of wages paid in prison (an average of $0.56 per hour for state prisoners in 1991) to reach the amount of the restitution ordered by the court. As one prosecutor noted, "sometimes, if the offender receives a very long sentence, victims can receive full restitution through prison wages" (Beck et al. 1991; Bureau of Justice Statistics, March 1993; Human Rights Watch interview with Maria Bee, September 14, 2007). All but two states—New Hampshire and North Dakota—allow victims to enforce restitution orders through a civil judgment. [Footnote 108 omitted].

State systems of crime victim compensation in the United States are intended to supplement or act in lieu of restitution that cannot or will not be provided directly by offenders. In most states, this is organized through state compensation funds. As of 2004, all 50 states and the District of Columbia compensated victims for medical expenses, mental health costs (except Utah), lost wages, and funerals. A majority of states compensated victims for travel expenses and for attorney fees and rehabilitation costs, while only a minority of states covered moving costs and crime scene clean-up in victims' homes or other property. Maximum award limits ranged between $4,000 and $150,000, with $26,000 as the mean limit on compensation to victims among the 50 states and the District of Columbia (National Conference of State Legislatures 2004).

Some victims' rights advocates told Human Rights Watch that they find these state systems sorely lacking: "The kinds of compensation funds that exist in the states and at the national level are very minimal. They don't even cover the cost of the funeral. Getting compensation for time off work is almost impossible" (Human Rights Watch interview with victims' rights advocate Jennifer Bishop Jenkins, August 28, 2007). Another advocate raised the problem of statutes of limitations: "Most states have a statute of limitations of three years for access to the victims' compensation fund. [Relatives of] victims of homicide may have ongoing mental health issues that don't present themselves until five years after the crime" (Human Rights Watch interview with victims' rights advocate Renny Cushing, August 28, 2007).

Compensation problems are particularly acute in the area of health care, especially given that many US residents who are not victims of crime struggle to cover the expense of health care. One victims' rights advocate explained, "At its worst, victims say to themselves, 'why does the homicide perpetrator sit in prison and get health care, whereas victims do not?'" (Id.). Another advocate gave the following example:

I know one family where a girl was shot in the head—she's permanently disabled. The mom was already working two jobs, but had to give up one job because her daughter can't dress herself or feed herself. She's 21 years old and she's going to be in diapers the rest of her life and have to be fed and dressed and showered and there was no compensation for ongoing nursing care. They were already on welfare, so they get some medical aid, but the mother had to quit one of her jobs, she's not getting compensation for that and they didn't even get enough help to be able to cover the initial medical care, much less the ongoing. (Human Rights Watch interview with Jennifer Bishop Jenkins, August 28, 2007)

In some jurisdictions in the United States, victims' services, which are most often provided through a team of victim advocates, do not commence until after a suspect is arrested or charged with the crime. A federal judge explained to Human Rights Watch, "Most crime victims' rights are triggered by the filing of a formal charging document; if that is never filed, victims are on their own" (Human Rights Watch interview with Hon. Paul Cassell, September 25, 2007). Another victims' rights advocate said:

Victim services, I believe, should be tied to the crime, not to [arrest or prosecution of] the offender. Because if you tie any services—whether it be counseling and support, or "here's an 800 number where you can get funeral help," or "here's information about your legal rights," or whatever—none of that is given to victims; victim services do not arrive into the life of the victim until there's an offender who has been caught and is being prosecuted. And if the offender's not caught . . . you can imagine how often the offender is never caught and put on trial. In fact, in Cook County, Illinois, victim services claims that 80 percent of the time there's no trial. That means either no offender is ever caught or there's a plea bargain, which is very common. Victim services will quite often not be forthcoming. So the highest standard is the one that ties victims' rights and victims' services to the crime and not the offender. (Human Rights Watch interview with Jennifer Bishop Jenkins, August 28, 2007)

In contrast to the problems in Illinois identified above, in San Francisco, victims' advocates get in touch with victims and provide compensation and assistance within 48 hours of the time the case is opened, and irrespective of whether a suspect is arrested or put on trial (Human Rights Watch interview with Maria Bee, September 14, 2007).

Expeditious and Fair Procedures

According to the Basic Principles for Victims, victims should be able to obtain redress through procedures that are "expeditious, fair, inexpensive and accessible" (Basic Principles for Victims, para. 5). Expeditious criminal trials may at times be in the interests of victims (who may want a prompt resolution) as well as defendants (who, under Article 9 of the ICCPR, are entitled to "trial within a reasonable time or to release"). Nevertheless, defendants have pointed out that their rights to "have adequate time and facilities for the preparation of [their] defence" may militate against very rapid criminal procedures (ICCPR, Article 14(b)).

Each victim's experience is unique and reactions to the speed of trial differ. For example, one commentator, who is herself a victim of violent crime, writes:

Trauma might lead victims to want to speed up the process—to get it over with—in the hope that somehow this will make the anguish go away. Conversely, victims may want to slow down the process in order to gain some distance and relief from pressure. For some victims, notice about hearings may rekindle trauma. For others, notice may provide feelings of predictability and control that offset the feeling of helplessness many experience. (Henderson 1999).

One prosecutor explained that in her experience, she hears most from victims who are unhappy with delays in criminal trials: "The victim will come to us and say 'I want closure, and now here's another continuance [delay in the case]? Can't you do something, prosecutor?' And, often the prosecutor can't do anything and has to explain the process to the victim" (Human Rights Watch interview with Maria Bee, September 14, 2007).

In the United States, 25 states have enacted statutes recognizing a right of victims to a speedy trial. [Footnote 121 omitted]. In Europe, the Court of Human Rights has condemned some governments for their failure to prosecute cases within a reasonable time (Reese 2000).

Apart from the speed of trial, international standards recognize that victims should be "treated with compassion and respect for their dignity" throughout criminal proceedings (Basic Principles for Victims, para. 4). Compassionate treatment may require assistance from mental health and other professionals. In addition, "police, justice, health, social service and other personnel should receive training to sensitize them to the needs of victims" (Id., para. 15).

There are numerous international guidelines and codes of conduct that instruct public officials on achieving high standards of professional conduct when interacting with crime victims, including the following instruments developed by the United Nations: the Code of Conduct for Law Enforcement Officials; the Principles of Medical Ethics relevant to the Role of Health Personnel, particularly Physicians, in the Protection of Prisoners and Detainees against Torture and Other Cruel, Inhuman or Degrading Treatment or Punishment; and the International Code of Conduct for Public Officials (UN General Assembly 1979; 1982; 1996). Jurisdictions in the United States each take their own approach to these issues, with varying results. In California, prosecutorial staff members receive training on the needs of victims, and victims' services personnel work to get victims psychological assistance (Human Rights Watch interview with Maria Bee, September 14, 2007).

The Basic Principles for Victims also require that governments take measures during criminal proceedings to:

Minimize inconvenience to victims, protect their privacy, when necessary, and ensure their safety, as well as that of their families and witnesses on their behalf, from intimidation and retaliation. (Basic Principles for Victims, para. 6(d))

The ICCPR similarly provides that:

> The Press and the public may be excluded from all or part of a trial for reasons of morals, public order or national security in a democratic society, or when the interest of the private lives of the Parties so requires. (ICCPR, Article 14)

Victims may have serious concerns about their safety and privacy. In accordance with international standards, criminal justice professionals should implement policies that protect victims from further harm, intimidation, or harassment. Harm, intimidation, or harassment can come from many sides, including from the accused and from individuals acting on behalf of the accused, and the dangers may be heightened when the accused is a family member of the victim (*Handbook for Victims*, 35).

In the United States, most of these issues are governed by state and federal statutes. Of the 50 states and the District of Columbia, 37 protect victims' right to keep home addresses and personal information confidential, and 39 protect victims' right to protection from harm or threats of harm (National Conference of State Legislatures 2004). However, there are limits to the protection victims receive when safety is not an issue. A prosecutor in California told Human Rights Watch:

> For example, in California the defendant is not allowed to know the victim's address or personal information. As prosecutors, we would never give out that information to a defendant, but we are required by law to give discovery to defense attorneys. The law allows minors under age 13 who are victims of sexual offenses or a violent felony to testify via closed circuit if they are likely to suffer serious emotional distress, and in sex crimes victims don't have to use their full names. But a lot of other information is a matter of public record. (Human Rights Watch interview with Maria Bee, September 14, 2007)

Protection for other Rights of Victims

Victims of violent crime in the United States are disproportionately young, black, and poor. For example, in 2005, persons aged 16–24 were victims of violent crime at a rate that was 2.5 times that of persons aged 35–49. African Americans were crime victims at a rate that was 1.35 times that of whites; and persons in households earning less than $14,999 per year were victims at a rate that was 2.1 times higher than persons earning $75,000 or more (Catalano 2005; Bureau of Justice Statistics, 2006). Therefore, victims' rights are not only important on their own terms, but are worthy of special attention since marginalized portions of American society may have more difficulty enforcing these rights, or enjoying them on an equal basis with other segments of the population (Office of the President of the United States 1982; Beloof, Cassell, and Twist 2006, 17–19).

As a starting point, the right to equal access to the mechanisms of justice for all victims must inform criminal procedures:

> The structure of the justice system should take into account the obstacles which many victims encounter in seeking such access, owing to factors such

as culture, race, language, resources, education, age or citizenship. (*Handbook for Victims*, 34)

Nondiscrimination is also an essential human right that must be part and parcel of the enjoyment and enforcement of crime victims' rights. Female victims should have the same ability to participate in the justice system as males. And there should be no distinction between victims of different races, nationalities, or linguistic abilities. Citizenship status should not play a role in a victim's ability to claim a remedy.

Beyond accessing a remedy, there are other points in the proceedings at which additional important human rights concerns must be addressed. For example, child victims of crime should be subject to criminal procedures that are tailored to their best interests and that respect their rights to be informed, heard, and treated with dignity and compassion. Child victims of crime also have rights to be protected from discrimination and hardship during the justice process, and to have their rights to privacy, safety, and reparation respected (UN Economic and Social Council 2005; each of these rights is enumerated and described in this resolution). Despite these standards, and despite a detailed federal law on the need to provide special assistance, including the appointment of a guardian *ad litem* for child victims of crime, "absolutely no money has been appropriated to actually hire and pay for the appointment of a guardian *ad litem* in federal courts for child victims" (18 U.S.C. sec. 3509(h); Human Rights Watch interview with Hon. Paul Cassell, September 25, 2007).

In addition, studies in the United States have shown that African-American victims are often denied equal rights to participate in criminal proceedings, even in the most serious cases (Kennedy 1997, 12–28). Recent moves by state and local officials to enforce federal immigration law appear to have suppressed immigrants' willingness to come forward when they are victims of crime (Kripalani 2000; Wong 1999; Human Rights Watch 2004). Finally, one prosecutor gives the following perspective on possible discrimination against victims of different races, citizenship status, or economic backgrounds:

> By virtue of the complexity of their lives, neutral policies can have a discriminatory effect especially when it comes to language, citizenship status, and economic issues: A victim may not respond to calls from the DA's office, because she is afraid that she will get deported. Recognizing that reality, we've put a lot of measures in place, like Spanish-speaking and Mandarin-speaking advocates. We have a contract with one of the cab companies, and we can have a cab come and pick someone up who can't afford to travel to the office. . . . We also try to explain to victims' employers, explaining that the victim's presence is required. We do the same thing with creditors. But the truth is that sometimes employers don't care and they can still make things uncomfortable for the employee at work. We have neutral policies on all of these issues, but there can still be a disparate impact. (Human Rights Watch interview with Maria Bee, September 14, 2007)

While several aspects of other human rights treaties such as the ICCPR and the Convention on the Elimination of All Forms of Racial Discrimination (CERD) are relevant to the issue of non-discrimination, the Basic Principles for Victims provide a helpful summary:

> The provisions contained herein shall be applicable to all, without distinction of any kind, such as race, colour, sex, age, language, religion, nationality, political or other opinion, cultural beliefs or practices, property, birth or family status, ethnic or social origin, and disability. (Basic Principles for Victims, para. 3)

VI. Recommendations

All US states and localities, the District of Columbia, and the federal government should use the Basic Principles for Victims to inform their laws and policies protecting the rights of crime victims. In particular, all jurisdictions should:

- Ensure that the definition of "victim" in state and federal laws embraces all victims of crime, and does not arbitrarily limit the category in any way.
- Ensure that victim status is accorded to all victims of crime and their family members, irrespective of the degree to which the victim cooperates with the prosecution's pursuit of a particular punishment in the case.
- Commence victims' services once a crime victim has been identified, without regard to whether an individual is arrested or tried for the crime.
- Ensure that the special needs of women and children who are victims of crime are given adequate attention in definitions of victims and in victims' services.
- Give victims adequate notice of their right to receive information about all stages in criminal proceedings and the right to opt out of that information. Ensure that such decisions are not required to be made during periods of trauma for the victim, and that victims may change their minds at any time.
- Compensate victims for the medical and mental health care costs associated with the criminal offense that they or their family members have experienced.
- Lift statutes of limitations on compensation when victims can show new harms arising from their victimization (for example, mental health problems that may surface years after the crime).
- Maintain and enforce standards for the collection and preservation of evidence, particularly rape kit evidence.
- Use the vast array of handbooks and training materials produced by the United Nations and related agencies to inform policies toward crime victims.
- Educate law enforcement personnel and state agencies on the rights of crime victims and their role in ensuring that these rights are respected.

The President of the United States should:

With the consent of the US Senate, ratify the Convention on the Elimination of all Forms of Discrimination against Women (CEDAW) and the Convention on the Rights of the Child (CRC).

* * *

Analysis

The Human Rights Watch Report is rich with significance. The victims' rights in the United States came about without much influence from the outside world. Meanwhile, much of the rest of the world has been engaged in formulating international standards on the rights and interests of crime victims. In this report, the victims' rights in the United States are critiqued through the lens of these international standards.

Previous critiques of victims' rights in the United States have come largely from those in the U.S. who oppose victims' rights in general. Most of the debate has been about whether there should or should not be victims' rights in the American criminal process. That is to say, whether there should be any such rights at all. The Human Rights Watch Report moves the debate to another level. The report points out that international documents favor victims' rights. Relying in part on international documents, the report favors victims' rights in the United States. Moreover, the report favors victims' rights that are enforceable at law. That is, the report favors real, as opposed to aspirational, rights.

Because the report transcends the yes-or-no debate, it is capable of looking more subtly at various aspects of victims' rights in America that may be undesirable or in need of improvement. These aspects are addressed again at the end of the report in the section on recommendations. Furthermore, putting aside the identified flaws in existing victims' rights schemes in the United States, the report is quite supportive of enforceable victims' rights. This is important for several reasons. First, much of the opposition to victims' rights in the United States came from a perspective that there were only two legitimate interests in the criminal process—the state and the defendant. The Human Rights Watch report gives significant legitimacy to the idea that victims' rights are human rights. This legitimacy is provided both in the content of the report as well as the fact that the report comes from such a well-regarded human rights organization.

The Human Rights Watch Report reflects the maturation of victims' rights. Victims' rights are now an international concern. Moreover, domestic rights have come so far in the United States that they are capable of critique via an international lens. Future development and improvement of victims' rights in the United States will benefit from this global perspective.

REFERENCES

18 U.S.C. sec. 3509.
A.H. ex rel Weiss v. Superior Court, 911 P.2d 633, 636 (Ariz. Ct. App. 1996).
Alabama Code, Section 15-23-60(19).
Alaska Statutes, Section 12.55.185(19).
Anonymous victims' rights advocate. Human Rights Watch interview with, Jun. 3, 2008.
Appriss, Inc. "VINE Fact Sheet," http://www.appriss.com/sitedocs/VINECutSheet.pdf, revised May, 2009.
Arizona Constitution, Article II, Section 2.1(C).
Arizona Rules of Criminal Procedure 39 (2007).

Bandoni v. State, 715 A.2d 580 (R.I. 1998).

Bautista v. Colombia, communication No. 563/1993, para. 8.2, CCPR/C/55/D/563/1993 (1995).

Beck, A., D. Gilliard, L. Greenfeld, C. Harlow, T. Hester, L. Jankowski, T. Snell, J. Stephan, and D. Morton. "Survey of State Prison Inmates, 1991." Washington, DC: Bureau of Justice Statistics, 1993. http://bjs.ojp.usdoj.gov/content/pub/pdf/SOSPI91.PDF

Bee, Maria. Human Rights Watch interview with, Sept. 14, 2007.

Beloof, Douglas E. *Constitutional Implications of Crime Victims as Participants*, 88 Cornell L. Rev. 282, 286 (2003).

Beloof, Douglas E. Human Rights Watch interview with, Oct. 2, 2007.

Beloof, Douglas E. *The Third Model of Criminal Process: The Victim Participation Model*, 1999 Utah L. Rev. 289, 328–29 (1999).

Beloof, Douglas E. *The Third Wave of Crime Victims' Rights: Standing Remedy, and Review*, 2005 B.Y.U. L. Rev. 255 (2005).

Beloof, Douglas and Paul Cassell, *The Crime Victim's Right to Attend the Trial: The Reascendant National Consensus*, 9 L & C L. Rev., 481 (2005).

Beloof, Douglas E., Paul G. Cassell, and Steven J. Twist. *Victims In Criminal Procedure*. Durham, NC: Carolina Academic Press, 2006.

Caggiano v. Commonwealth, 550 N.E.2d 389 (1990).

California Constitution, Article 1, Section 28.

Cassell, Paul. Human Rights Watch interview with, Sept. 25, 2007.

Catalano, Shannan M. "Criminal Victimization, 2005." Washington, DC: Bureau of Justice Statistics, September 2006.

Colorado Revised Statutes, sec. 18-1.3-602(4)(a)(V).

Commissioner of Corps. & Taxation v. Chilton Club, 61 N.E.2d 335 (1945).

Commissioner of Revenue v. Cargill, Inc., 706 N.E.2d 625 (1999).

Commonwealth v. Amirault, 677 N.E.2d 652 (1997).

Commonwealth v. Beal, 709 N.E.2d 413 (1999).

Commonwealth v. Bing Sial Liang, 747 N.E.2d 112 (2001).

Commonwealth v. Gonsalves, 739 N.E.2d 1100 (2000).

Commonwealth v. Russ R., 744 N.E.2d 39 (2001).

Costarelli v. Commonwealth, 374 Mass. 677 (1978).

Cushing, Renny. Human Rights Watch interview with, Aug. 28, 2007.

Delaware Code, Title 11, Section 9410(5).

Delaware Code Annotated, Title 11, Section 4331(g).

Dix v. Superior Court, 807 P.2d 1063 (Cal. 1991).

Doe v. U.S., 666 F.2d 43 (4th Cir. 1981).

First Nat'l Bank v. Judge Baker Guidance Ctr., 431 N.E.2d 243 (1982).

Florida Constitution, Article. I, Section 16.

Garvin, Meg. Human Rights Watch interview with, Oct. 2, 2007.

General Laws of Massachusetts, c. 258B.

Georgia Code Annotated, Section 17-17-3(11).

Gillis, John and Douglas Beloof. *The Next Step for a Maturing Victim Rights Movement: Enforcing Crime Victim Rights in the Courts*, 33 McGeorge L. Rev. 689 (2002).

Hagen v. Commonwealth, 722 NE.2d 32 (Ma. 2002).

Henderson, Lynne. *Revisiting Victims' Rights*, 1999 Utah L. Rev. 383 (1999).

Human Rights Watch. "Letter to US Senate and House of Representatives regarding the 'Clear Law Enforcement for Criminal Alien Removal Act of 2003' (CLEAR) and the 'Homeland Security Enhancement Act of 2003' (HSEA)." April 21, 2004.

Human Rights Watch. *Mixed Results: US Adherence to International Standards on the Rights and Interests of Crime Victims* New York: Human Rights Watch, 2008.

Human Rights Watch. *The Rest of Their Lives: Life without Parole for Child Offenders in the United States*. New York: Human Rights Watch, 2005.

Illinois Compiled Statutes 120/3, Section 725 (a).

Indiana Code, section 35-40-12-1.

Innocence Project, The. "Fact Sheet: Preservation of Evidence." http://www.innocence project.org/Content/253.php#

In re Alton D., 994 P.2d 402, 406 (Ariz. 2000).

In re Walling, 91 Ohio Misc. 2d 181, 698 N.E.2d 154, 1997 Ohio Misc. LEXIS 335 (Ct. Cl. 1997).

International Covenant on Civil and Political Rights (ICCPR), adopted December 16, 1966, G.A. Res. 2200A (XXI), 21 U.N. GAOR Supp. (No. 16) at 52, U.N. Doc. A/6316 (1966), 999 U.N.T.S. 171, entered into force March 23, 1976.

Iowa Code, Section 915.10(3).

Jenkins, Jennifer B. Human Rights Watch interview with, Aug. 28, 2007.

Jenkins, Jennifer B. Human Rights Watch email communication with, Nov. 3, 2007.

Kennedy, Randall. *Race, Crime, and the Law*. New York: Random House, 1997.

Knight, Marsha. "A Proposed Constitutional Amendment to Protect Victims of Crime," statement at hearings on S.J. Res. 6, 105th Congress, 1997.

Kripalani, Jasmine. "Hispanics Unlikely to Report Crime, Police Say." *Memphis Commercial Appeal*, August 7, 2000.

Louisiana Revised Statutes, Section 46:1842(9).

Lynn v. Reinstein, 68 P.3d 412 (Ariz. 2003).

Maine Revised Statutes Annotated, Title 17-A, Section 1171.

Marbury v. Madison, 5 U.S. 137 (1803).

Michigan Compiled Laws, Section 780.752, Subsection 2(1)(l).

Michigan Constitution, Article I.

Mississippi Code Annotated, Section 99-36-3.

Moffeit, Miles & Susan Greene. "Room for Error in Evidence Vaults," *Denver Post*, July 23, 2007. http://www.denverpost.com/evidence/ci_6439646

Moffeit, Miles & Susan Greene. "Trashing the Truth (Evidence Project)," *Denver Post*, July 21–24, 2007. http://www.denverpost.com/evidence

Murder Victims' Families for Reconciliation, "Dignity Denied: The Experience of Murder Victims' Family Members Who Oppose the Death Penalty," August 2002.

National Conference of State Legislatures. "Victims' Rights Laws in the States, Table 4: Victim Notice of Rights of Events in Criminal Proceedings." 2004.

National Conference of State Legislatures. "Victims' Rights Laws in the States, Table 5: Victim Participation." 2004.

National Conference of State Legislatures. "Victims' Rights Laws in the States, Table 6: Production and Confidentiality." 2004.

National Conference of State Legislatures. "Victims' Rights Laws in the States, Table 8: Victim Compensation." 2004.

New Hampshire Revised Statutes Annotated, Section 21-M:8-k.

New Jersey Constitution, Article I.

New Mexico Statutes Annotated, Section 31-26-3(F).

Office for Victims of Crime, President's Task Force on Victims of Crime, Final Report. Washington, DC: U.S. Government Printing Press, 1982.

Office for Victims of Crime, *Victims' Rights Compliance Efforts: Experiences in Three States*. Washington, DC: United States Office of Justice Programs, 1998.

Ohio Revised Code Annotated, Section 2930.02.

Oregon Constitution, Article 1, Section 42.

Oregon Revised Statutes, Section 419A.004(31).

People v. Nestrock, 735 N.E.2d 1101, 1109 (Ill. App. ct. 2000), appeal denied, 747 N.E.2d 332 (Ill. 2000).

People v. Stringham, 253 Cal. Rptr. 484 (Cal. Ct. App. 1988).

People v. Valdez, 30 Cal. Rptr. 2d 4 (Cal. Ct. App. 1994).

Reese, Carolyn. "The Implementation of the UN Declaration of Basic Principles of Justice for Victims of Crime and Abuse of Power in France." *The Victimologist*, vol. 4, no. 1 (May 2000).

Riley, Donald E. "DNA Testing: An Introduction for Non-Scientists," *Scientific Testimony: An Online Journal*, April 6, 2005. http://www.scientific.org/tutorials/articles/riley/riley.html

Siegleman, Don and Courtney W. Tarver, *Victims Rights in State Constitutions*, 1 Emerg. Iss. St. Const. L. 163, 163–173 (1988).

South Dakota Codified Laws, Section 23A-28C-4.

State ex rel. Dean v. City of Tucson, 844 P.2d 1165, 1167 (Ariz. Ct. App. 1992)

State ex rel. Hilbig v. McDonald, 839 S.W.2d 854 (Tex. App. 1992).

State v. Broberg, 677 A.2d 602 (Md.1996).

State v. Gonzales, 912 P.2d 297 (Ariz. 1996).

State v. Lamar, 72 P.3d 831 (Ariz. 2003).

State v. O'Neil, 836 P.2d 393, 394 (Ariz. Ct. App. 1991).

State v. Robinson, No. C1-02-1957 2003 WL 21694412 (Minn. Ct. App. Jul. 22, 2003).

State v. Roscoe, 912 P.2d 1297 (Ariz. 1996).

State v. Rymer, 2001 WI Ct. App. 31U, P 16, 622 N.W.2d 770, cert. denied, 2001 WI 15, 626 N.W.2d 807 (2001).

State v. Timmendequas, 737 A.2d 55 (1999).

Stein, John H. "Oregon Surprises Activists, Victims' Rights Movement Moving Again," in *The Crime Victims Report*. New York: Civic Research Institute, 2007.

Taylor v. Newton Div. of the Dist. Court Dep't, 622 N.E.2d 261 (1993).

Texas Code of Criminal Procedure Annotated Article 42.03.

Tribe, Laurence H. *A Black Hole for Victims' Rights*, 9 Lewis and Clark L. Rev. 665 (2005).

UN Economic and Social Council, Commission on Crime Prevention and Criminal Justice. *Report of the Secretary General on Use and Application of the Declaration of Basic Principles of Justice for Victims of Crime and Abuse of Power*. United Nations: UN Economic Social Council, 1996.

UN Economic and Social Council. *Guidelines on Justice in Matters Involving Child Victims and Witnesses of Crime*. Resolution 2005/20, annex, July 22, 2005.

UN General Assembly. *Code of Conduct for Law Enforcement Officials*. General Assembly Resolution 34/169, annex, December 17, 1979.

UN General Assembly. *Crime Prevention and Criminal Justice Measures to Eliminate Violence Against Women*. General Assembly Resolution 52/86, annex, December 12, 1997.

UN General Assembly. *Declaration of Basic Principles of Justice for Victims of Crime and Abuse of Power*. General Assembly Resolution 40/34, November 29, 1985.

UN General Assembly. *International Code of Conduct for Public Officials*. General Assembly Resolution 51/59, annex, December 12, 1996.

UN General Assembly. *Principles of Medical Ethics relevant to the Role of Health Personnel, particularly Physicians, in the Protection of Prisoners and Detainees against Torture and Other Cruel, Inhuman or Degrading Treatment or Punishment*. General Assembly Resolution 37/194, annex, December 18, 1982.

UN Office for Drug Control and Crime Prevention. *Handbook on Justice for Victims on the Use and Application of the Declaration of Basic Principles of Justice for Victims of Crime and Abuse of Power*. New York: United Nations, 1999.

U.S. Department of Justice, Office of Justice Programs (OJP). *Final Program Guidelines for Victims of Crime Act Victim Assistance Grant Program*. Washington, DC: U.S. Government Printing Press, 1996.

Utah Code Annotated, Section 77-38-2(9)(a).

Van Dijk, Jan. "Victims Rights in International Criminal Law." January 21, 2006. http://www.tilburguniversity.nl/intervict/news/06-01-19-paper.pdf

Vermont Statutes Annotated, Title 13, Section 5301(4).

Victory Distribs., Inc. v. Ayer Div. of the Dist. Court Dep't, 755 N.E.2d 273 (2001).

Virginia Code Annotated, Section 19.2-295.3.

Wong, Doris Sue. "Gaps Seen in Help for Abused Immigrants." *Boston Globe*, June 23, 1999.

Additional Reading

Fletcher, George P. *With Justice for Some: Protecting Victims' Rights in Criminal Trials*. Boston, MA: Addison Wesley, 1995.

Groenhuijsen, Marc, and Rianne Letschert, eds. *Compilation of International Victims' Rights Instruments*. Netherlands: Wolf Legal Publishers, 2006.

National Crime Victim Law Institute. NCVLI Library of Legal Resources. Accessed June 18, 2011. http://www.lclark.edu/law/centers/national_crime_victim_law_institute/professional_resources/ncvli_library/

Tobolowsky, Peggy M., Mario T. Gaboury, Arrick L. Jackson, and Ashley G. Blackburn. *Crime Victim Rights and Remedies*. 2nd edition. Durham, NC: Carolina Academic Press, 2009.

CONCLUSION

In colonial America and well into the early years of the United States of America, crime victims were directly prosecuting criminal actions. Over the course of a century, the role of victims was diminished to that of a mere witnesses. Victims could not attend the trials of their victimizers, could not speak at sentencing, and could not give their opinions on plea bargains.

In the 1970s, the dissatisfaction had reached a breaking point, and the Victims' Rights Movement was born. In the years since then, the Movement has made significant strides in law reform. Victims have rights of participation, privacy safeguards, and protections in the criminal process. The Movement is described as occurring in three waves. The First Wave was statutory rights for victims. Some states are still in the First Wave. The Second Wave involved enacting state constitutional crime victims' rights. There are currently 33 states with constitutional victims' rights. The Third Wave is an effort to ensure that the laws of the First and Second Wave are enforceable.

The constitutional amendment effort is an effort to establish enforceable, uniform rights throughout the United States. That effort was delayed to determine the results of the Crime Victims' Rights Act, an experimental federal statute. The enforceability of the CVRA is an issue that awaits final determination by the United States Supreme Court. So far, the federal circuit court decisions interpreting the CVRA have been very mixed.

Meanwhile, the states of California and Oregon have joined the Third Wave by providing remedies for violations of victims' rights. In addition, Human Rights Watch issued a significant report providing important criticism but essentially supporting American victims' rights.

The future of victims' rights probably involves a return to the federal constitutional amendment effort.

Should this occur, it will likely be because the Movement has established the following:

1. Victims' rights are such a fundamental value that they should be in the Constitution.

   Three-quarters of the states must ratify a crime victims' rights amendment to the United States Constitution. Thirty-three of the states have already enacted constitutional rights for crime victims. The nation as a whole has recognized the substantial value of crime victims' rights as fundamental to fairness. It is fitting that the Constitution should embody this value.

2. The entrenched justice system will not become more victim centered unless there is a federal victims' rights amendment.

   Criminal defendants' rights apply in every jurisdiction in the country. The statutory federal Crime Victims' Rights Act only applies in federal prosecutions. There can be no balanced criminal process in America until victims' rights are mandated in the United States Constitution.

3. The Crime Victims' Rights Act has proven to be largely ineffective in enforcing victims' rights in court.

   Increasingly, federal appellate courts are interpreting the CVRA to provide little in the way of remedy or review for victims' rights. For example, under the CVRA, federal courts have permitted the justice department to engage in secret plea agreements made without the victims' knowledge; refuse to consult with victims; and refuse to provide information to victims that would ensure victim status under the CVRA. Additionally, a majority of federal courts have decided that the CVRA provides relief to victims only in clear and indisputable circumstances—circumstances that will rarely exist. This essentially makes the statute unenforceable in federal courts.

4. Is the CVRA a failed experiment?

   In 1984, President Reagan's Crime Victims' Task Force recommended a victims' rights amendment to the United States Constitution. In the late 1900s and early 2000s, both Presidents Clinton and Bush (II) advocated for a victims' rights amendment. In 2004, in exchange for putting off the constitutional amendment, victims agreed to a statutory experiment: the CVRA. A strong argument can be made that the CVRA is a failed experiment, as courts are not enforcing it, the Justice Department is working to undercut it, and it applies to only to 2 percent of prosecutions. Many state amendments have even weaker enforcement mechanisms than the CVRA. A well drafted federal amendment will ensure enforcement of victims' rights.

What is clear is that the effort to establish enforceable victims' rights is ongoing and far from complete, and it will be up to the next generation to determine the proper role of victims in the criminal process and how those rights will be enforced.

INDEX

Academic victim services programs, 31–32
Addams, Jane, 21
Against Our Will: Men, Women and Rape (Brownmiller), 23
Alabama, laws and constitution of, 10, 33, 221, 282, 290
Alaska, laws and constitution of, 10, 33, 290
Alienation, victims', 49–51
Amber Alerts, 1
American Bar Association: defendants' rights stance of, 179; Victim Witness Project guidelines, 79, 80–82, 174
American Society for the Prevention of Cruelty to Animals, 21
Anthony, Susan B., 21
Antiwar movement, 22
Antrobus, In re, 231, 238–50
Arizona: constitution of, 10, 33, 262, 263, 264–65; victim defined in, 282; victim participation in, 10, 289; victims' rights violations redress in, 226, 274–75; victims' right to refuse defense interview in, 290
Arkansas, laws of, 10, 218, 291
Attorney General's Task Force on Family Violence, 79
Attorney General's Task Force on Violent Crime, 27, 28

Bail hearings: Eighth Amendment excessive bail constraints, 164; President's Task Force recommendations on, 72, 74–75; safety of victim considered in, 153–54, 163–64; victim notification of, 143, 215; victim participation in, 57, 148–49, 159, 215–17
Bail Reform Act (1984), 75, 216
Bard, Morton, *The Crime Victim's Book*, 26
Beccaria, Cesare, *Essay on Crimes and Punishment*, 14, 89
Bell, Virginia, 142
Biden, Joseph, 138, 139, 184
Blackstone, *Commentaries on the Laws of England*, 4–5
Booth v. Maryland (1987), 5–6, 83–84, 87–89, 90–93, 94–97, 99–100
Brownmiller, Susan, *Against Our Will: Men, Women and Rape*, 23
Burgess, Ann, 26
Bush administration, 208, 211, 304
Byron, Mary, 151

California: constitution of, 10, 33, 74, 263, 273, 277–78; evidence preservation in, 291; victim compensation program in, 24, 273, 293; Victim Participation Model under laws of, 10; victims' courtroom seating in, 221; victim

service provider credentialing in, 31; victims' rights determination under laws of, 4, 10, 24, 218, 221, 273, 277–78, 293; victims' right to attend trial in, 218
Campbell, Collene, 137
Capital cases. *See* Death penalty cases
Carrington, Frank, 25, 27
Cassell, Paul: on Constitutional amendment, 137, 138, 139, 142, 170, 187, 189, 196–98; on Crime Victims' Rights Act, 222, 238
Center for the Study of Crime Victims' Rights, Remedies, and Resources, 32
Chemerinsky, Erwin, 193, 195, 196
Christian, Sharon, 142, 150–51
Civil libertarians, 54, 59, 60
Civil process, 14, 41–42, 43
Civil rights movement, 21–22, 53
Clinton administration, 140, 188, 304
Colorado, laws and constitution of, 10, 33
Commentaries on the Laws of England (Blackstone), 4–5
Common law, 2, 15–16, 115–16, 153, 229, 230, 231, 242, 252, 261
Community Crisis Response Teams, 29
Connecticut, laws and constitution of, 10, 16, 31–32, 33, 291
Constitution, U.S.: *Booth v. Maryland* (1987) interpretation of, 5–6,

83–84, 87–89, 90–93, 94–97, 99–100; civil rights under, 22; defendants' rights under, 44, 72, 75, 98, 151, 154–55, 161, 162–63, 179–82, 194, 197, 199–202, 228–29 (*see also* Due process); Double Jeopardy Clause of, 228–29; Eighteenth Amendment to, 168; Eighth Amendment to, 5–6, 84, 87, 88, 91, 93–95, 98, 99, 164, 289; equal protection under, 112, 181; Fifteenth Amendment to, 140; Fifth Amendment to, 218; First Amendment to, 76, 200, 201; Fourteenth Amendment to, 92, 94, 107, 110, 112, 191, 223; Fourth Amendment to, 72, 75, 191, 192; Nineteenth Amendment to, 140; Ninth Amendment, 200–201; *Payne v. Tennessee* (1991) interpretation of, 5–6, 83, 84–101, 160; President's Task Force proposed amendment to, 73, 76–77, 136–37, 304; private prosecutions under, 106–11; Sixth Amendment to, 151, 181, 200, 223, 290–91; *South Carolina v. Gathers* (1989) interpretation of, 84, 87–88, 88–89, 91, 93, 94, 96, 99; standing under, 112–17, 121–32, 134; Twenty-first Amendment to, 168; Twenty-sixth Amendment to, 140; victim impact statement constitutionality, 5–6, 83–106, 289; victims' rights, Constitutional amendment efforts on (*see* Crime Victims' Rights Constitutional Amendment); victims' rights, Constitutional context of, 83–117, 289; victims' rights exclusion from, 3; women's voting rights under, 22

Constitutions, state: broad state constitutional rights, 261–62; defendants' rights under, 10–11, 44, 262, 263–65; President's Task Force leading to amendments to, 73–74, 137; remedy enforcement under, 271, 273, 274–75, 278; specific state constitutional rights, 263–65; Victim Participation Model under, 7–8, 10–11; victims'

rights under, 3, 5, 7–8, 10–11, 30, 33, 73–74, 130, 137, 143, 261–65, 271–78, 303, 304; victims' standing under, 271–78

Convicted offenders. *See* Defendants and convicted offenders

Courts. *See* Judges and courts

Crime Control Model, 5, 6–7

Crime victims. *See* Victims; Victims' rights

The Crime Victim's Book (Bard and Sangrey), 26

Crime Victims Fund, 28, 30

Crime Victims Project, 79

Crime Victims' Rights Act (CVRA/2004): analysis of, 214–38; *Antrobus, In re* interpretation of, 231, 238–50; bail hearing-related rights under, 215–17; as Crime Victims' Rights Constitutional Amendment statutory alternative, 202, 207–11, 303, 304; *Dean, In re* interpretation of, 229–30, 250–56; enforcement remedies under, 224, 225–29, 304; funding for implementation of, 231; *Kenna v. United States District Court for the Central District of Columbia* interpretation of, 230, 231, 232–38; limitations of, 227–29, 304; parole-related rights under, 224; plea and sentencing-related rights under, 221–24, 232–38, 240–56; President's Task Force leading to, 73–74, 77; restitution or damages under, 224, 227–28; text of, 211–14; trial-related rights under, 217–21; victims' courtroom seating under, 220–21; victims' emotional courtroom displays under, 220; victims' rights at different stages of criminal process under, 215–17; victims' right to fairness, dignity, and privacy under, 223, 224–25; victims' standing under, 131–32, 227; victims' *vs.* defendants' rights under, 215–17, 223–24, 227; writ of mandamus under, 210, 226–27, 229–31, 233, 236–56

Crime Victims' Rights Constitutional Amendment: background and

legislative history of, 136–39; criminal process rights notification under, 154, 164; damages from government restrictions under, 166, 192; exceptions under, 167–68; federalism principles in, 144–45, 183, 184, 185–86, 198; future of victims' rights and, 271–72, 303–4; inadequacy of victims' rights without, 141–42, 143–44, 303–4; legislative enforcement of, 166; need for constitutional protection, 139–40; negative potential consequences of, 168–84, 189–96; participatory rights protection under, 140–41; President's Task Force recommendation for, 73, 76–77, 136–37, 304; purpose of, 135–36; right to attend under, 146–48, 158, 180–81; right to be heard under, 148–50, 158–61, 181; right to have safety considered under, 153–54, 163–64; right to notice of proceedings under, 145–46, 157–58; right to notice of release/escape under, 150–51, 161–62; right to order of restitution under, 152–53, 163; right to victim's consideration in delayed trial under, 151–52, 162–63, 181; scholarly debate on, 187–202; section-by-section analysis of, 154–68; Senate majority report on, 135–68; Senate minority report on, 168–84; states' rights impacted under, 182–83; statistical quantification of victims' rights violations in, 143–44; statutory alternative to, 202, 207–11, 303, 304; support for, 135–68, 187–89, 196–202, 271–72, 303–4; text of, 133; victim participation denial, examples of, in, 142–43; victims defined under, 155–57; victims' right to challenge decisions under, 165–66; victims' standing under, 164–65, 271–72; victims' *vs.* defendants' rights in, 154–55, 161, 162–63, 179–82, 194, 197, 199–202; vote on, 168

Crime Victims' Rights Movement. *See also* Victims' rights: advancing advocacy in, 32–34; antiwar movement influence on, 22; civil libertarians *vs.*, 54, 59, 60; civil rights movement influence on, 21–22, 53; conflict and unstable funding in, 26–27; Constitutional victims' rights amendment efforts of (*see* Crime Victims' Rights Constitutional Amendment); emerging professionalism in, 30–32; future of, 270–78, 303–4; history of, 1–2, 4, 20–34, 53–54, 111–17; law and order movement influence on, 23–24, 53–54; legislative changes during, 24, 25, 27, 28–29, 30; mental health support in, 25–26, 29; opposition to, 4, 16, 52–60; present status of, 261–69; President's Task Force on Victims of Crime boosting, 28, 32, 63–82; public awareness in, 27–30; stages of, 24–34; victims' assistance program development in, 24–26, 53; women's movement influence on, 21, 22–23, 53, 60
Crime Victims United, 275
Crime Victims With Disabilities Awareness Act, 173
Criminal Appeals Act, 124
Criminal fraud, 16–17
Criminal process: bail hearings in (*see* Bail hearings); civil *vs.*, 14, 41–42, 43; defendants in (*see* Defendants and convicted offenders); defined, 41; due process in (*see* Due process); evidence in (*see* Evidence); laws and statutes in (*see* Laws and statutes); models underlying (*see* Models); notifications in (*see* Notifications); parole hearings in (*see* Parole board hearings); plea bargains in (*see* Plea bargains); public prosecutors in (*see* Public prosecutors); secondary victimization of victims in, 8, 29, 48, 65–71, 78, 139; sentencing in (*see* Sentencings); standing in (*see* Standing); trials in (*see* Trial); victims' participation in

(*see* Victim participation); victims' rights in (*see* Victims' rights)
Critical Incident Stress Debriefings, 29
CVRA. *See* Crime Victims' Rights Act

Damages or compensation: civil process addressing, 14, 41–42, 43; Crime Victims Fund for, 28, 30; Crime Victims' Rights Act on, 224, 227–28; Human Rights Watch report on, 284–85, 291–93; Mandatory Victim Restitution Act on, 153, 163, 172; President's Task Force recommendations on, 72, 76, 153; proposed Constitutional amendment on, 134, 152–53, 163, 166, 192; state and federal programs for, 24, 28, 30, 273, 284–85, 292–93; state constitutional rights on, 263–64, 265, 273; victims' right to, 12–13, 14, 15, 24, 28, 30, 41–42, 43, 72, 76, 134, 152–53, 163, 166, 172, 192, 224, 227–28, 263–64, 265, 273, 284–85, 291–93
Dean, In re, 229–30, 250–56
Death penalty cases: evolving due process standards in, 106–10; victim impact statements in, 5–6, 83–101, 289; victims' right to attend trial in, 130
Dees, Morris, 110
Defendants and convicted offenders: Constitutional rights of, 10–11, 44, 72, 75, 98, 151, 154–55, 161, 162–63, 179–82, 194, 197, 199–202, 228–29, 262, 263–65; Crime Victims' Rights Act on victims' *vs.* defendants' rights, 215–17, 223–24, 227; criminal process involving (*see* Criminal process); damages paid by (*see* Damages or compensation; Remedies); due process for (*see* Due process); fairness to, victim exclusion as, 44, 180–81; full party standing of, 3; notifications related to (*see* Notifications); presumption of innocence, 180, 216; prison system for, 15, 158, 282; victims' interest subordinate to, 16, 276–77

Delaware, laws of, 10, 281, 289
Department of Justice. *See* Justice Department, U.S.
Dignity of victims: Crime Victims' Rights Act on, 223, 224–25; international standards on, 294; state constitutional rights on, 261–62; Victim Participation Model on, 8, 10–11
Discrimination, protection from, 295–97
District attorneys. *See* Public prosecutors
Doell, Steve, 275
Domestic violence cases: battered women's shelter for, 25; grassroot organization agendas addressing, 26–27, 28–29; mental health support for victims of, 26; National Domestic Violence Hotline, 32; notification of release/escape in, 151; police pressure in, 56; state laws addressing, 27, 28–29; victim definition challenges in, 283; women's movement addressing, 23
Double Jeopardy Clause, 228–29
Doyle, Jim, 138
Due process: Due Process Model, 5, 6–7; evolving, Constitutional interpretation and, 106–11; Fourteenth Amendment Due Process Clause, 92, 94, 107, 110, 223; opposition to victims' rights based on, 54, 59, 218; private prosecution impact on, 106–11; state constitutional/statutory rights on, 10–11, 262, 263–65; victim impact statements at sentencing impact on, 92, 94, 96
Durbin, Richard, 139, 184

Early, Norm, 139
East v. Scott (1995), 101–6
Educational victim services programs, 31–32
Edwards, Donna F., 138
Eighteenth Amendment, 168
Eighth Amendment: excessive bail constraints under, 164; victim impact statement at sentencing constitutionality under, 5–6, 84, 87, 88, 91, 93–95, 98, 99, 289

Elledge, Mary, 275
Enforcement remedies. *See* Remedies
English law, 4–5, 12–14, 15–16, 40, 43, 89
Enlightenment, 13–14
Equal protection/Equal Protection Clause, 112, 181
Essay on Crimes and Punishment (Beccaria), 14, 89
Evidence: destruction and preservation of, 291; Federal Rules of Evidence, 9, 19, 111, 217; privileged, victims' protection of, 2; victims' presentation of, 290–91

Fairness: to defendants, 44, 180–81; to victims, 8, 10–11, 46–47, 77, 223, 224–25, 261–62
FBI *Uniform Crime Report*, 25, 27–28
Federal government: Constitution of (*see* Constitution, U.S.); federalism principles impacting, 144–45, 183, 184, 185–86, 198; Justice Department of (*see* Justice Department, U.S.); laws of (*see* Laws and statutes); Oklahoma City Bombing victims' rights failure under, 121–32, 147–48, 289; President's Task Force on Victims of Crime recommendations to, 71–77, 78–80, 146, 153, 158; victim assistance programs by, 25, 27, 28, 29, 30; victim compensation programs under, 28, 30; Victim Participation Model under laws of, 7–8, 10; victims' rights determination under laws of, 3, 5, 7–8, 10, 28, 172–74 (*see also* *specific laws*)
Federal Rules of Evidence (FRE), 9, 19, 111, 217
Federal Sentencing Guidelines, 89
Fein, Bruce, 137, 176, 190
Feingold, Russell, 184
Feinstein, Dianne: Constitutional amendment position of, 33, 137, 138, 173, 187; Crime Victims' Rights Act position of, 208, 209, 226, 235
Fifteenth Amendment, 140
Fifth Amendment, 218
First Amendment, 76, 200, 201

Fisher, Raymond C., 139
Florida, laws and constitution of, 10, 31, 33, 263, 291
Force 100, 208
Fourteenth Amendment: Due Process Clause, 92, 94, 107, 110, 223; Equal Protection Clause, 112; search and seizure under, 191
Fourth Amendment, 72, 75, 191, 192
Fry, Margery, 24

Gallagher, Connie, 273–74, 277
Garvin, Margaret, 280
Georgia, laws of, 10, 291
Gillis, John, 233
Goldsmith, Rita, 137

Hagen v. Commonwealth (2002), 267–69
Haight-Herrington, Lois, 28, 77–79
Hate crime cases, 30, 57
Hawaii, laws of, 10
Heiser, Scott, 274, 275, 277
Henderson, Lynne, 138, 170, 193, 195, 196
Heymann, Philip, 182
Higgins, Stephen, 222
History of victim's rights: American correctional reform, 14–19; colonial American, 12–14, 15–16; Constitutional amendment efforts (*see* Crime Victims' Rights Constitutional Amendment); Crime Victims' Rights Movement history, 1–2, 4, 20–34, 53–54, 111–17; Enlightenment period, 13–14; overview of, 1–5; professional police role emergence, 17–19; public prosecutor role emergence, 15–17, 40; social justice movement influence on, 20–24; Victim Participation Model, 5–9, 10–11; victim participation overview, 1, 2, 3, 5–9, 10–11, 12–34, 39–46, 111–17; victim removal from criminal process, 9, 12, 13–19, 39–46, 111
Hubbard, Ralph, 137
Hullinger, Robert and Charlotte, 27
Human Rights Watch Report on Victims' Rights in America, 280–98; ability to participate in,

288–90; access to information in, 286–88; access to prompt redress in, 284–85; crime victim defined in, 281–84; expeditious and fair procedures in, 293–95; participation through evidence presentation in, 290–91; protection for other rights of victims in, 295–97; restitution and compensation provision in, 291–93
Humphreys, Robert J., 138
Hyde, Henry, 137

ICCPR (International Covenant on Civil and Political Rights), 285, 293, 295
Idaho, laws and constitution of, 10, 33, 290
Illinois: constitution of, 10, 33, 262, 263, 278; evidence preservation in, 291; Victim Participation Model under laws of, 10; victim services in, 293
Indiana, laws and constitution of, 10, 33, 226
Information, victims' access to, 286–88. *See also* Notifications
International Code of Conduct for Public Officials, 294
International victims' rights standards, 32, 283, 284–85, 290, 293–95, 298
Iowa, laws of, 10

Judges and courts: discretion and latitude allowed, 2, 3, 4, 266, 271; review mechanisms of, 271; sentencing by (*see* Sentencings); sequestration power of, 121–32, 146–48; standing in court (*see* Standing); victim addressing, 8 (*see also* Victim participation); victims' rights enforcement by, 3–4, 271, 274–75, 278–80, 304. (*see also* Remedies); victims' rights opposition by, 4, 54, 55, 57–59
Jurisdictional issues, 266
Justice Department, U.S.: Constitution amendment stance of, 178, 179, 182, 183, 188, 192; Crime Victims' Rights Act weakening by, 229, 231, 238–56,

304; notification issues reports by, 146, 151; Office for Victims of Crime, 28, 29, 32, 79, 80, 174, 175, 233; Office of Justice Programs, 77; "substantially equivalent" victims' rights law defined by, 209; victims' right to attend trial position of, 49, 131, 147

Justice for All Act, 202

Kansas, laws and constitution of, 10, 31, 34

Kempe, C. Henry, 22

Kenna v. United States District Court for the Central District of Columbia, 230, 231, 232–38

Kennedy, Edward "Ted," 139, 168, 184

Kennedy administration, 21

Kentucky, laws of, 10, 291

Kight, Marsha, 138

King, Martin Luther, Jr., 21

Kohl, Herb, 139, 168, 184

Kreneck, Kathleen, 139

Kyl, Jon: Constitutional amendment position of, 33, 137, 138, 168, 173, 187; Crime Victims' Rights Act position of, 208–9, 222, 225, 226, 235

Lamb, Cindy, 27

Larson, Kimberly, 276

LaWall, Barbara, 138

Law and order movement, 23–24, 53–54

Law Enforcement Assistance Administration (LEAA), 25, 26

Laws and statutes. *See also* Federal government; State governments: Bail Reform Act (1984), 75, 216; Crime Victims' Rights Act (CVRA/2004), 73–74, 77, 131–32, 202, 207–56, 303, 304; Crime Victims With Disabilities Awareness Act, 173; Criminal Appeals Act, 124; Justice for All Act, 202; Mandatory Victim Restitution Act (1996), 153, 163, 172; Marsy's Law For All, 278; President's Task Force on Victims of Crime recommendations for, 71–77, 78–80, 146, 153, 158; Speedy Trial Act (1974), 163,

227; Victim and Witness Protection Act (1972), 28, 129, 153, 172; Victims of Crime Act (VOCA/1984), 28, 29, 30, 172, 282; Victims' Rights and Restitution Act (1990), 128–29, 131, 172; Victims' Rights Clarification Act (1997), 130–31, 147, 173; Violence Against Women Act (1994), 172

Leahy, Patrick, 139, 168, 184, 208, 209, 210, 227

Legal representation, victims', 4, 278–80, 290

Legislative Sourcebook, 32

Lightner, Candy, 24, 27

Linda R.S. v. Richard D. (1973), 111–17

Louisiana: constitution of, 10, 34; evidence preservation in, 291; victim defined in, 283; victims' courtroom seating in, 221; Victims Participation Model under laws of, 10; victims' right to refuse defense interview in, 290

Luttig, Michael, 101–6

Lynn, Duane, 289

MADD (Mothers Against Drunk Driving), 27, 31, 137, 149, 208

Maine, laws of, 10, 291

Mandamus. *See* Writ of mandamus

Mandatory Victim Restitution Act (1996), 153, 163, 172

Marsy's Law For All, 278

Maryland, laws and constitution of, 10, 34, 226, 262, 291

Massachusetts, laws of, 10, 266–69

McVeigh, United States v. (1997), 121–32, 173, 289

Media, 27–30

Mental health support, 25–26, 29, 294

Michigan: constitution of, 10, 34, 263–64; evidence preservation in, 291; victim defined in, 282; victim service provider credentialing in, 32; Victims Participation Model under laws of, 10; victims' rights violations redress in, 226

Milk, Harvey, 187

Minnesota, laws of, 10, 27

Minorities and marginalized people: civil rights movement of, 21–22,

53; victimization of, 44, 59, 143–44, 295–97

Missing persons cases, 56

Mississippi, laws and constitution of, 10, 34

Missouri, laws and constitution of, 10, 34

Models: Crime Control Model, 5, 6–7; Due Process Model, 5, 6–7; Victim Participation Model, 5–9, 10–11

Montana, laws and constitution of, 10, 34, 291

Mosteller, Robert, 139, 170, 189, 192, 193, 196

Mothers Against Drunk Driving (MADD), 27, 31, 137, 149, 208

Movements, historical: antiwar movement, 22; civil rights movement, 21–22, 53; Crime Victims' Rights Movement (*see* Crime Victims' Rights Movement); law and order movement, 23–24, 53–54; women's movement, 21, 22–23, 53, 60

Myers, Hardy, 274, 275, 277, 278

National Advocate Credentialing Program (NACP), 32

National Center for the Victims of Crime, 32

National Center on Child Abuse and Neglect, 22

National Clearinghouse for the Defense of Battered Women, 171

National Coalition Against Domestic Violence (NCADV), 26

National Coalition Against Sexual Assault (NCASA), 26

National Crime (Victimization) Survey, 25

National Crime Victim Law Institute (NCVLI), 4, 31, 275, 280

National Criminal Justice Association, 174

National District Attorneys Association, 177, 179

National Domestic Violence Hotline, 32

National Governors Association, 137, 144

National Network to End Domestic Violence, 138

National Organization for Victim
    Assistance (NOVA), 25, 29, 31,
    137, 139, 142, 208, 273
National Victim Assistance Academy
    (NVAA), 32
National Victim Assistance Standards
    Consortium, 32
National Victim Center, 143, 174–75
National Victim Constitutional
    Amendment Network
    (NVCAN), 133, 137, 139, 210–11
National Victim Constitutional
    Amendment Passage (NVCAP),
    273, 277
National Victims' Rights Week, 27
Nebraska, laws and constitution of,
    10, 34, 291
Nevada, laws and constitution of, 10,
    34, 218, 226
New Directions from the Field: Victims'
    Rights and Services for the 21st
    Century, 32
New Hampshire, laws of, 11, 291, 292
New Jersey, laws and constitution of,
    11, 34, 262
New Mexico, laws and constitution of,
    11, 34, 262, 291
New York, laws of, 11
Nicholas, Henry, 278
Nineteenth Amendment, 140
Ninth Amendment, 200–201
North Carolina, laws and constitution
    of, 11, 34, 218, 291
North Dakota, laws of, 11, 292
Notifications: Amber Alert, 1; bail
    hearing, 143, 215; criminal
    process rights, 154, 164; criminal
    process schedule and status, 81,
    134, 145–46, 157–58; Human
    Rights Watch report on, 286–88;
    offender release/escape, 1, 134,
    143, 150–51, 161–62; opting-out/
    waiver of, 287–88; plea bargain,
    143; sentencing, 143; sex offender
    location, 1; victims' right to be
    informed by, 55–56, 150–51,
    157–58, 161–62
NOVA (National Organization for
    Victim Assistance), 25, 29, 31,
    137, 139, 142, 208, 273

Offenders. See Defendants and
    convicted offenders

Office for Victims of Crime (OVC),
    28, 29, 32, 79, 80, 174, 175, 233
O'Hara, Erin, 196
Ohio, laws and constitution of, 11, 31,
    34, 282
Oklahoma: constitution of, 11, 34,
    130; evidence preservation in,
    291; Oklahoma City Bombing,
    121–32, 147–48, 173, 289;
    Victims Participation Model
    under laws of, 11; Victims' Rights
    Clarification Act in, 130–31
Opposition to victims' rights: areas of
    conflict in, 55–59; civil
    libertarians in, 54, 59, 60; due
    process as basis for, 54, 59, 218;
    history of, 52–54; judge–victim
    issues in, 5, 54, 55, 57–59; Justice
    Department role in, 238–56;
    police–victim issues in, 54, 55,
    56–57; public prosecutor–victim
    issues in, 5, 16, 54, 55, 57; victims'
    contradictory role impacting, 54;
    victims' goals for justice and,
    54–55; victims' right to be
    informed and, 55–56
Oregon: constitution of, 11, 34, 74,
    273–78; enforceability of victims'
    rights in, 4, 273–78; victim
    assistance programs in, 27; victim
    defined in, 281–82; Victims
    Participation Model under laws of,
    11; victims' right to refuse defense
    interview in, 290

Packer, Herbert, 5–7, 8, 9
Parents of Murdered Children
    (POMC), 27, 137, 145, 208, 275
Parks, Ross and Betty, 142
Parole board hearings: President's Task
    Force recommendations on, 72, 75;
    victim participation in, 1, 56, 58,
    134, 150, 159, 161, 224, 289
Payne v. Tennessee (1991), 5–6, 83,
    84–101, 160
Pennsylvania, laws of, 11, 291
Plea bargains: Crime Victims' Rights
    Act on, 221–24, 250–56; victim
    notification of, 143; victim
    obstruction of, 177–78, 195;
    victim participation in, 1, 17, 48,
    134, 148, 159–60, 197, 221–24,
    250–56, 289

Police: Code of Conduct for Law
    Enforcement Officials, 294;
    correctional reform creating
    professional position of, 17–19;
    evidence destruction and
    preservation by, 291; victim
    acting as, 12; victim consultation
    with, 8; as victims, 282; victims'
    rights opposition by, 54, 55, 56–57
Pollard, Patricia, 150, 154
Posttraumatic stress disorder (PTSD),
    29
Prescott, Katherine, 137, 149
President's Task Force on Victims of
    Crime: American Bar Association
    Victim Witness Project guidelines
    based on, 79, 80–82, 174;
    Attorney General's Task Force
    recommendation to create, 27, 28;
    composite of victims of crime in
    America, 64–71; Constitutional
    amendment recommendation of,
    73, 76–77, 136–37, 304; historical
    impact of, 77–79; OVC
    recommendation implementation,
    28, 32, 79; present status of
    recommendations by, 74–77;
    secondary victimization
    highlighted by, 65–71, 78; state
    and federal action
    recommendations, 71–77, 78–80,
    146, 153, 158
Preston, Robert E., 137, 208
Presumption of innocence, 180, 216
Pretrial release hearings. See Bail
    hearings
Prison system, 15, 158, 282. See also
    Defendants and convicted
    offenders
Privacy rights: Crime Victims' Rights
    Act on, 224–25; international
    standards on, 294–95; state
    constitutional rights on, 261–62;
    third-party rights as, 265; Victim
    Participation Model on, 10–11;
    victims' rights including, 1, 2, 10–
    11, 224–25, 261–62, 265, 294–95
Private prosecution, 2, 5, 9, 12–13,
    15–16, 43, 106–11
Privileged information, 2
Pryce, Deborah, 138
Psychological support, 25–26, 29, 294
Public awareness, 27–30

Public prosecutors: correctional reform creating position of, 15–17; criminal process role of, 2, 3, 4, 15–17, 40; discretion and latitude allowed, 2, 40, 115–17, 177–78, 195, 222, 228, 266, 284–85; full party standing of, 3; notifications by (*see* Notifications); plea bargaining by (*see* Plea bargains); private prosecution *vs.*, 2, 5, 9, 12–13, 15–16, 43, 106–11; proposed Constitutional amendment impact on, 175–76, 177–78, 194–95; trials involving (*see* Trial); victim alienation by, 50–51; victim consultation with, 8, 49; victims' rights opposition by, 4, 16, 54, 55, 57

Racial minorities. *See* Minorities and marginalized people
Rape and sexual assault cases: grassroot organization agendas addressing, 26–27, 28–29; mental health support in, 25–26; notification of release/escape in, 150–51; police pressure in, 57; secondary victimization in prosecution of, 65–71; state laws addressing, 28–29; victims' rights in, 1, 16, 23, 25–29, 60, 150–51; women's movement addressing, 23, 60
Raskin, Jamin, 137
Reagan administration, 27, 28, 63, 64, 73, 136, 304. *See also* President's Task Force on Victims of Crime
Remedies: Crime Victims' Rights Act on, 224, 225–29, 304; damages or compensation as, 12–13, 14, 15, 24, 28, 30, 41–42, 43, 72, 76, 134, 152–53, 163, 166, 172, 192, 224, 227–28, 263–64, 265, 273, 284–85, 291–93; Human Rights Watch report on, 284–85, 291–93; judicial enforcement of, 3–4, 271, 274–75, 278–80, 304; as standing prerequisite, 271; state constitutional enforcement of, 271, 273, 274–75, 278
Reno, Janet, 138, 140, 141
Respect for victims, 8, 10–11. *See also* Dignity of victims

Restitution. *See* Damages or compensation
Restraining orders, 1
Review mechanisms, 271
Rhode Island, laws and constitution of, 11, 34, 291
Roper, Roberta, 24, 142, 208
Rowland, James, 25

Safety, victims', 153–54, 163–64, 294–95
Sangrey, Dawn, *The Crime Victim's Book*, 26
Schwarzenegger, Arnold, 273
Scott, Robert C., 138, 181
Secondary victimization, 8, 29, 48, 65–71, 78, 139
Senate Joint Resolution 44: background and legislative history of, 136–39; criminal process rights notification under, 154, 164; damages from government restrictions under, 166, 192; exceptions under, 167–68; federalism principles in, 144–45, 183, 184, 185–86, 198; inadequacy of victims' rights without, 141–42, 143–44; legislative enforcement of, 166; need for constitutional protection, 139–40; negative potential consequences of, 168–84, 189–96; participatory rights protection under, 140–41; purpose of, 135–36; right to attend under, 146–48, 158, 180–81; right to be heard under, 148–50, 158–61, 181; right to have safety considered under, 153–54, 163–64; right to notice of proceedings under, 145–46, 157–58; right to notice of release/escape under, 150–51, 161–62; right to order of restitution under, 152–53, 163; right to victim's consideration in delayed trial under, 151–52, 162–63, 181; scholarly debate on, 187–202; section-by-section analysis of, 154–68; Senate majority report on, 135–68; Senate minority report on, 168–84; states' rights impacted under, 182–83;

statistical quantification of victims' rights violations in, 143–44; statutory alternative to, 202, 207–11; support for, 135–68, 187–89, 196–202; text of, 133; victim participation denial, examples of, in, 142–43; victims defined under, 155–57; victims' right to challenge decisions under, 165–66; victims' standing under, 164–65; victims' *vs.* defendants' rights in, 154–55, 161, 162–63, 179–82, 194, 197, 199–202; vote on, 168
Sentencings: Crime Victims' Rights Act on victim rights at, 221–24, 232–38, 240–50; Federal Sentencing Guidelines, 89; President's Task Force recommendations on, 72, 75, 76; victim impact statements on, 5–6, 57–58, 76, 81–82, 83–106, 149–50, 160, 240, 276, 289; victim notification of, 143; victim participation in, 1, 3, 5–6, 56, 57–58, 76, 81–82, 83–106, 134, 149–50, 160, 221–24, 232–38, 240–50, 276, 289
Sequestration power, 121–32, 146–48. *See also* Trial, *See also* victims' right to attend
Shepherd, Pete, 275
Sixth Amendment, 151, 181, 200, 223, 290–91
Social justice movements. *See* Movements, historical
Societal interests: protecting through victim participation, 47–48, 266; public prosecutors representing (*see* Public prosecutors)
Society for the Prevention of Cruelty to Children, 21
South Carolina, laws and constitution of, 11, 31, 34, 226
South Carolina v. Gathers (1989), 84, 87–88, 88–89, 91, 93, 94, 96, 99
South Dakota, laws of, 11
Speedy Trial Act (1974), 163, 227
Standing: Constitutional issues related to, 112–17, 121–32, 134, 164–65, 271–78; Crime Victims' Rights Act on, 131–32, 227; denial of victims' right

enforcement due to lack of, 121–32, 268–69; full party, 3; future of victims' right movement focus on, 270–78; victims', 3–4, 39, 50–51, 80–81, 112–17, 121–32, 134, 164–65, 227, 268–69, 270–78

Stanton, Elizabeth Cady, 21

State governments. *See also specific states*: constitutions of, 3, 5, 7–8, 10–11, 30, 33–34, 44, 73–74, 130, 137, 143, 261–65, 271–78, 303, 304; Crime Victims' Rights Act implementation by, 207–56; defendants' rights under, 44, 262, 263–65; domestic violence and rape/sexual assault addressed by, 27, 28–29; federal court supervision of, 183–84; federalism principles impacting, 144–45, 183, 184, 185–86, 198; "have" and "have-not" state enforcement of victims' rights, 266–69; laws of (*see* Laws and statutes); notifications by (*see* Notifications); President's Task Force on Victims of Crime recommendations to, 71–77, 78–80, 146, 153, 158; proposed Constitutional amendment impacting states' rights, 182–83; victim assistance programs by, 27, 28, 30; victim compensation programs under, 24, 28, 30, 273, 284–85, 292–93; victim defined by, 281–84; Victim Participation Model under laws of, 7–8, 10–11; victim service provider credentialing by, 31–32; victims' rights determination under laws of, 3–4, 5, 7–8, 10–11, 143, 174–75, 266–69 (*see also specific laws*); victims' right to attend trial under, 147–48

State of Texas v. Napoleon Beazley (1997), 101–6

STOP (Services, Training, Officers, Prosecutors) grants, 172

Stovall, Carla, 138

Street crime victims, 59

Symonds, Martin, 29

Task forces: Attorney General's Task Force on Family Violence, 79; Attorney General's Task Force on Violent Crime, 27, 28; President's

Task Force on Victims of Crime, 27, 28, 32, 63–82, 136–37, 146, 153, 158, 174, 304

Tennessee, laws and constitution of, 11, 34, 291

Texas: constitution of, 11, 34, 263; evidence preservation in, 291; victim participation in, 11, 289; victims' rights violations redress in, 226

Third-party rights, 2, 115, 265

Trial. *See also* Criminal process: accused's right to fair, 180–81; Crime Victims' Rights Act on, 217–21; delay of, consideration of victim in, 151–52, 162–63, 181, 293–94; emotional displays during, 220; Speedy Trial Act on, 163, 227; victims' courtroom seating during, 220–21; victims' right to attend, 4, 49, 121–32, 146–48, 158, 173, 180–81, 217–21

Tribe, Laurence H., 142, 144, 187, 189, 198–202, 266–67

Truth seeking, 44–45, 48–49

Twenty-first Amendment, 168

Twenty-sixth Amendment, 140

Twist, Steven, J., 133, 137, 139, 207, 210–11, 222, 273–75, 277

Uniform Crime Report, 25, 27–28

United Nations: codes of conduct by, 294; declaration on victims' rights, 32; International Covenant on Civil and Political Rights, 285, 293, 295

U.S. Department of Justice. *See* Justice Department, U.S.

Utah: constitution of, 11, 34; victim defined in, 281; Victims Participation Model under laws of, 11; victims' rights violations redress in, 226; victims' right to attend trial in, 148, 218

Vermont, laws of, 11

Victim and Witness Protection Act (1972), 28, 129, 153, 172

Victim participation: in bail hearings, 57, 148–49, 159, 215–17; in civil process, 14, 41–42, 43; colonial American, 12–14, 15–16; Constitutional protection of

participatory rights, 7–8, 10–11, 140–41, 263–65; consultation role of, 8–9, 49; cultural and institutional dynamics impacting, 45–46; decline and exclusion of, 9, 12, 13–19, 39–46, 111–17, 276; denied opportunities for, examples of, 142–43; evidence presentation as, 290–91; fairness to defendant impacted by, 44, 180–81; fairness to victim impacted by, 8, 10–11, 46–47, 77, 223, 224–25, 261–62; historical overview of, 1, 2, 3, 5–9, 10–11, 12–34, 39–46, 111–17; Human Rights Watch report on, 288–91; justifications for victim inclusion, 46–52; law and order movement encouraging, 23–24, 53–54; opposition to, 4, 16, 52–60, 218, 238–56; in parole board hearings, 1, 56, 58, 134, 150, 159, 161, 224, 289; in plea bargains, 1, 17, 48, 134, 148, 159–60, 197, 221–24, 250–56, 289; practicality of victim exclusion, 40–43; private prosecutions as, 2, 5, 9, 12–13, 15–16, 43, 106–11; secondary victimization impacted by, 8, 29, 48, 65–71, 78, 139; in sentencing, 1, 3, 5–6, 56, 57–58, 76, 81–82, 83–106, 134, 149–50, 160, 221–24, 232–38, 240–50, 276, 289; societal interest protection through, 47–48, 266; state constitutional right to, 263–65; trial attendance as, 4, 49, 121–32, 146–48, 158, 173, 180–81, 217–21; truth seeking impacted by, 44–45, 48–49; victim alienation prevention through, 49–51; victim impact statements as, 5–6, 25, 30, 57–58, 76, 81–82, 83–106, 149–50, 160–61, 240, 276, 289; Victim Participation Model, 5–9, 10–11; victims' right to be heard and, 148–50, 158–61, 181, 221–24, 233–38

Victims: alienation of, 49–51; civil process plaintiff role of, 14, 41–42, 43; composite of/hypothetical situations of, 64–71; damages or compensation paid to (*see*

Damages or compensation); defined, 155–57, 241, 264, 281–84; dignity of, 8, 10–11, 223, 224–25, 261–62, 294; emotional courtroom displays of, 220; fairness to, 8, 10–11, 46–47, 77, 223, 224–25, 261–62; goals of, in criminal process, 54–55; legal representation for, 4–5, 278–80, 290; mental health support for, 25–26, 29, 294; multiple, 157, 167, 212, 213, 221, 251–56; nondiscrimination protection for, 295–97; notifications to (*see* Notifications); participation of, in criminal process (*see* Victim participation); President's Task Force on Victims of Crime, 27, 28, 32, 63–82, 136–37, 146, 153, 158, 174, 304; primary harm to, 8; privacy rights of, 1, 2, 10–11, 224–25, 261–62, 265, 294–95; private prosecutions by, 2, 5, 9, 12–13, 15–16, 43, 106–11; respect for, 8, 10–11 (*see also* Dignity of victims); restraining orders obtained by, 1; rights of (*see* Victims' rights); safety of, 153–54, 163–64, 294–95; seating of, in courtroom, 220–21; secondary victimization of, 8, 29, 48, 65–71, 78, 139; standing of, 3–4, 39, 50–51, 80–81, 112–17, 121–32, 134, 164–65, 227, 268–69, 270–78; street crime, 59; third-party interests of, 2, 115, 265; victim impact statements, 5–6, 25, 30, 57–58, 76, 81–82, 83–106, 149–50, 160–61, 240, 276, 289
The Victims (Carrington), 25
Victims' Assistance Legal Organization (VALOR), 27
Victims' Information and Notification Everyday (VINE), 288
Victims of Crime Act (VOCA/1984), 28, 29, 30, 172, 282

Victims' rights: American Bar Association Victim Witness Project guidelines on, 79, 80–82, 174; background and history of, 1–34, 39–46, 53–54, 111–17; common law on, 2, 15–16, 115–16, 153, 229, 230, 231, 242, 252, 261; Constitutional issues related to (*see* Constitution, U.S.; Constitutions, state); Crime Victims' Rights Movement on (*see* Crime Victims' Rights Movement); defined, 4; exercising *vs.* enforcement of, 3–4 (*see also* Remedies); future of, 270–78, 303–4; Human Rights Watch Report on Victims' Rights in America, 280–98; international standards for, 32, 283, 284–85, 290, 293–95, 298; jurisdictional issues with, 266; laws and statutes on (*see* Federal government; Laws and statutes; State governments); legal representation supporting, 4–5, 278–80, 290; modern, 2, 20–34, 111, 261–98; nondiscrimination protection as, 295–97; notification as (*see* Notifications); Oklahoma City Bombing trial failure of, 121–32, 147–48, 289; opposition to, 4, 16, 52–60, 218, 238–56; present status of, 261–69; President's Task Force on Victims of Crime addressing, 27, 28, 32, 63–82, 136–37, 146, 153, 158, 174, 304; privacy as, 1, 2, 10–11, 224–25, 261–62, 265, 294–95; remedies for violation of (*see* Remedies); restitution as (*see* Damages or compensation); review mechanisms for violation of, 271; right to be heard as, 148–50, 158–61, 181, 221–24, 233–38 (*see also* Victim participation); standing impacting (*see*

Standing); statistical quantification of violation of, 143–44; third-party rights as, 2, 115, 265; trial attendance as, 4, 49, 121–32, 146–48, 158, 173, 180–81, 217–21; trial delay, consideration of victim in, as, 151–52, 162–63, 181, 293–94; victim participation as (*see* Victim participation); victims' safety considerations as, 153–54, 163–64, 294–95; waiver of, 1, 287–88
Victims' Rights and Restitution Act (1990), 128–29, 131, 172
Victims' Rights Clarification Act (1997), 130–31, 147, 173
Victim Witness Project, 79, 80–82, 174
Violence Against Women Act (1994), 172
Virginia: constitution of, 11, 34, 277; victim participation in, 11, 289, 291; victims' right to attend trial in, 218
VOCA (Victims of Crime Act/1984), 28, 29, 30, 172, 282

Walker, Lenore, 26
Walsh, John, 24, 137, 138
Washington, laws and constitution of, 11, 34, 291
West Virginia, laws of, 11
Wisconsin, laws and constitution of, 11, 27, 34, 218, 291
Women's movement, 21, 22–23, 53, 60
Writ of mandamus: Crime Victims' Rights Act on, 210, 226–27, 229–31, 233, 236–56; standing impacting use of, 115–16, 123, 127–28, 129–30
Wyoming, laws of, 11, 291

Young, Marlene, 139, 142, 154

Zero sum game, 59, 60, 154